Shojo Beat

Crimson Hero

Story & Art by

MITSUBA TAKANASHI

9

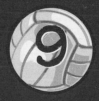

CONTENTS

STORY THUS FAR

Nobara Sumiyoshi is a first-year student in high school who lives for her one passion, volleyball. She's the successor to "Seiryu," the high-class ryotei restaurant her family runs, but she enrolled in Crimson Field High School expressly to play volleyball.

Nobara begins living and working in Crimson Dorm, the dorm for the boys' volleyball recruits. There she meets Yushin...and falls in love with him. But Yushin rejects her in front of everyone! In the midst of all this, Coach Shima arrives and begins to whip the mentally unprepared girls' team into shape. The goal: the Spring Tournament! Nobara leaves her teammates behind and sets out to become a strong attacker by training intensively with the Eagles, a team led by Shima's younger brother Ryo. There Nobara succeeds in improving both technically and mentally.

Back at Crimson Dorm, Nobara's absence makes the boys notice just how important her presence is. A transformation begins to take place in Yushin's heart! And just when Nobara is about to play the game between the Eagles and Sokai University—the team that wouldn't let Ryo be an attacker because of his height—who should appear but Yushin...?!

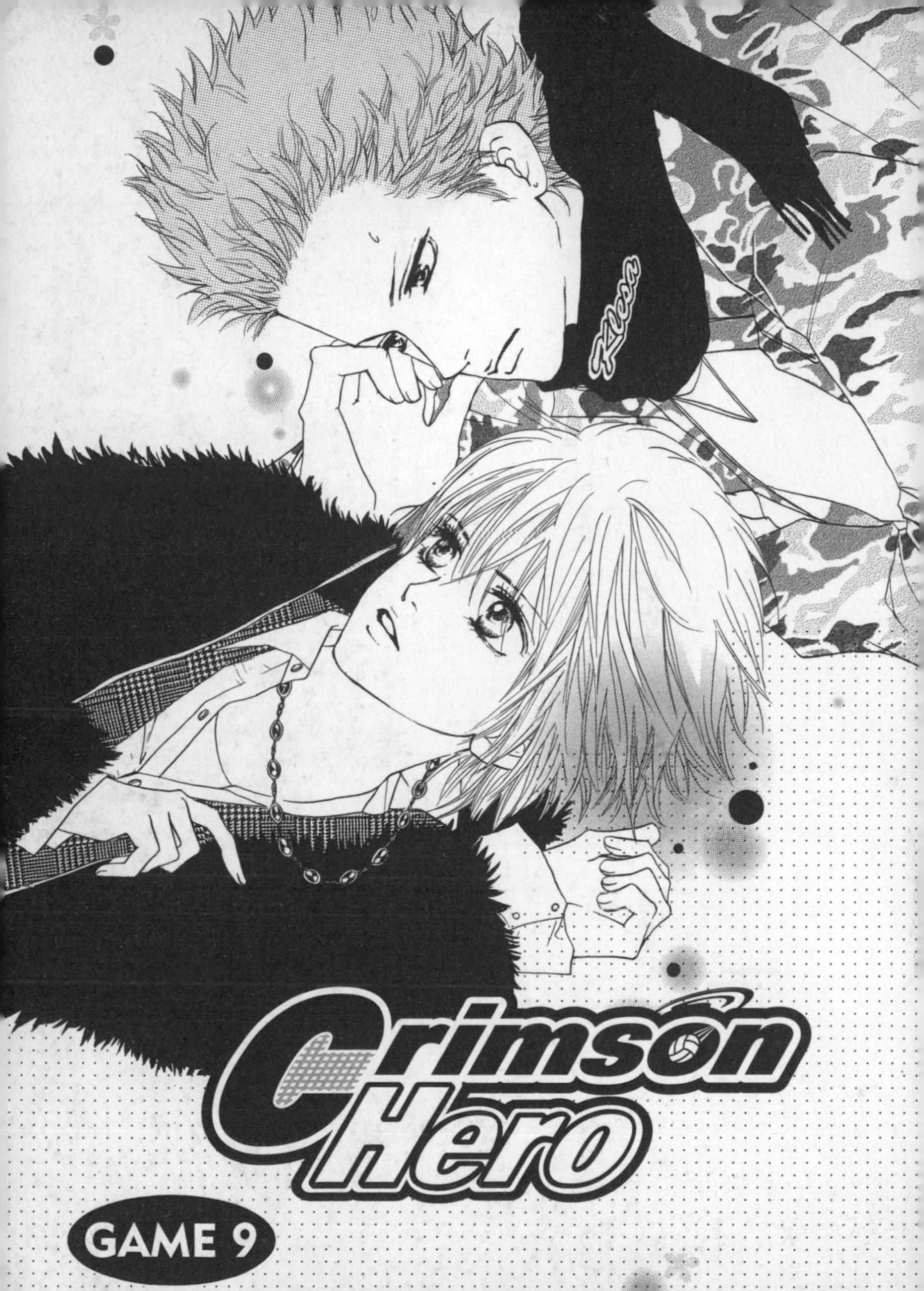

Crimson Hero

GAME 9

BIRTH OF A SUPER HIGH SCHOOL GIRL

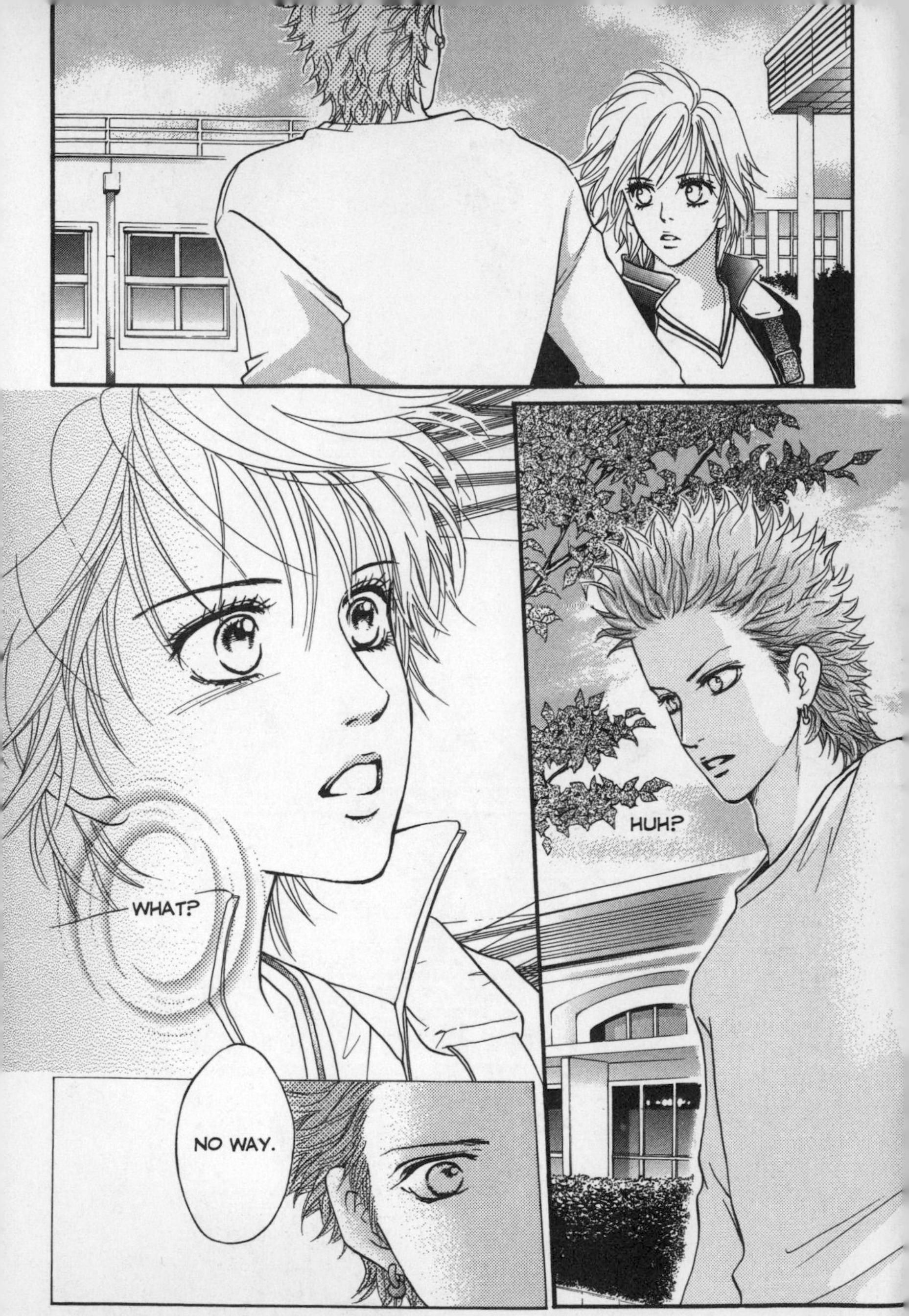
HUH?
WHAT?
NO WAY.

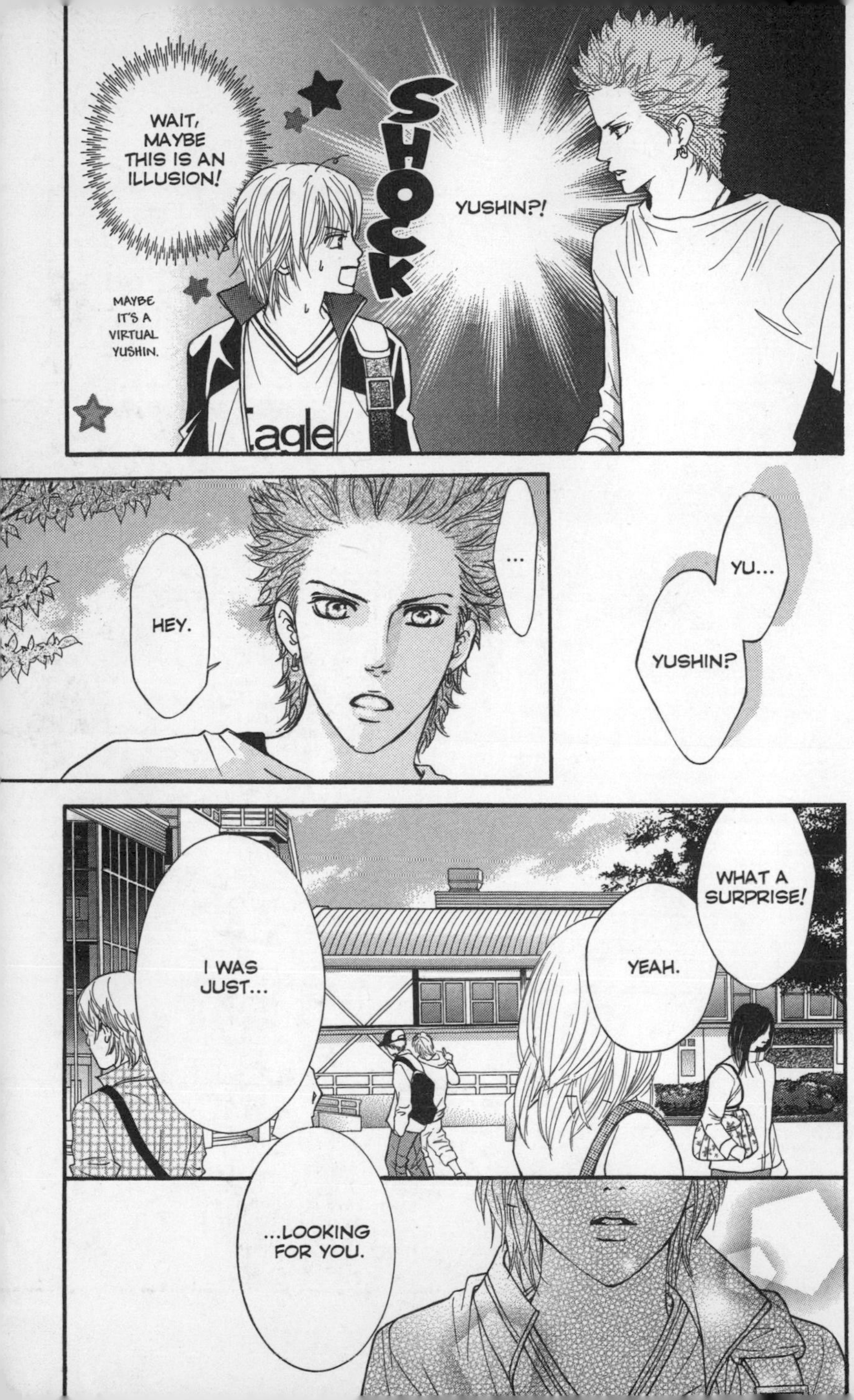
YUSHIN?!
SHOCK
WAIT, MAYBE THIS IS AN ILLUSION!
MAYBE IT'S A VIRTUAL YUSHIN.
Eagle
YU...
YUSHIN?
...
HEY.
WHAT A SURPRISE!
YEAH.
I WAS JUST...
...LOOKING FOR YOU.

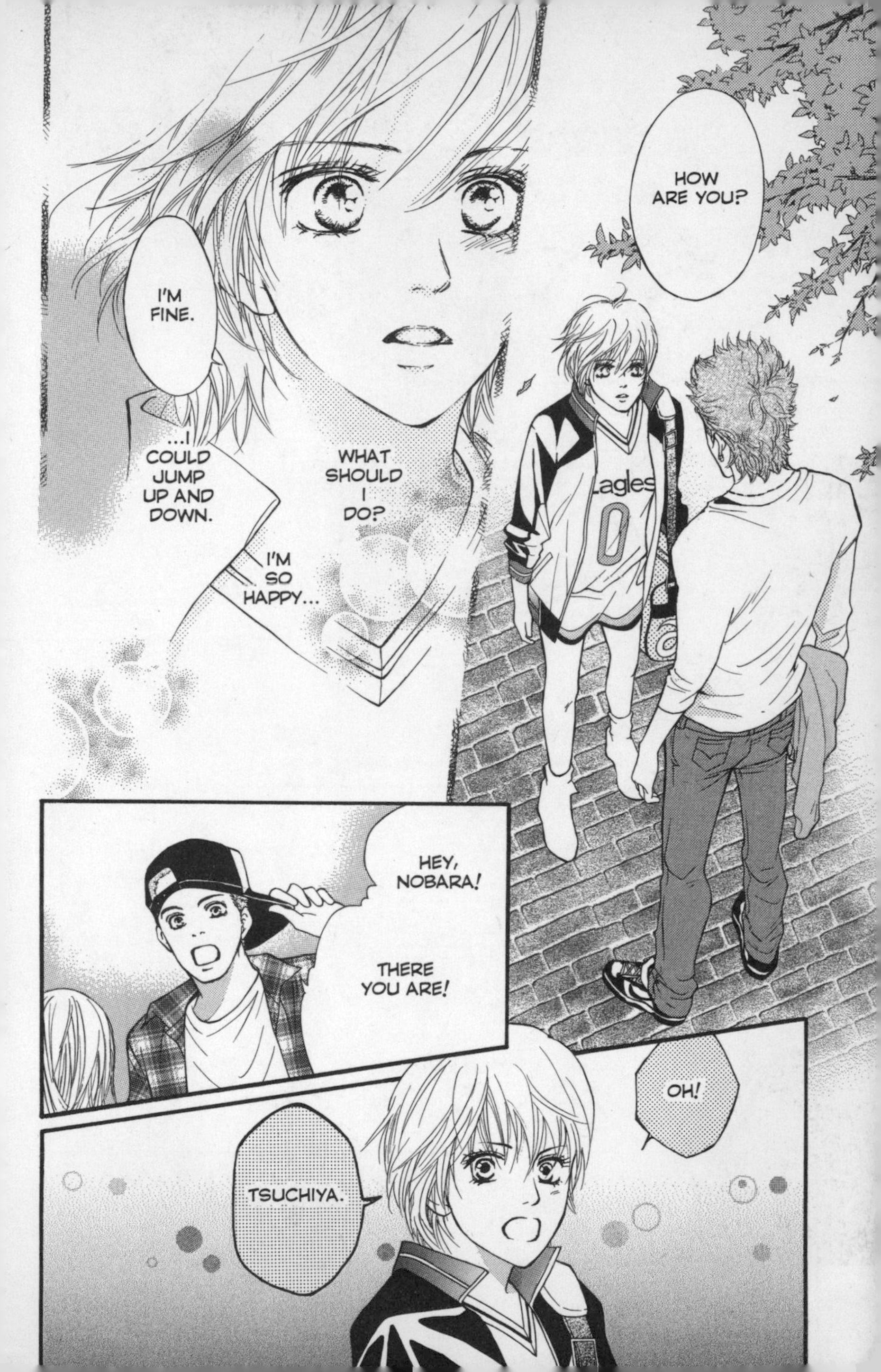
HOW ARE YOU?
I'M FINE.
WHAT SHOULD I DO?
I'M SO HAPPY...
...I COULD JUMP UP AND DOWN.
HEY, NOBARA!
THERE YOU ARE!
OH!
TSUCHIYA.

WHAT DO YOU THINK?

I'VE BEEN TRAINING!! WHAT ELSE?!

GUTS!!

WHAT'S GOING ON?

DID EVERYONE COME?

TOMONORI HAS BEEN SO LONELY WITHOUT YOU THAT HE CRIES.

WHAT ON EARTH HAVE YOU BEEN DOING DOWN HERE FOR A WHOLE MONTH?

NOPE. JUST ME AND YUSHIN.

NO WAY!

SORRY I HAVEN'T BEEN IN TOUCH.

BUT MY TIME HERE HAS PAID OFF.

HMM.

7

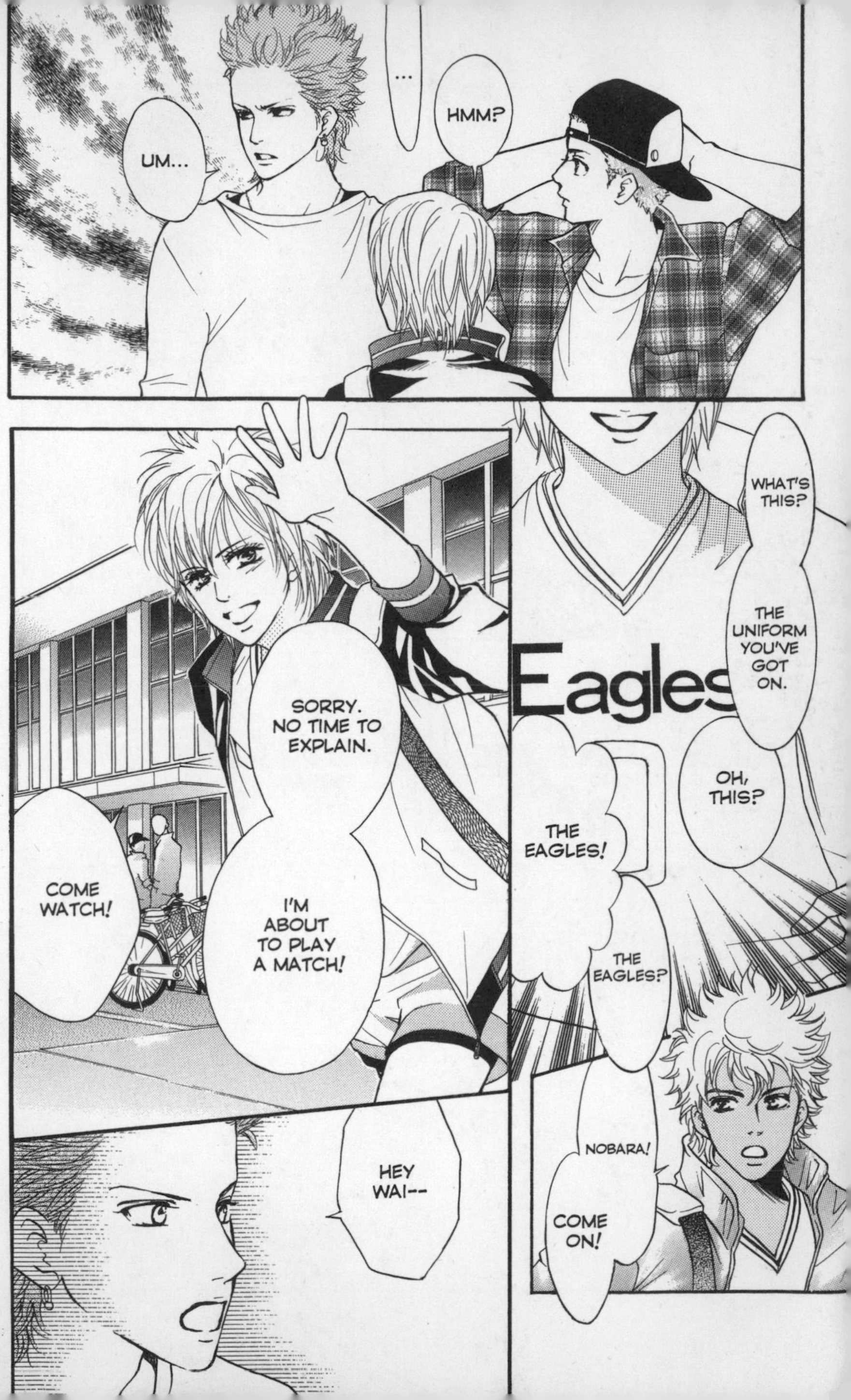
HMM?
...
UM...
WHAT'S THIS?
THE UNIFORM YOU'VE GOT ON.
Eagles
OH, THIS?
THE EAGLES!
THE EAGLES?
NOBARA!
COME ON!
SORRY. NO TIME TO EXPLAIN.
I'M ABOUT TO PLAY A MATCH!
COME WATCH!
HEY WAI--

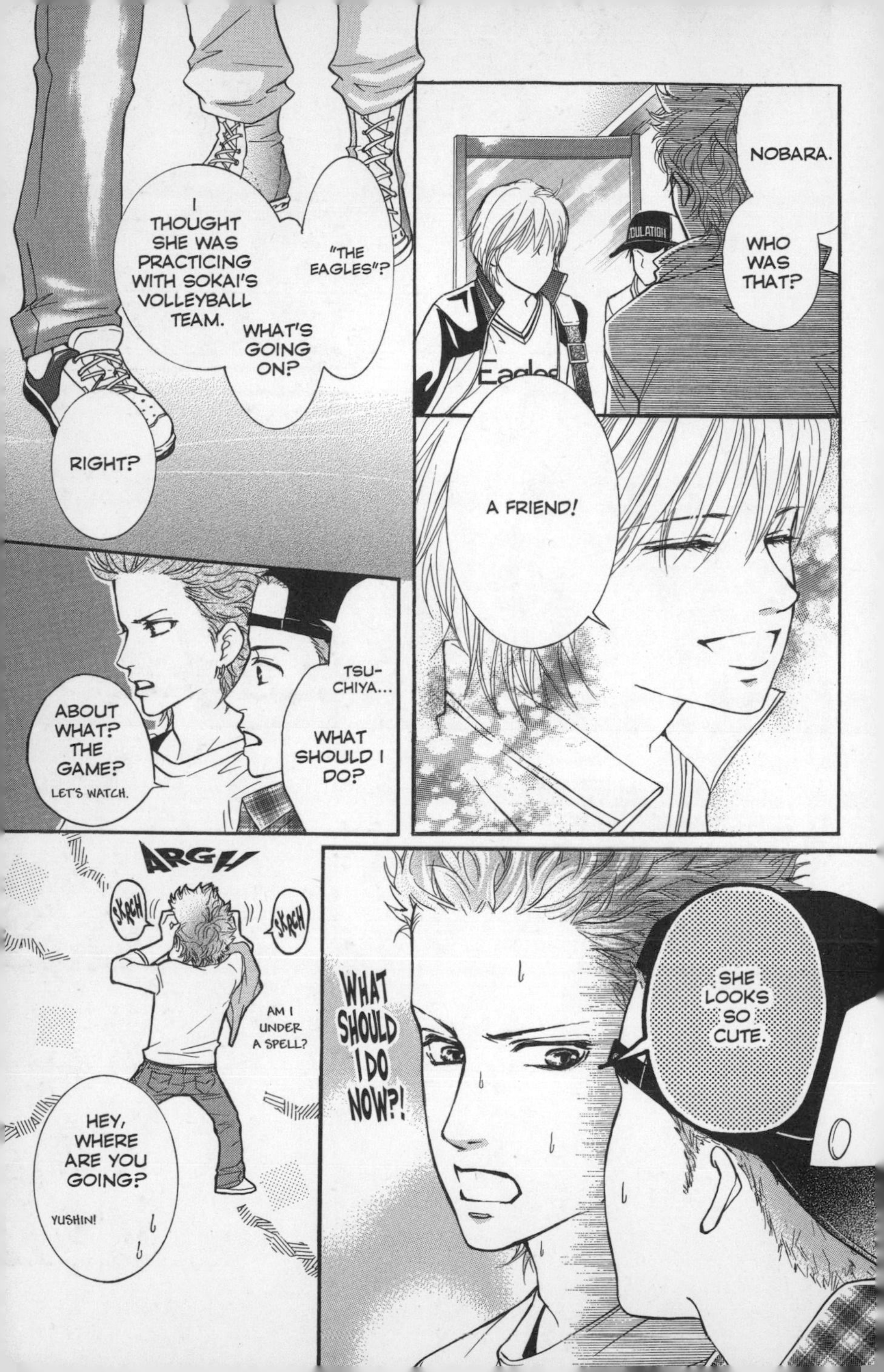
NOBARA.
WHO WAS THAT?
A FRIEND!
"THE EAGLES"?
I THOUGHT SHE WAS PRACTICING WITH SOKAI'S VOLLEYBALL TEAM.
WHAT'S GOING ON?
RIGHT?
TSU-CHIYA...
WHAT SHOULD I DO?
ABOUT WHAT? THE GAME?
LET'S WATCH.
SHE LOOKS SO CUTE.
WHAT SHOULD I DO NOW?!
ARGH
SKRCH
SKRCH
AM I UNDER A SPELL?
HEY, WHERE ARE YOU GOING?
YUSHIN!

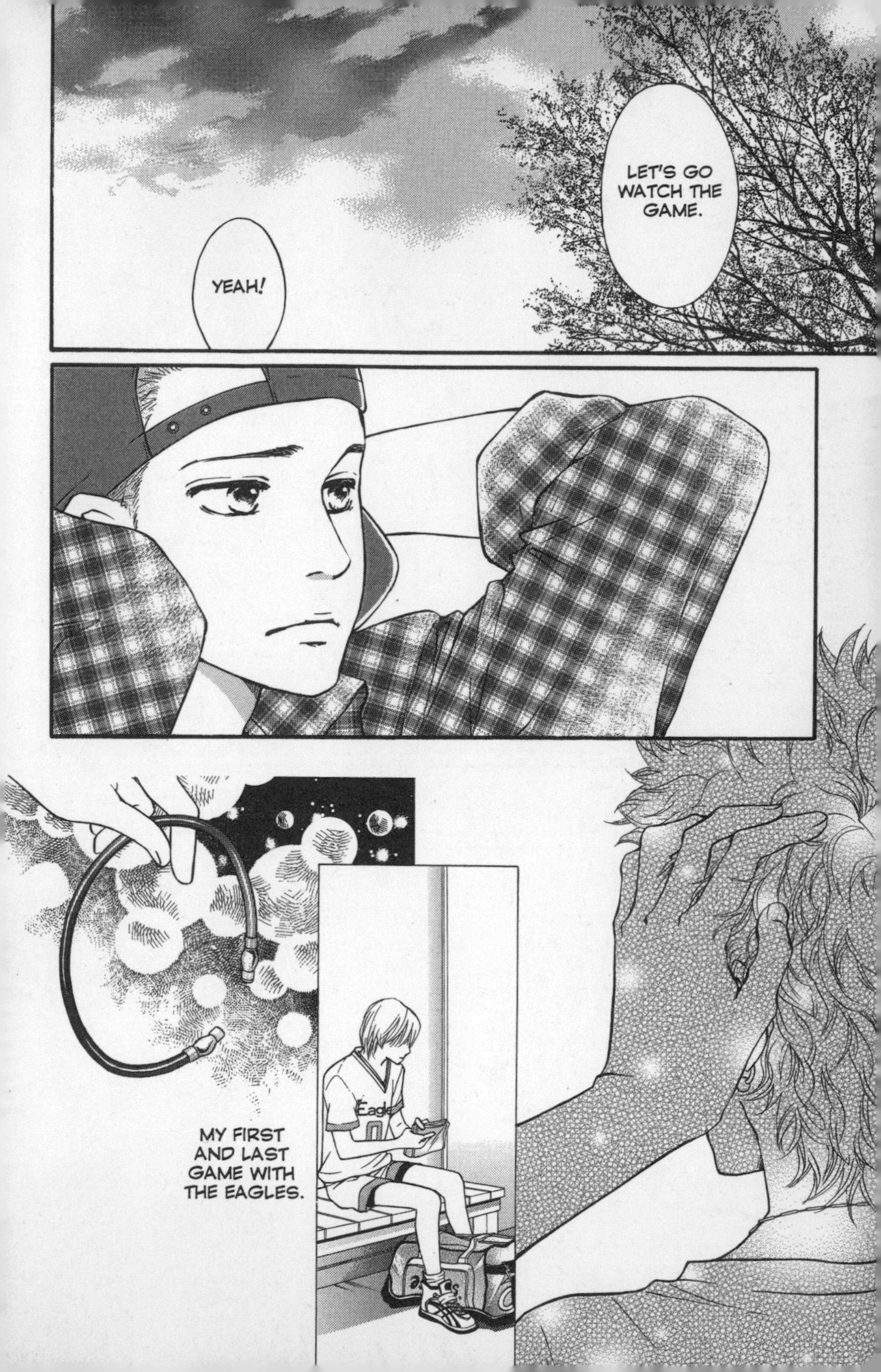
LET'S GO WATCH THE GAME.
YEAH!
MY FIRST AND LAST GAME WITH THE EAGLES.

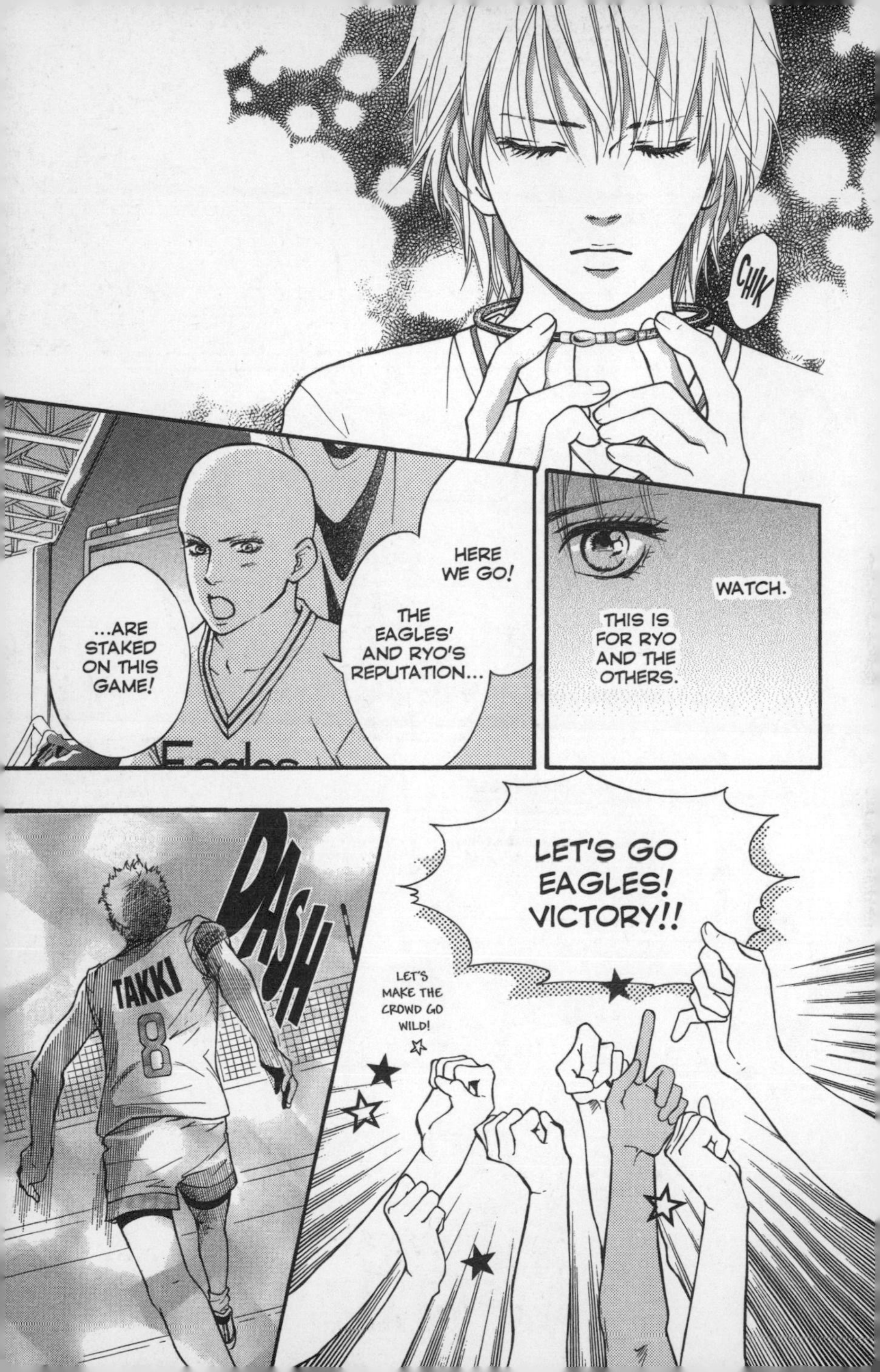
CHIK
WATCH.
THIS IS FOR RYO AND THE OTHERS.
HERE WE GO!
THE EAGLES' AND RYO'S REPUTATION...
...ARE STAKED ON THIS GAME!
LET'S GO EAGLES! VICTORY!!
LET'S MAKE THE CROWD GO WILD!
DASH
TAKKI
8

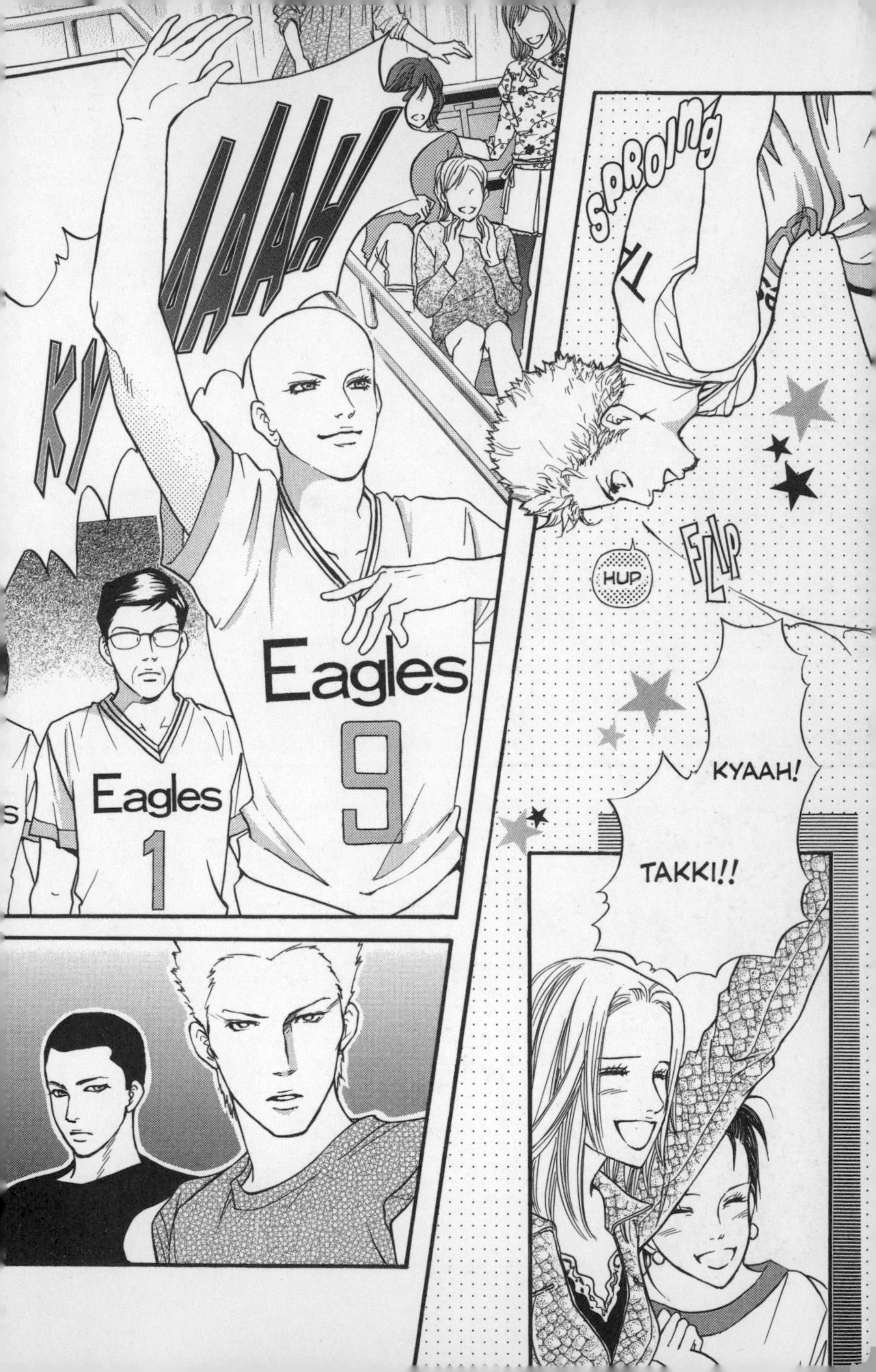
SPROING
HUP
FLIP
KYAAH!
TAKKI!!
KYAAAH!
Eagles
9
Eagles
1

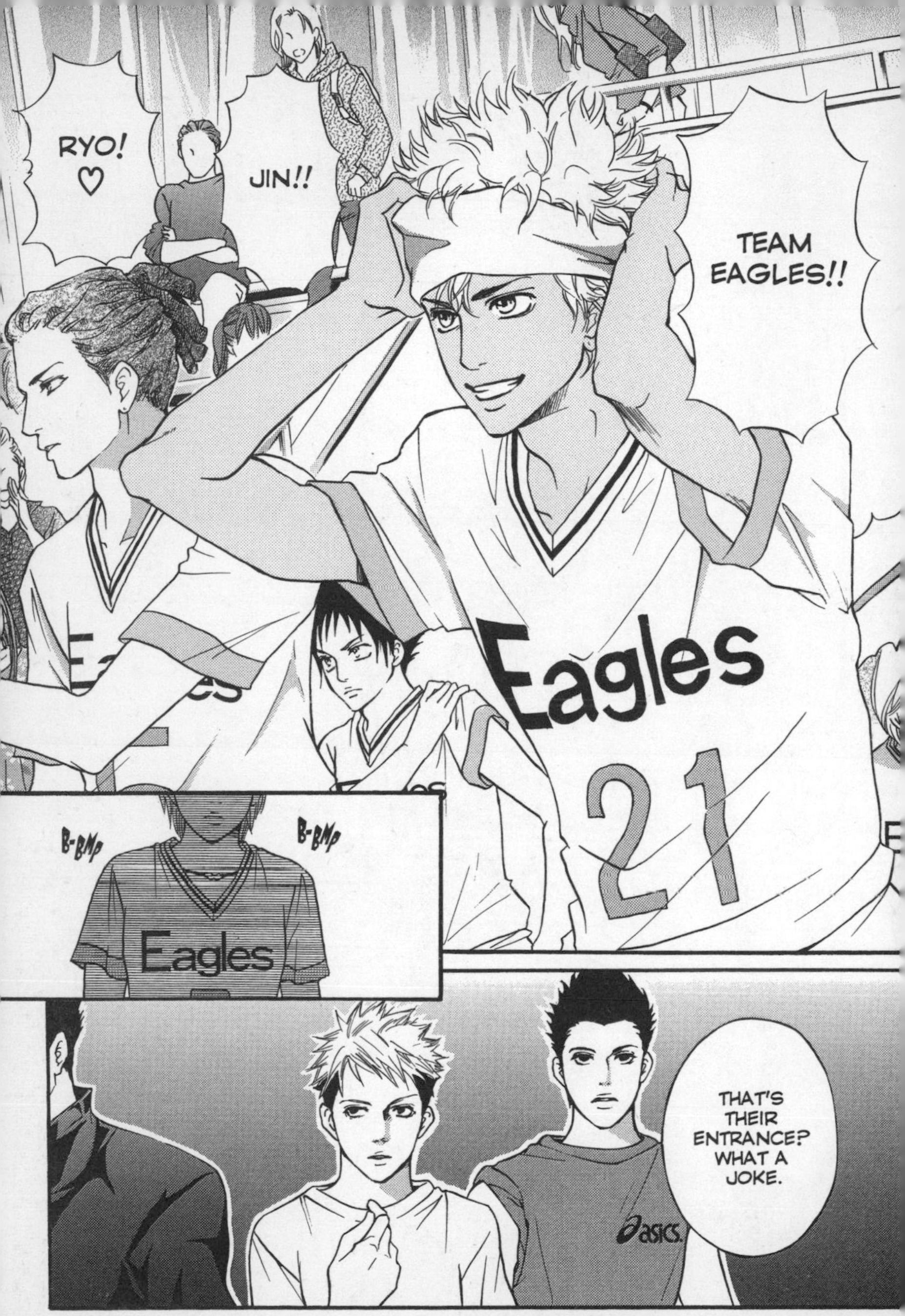
TEAM EAGLES!!
JIN!!
RYO! ♥
B-BMP
B-BMP
THAT'S THEIR ENTRANCE? WHAT A JOKE.

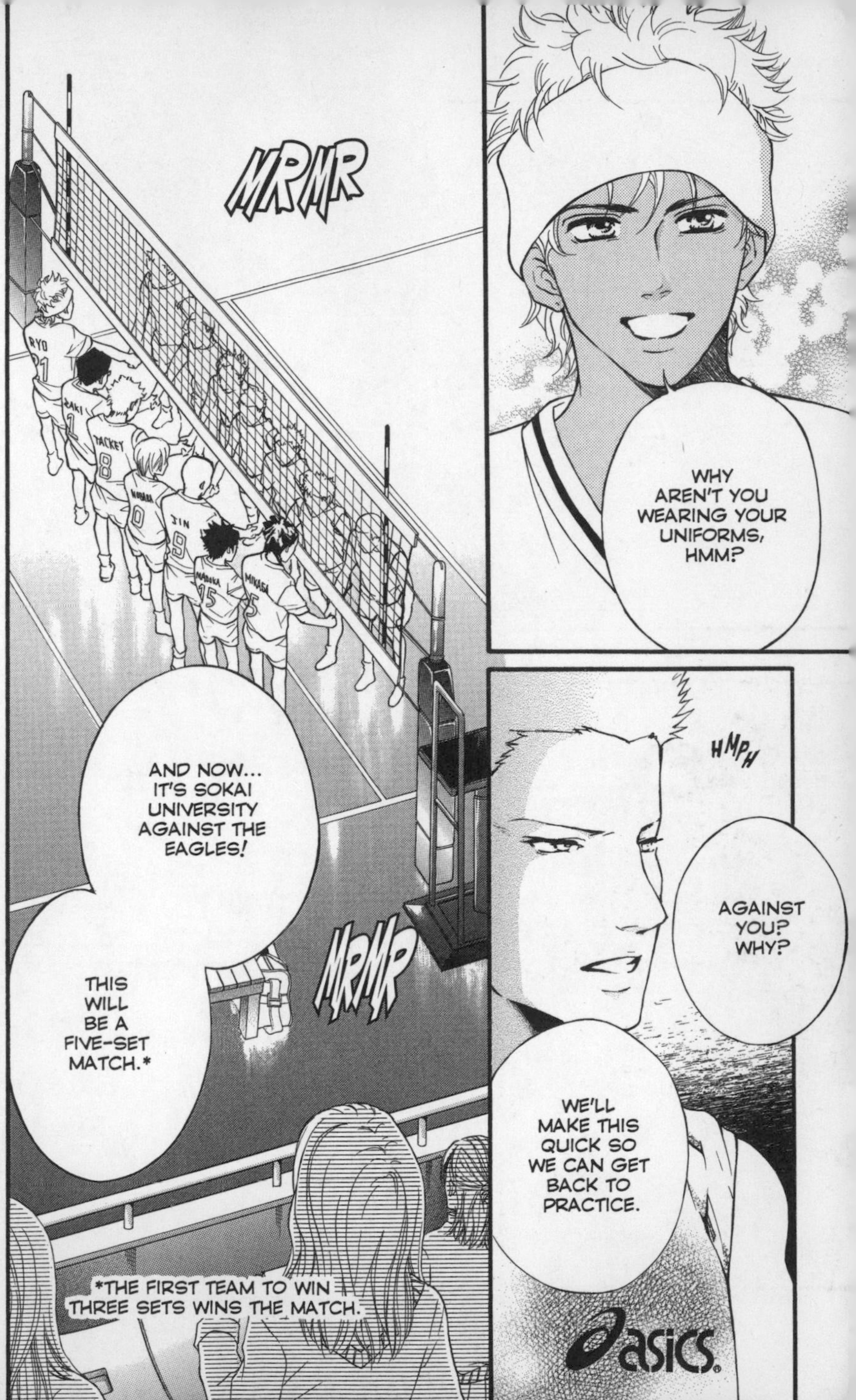
WHY AREN'T YOU WEARING YOUR UNIFORMS, HMM?
HMPH
AGAINST YOU? WHY?
WE'LL MAKE THIS QUICK SO WE CAN GET BACK TO PRACTICE.
asics
MRMR
AND NOW... IT'S SOKAI UNIVERSITY AGAINST THE EAGLES!
THIS WILL BE A FIVE-SET MATCH.*
MRMR
*THE FIRST TEAM TO WIN THREE SETS WINS THE MATCH.

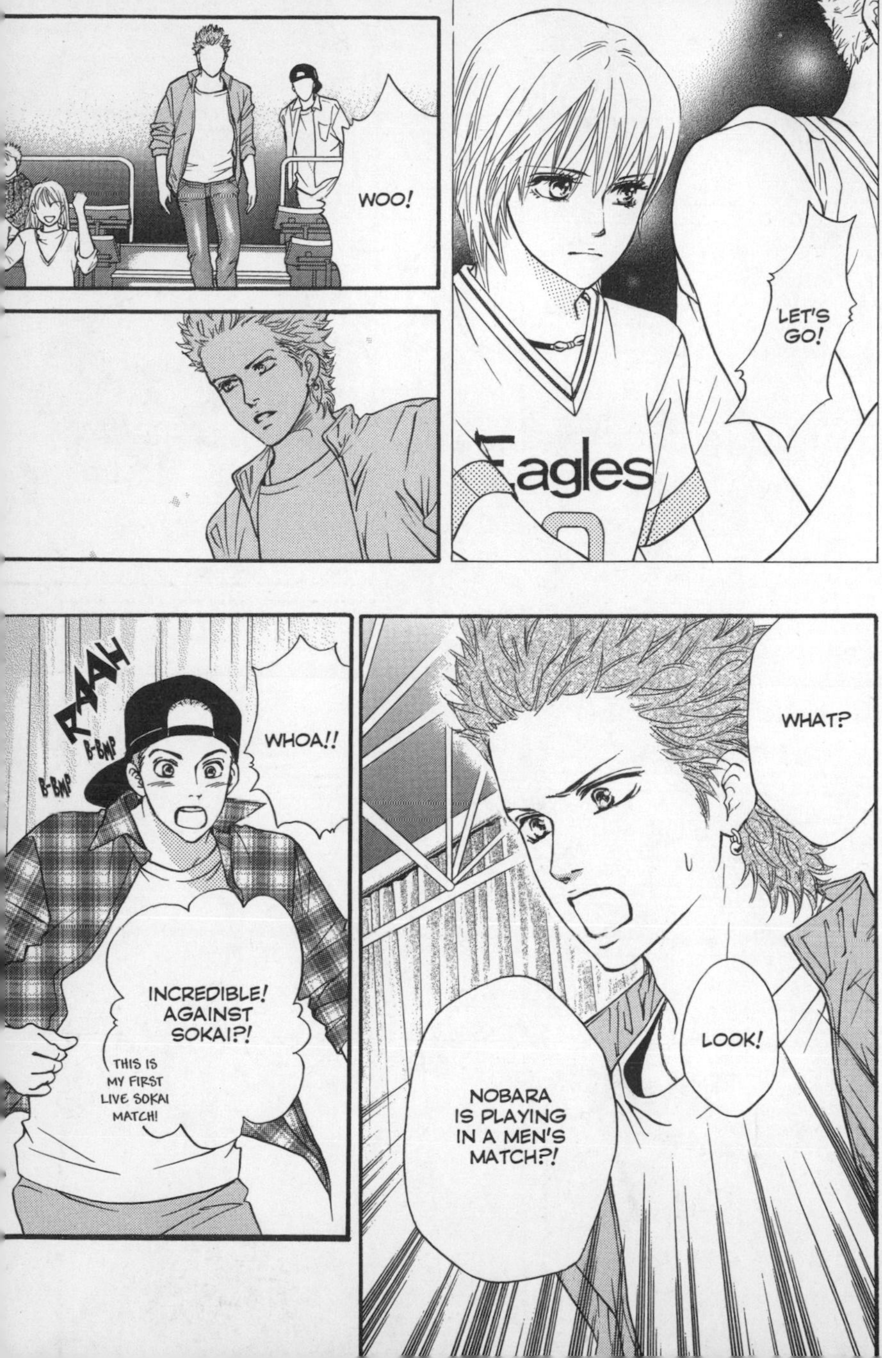
Eagles
LET'S GO!
WOO!
WHAT?
LOOK!
NOBARA IS PLAYING IN A MEN'S MATCH?!
RAAAH
WHOA!!
B-BMP
B-BMP
INCREDIBLE! AGAINST SOKAI?!
THIS IS MY FIRST LIVE SOKAI MATCH!

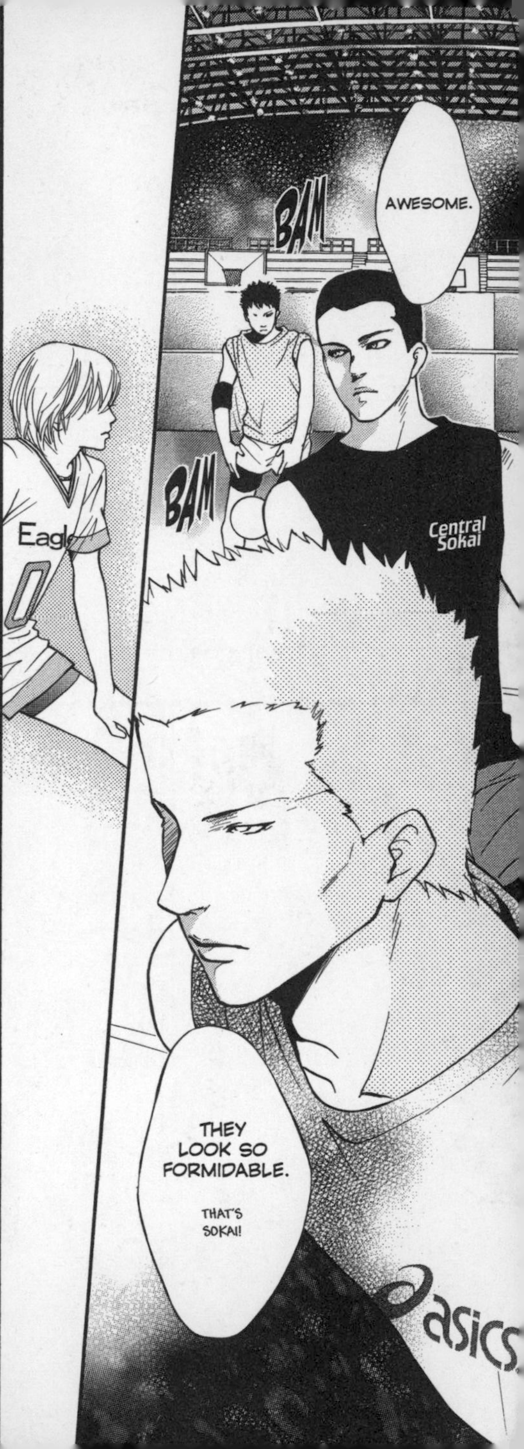
BAM
AWESOME.
BAM
Central Sokai
THEY LOOK SO FORMIDABLE.
THAT'S SOKAI!
asics

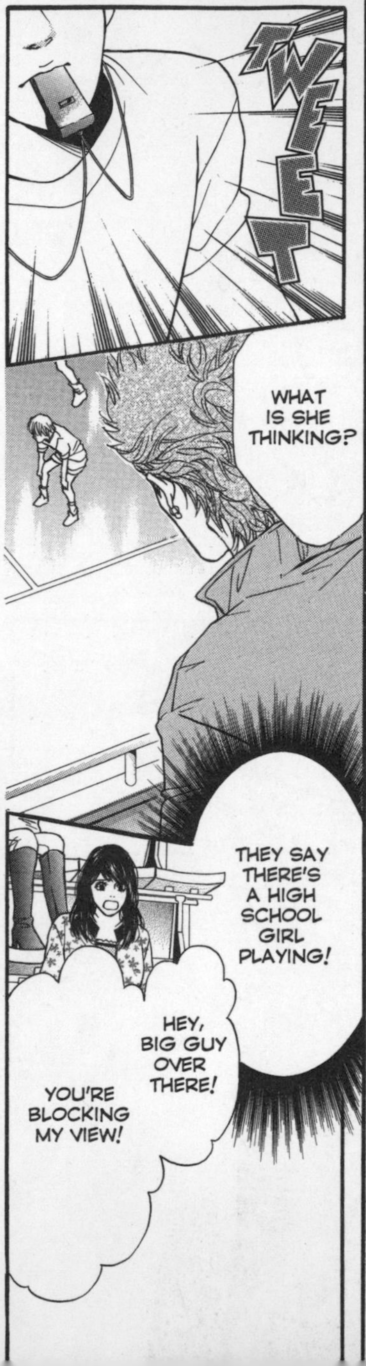
TWEET
WHAT IS SHE THINKING?
THEY SAY THERE'S A HIGH SCHOOL GIRL PLAYING!
HEY, BIG GUY OVER THERE!
YOU'RE BLOCKING MY VIEW!

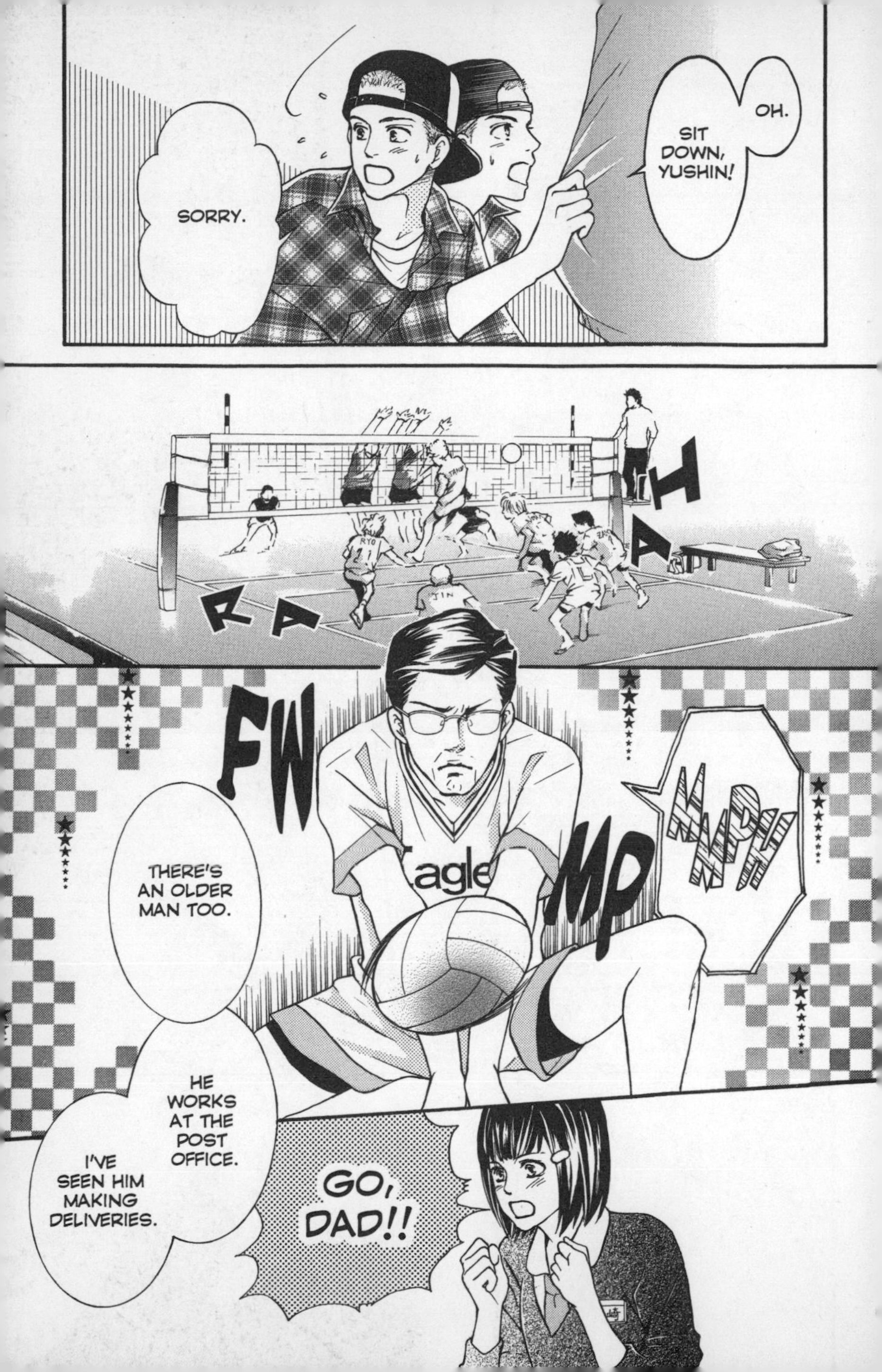
OH.
SIT DOWN, YUSHIN!
SORRY.
RA
AH
MMPH
FW
MP
THERE'S AN OLDER MAN TOO.
GO, DAD!!
HE WORKS AT THE POST OFFICE.
I'VE SEEN HIM MAKING DELIVERIES.

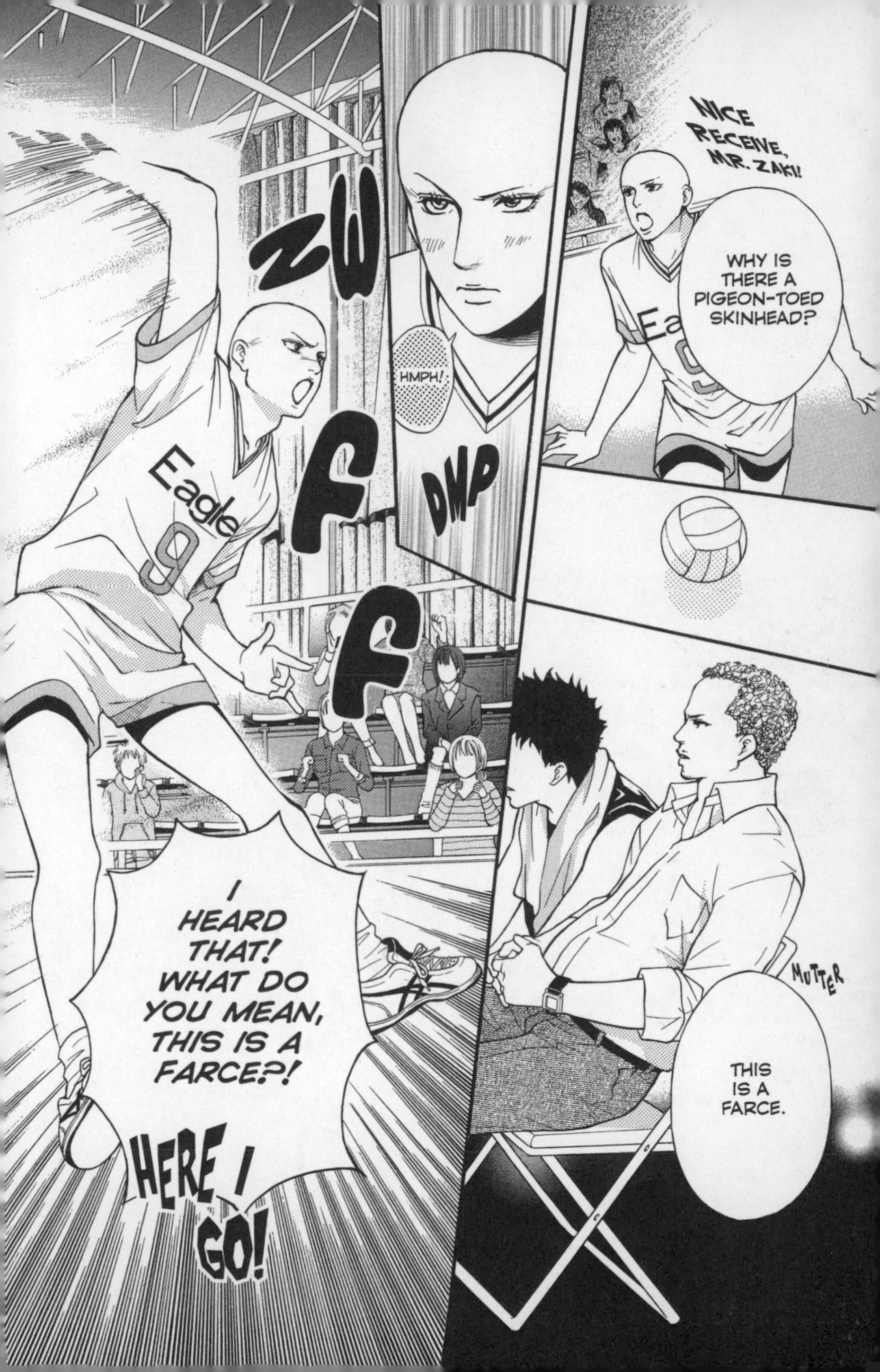
NICE RECEIVE, MR. ZAKI!
WHY IS THERE A PIGEON-TOED SKINHEAD?
MUTTER
THIS IS A FARCE.
HMPH!
DMP
ZW
I HEARD THAT! WHAT DO YOU MEAN, THIS IS A FARCE?!
FF
HERE I GO!

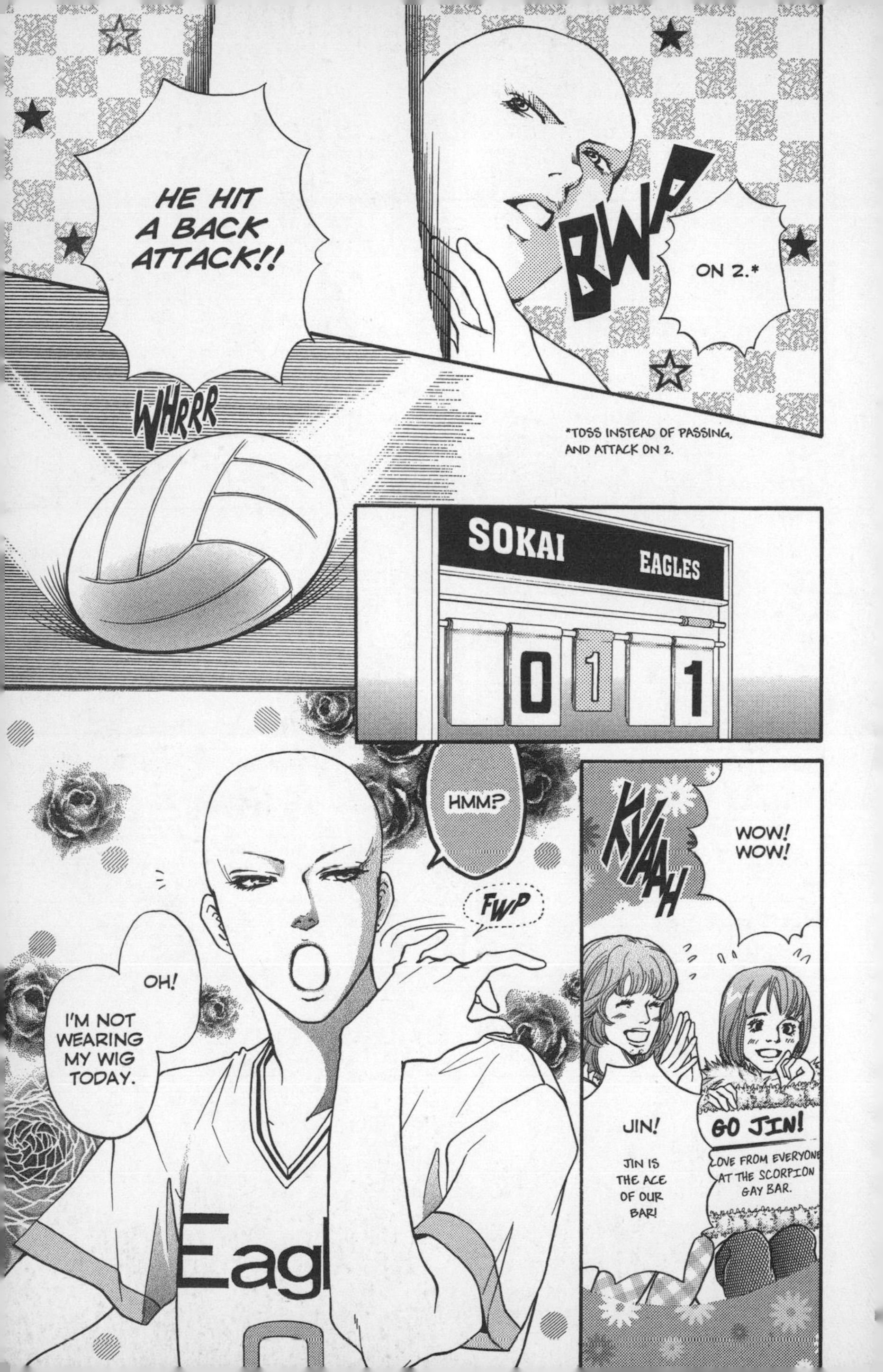
BWIP
ON 2.*
HE HIT A BACK ATTACK!!
WHRRR
SOKAI
EAGLES
0 1 1
KYAAAH
WOW! WOW!
JIN!
JIN IS THE ACE OF OUR BAR!
GO JIN!
LOVE FROM EVERYONE AT THE SCORPION GAY BAR.
HMM?
FWP
OH!
I'M NOT WEARING MY WIG TODAY.
Eagl

*TOSS INSTEAD OF PASSING, AND ATTACK ON 2.

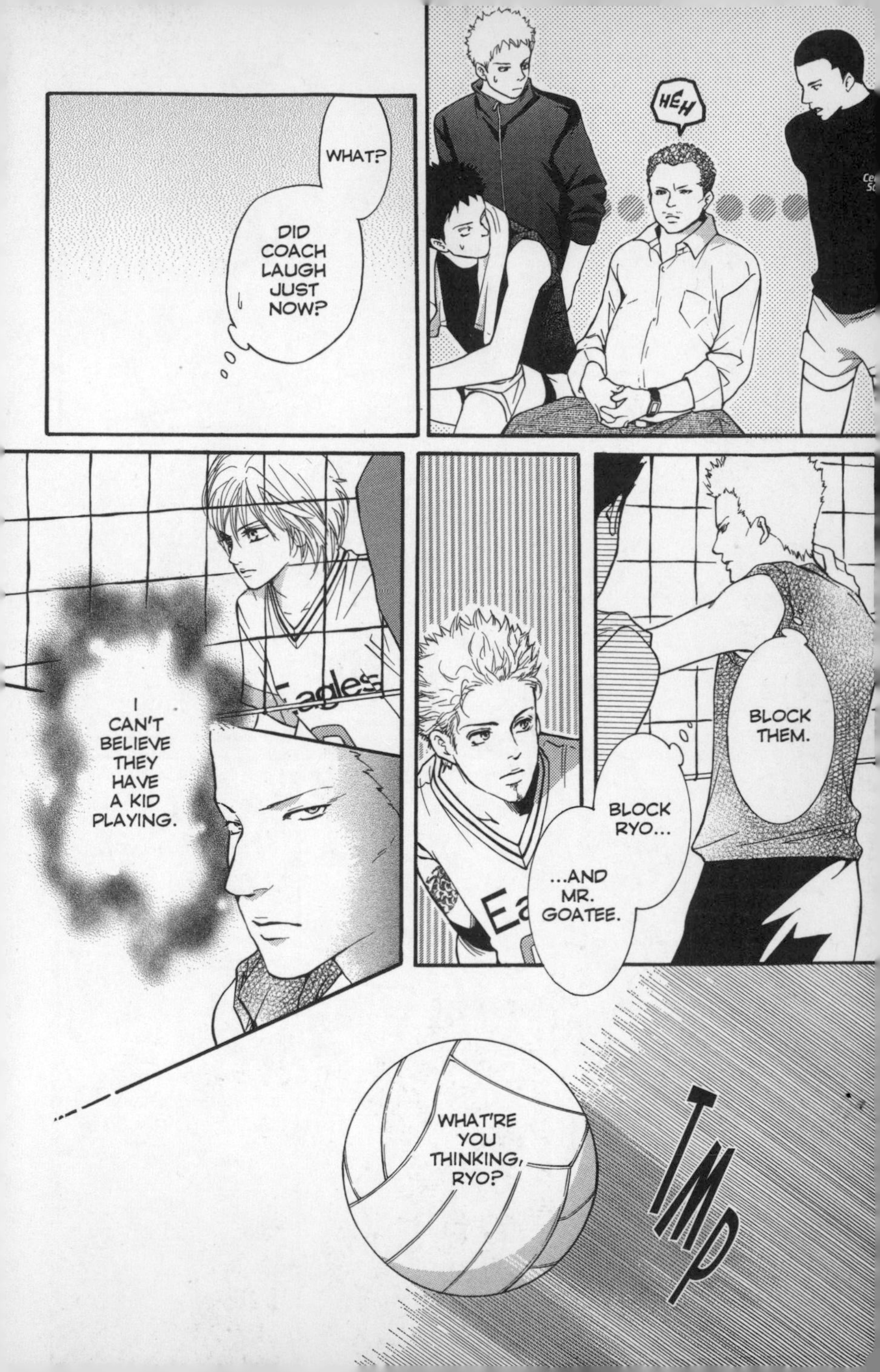
HEH
WHAT?
DID COACH LAUGH JUST NOW?
BLOCK THEM.
BLOCK RYO...
...AND MR. GOATEE.
I CAN'T BELIEVE THEY HAVE A KID PLAYING.
WHAT'RE YOU THINKING, RYO?
TMP

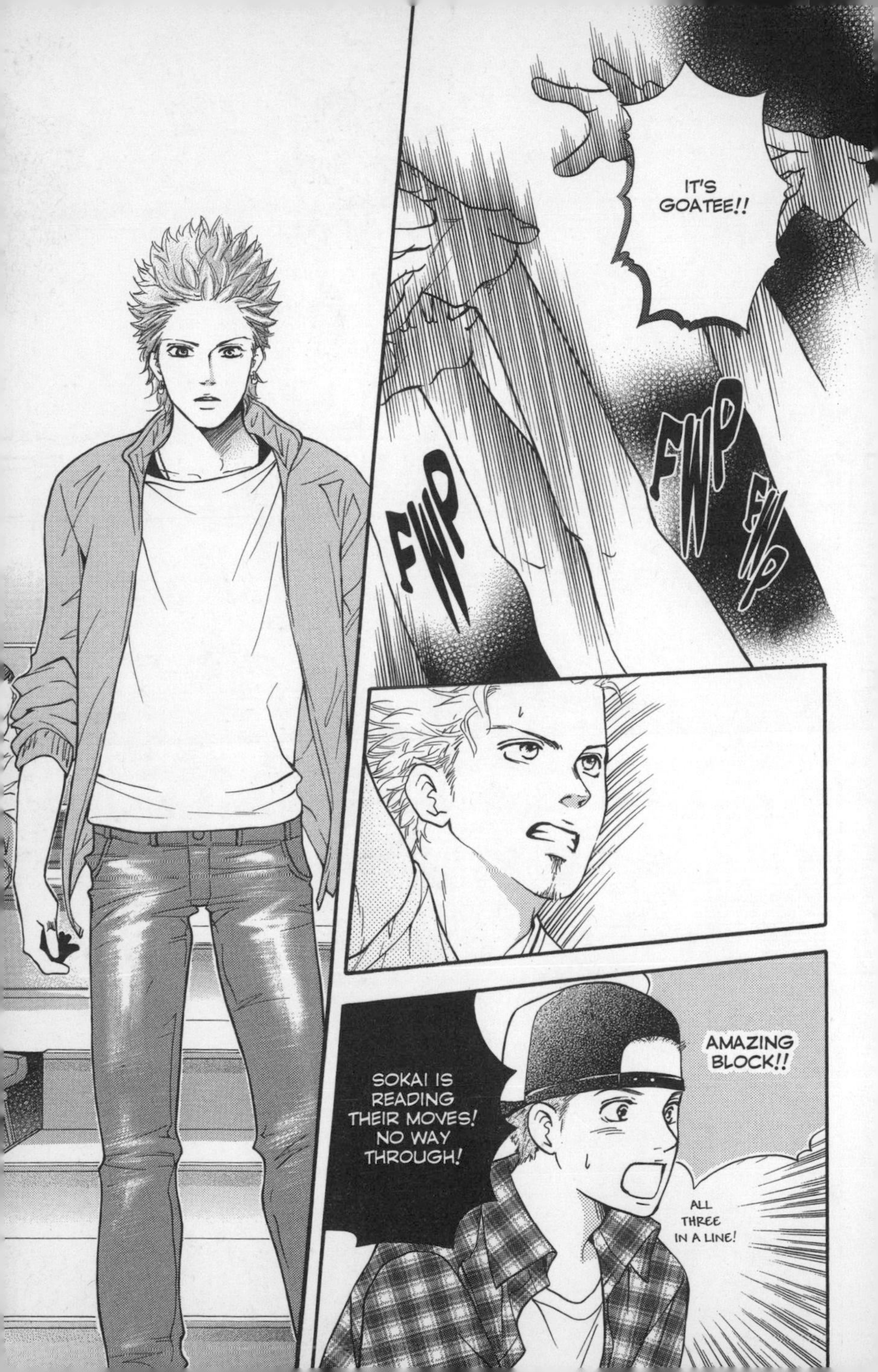
IT'S GOATEE!!
FWP
FWP
FWP
AMAZING BLOCK!!
SOKAI IS READING THEIR MOVES! NO WAY THROUGH!
ALL THREE IN A LINE!

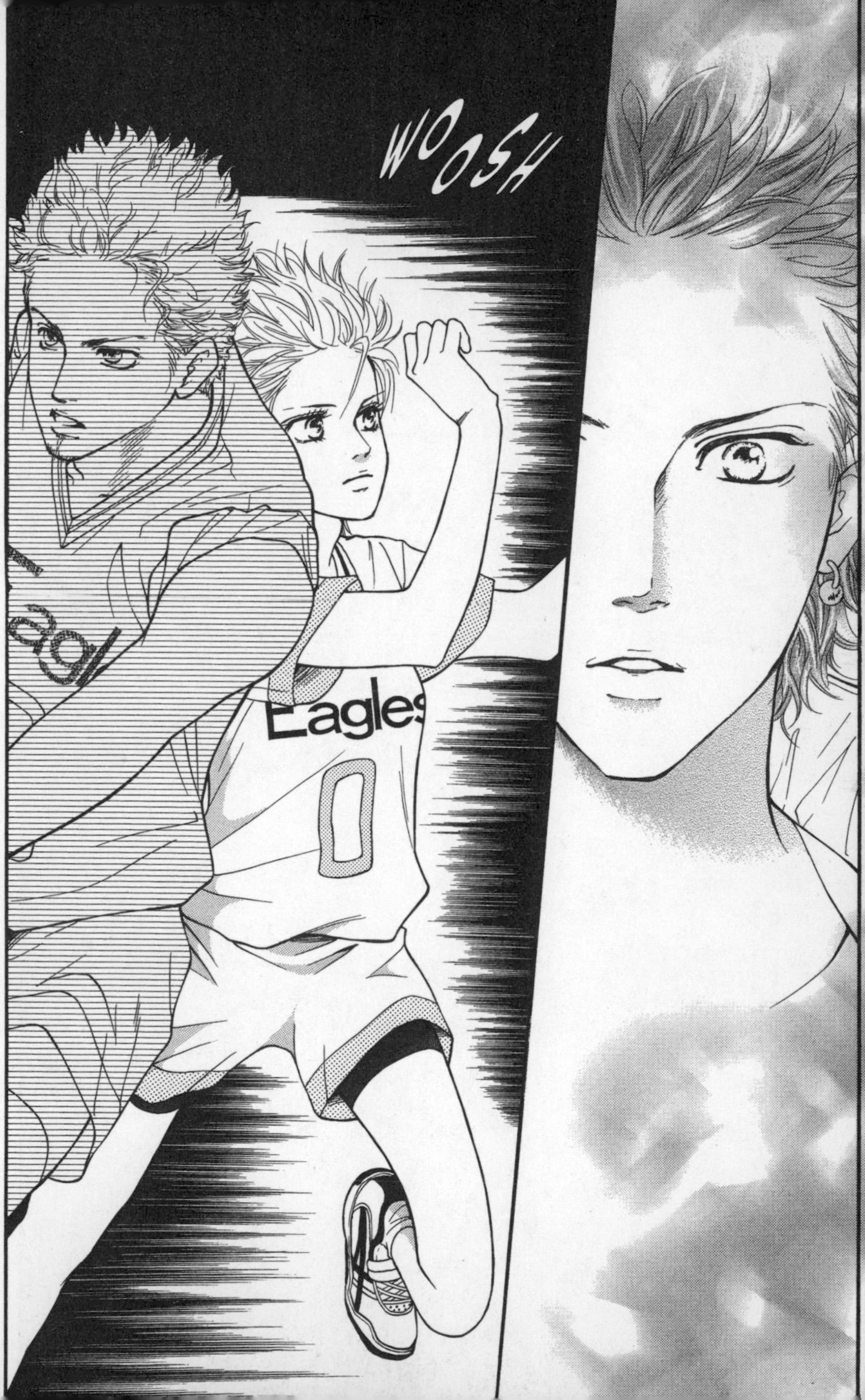
WOOSH
Eagles
0

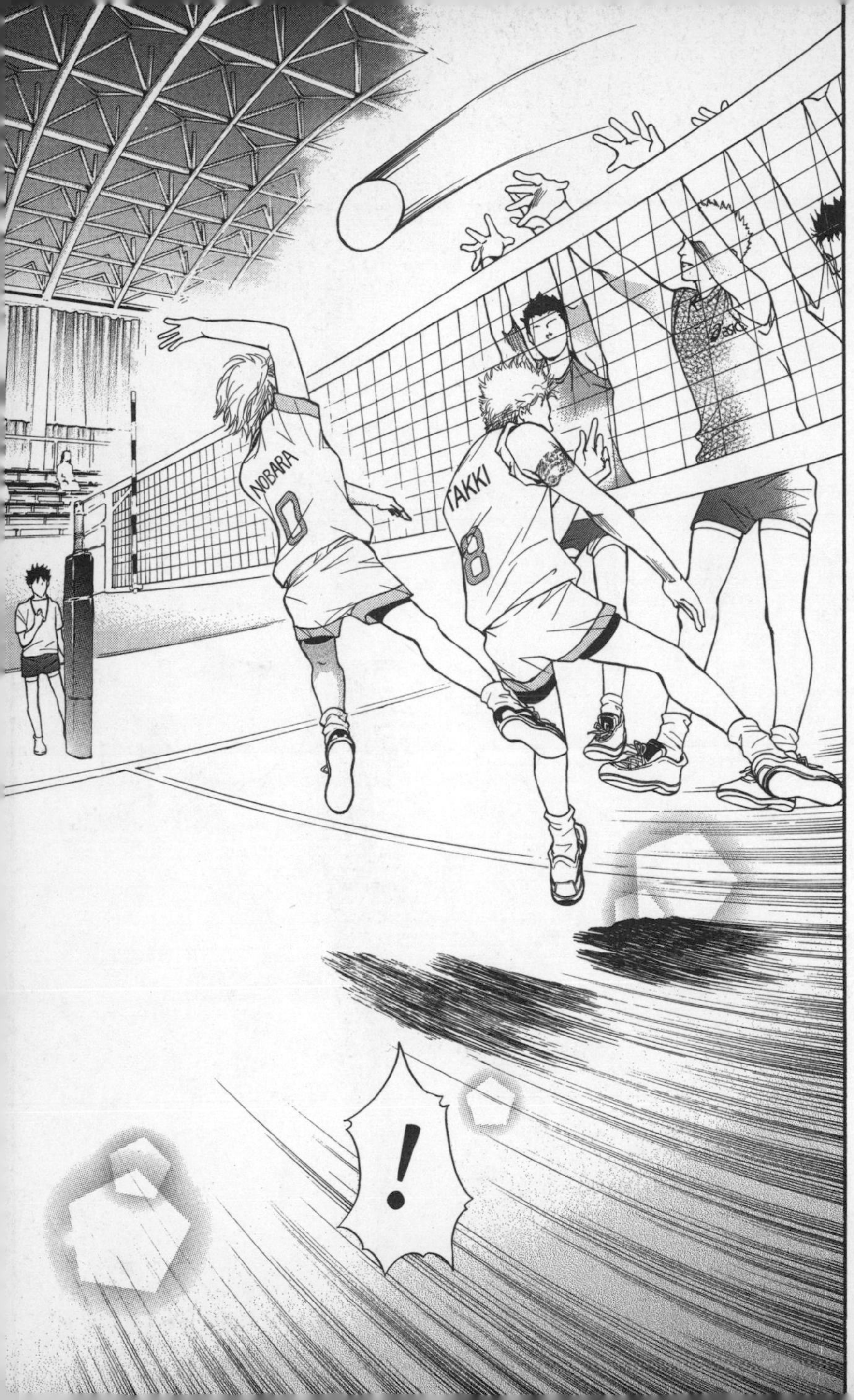

!

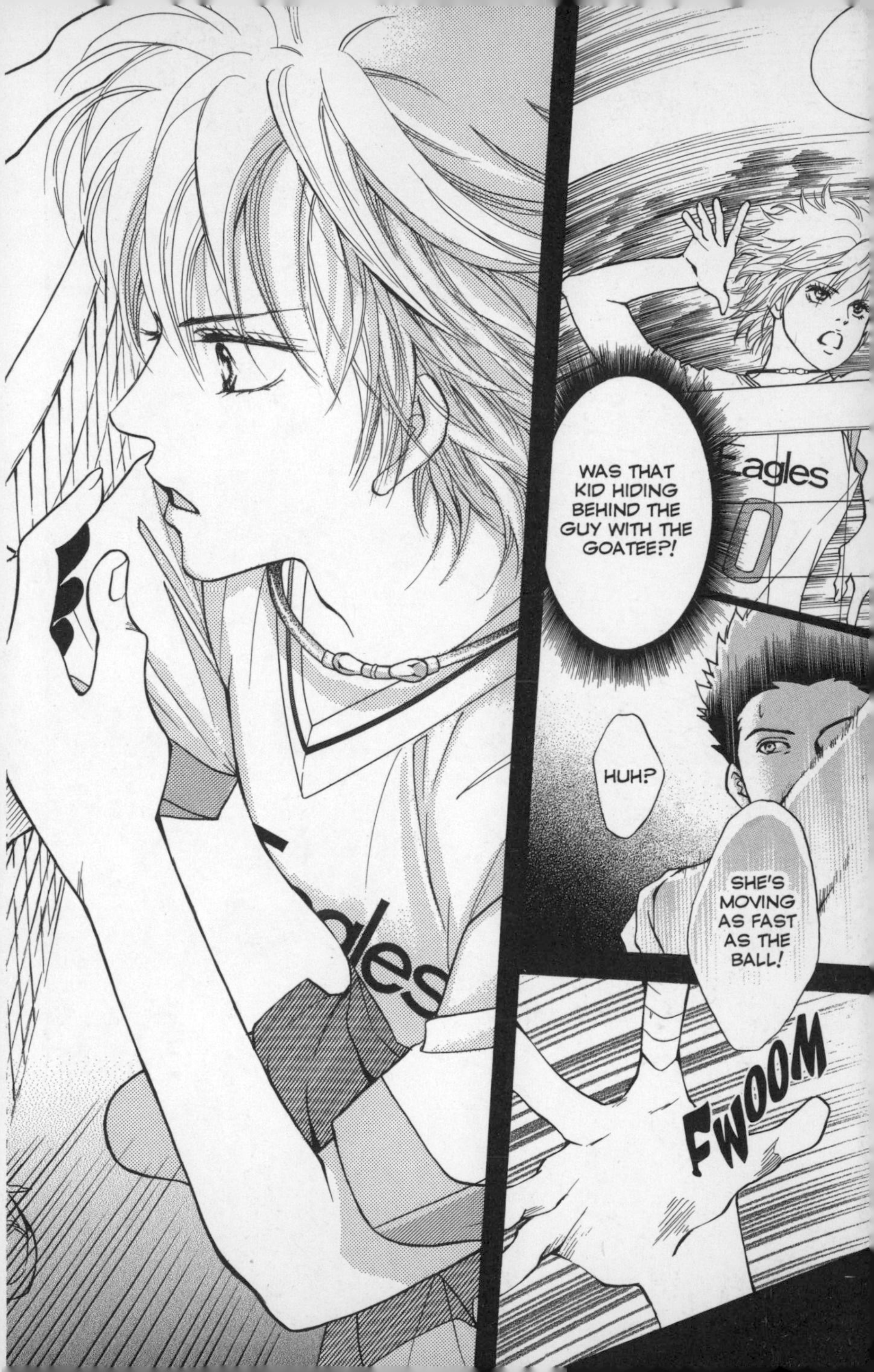
WAS THAT KID HIDING BEHIND THE GUY WITH THE GOATEE?!
HUH?
SHE'S MOVING AS FAST AS THE BALL!
FWOOM

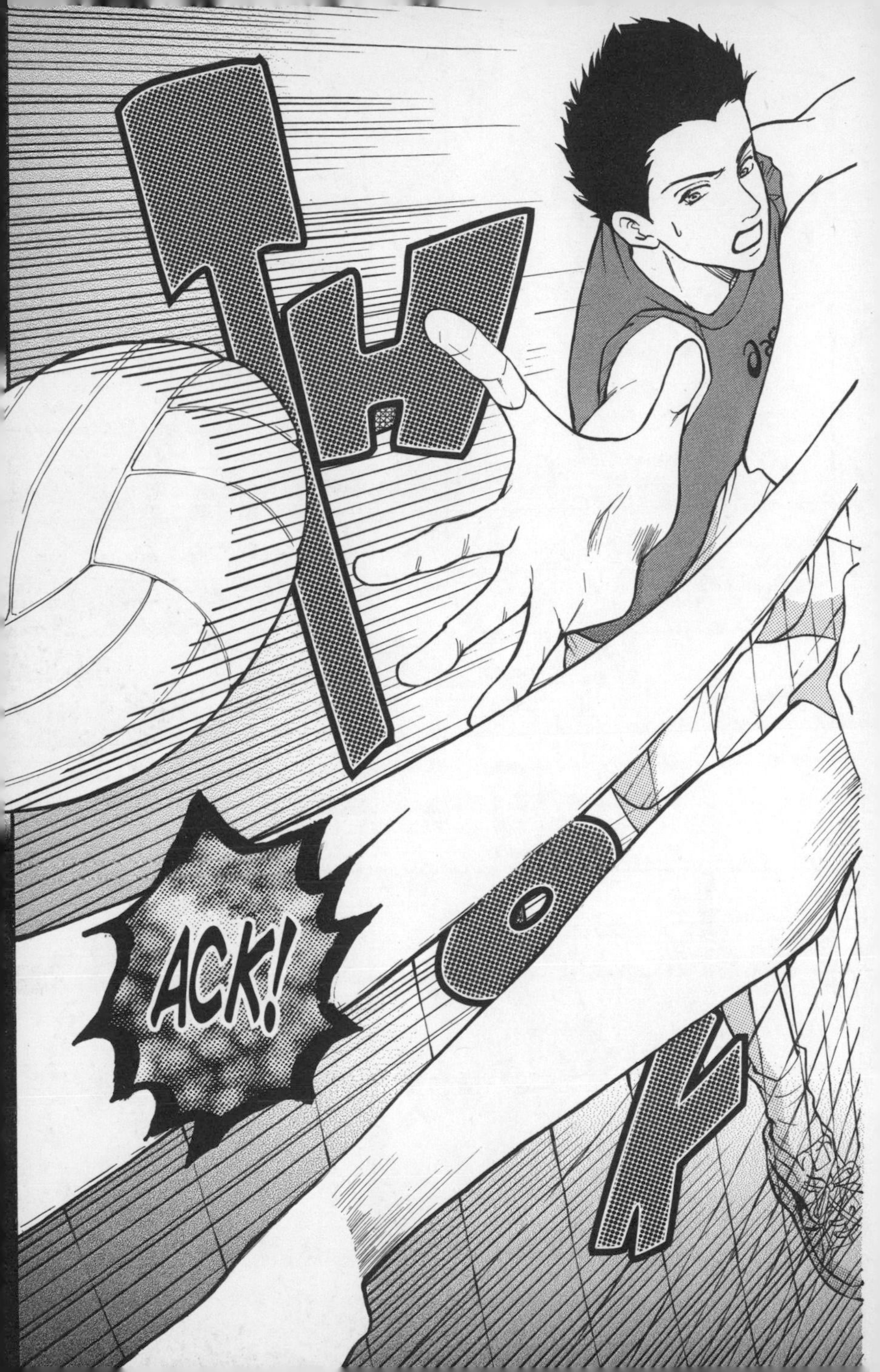
ACK!

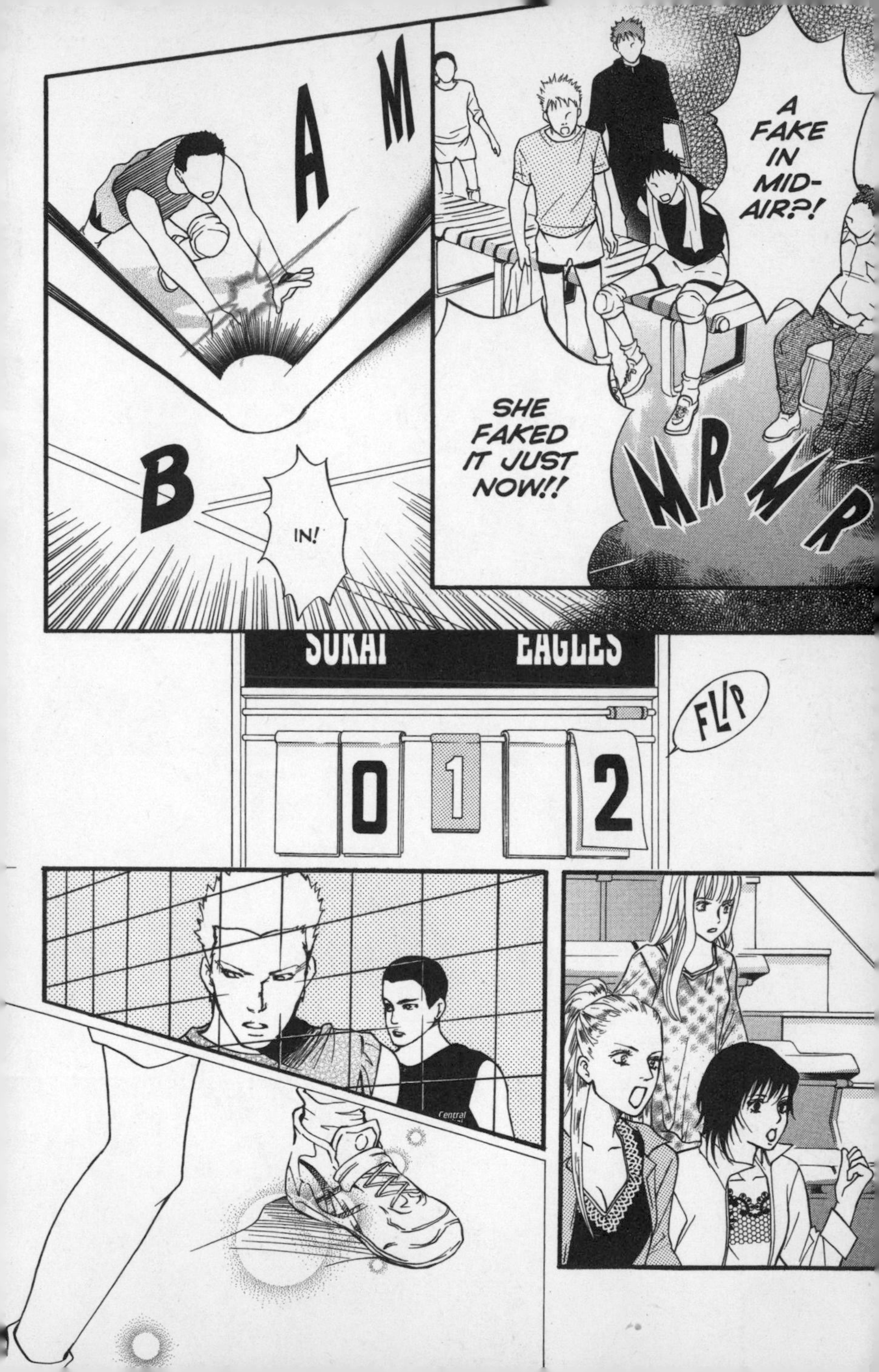

A FAKE IN MID-AIR?!
SHE FAKED IT JUST NOW!!
MRMR
BAM
IN!
FLIP

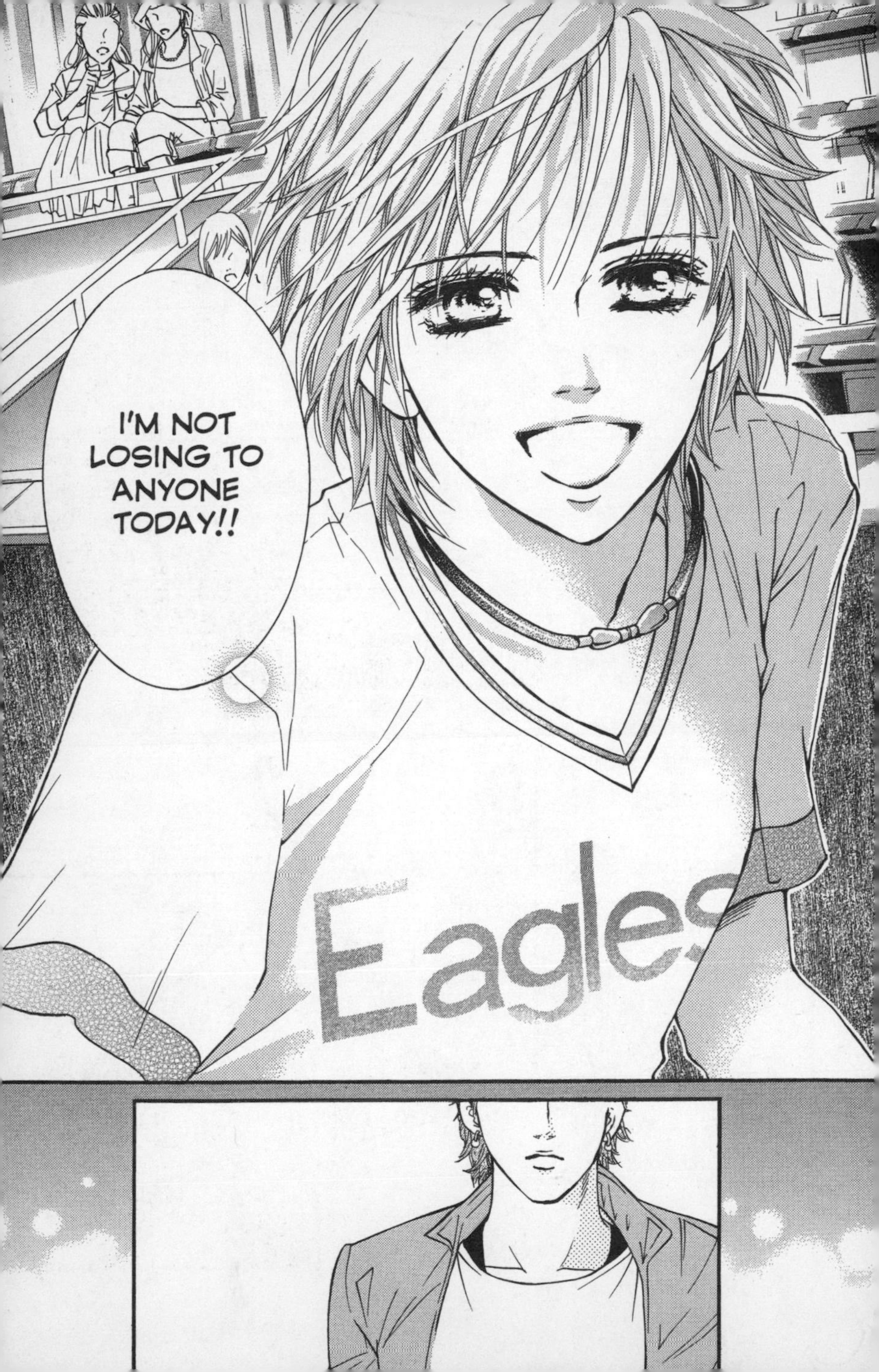
I'M NOT LOSING TO ANYONE TODAY!!
Eagles

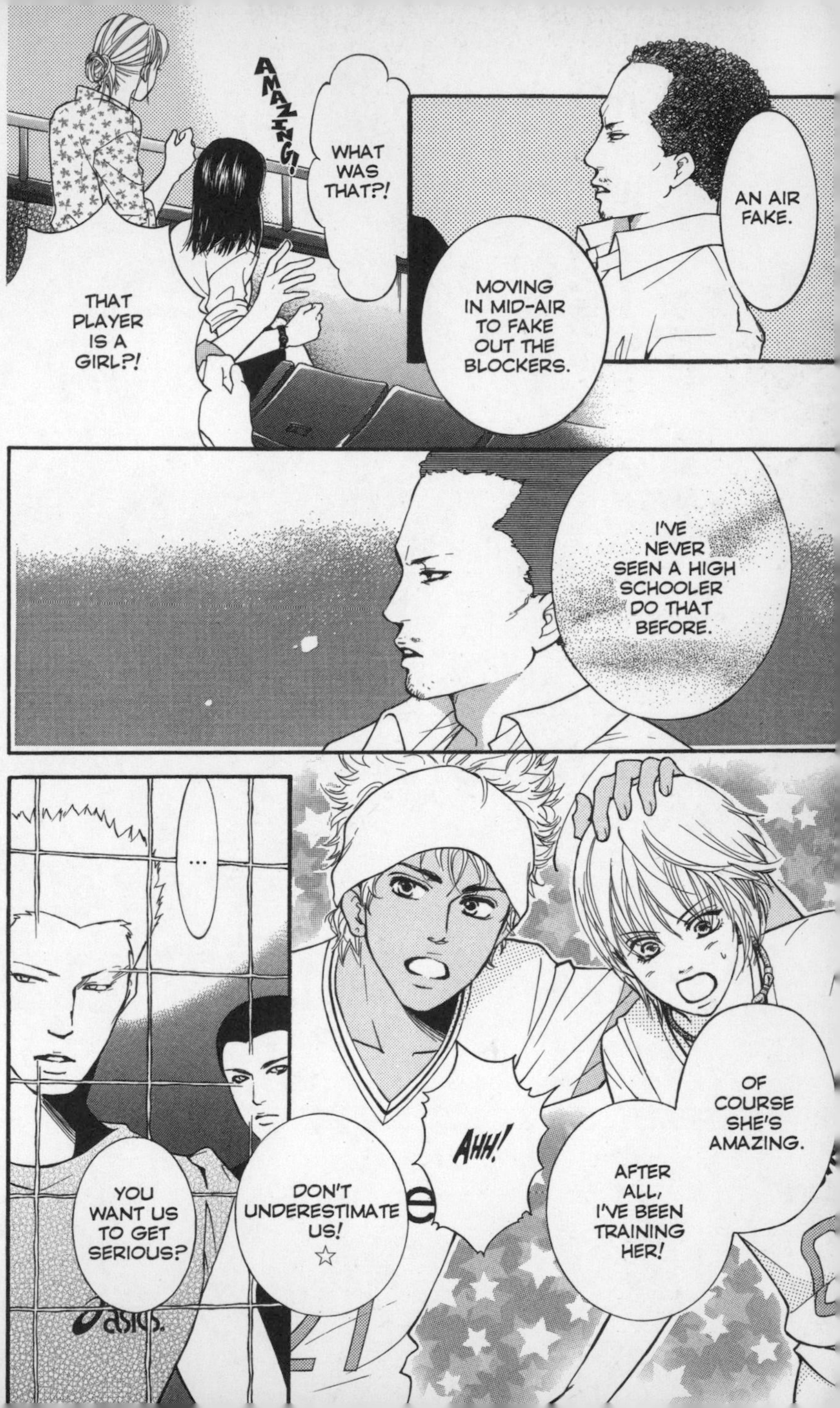
AN AIR FAKE.
MOVING IN MID-AIR TO FAKE OUT THE BLOCKERS.
AMAZING!
WHAT WAS THAT?!
THAT PLAYER IS A GIRL?!
I'VE NEVER SEEN A HIGH SCHOOLER DO THAT BEFORE.
OF COURSE SHE'S AMAZING.
AFTER ALL, I'VE BEEN TRAINING HER!
AHH!
DON'T UNDERESTIMATE US! ☆
...
YOU WANT US TO GET SERIOUS?

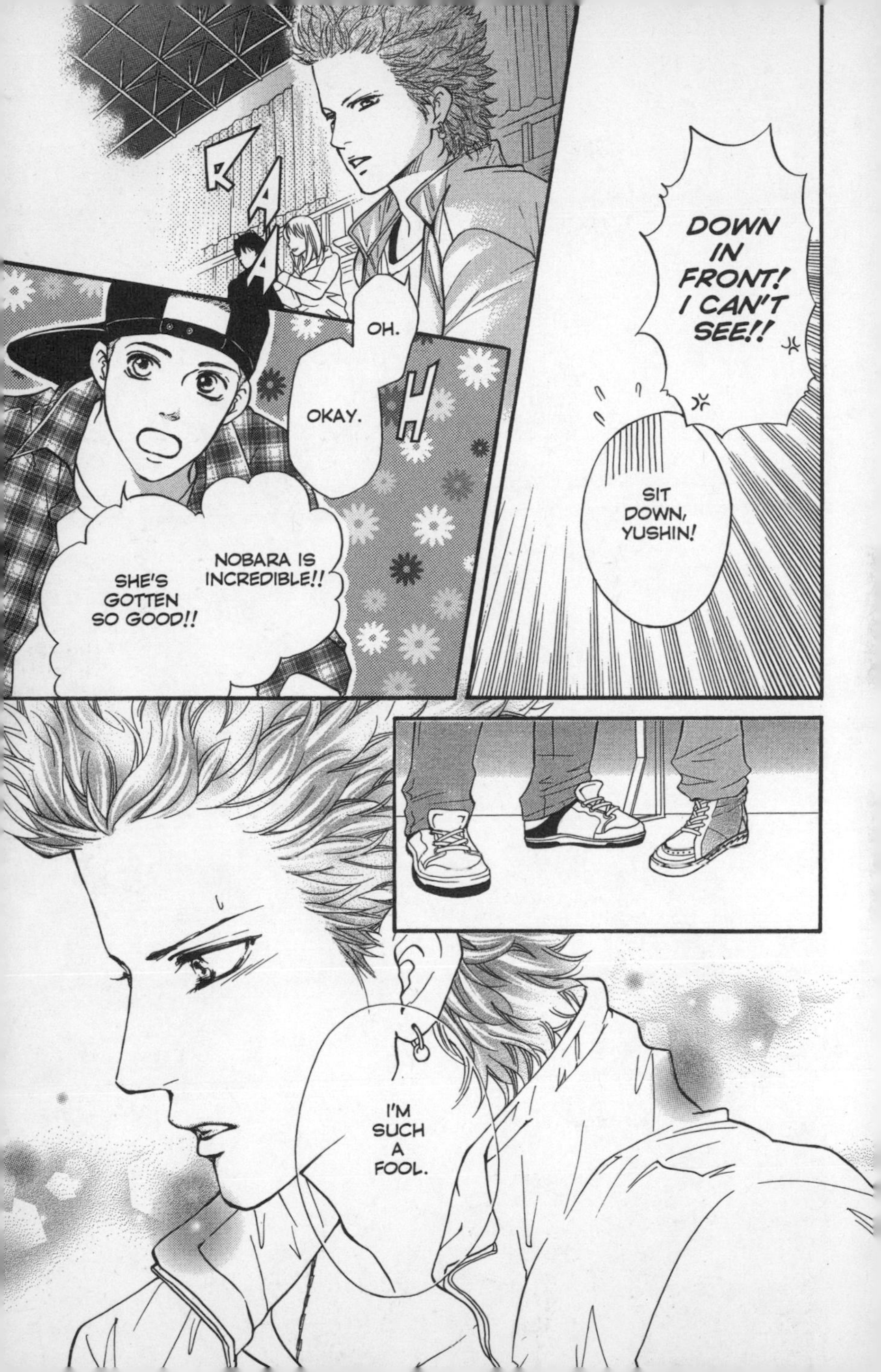
DOWN IN FRONT! I CAN'T SEE!!
SIT DOWN, YUSHIN!
RAA
OH.
OKAY.
H
NOBARA IS INCREDIBLE!!
SHE'S GOTTEN SO GOOD!!
I'M SUCH A FOOL.

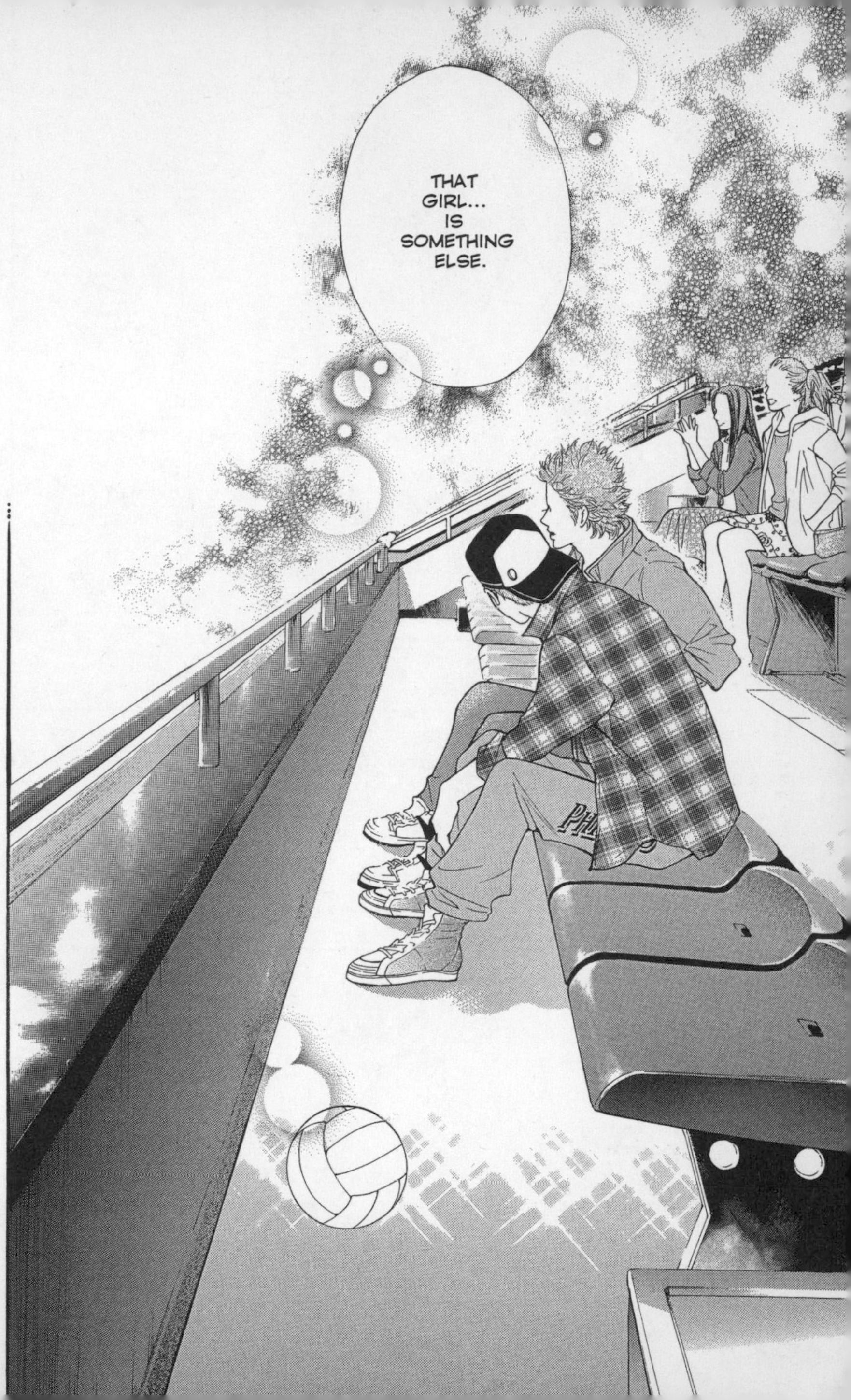
THAT GIRL... IS SOMETHING ELSE.

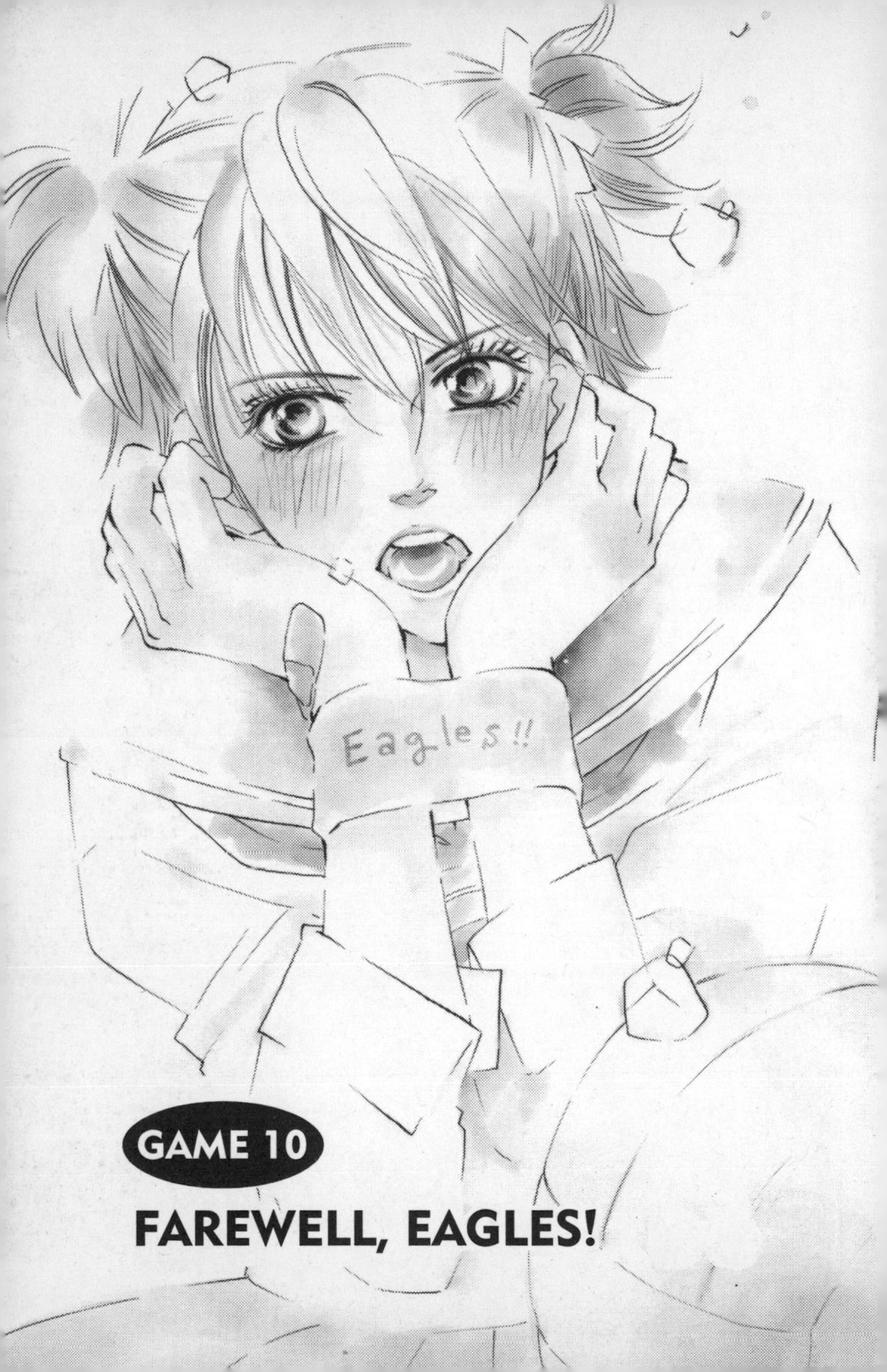
Eagles!!

GAME 10

FAREWELL, EAGLES!

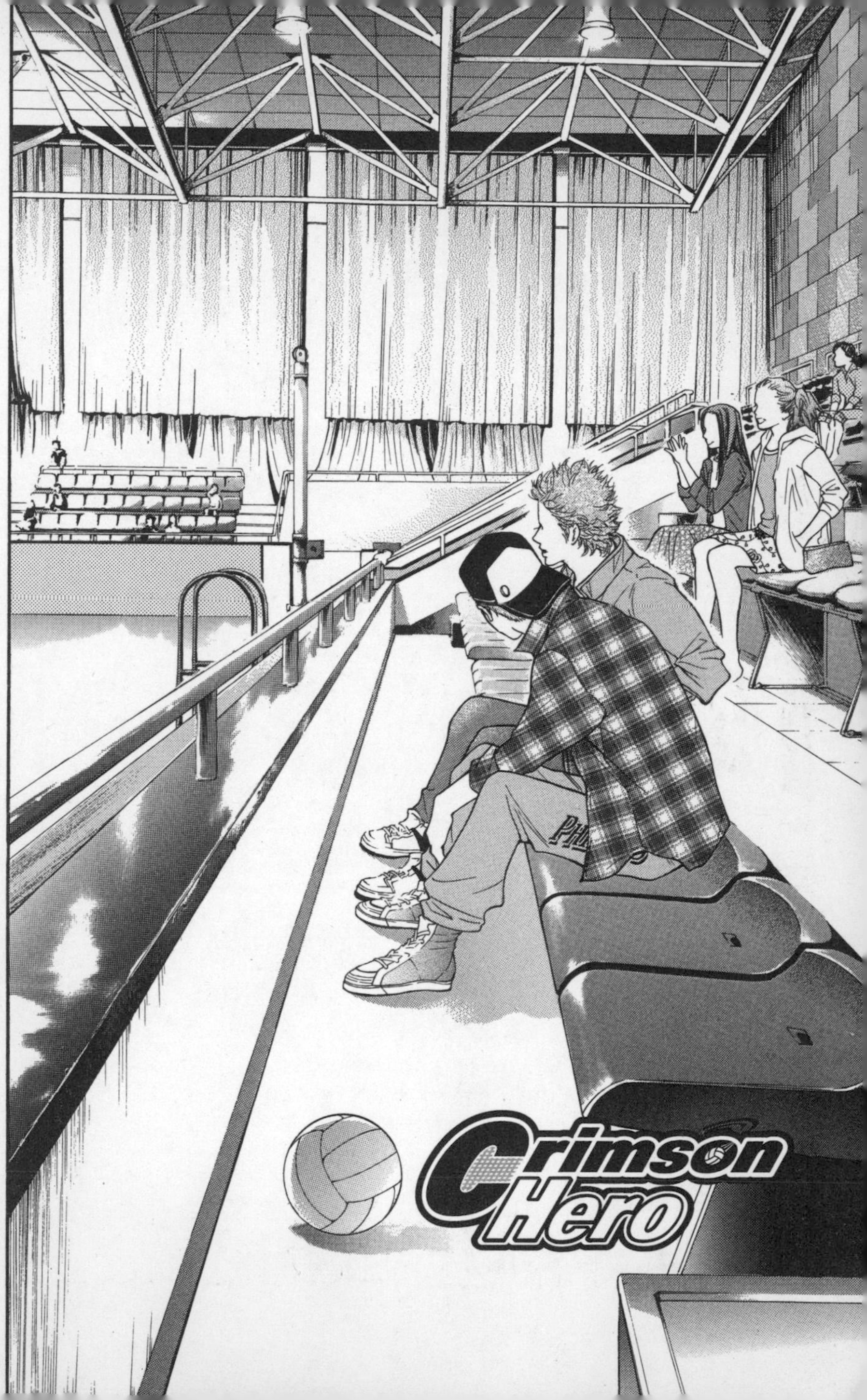
Crimson Hero

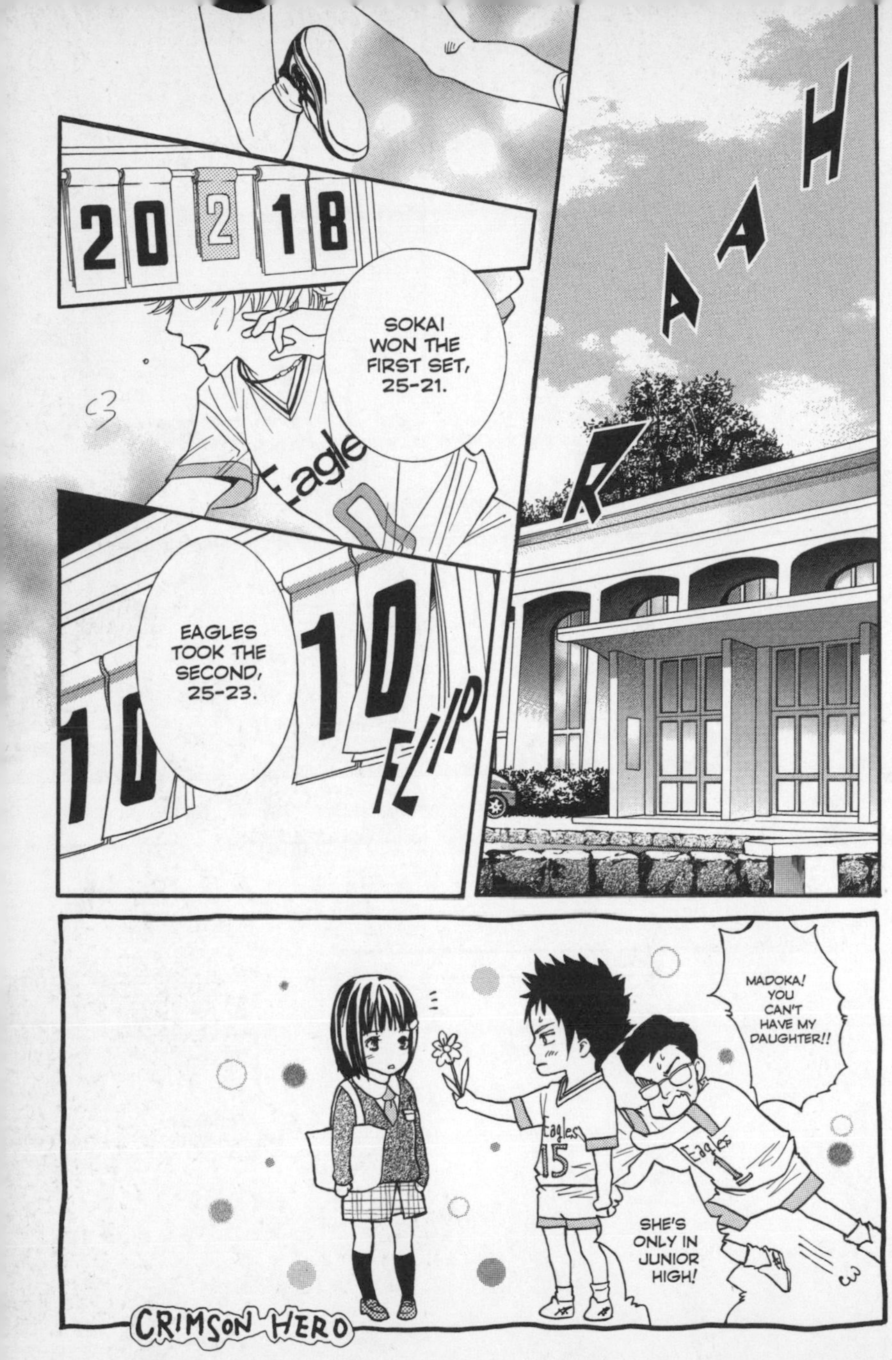
RAAAH
20 2 18
SOKAI WON THE FIRST SET, 25-21.
10 10
EAGLES TOOK THE SECOND, 25-23.
FLIP
MADOKA! YOU CAN'T HAVE MY DAUGHTER!!
SHE'S ONLY IN JUNIOR HIGH!
CRIMSON HERO

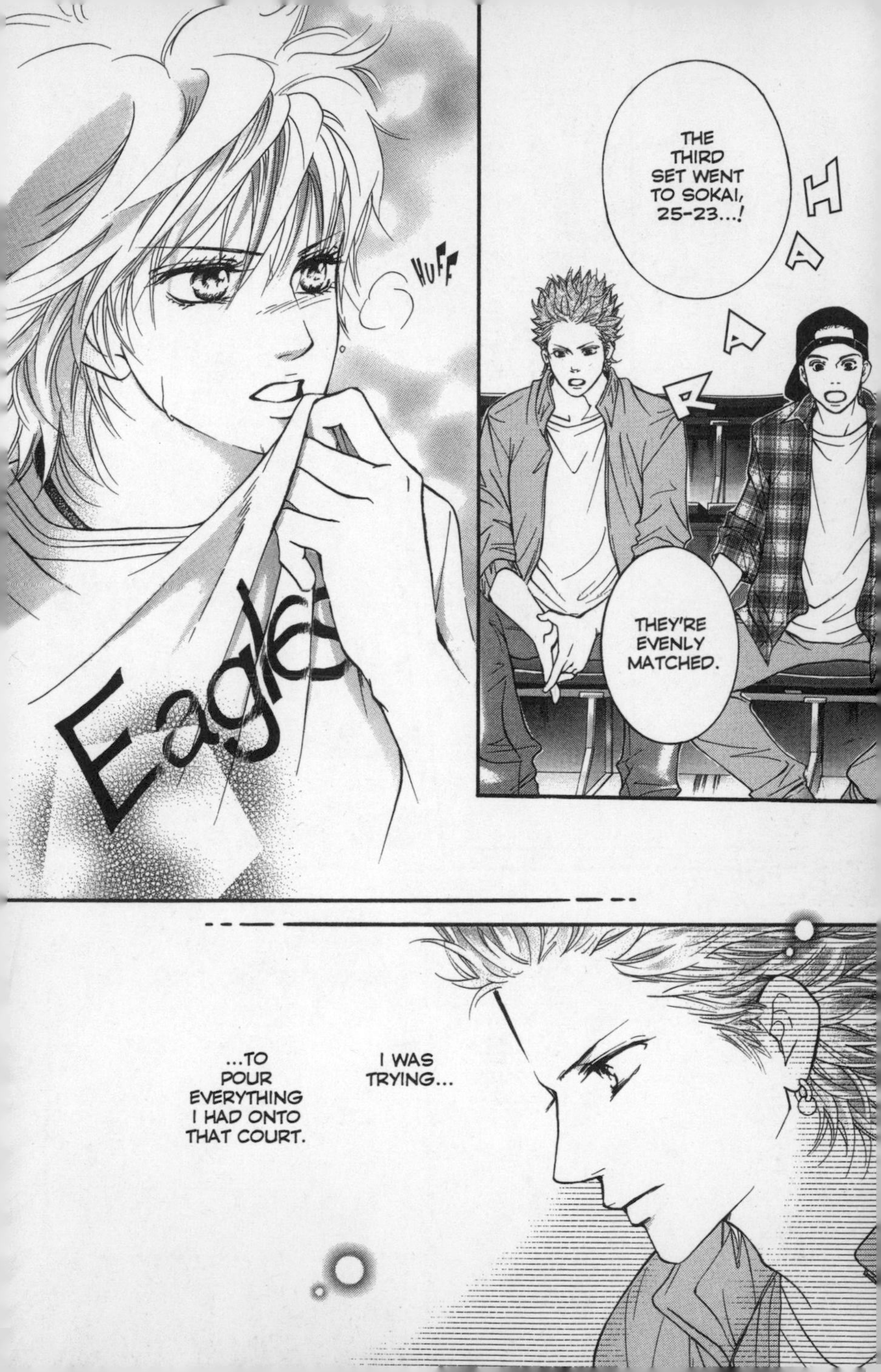
THE THIRD SET WENT TO SOKAI, 25-23...!
RAAH
THEY'RE EVENLY MATCHED.
HUFF
Eagles
I WAS TRYING...
...TO POUR EVERYTHING I HAD ONTO THAT COURT.

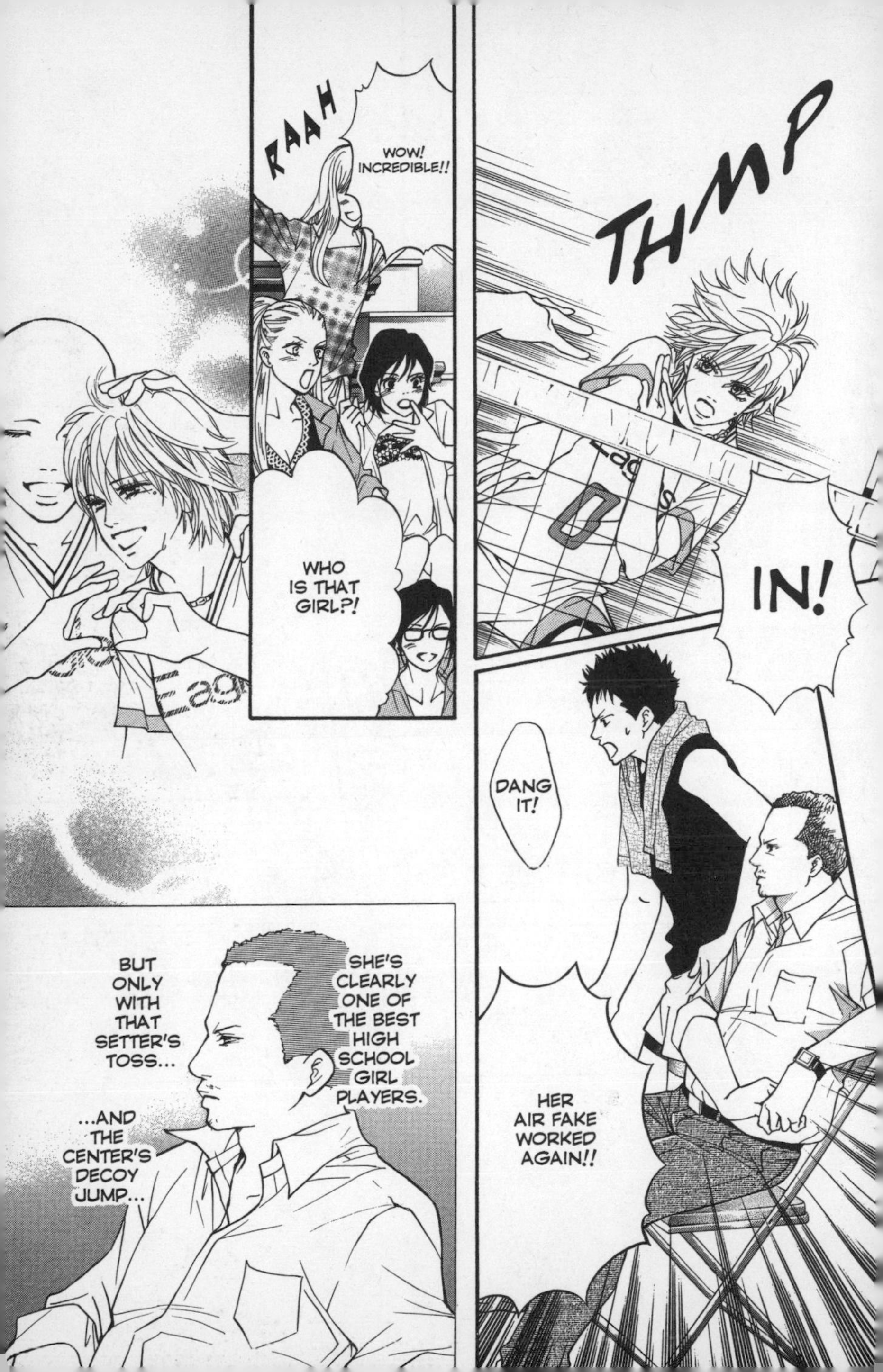
THMP
RAAH
WOW! INCREDIBLE!!
WHO IS THAT GIRL?!
IN!
DANG IT!
HER AIR FAKE WORKED AGAIN!!
SHE'S CLEARLY ONE OF THE BEST HIGH SCHOOL GIRL PLAYERS.
BUT ONLY WITH THAT SETTER'S TOSS...
...AND THE CENTER'S DECOY JUMP...

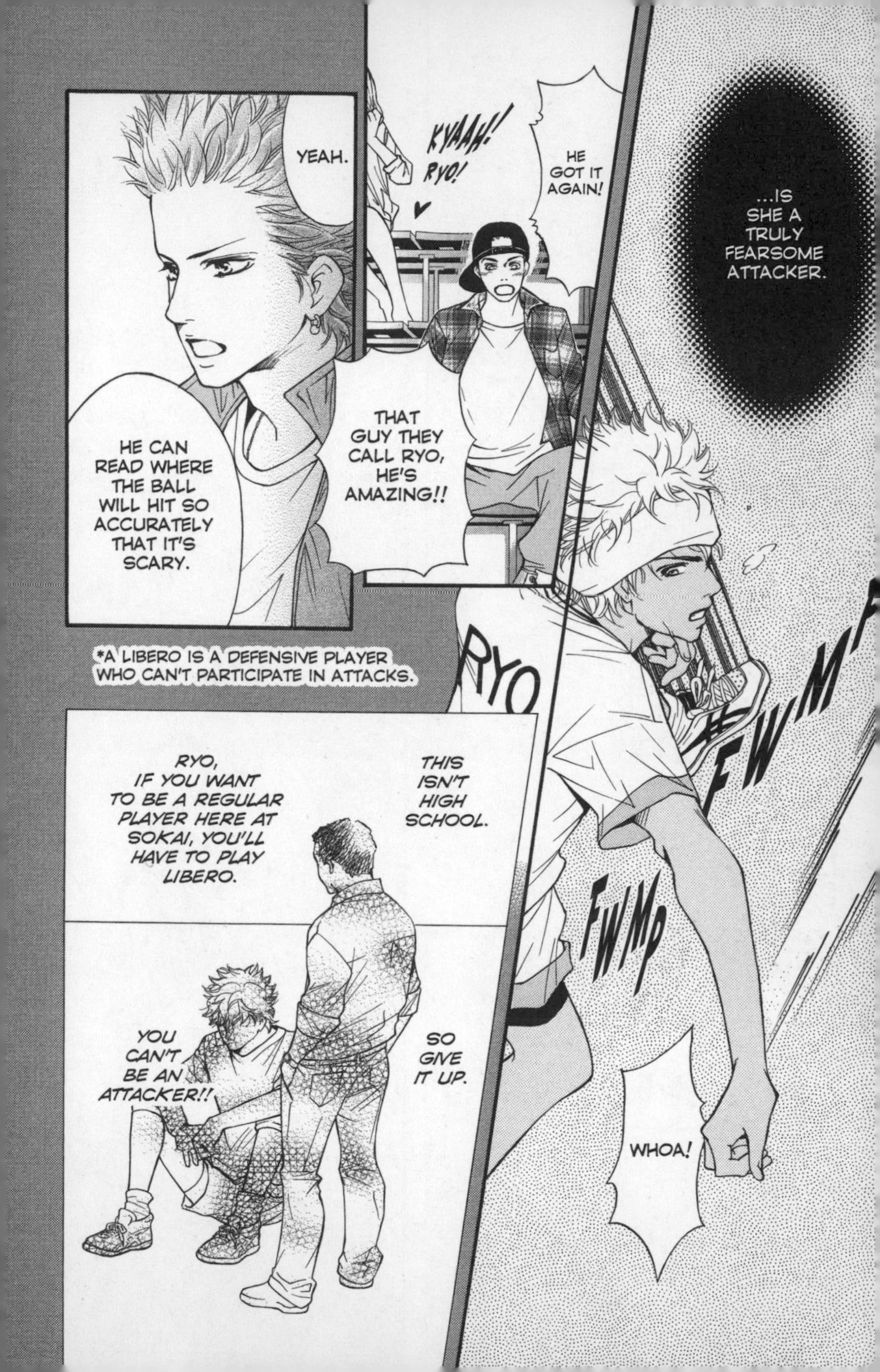
...IS SHE A TRULY FEARSOME ATTACKER.
FWMP
RYO
FWMP
WHOA!
KYAAH! RYO!
HE GOT IT AGAIN!
THAT GUY THEY CALL RYO, HE'S AMAZING!!
YEAH.
HE CAN READ WHERE THE BALL WILL HIT SO ACCURATELY THAT IT'S SCARY.
*A LIBERO IS A DEFENSIVE PLAYER WHO CAN'T PARTICIPATE IN ATTACKS.
THIS ISN'T HIGH SCHOOL.
RYO, IF YOU WANT TO BE A REGULAR PLAYER HERE AT SOKAI, YOU'LL HAVE TO PLAY LIBERO.
SO GIVE IT UP.
YOU CAN'T BE AN ATTACKER!!

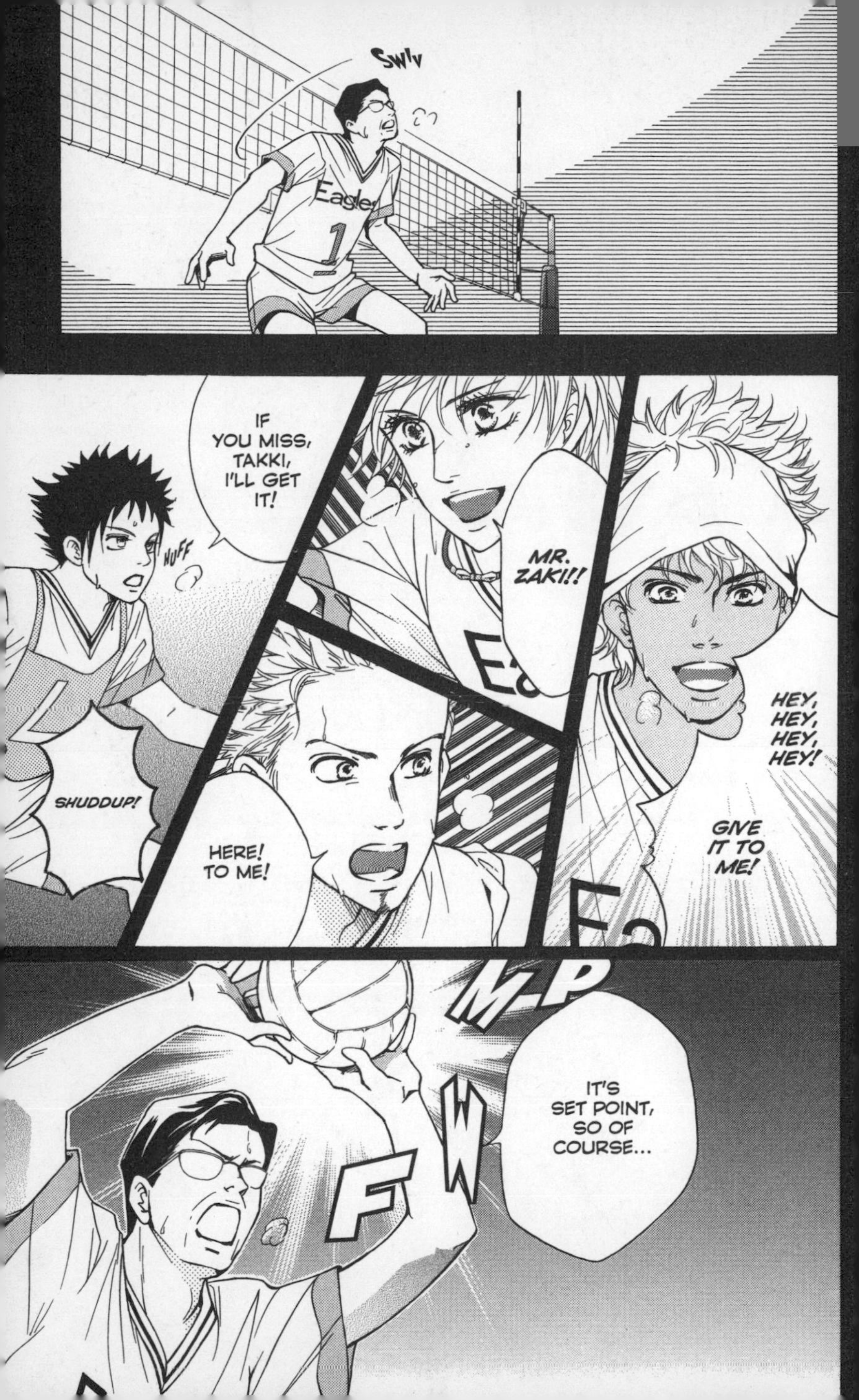
SWIV
HEY, HEY, HEY, HEY!
GIVE IT TO ME!
MR. ZAKI!!
HERE! TO ME!
IF YOU MISS, TAKKI, I'LL GET IT!
HUFF
SHUDDUP!
M-P
IT'S SET POINT, SO OF COURSE...
W
F

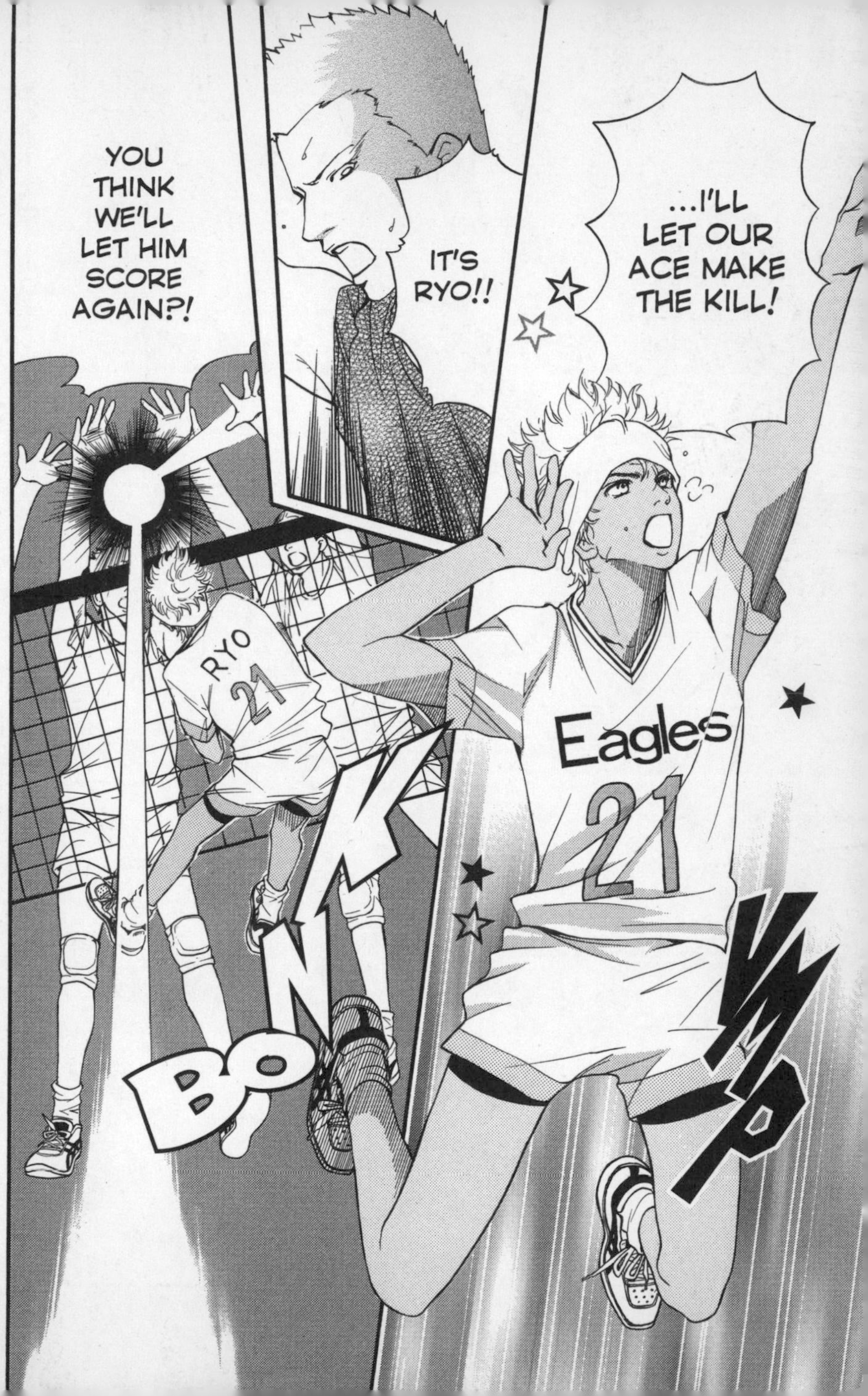
...I'LL LET OUR ACE MAKE THE KILL!
Eagles
21
WMP
IT'S RYO!!
YOU THINK WE'LL LET HIM SCORE AGAIN?!
RYO
21
BONK

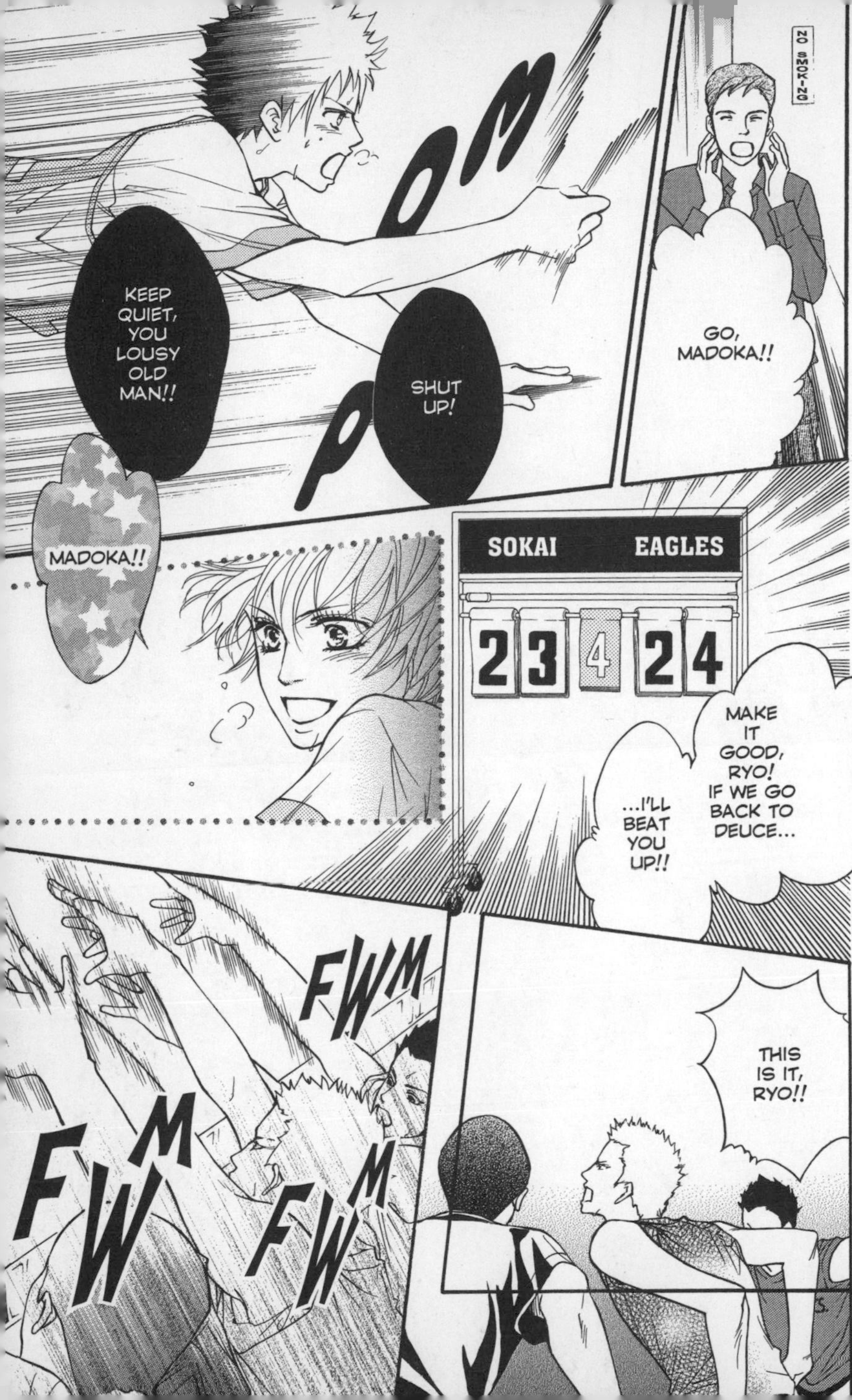
NO SMOKING
GO, MADOKA!!
POW
SHUT UP!
KEEP QUIET, YOU LOUSY OLD MAN!!
SOKAI EAGLES
23 4 24
MAKE IT GOOD, RYO! IF WE GO BACK TO DEUCE...
...I'LL BEAT YOU UP!!
MADOKA!!
THIS IS IT, RYO!!
FWM
FWM
FWM

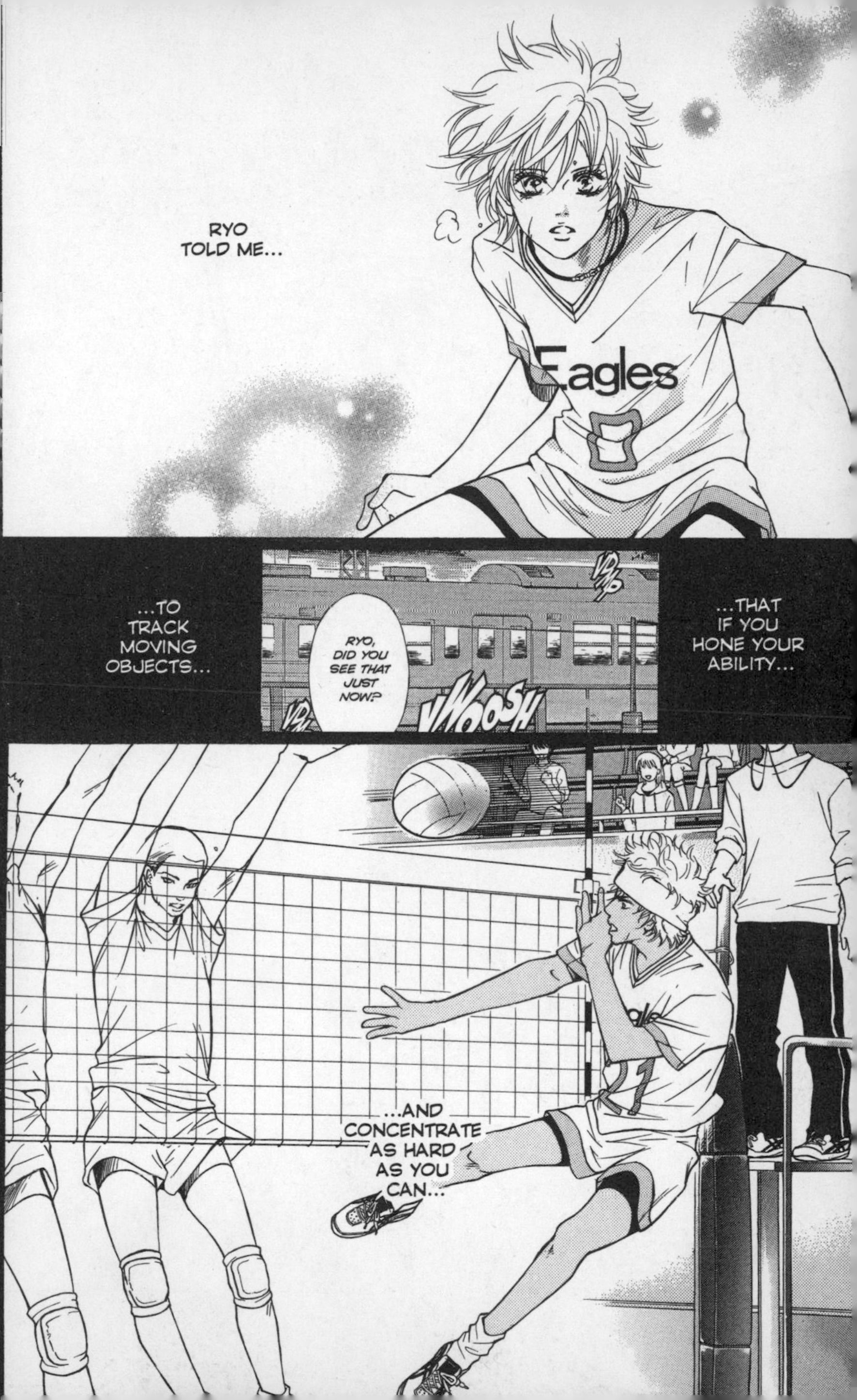
RYO TOLD ME...
...THAT IF YOU HONE YOUR ABILITY...
RYO, DID YOU SEE THAT JUST NOW?
VWOOSH
...TO TRACK MOVING OBJECTS...
...AND CONCENTRATE AS HARD AS YOU CAN...

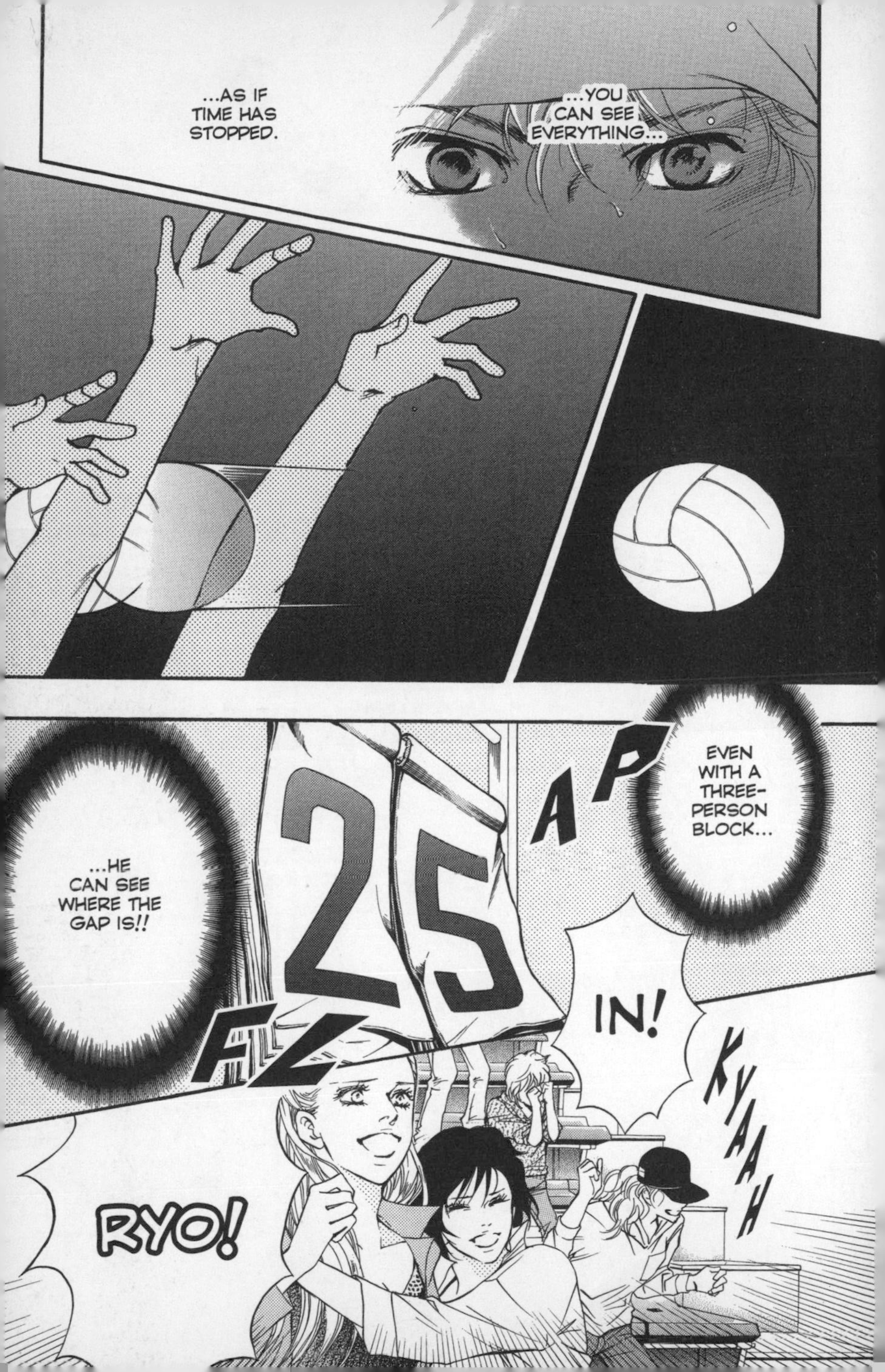
...YOU CAN SEE EVERYTHING...
...AS IF TIME HAS STOPPED.
EVEN WITH A THREE-PERSON BLOCK...
AP
25
FL
...HE CAN SEE WHERE THE GAP IS!!
IN!
KYAAH
RYO!

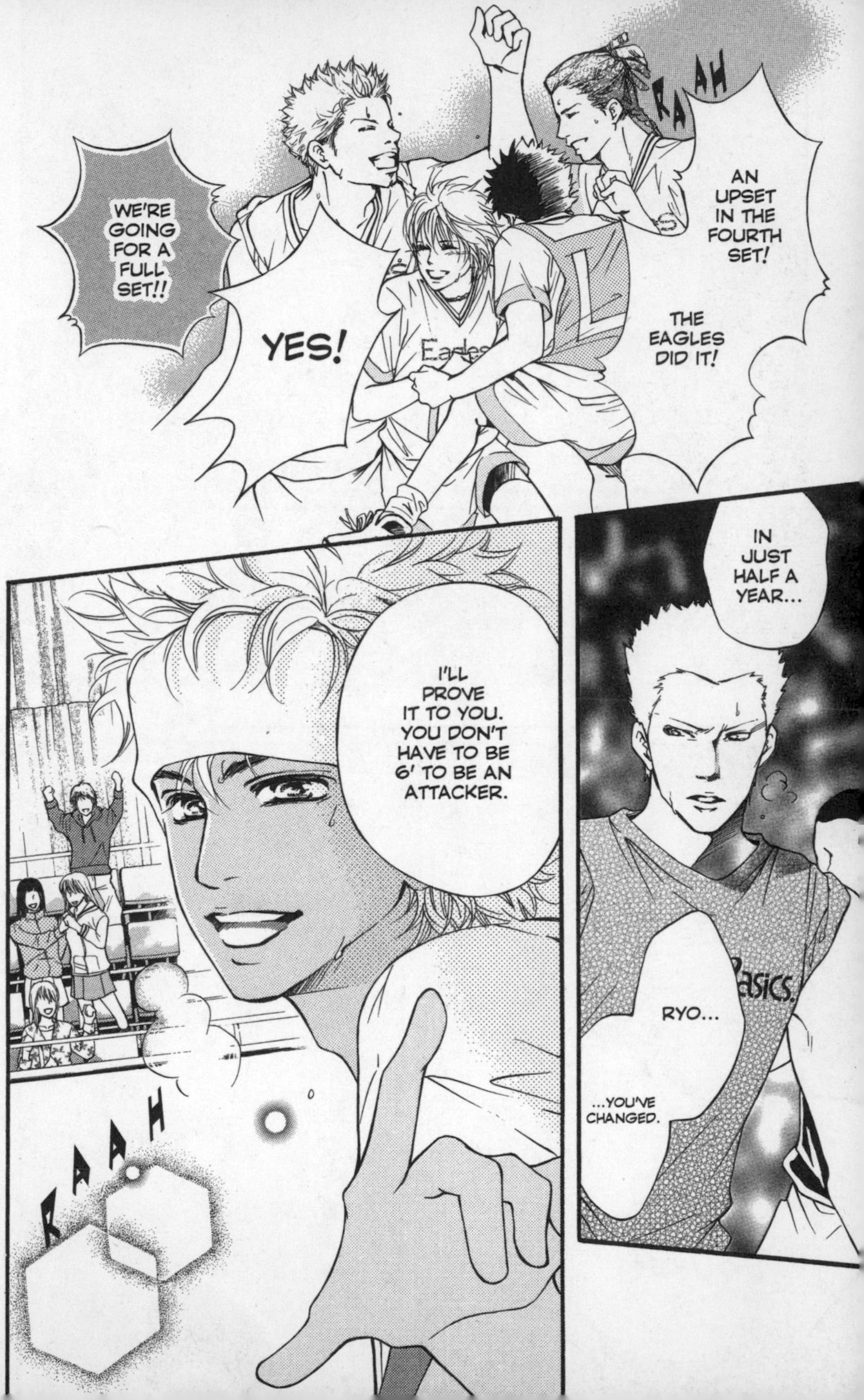
RAAH
AN UPSET IN THE FOURTH SET!
THE EAGLES DID IT!
YES!
WE'RE GOING FOR A FULL SET!!
Eagles
IN JUST HALF A YEAR...
RYO...
...YOU'VE CHANGED.
I'LL PROVE IT TO YOU. YOU DON'T HAVE TO BE 6' TO BE AN ATTACKER.
RAAH

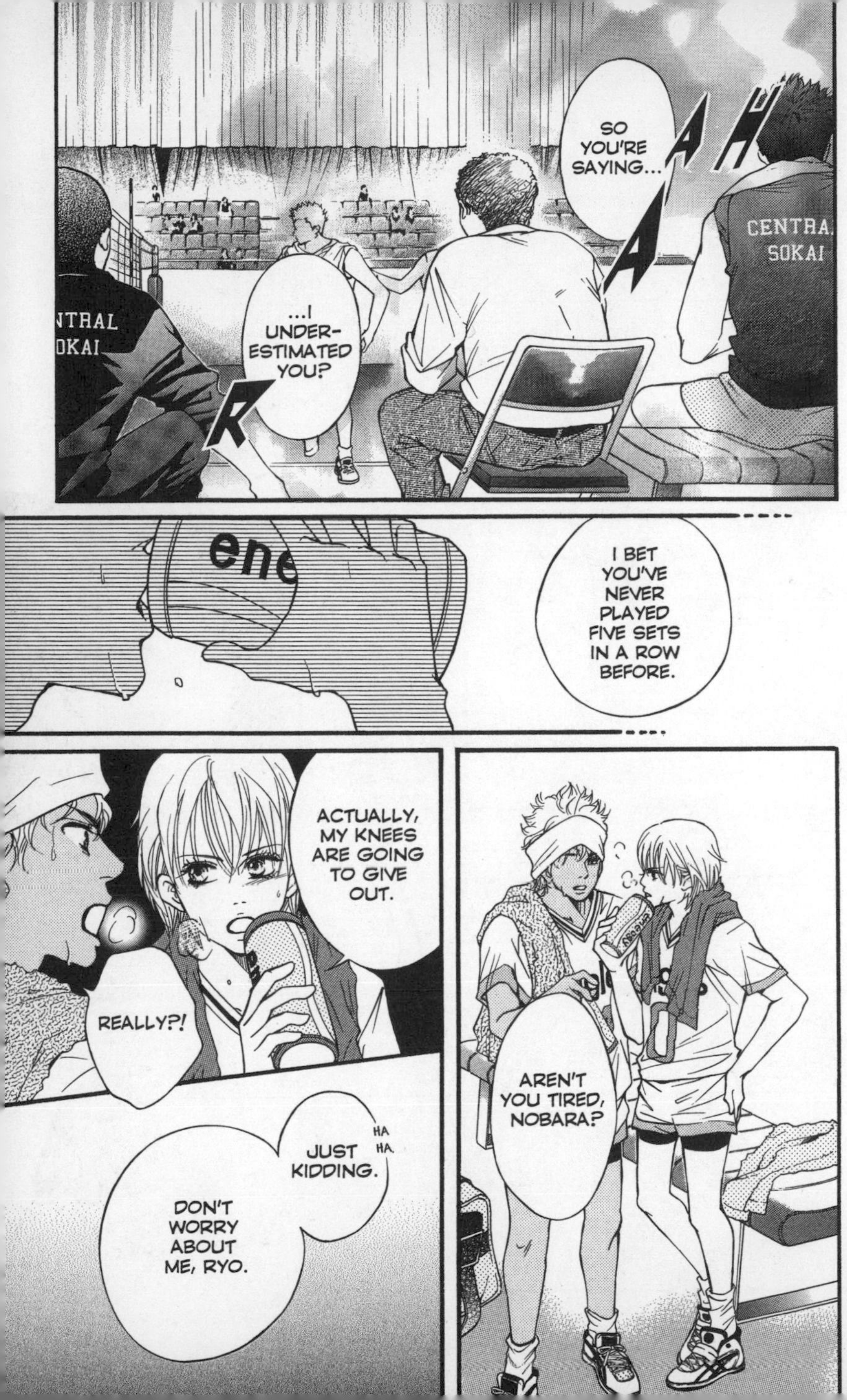
SO YOU'RE SAYING...
CENTRAL SOKAI
...I UNDER-ESTIMATED YOU?
NTRAL OKAI
I BET YOU'VE NEVER PLAYED FIVE SETS IN A ROW BEFORE.
AREN'T YOU TIRED, NOBARA?
ACTUALLY, MY KNEES ARE GOING TO GIVE OUT.
REALLY?!
JUST KIDDING.
HA HA
DON'T WORRY ABOUT ME, RYO.

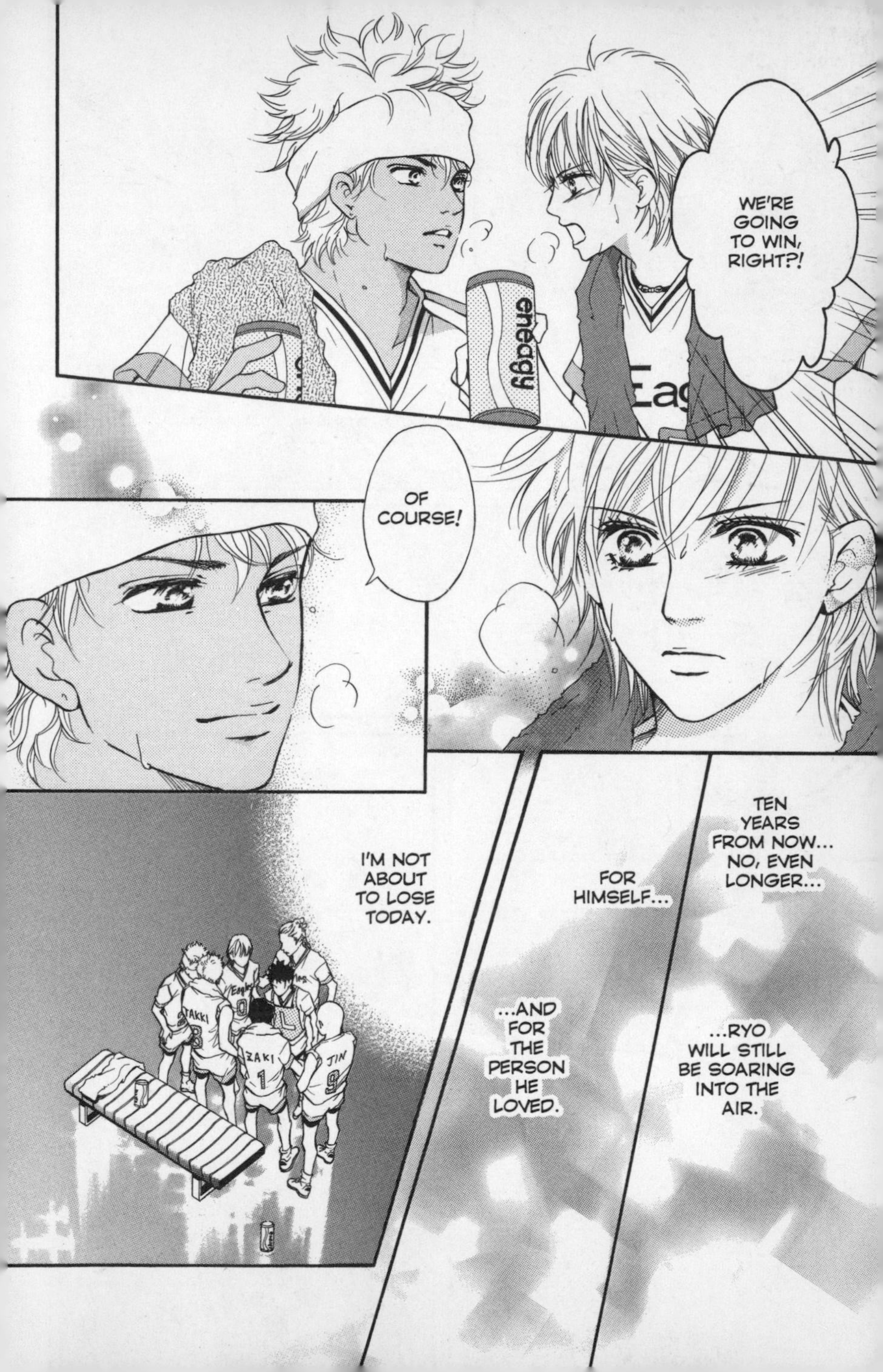
WE'RE GOING TO WIN, RIGHT?!
OF COURSE!
TEN YEARS FROM NOW... NO, EVEN LONGER...
...RYO WILL STILL BE SOARING INTO THE AIR.
FOR HIMSELF...
...AND FOR THE PERSON HE LOVED.
I'M NOT ABOUT TO LOSE TODAY.

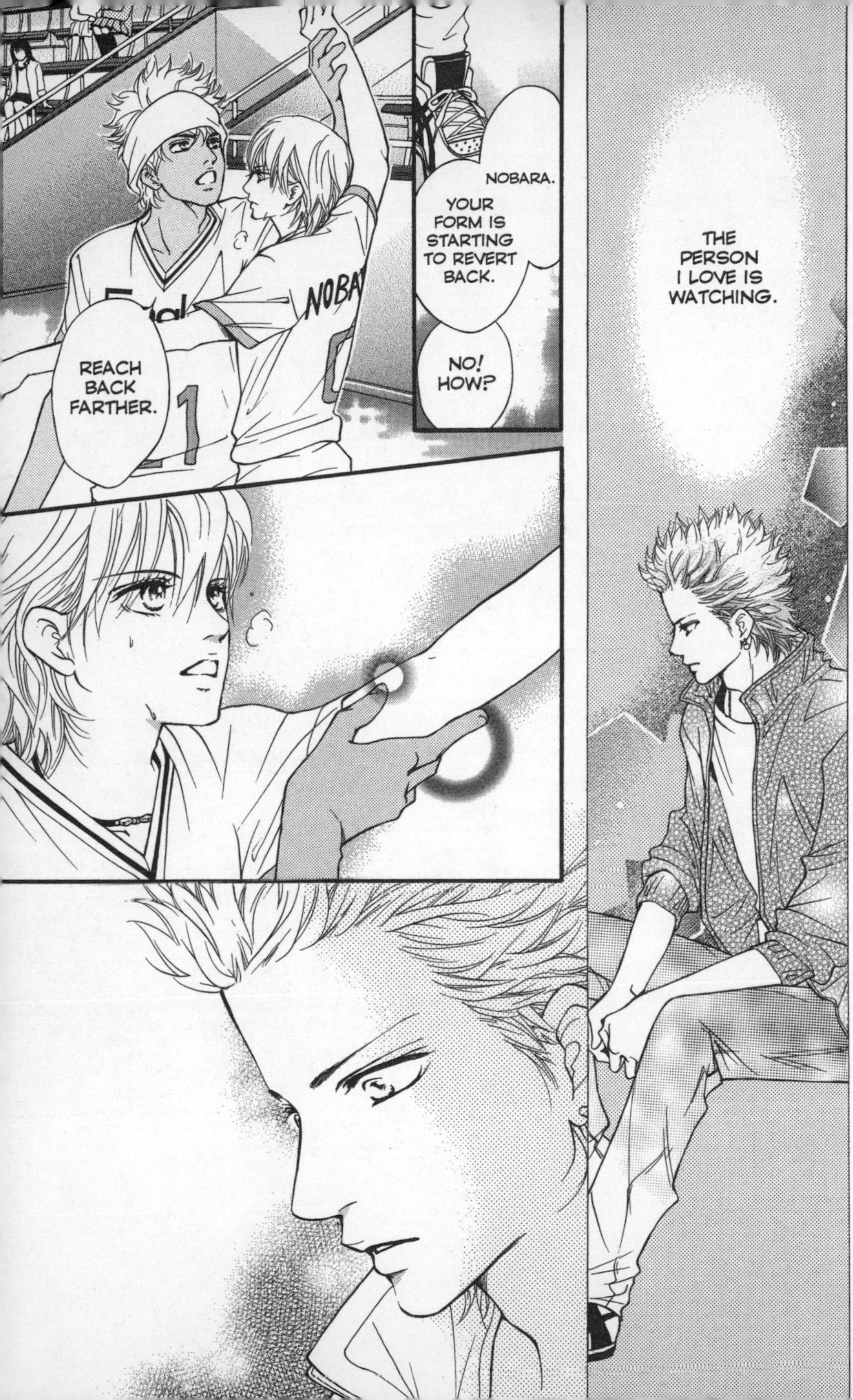
THE PERSON I LOVE IS WATCHING.
NOBARA.
YOUR FORM IS STARTING TO REVERT BACK.
NO! HOW?
REACH BACK FARTHER.

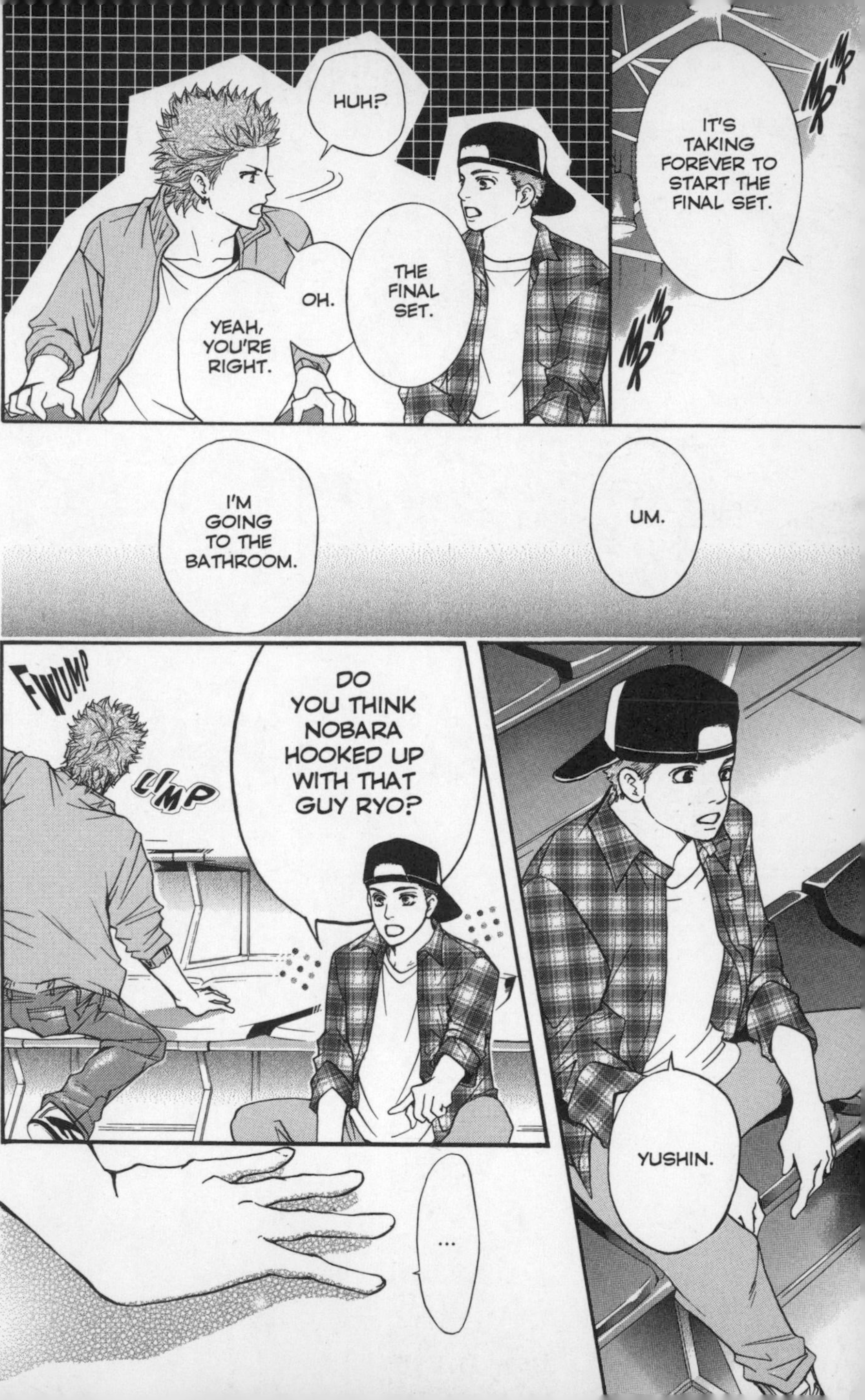
IT'S TAKING FOREVER TO START THE FINAL SET.
MR MR
MR MR
HUH?
THE FINAL SET.
OH.
YEAH, YOU'RE RIGHT.
UM.
I'M GOING TO THE BATHROOM.
YUSHIN.
FWUMP
LIMP
DO YOU THINK NOBARA HOOKED UP WITH THAT GUY RYO?
...

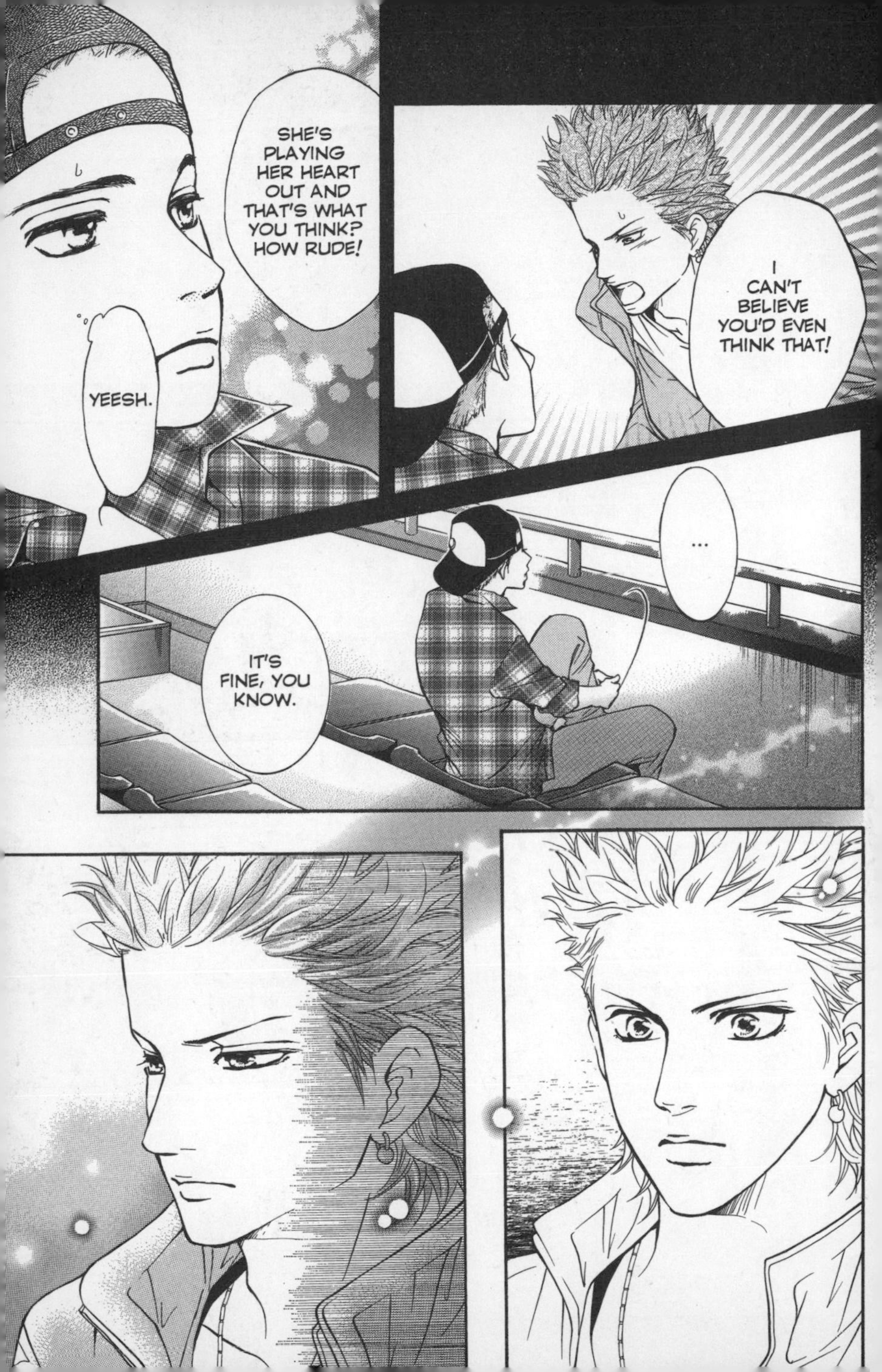
I CAN'T BELIEVE YOU'D EVEN THINK THAT!
SHE'S PLAYING HER HEART OUT AND THAT'S WHAT YOU THINK? HOW RUDE!
YEESH.
...
IT'S FINE, YOU KNOW.

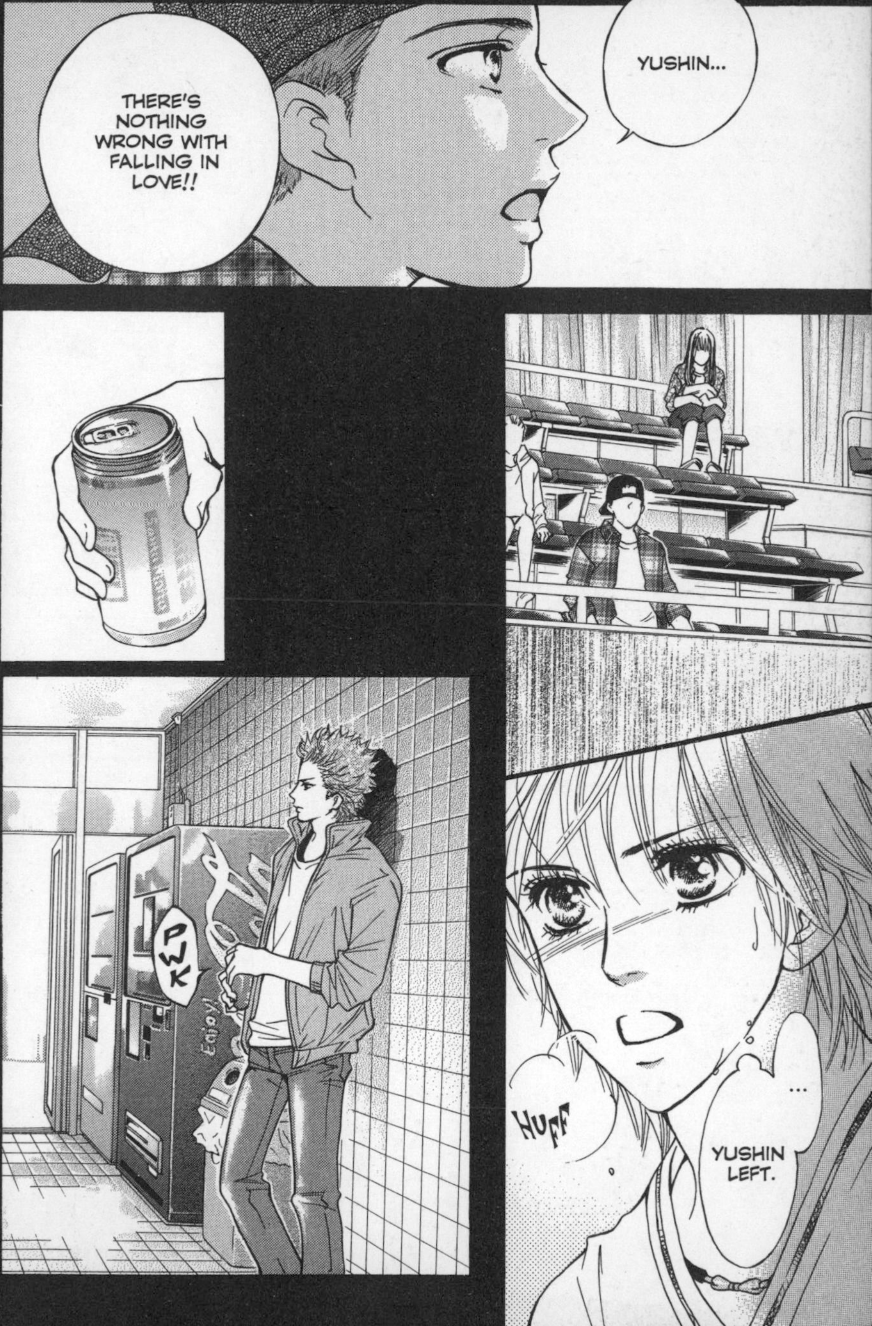
YUSHIN...
THERE'S NOTHING WRONG WITH FALLING IN LOVE!!
...
YUSHIN LEFT.
HUFF
PWK
Enjoy!

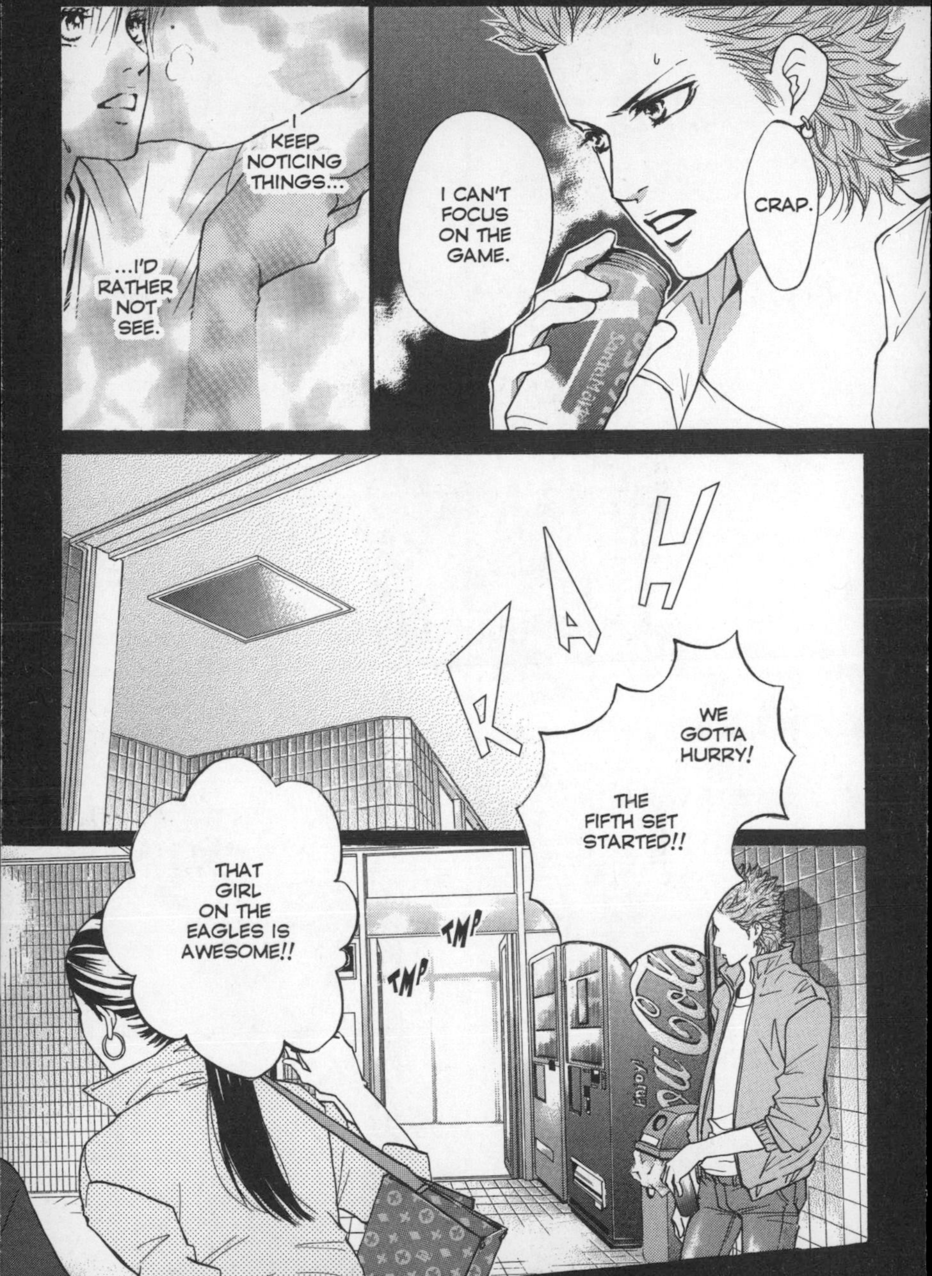
CRAP.
I CAN'T FOCUS ON THE GAME.
I KEEP NOTICING THINGS...
...I'D RATHER NOT SEE.
RAH
WE GOTTA HURRY!
THE FIFTH SET STARTED!!
TMP
TMP
THAT GIRL ON THE EAGLES IS AWESOME!!

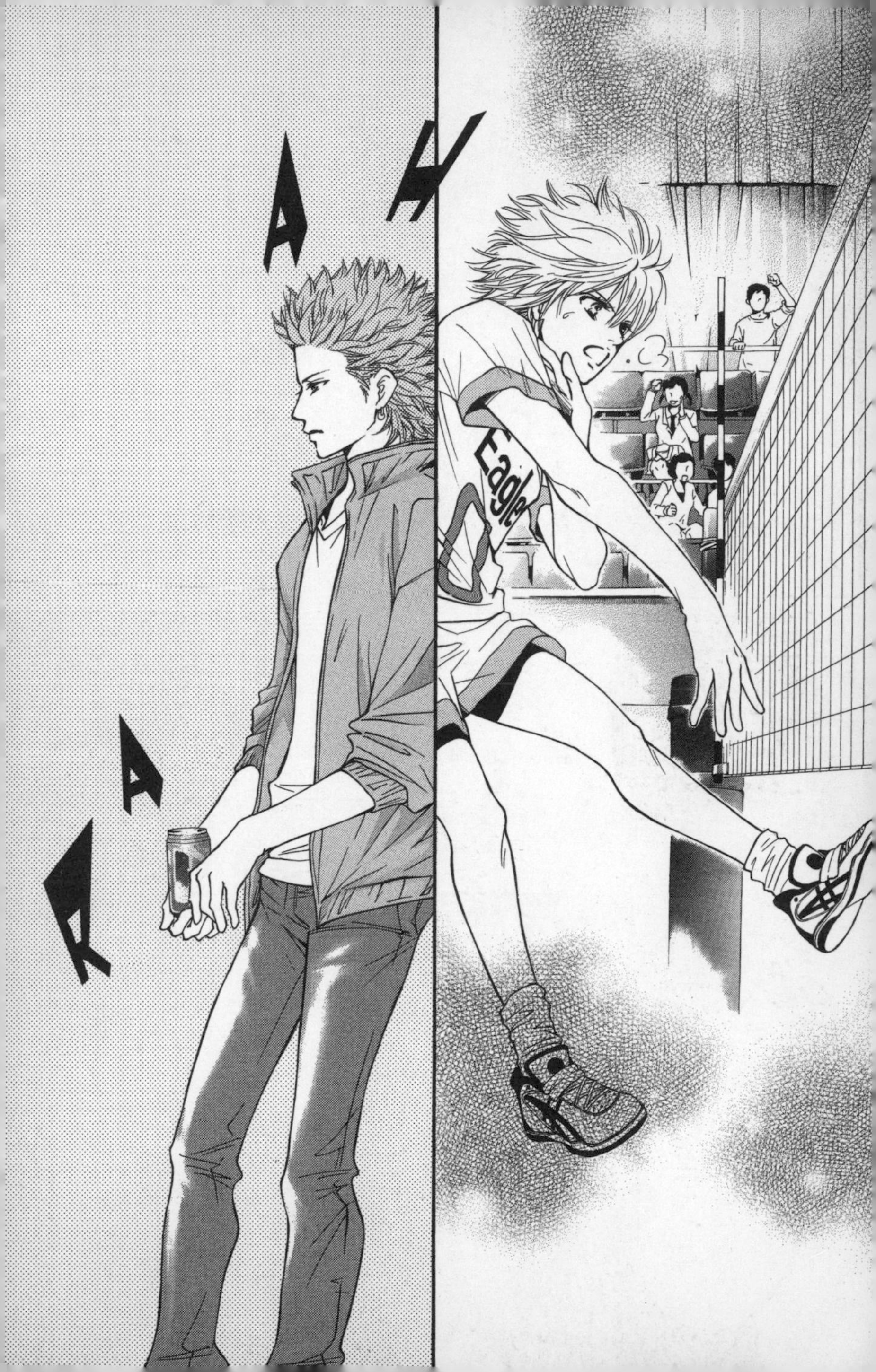
RAAH

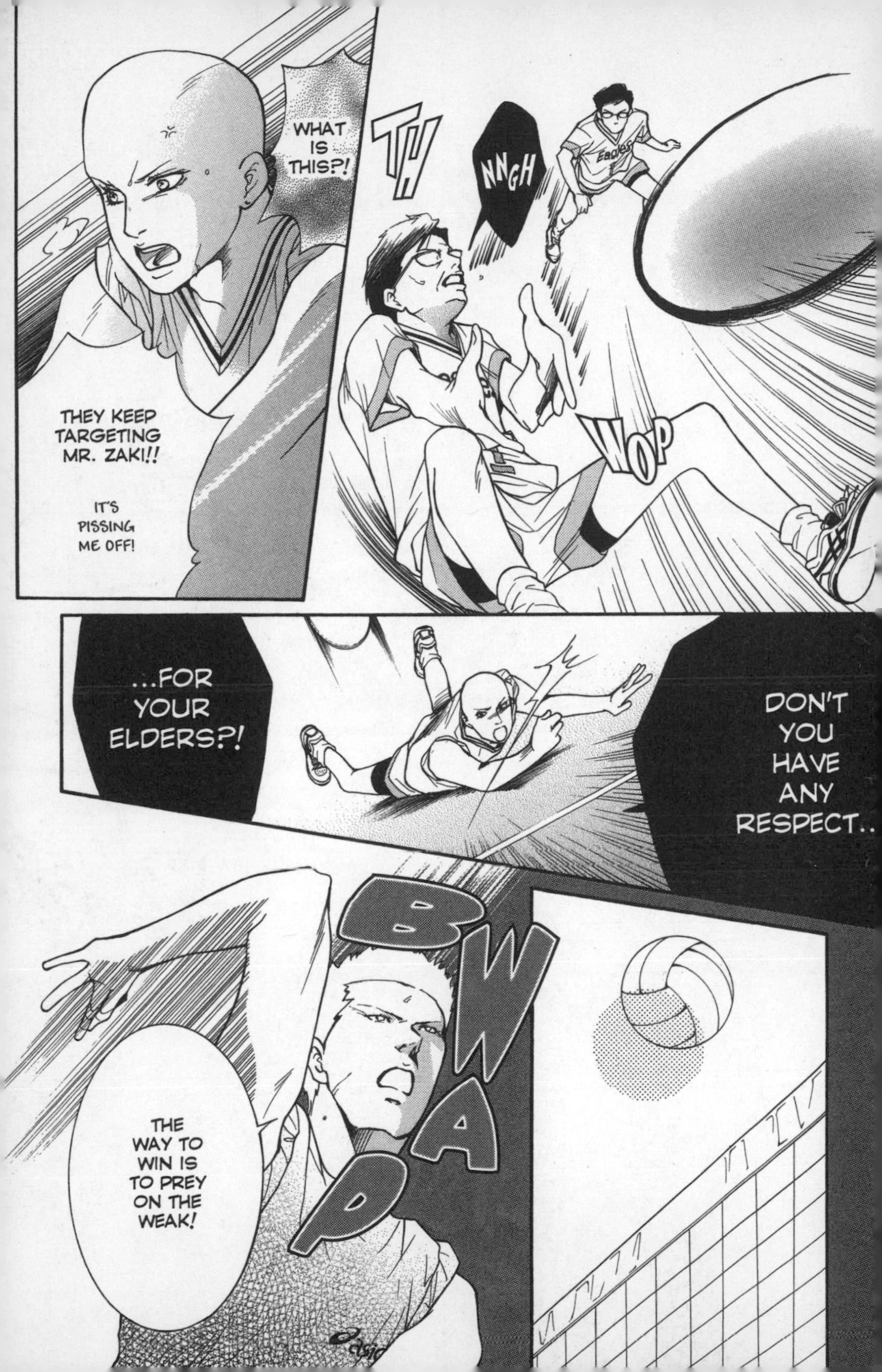
NNGH
TH
WOP
WHAT IS THIS?!
THEY KEEP TARGETING MR. ZAKI!!
IT'S PISSING ME OFF!
DON'T YOU HAVE ANY RESPECT..
...FOR YOUR ELDERS?!
BWAP
THE WAY TO WIN IS TO PREY ON THE WEAK!

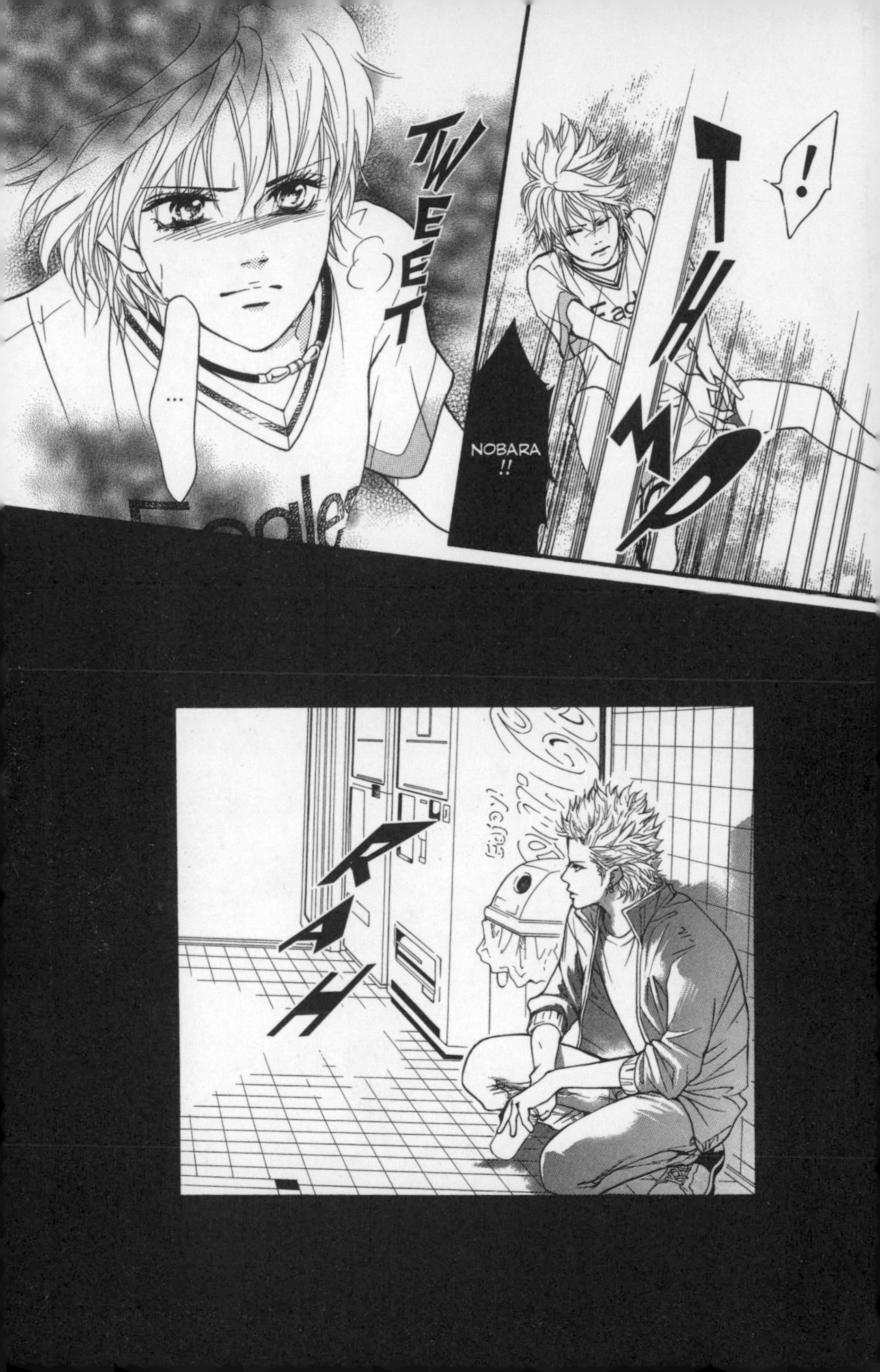
!
THHMP
NOBARA !!
TWEET
...
Enjoy!
RAH

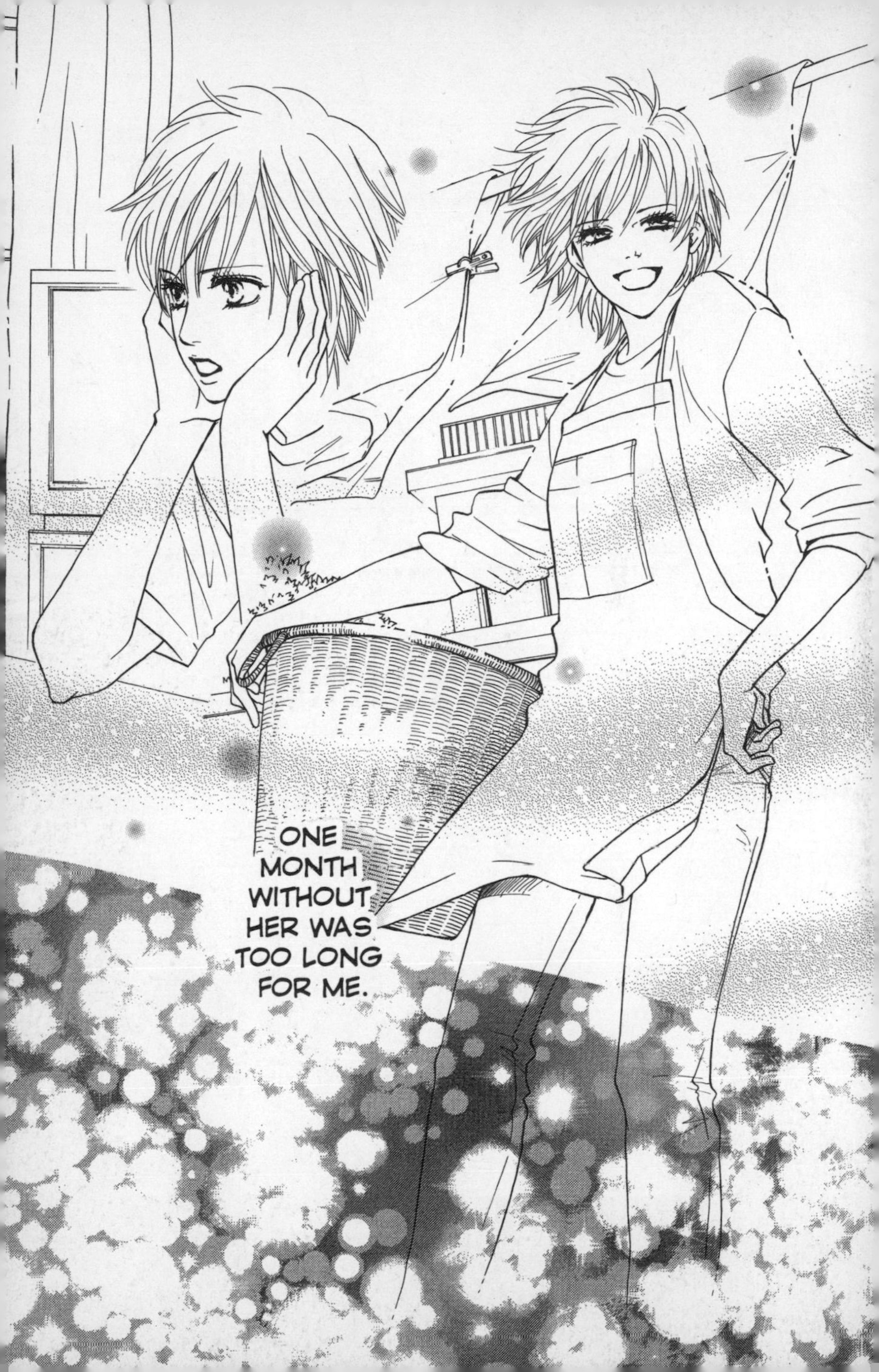
ONE MONTH WITHOUT HER WAS TOO LONG FOR ME.

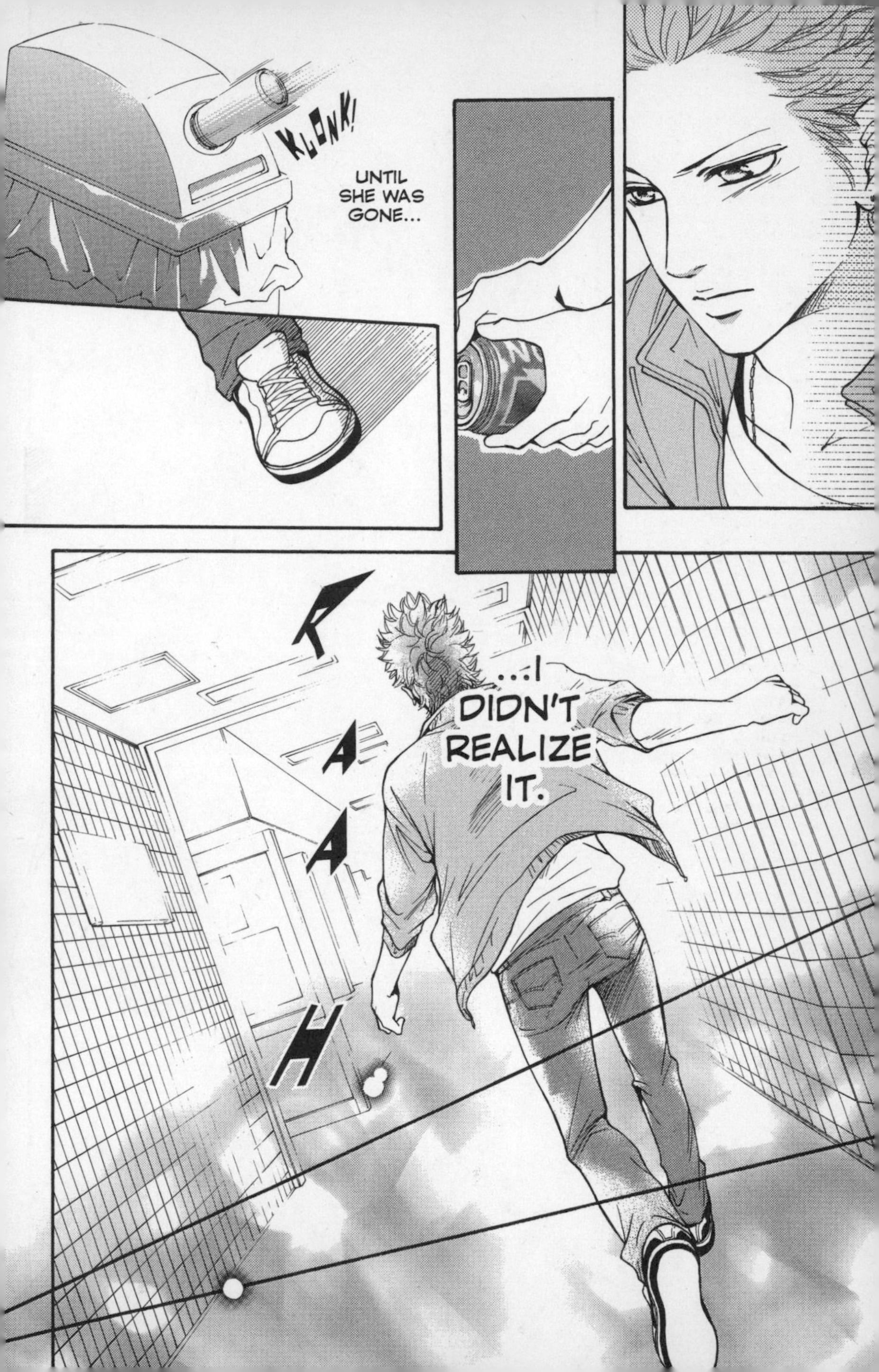
KLONK!
UNTIL SHE WAS GONE...
RAAAH
...I DIDN'T REALIZE IT.

MITSUBA CLUB

VoL. 1

HELLO. IT'S BEEN A WHILE. HERE WE ARE AT *CRIMSON HERO* VOLUME 9. VOLUME 9? NINE!! IF I'M ALREADY AT VOLUME 9 AT THIS POINT IN THE STORY...I BET THIS TITLE IS GOING TO BE LONGER THAN MY LAST SERIES. B-BMP B-BMP. MY GOSH, THE STORY'S UNFOLDING SO SLOWLY. WAAAAH. AND I STILL NEED TO COVER THIS, THAT, AND THE OTHER THING. PLEASE, EVERYONE, STAY WITH ME UNTIL THE END. I'LL KEEP ON DRAWING, FULL STEAM AHEAD, OKAY?! BY THE WAY, THE BEACH VOLLEYBALL ARC ENDS IN THIS VOLUME. THANKS SO MUCH TO THE GIRLS WHO WROTE, "I LIKE THOSE OLDER MEN!!" SOME EVEN LIKED MR. ZAKI, AND THE DAY I READ THE WORDS, "THANK YOU, MR. ZAKI," I ALMOST CRIED!!!! I CRY SO EASILY. EVEN WHEN I'M WATCHING TV WITH MY STAFF, I'LL START CRYING AND SURPRISE MY STAFF. THEY'RE LIKE, "WHOA! WHAT WAS THAT?!" GETTING BACK TO THE STORY, I DON'T KNOW WHETHER I'LL BE DEPICTING THE EAGLES AGAIN. MAYBE, IF THE OPPORTUNITY COMES. I LIKE THOSE BEACH MEN. RECENTLY I'VE BEEN GOING TO SHONAN BEACH A LOT. I LOVE THE ATMOSPHERE OF THE BEACH IN THE EARLY MORNING. AND BY THE WAY, I'VE GOT TO SAY THAT TAKKI IS MY FAVORITE. I'D LOVE TO GO DRINKING WITH HIM. THAT'S WHAT I THINK.

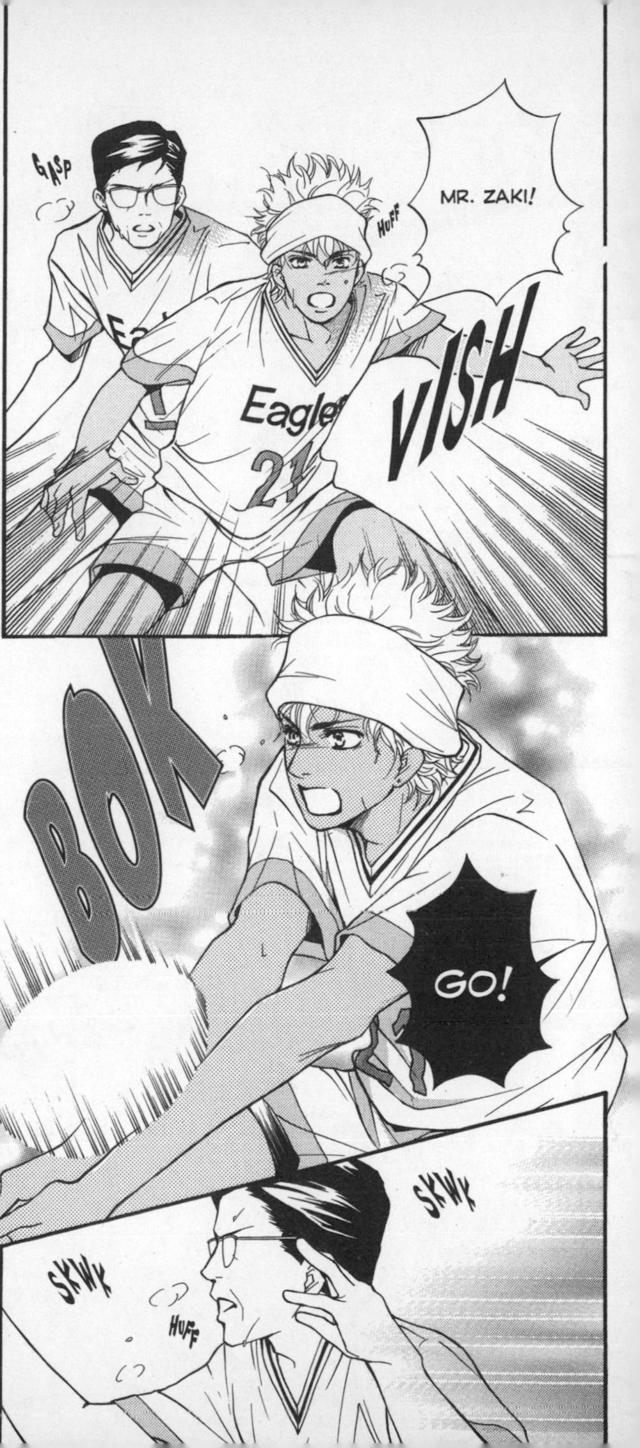
MR. ZAKI!
VISH
HUFF
GASP
Eagles
BOK
GO!
SKWK
HUFF
SKWK

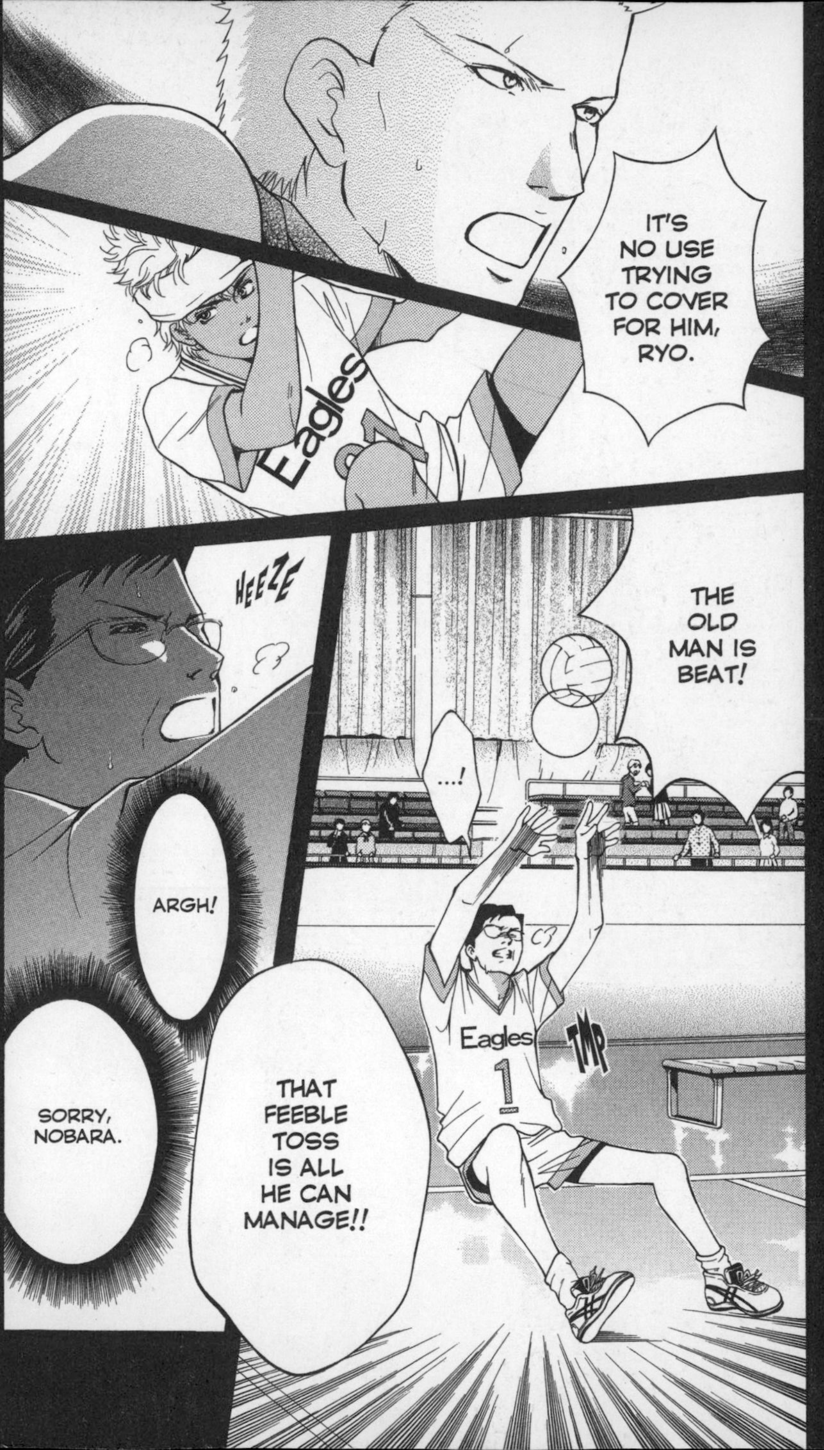
IT'S NO USE TRYING TO COVER FOR HIM, RYO.
THE OLD MAN IS BEAT!
...!
TMP
THAT FEEBLE TOSS IS ALL HE CAN MANAGE!!
Eagles
1
HEEZE
ARGH!
SORRY, NOBARA.

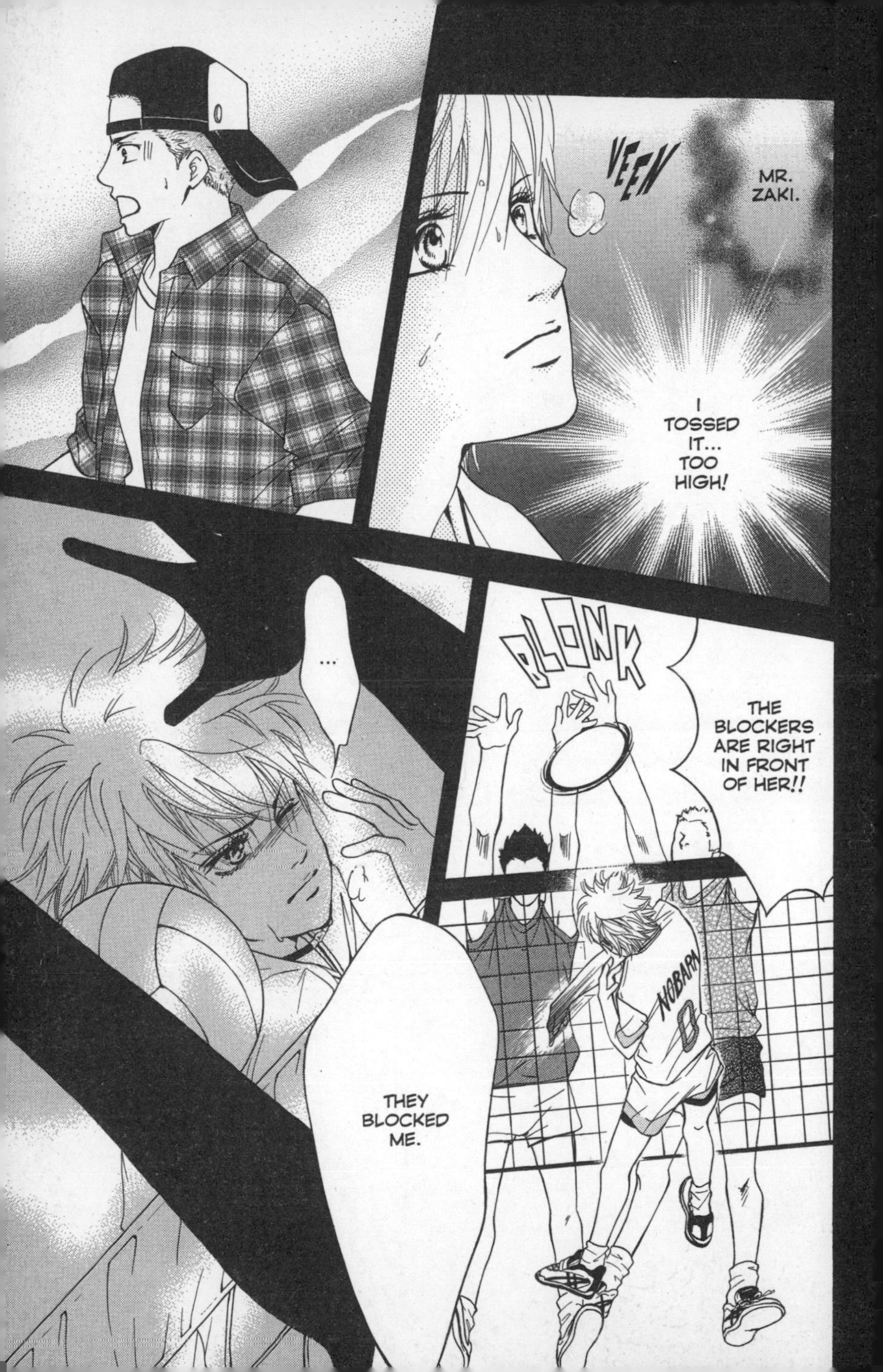
VEEN
MR. ZAKI.
I TOSSED IT... TOO HIGH!
BLONK
THE BLOCKERS ARE RIGHT IN FRONT OF HER!!
NOBARA
0
...
THEY BLOCKED ME.

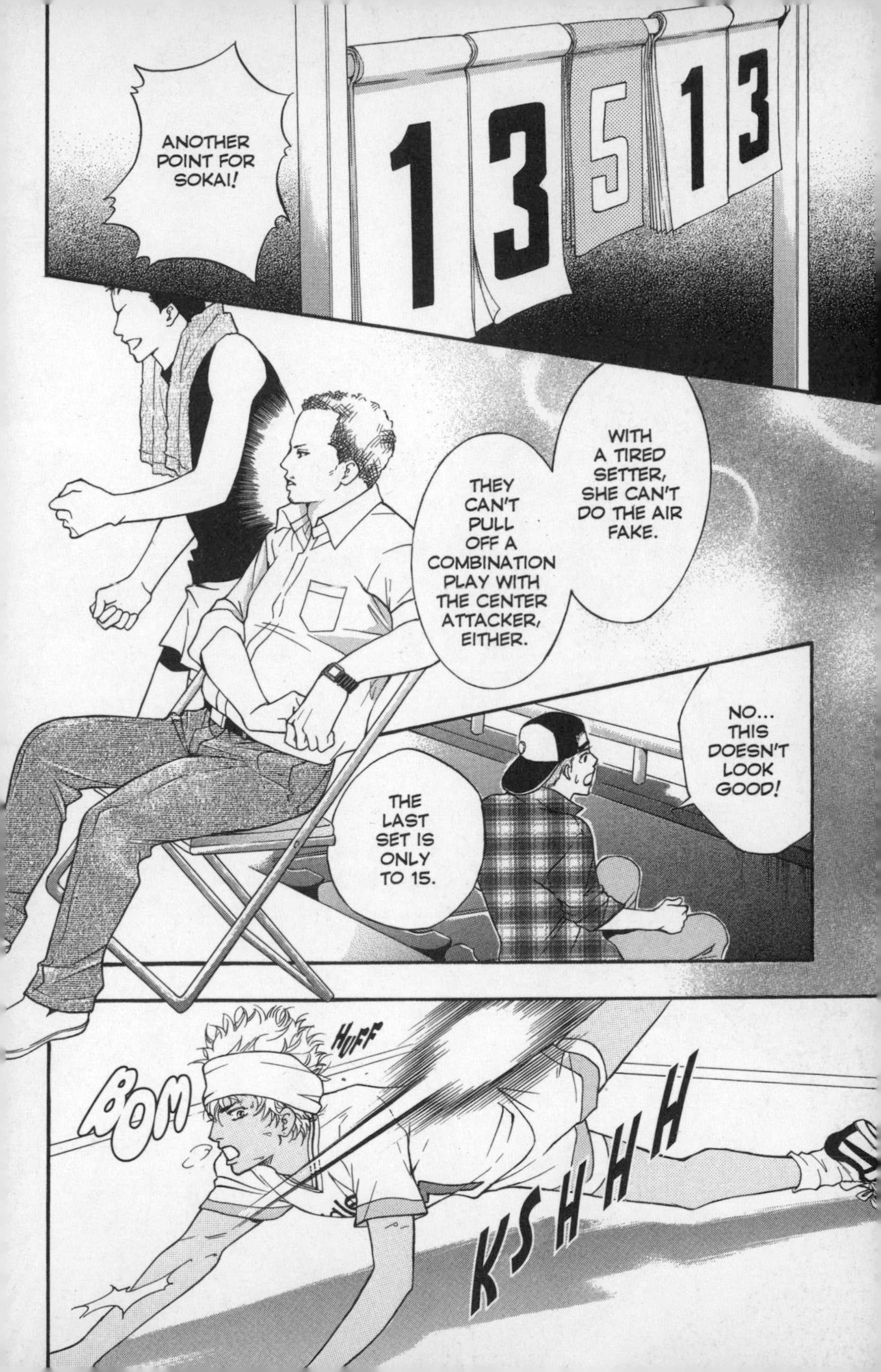
ANOTHER POINT FOR SOKAI!
WITH A TIRED SETTER, SHE CAN'T DO THE AIR FAKE.
THEY CAN'T PULL OFF A COMBINATION PLAY WITH THE CENTER ATTACKER, EITHER.
NO... THIS DOESN'T LOOK GOOD!
THE LAST SET IS ONLY TO 15.
HUFF
KSHHH
BOM

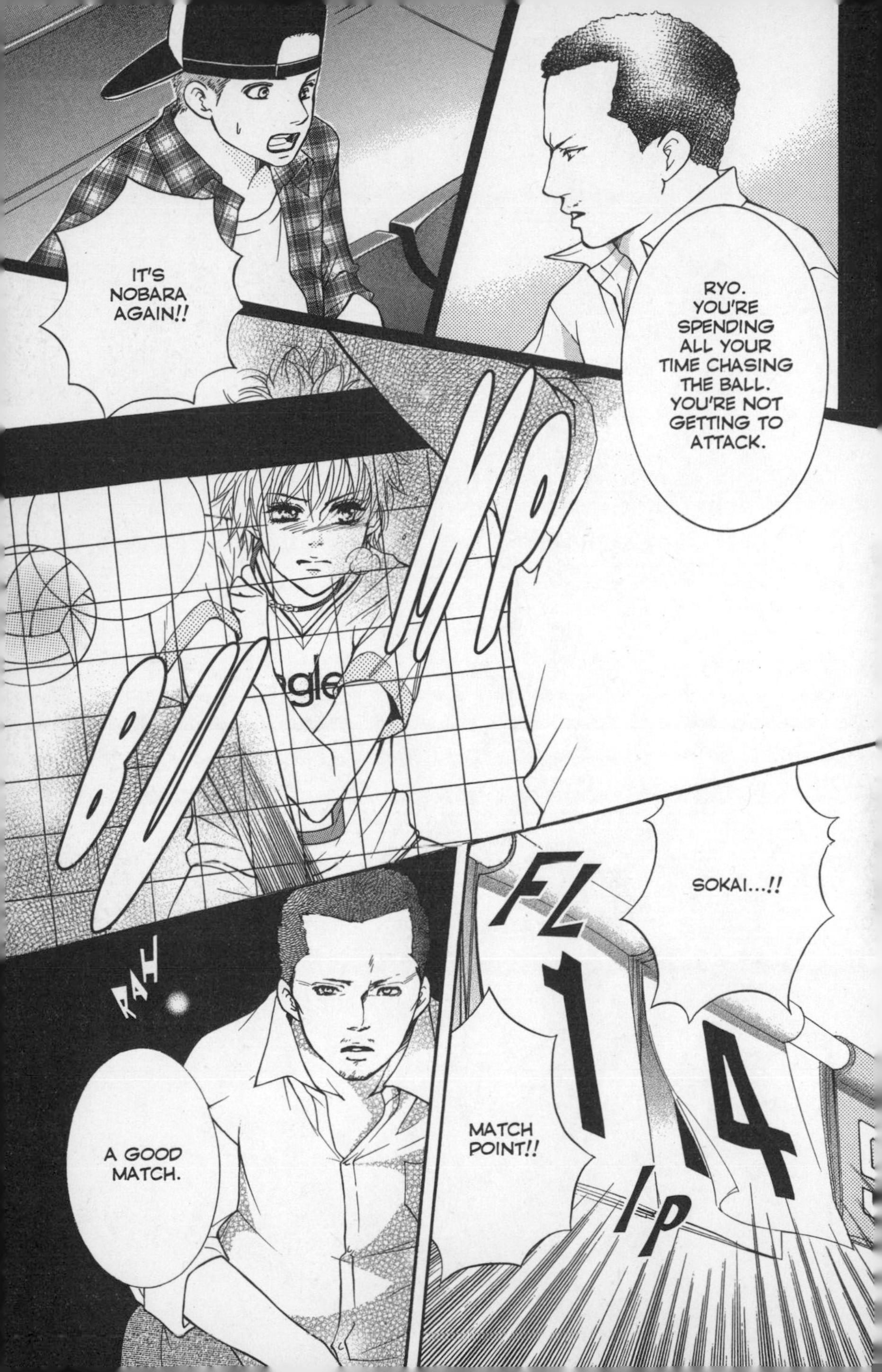
RYO. YOU'RE SPENDING ALL YOUR TIME CHASING THE BALL. YOU'RE NOT GETTING TO ATTACK.
IT'S NOBARA AGAIN!!
BUMP
SOKAI...!!
FLIP
14
MATCH POINT!!
RAH
A GOOD MATCH.

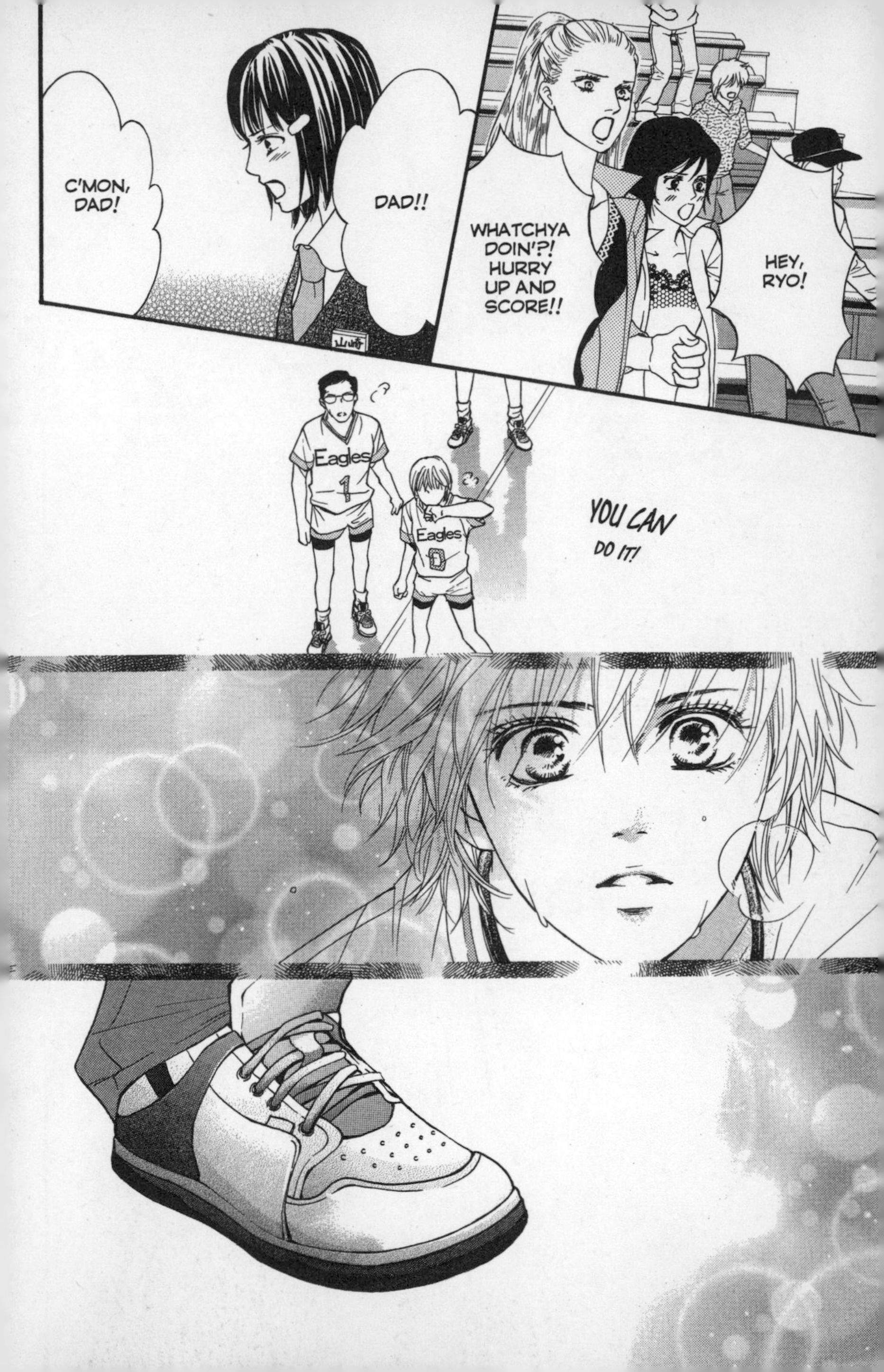
HEY, RYO!
WHATCHYA DOIN'?! HURRY UP AND SCORE!!
DAD!!
C'MON, DAD!
YOU CAN DO IT!

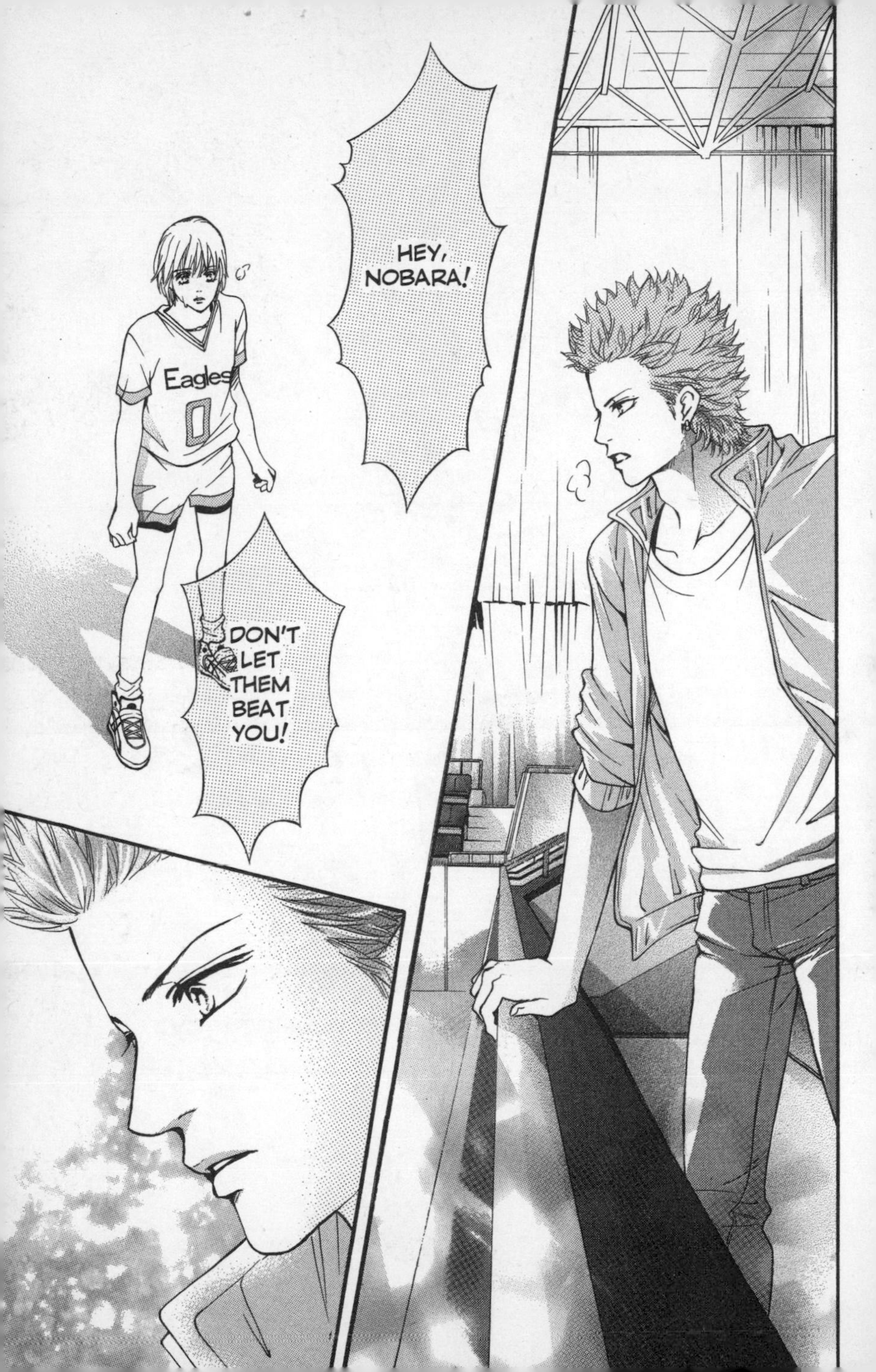
HEY, NOBARA!
Eagles 0
DON'T LET THEM BEAT YOU!

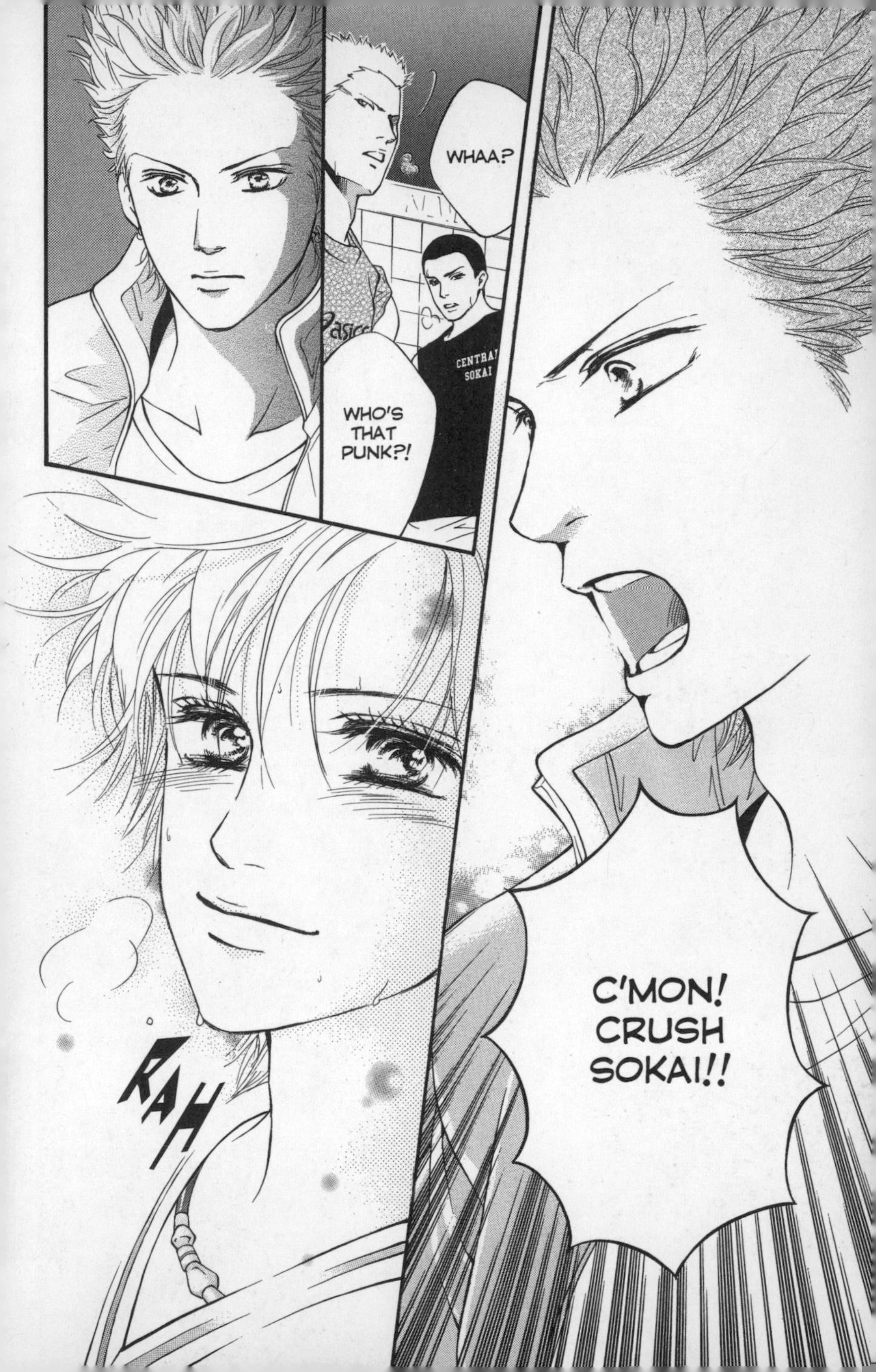
C'MON! CRUSH SOKAI!!
WHAA?
WHO'S THAT PUNK?!
CENTRAL SOKAI
RAH

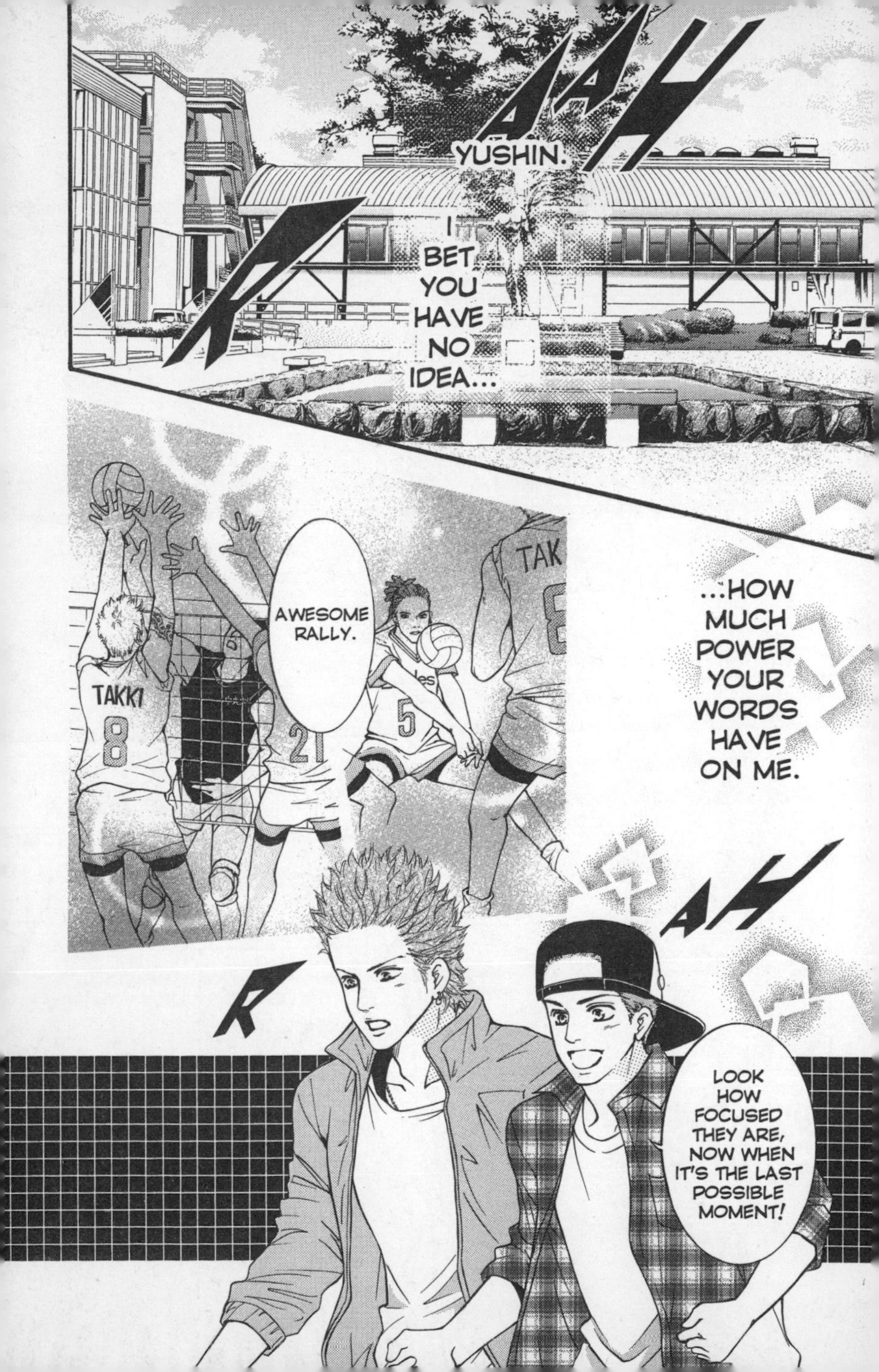

RAAH
YUSHIN.
I BET YOU HAVE NO IDEA...
...HOW MUCH POWER YOUR WORDS HAVE ON ME.
TAK
AWESOME RALLY.
TAKKI
AH
R
LOOK HOW FOCUSED THEY ARE, NOW WHEN IT'S THE LAST POSSIBLE MOMENT!

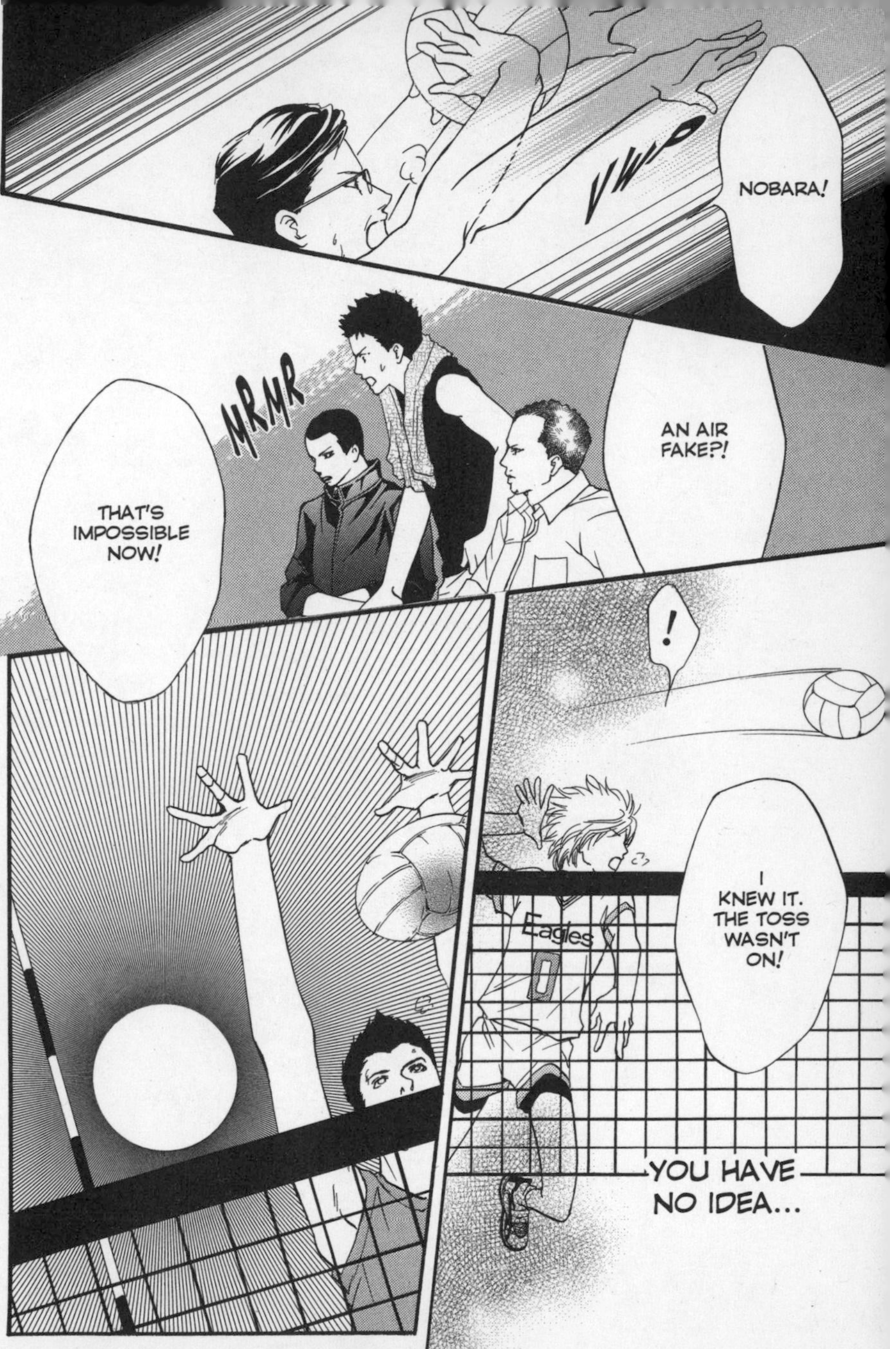
VWP
NOBARA!
AN AIR FAKE?!
MRMR
THAT'S IMPOSSIBLE NOW!
!
I KNEW IT. THE TOSS WASN'T ON!
YOU HAVE NO IDEA...

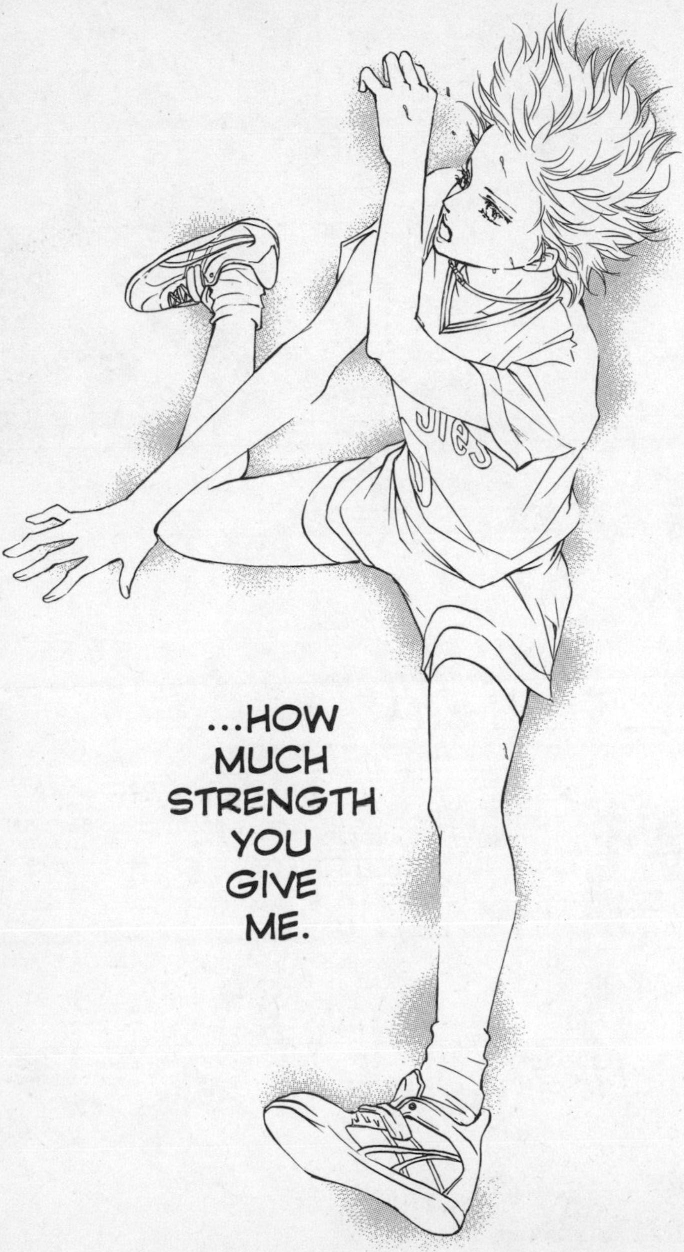
...HOW MUCH STRENGTH YOU GIVE ME.

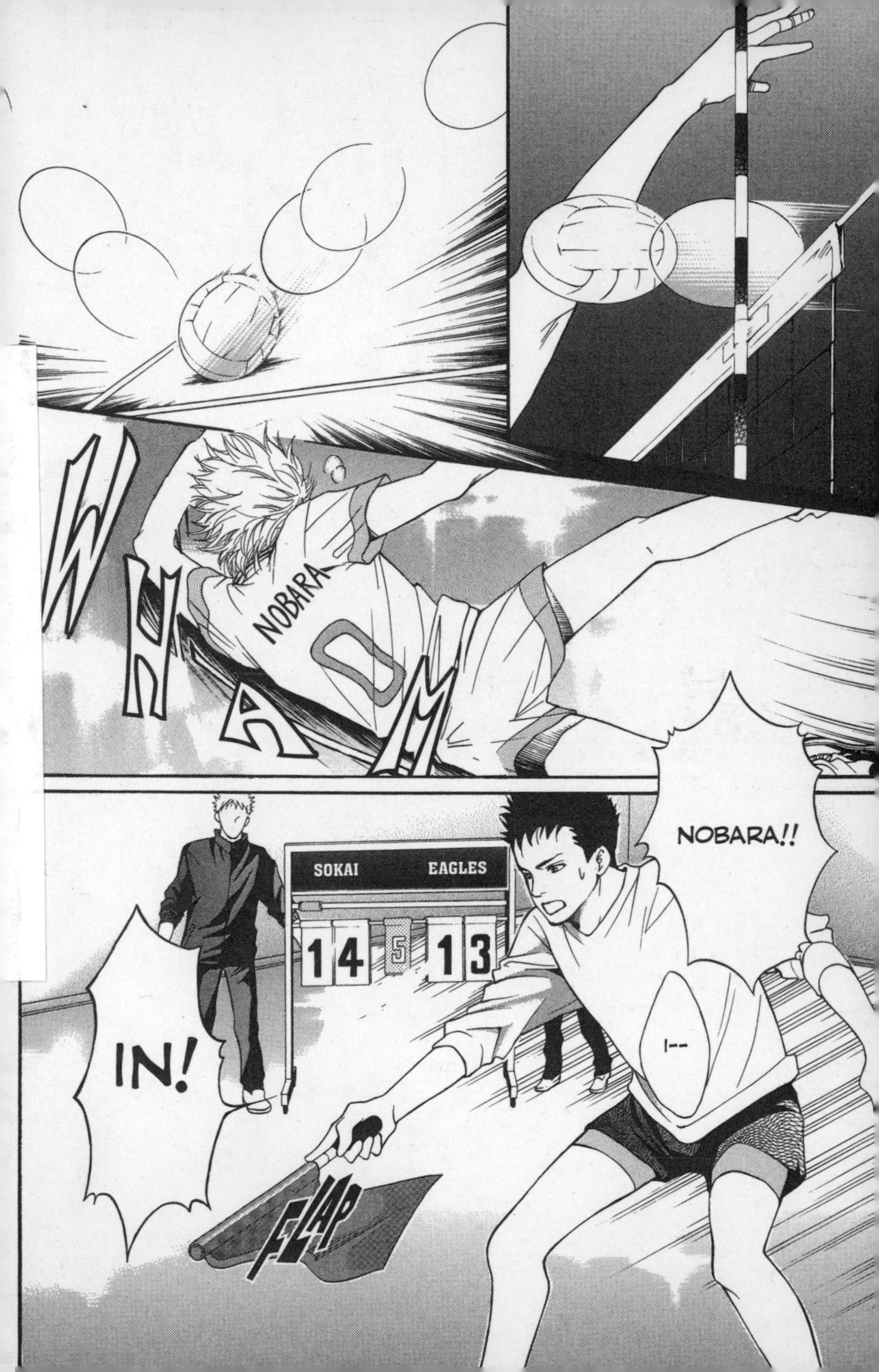
WHAM
NOBARA 0
NOBARA!!
I--
SOKAI EAGLES
14 5 13
IN!
FLAP

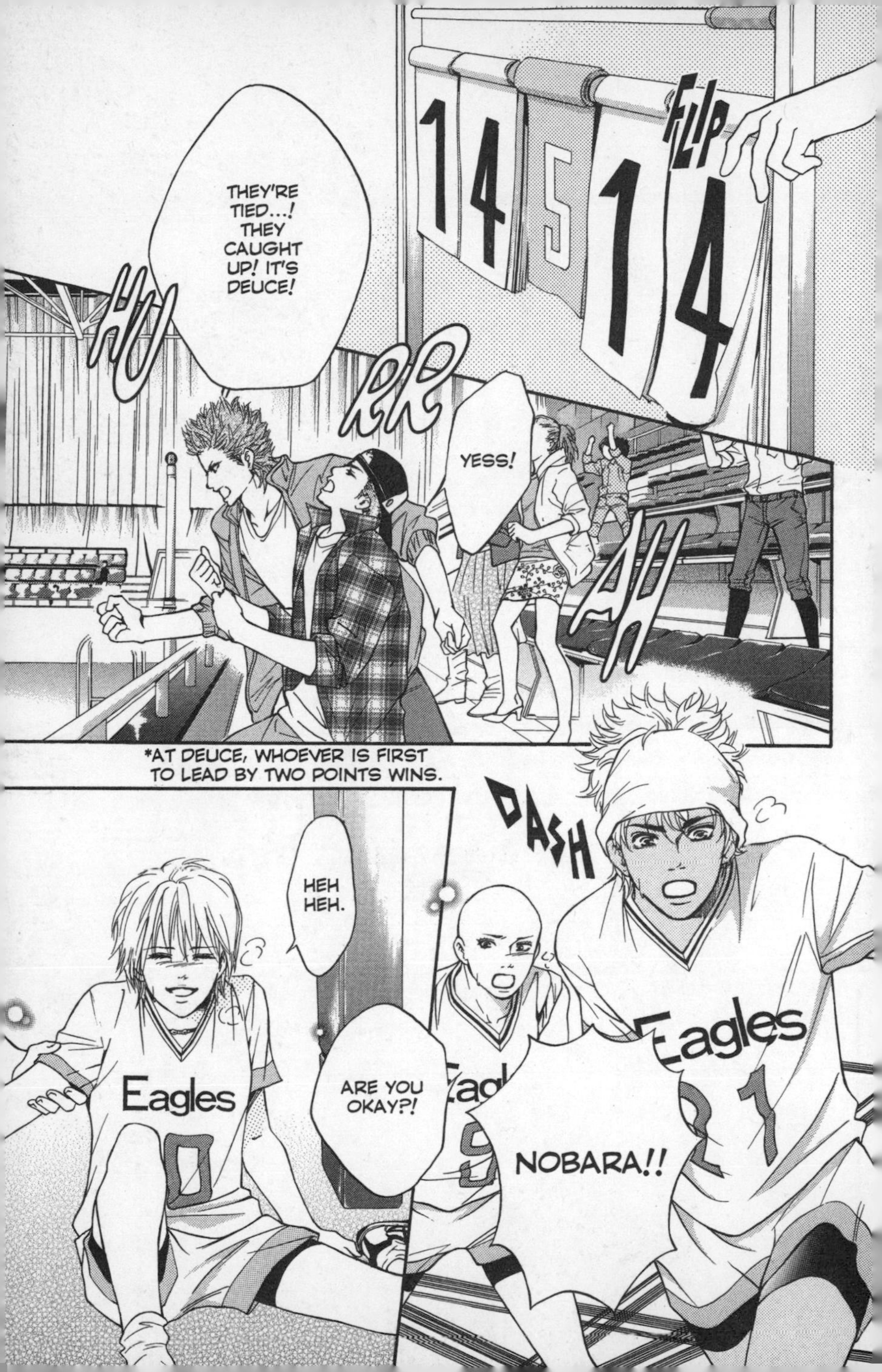
FLIP
THEY'RE TIED...! THEY CAUGHT UP! IT'S DEUCE!
YESS!
HURR
AH
*AT DEUCE, WHOEVER IS FIRST TO LEAD BY TWO POINTS WINS.
DASH
NOBARA!!
ARE YOU OKAY?!
HEH HEH.

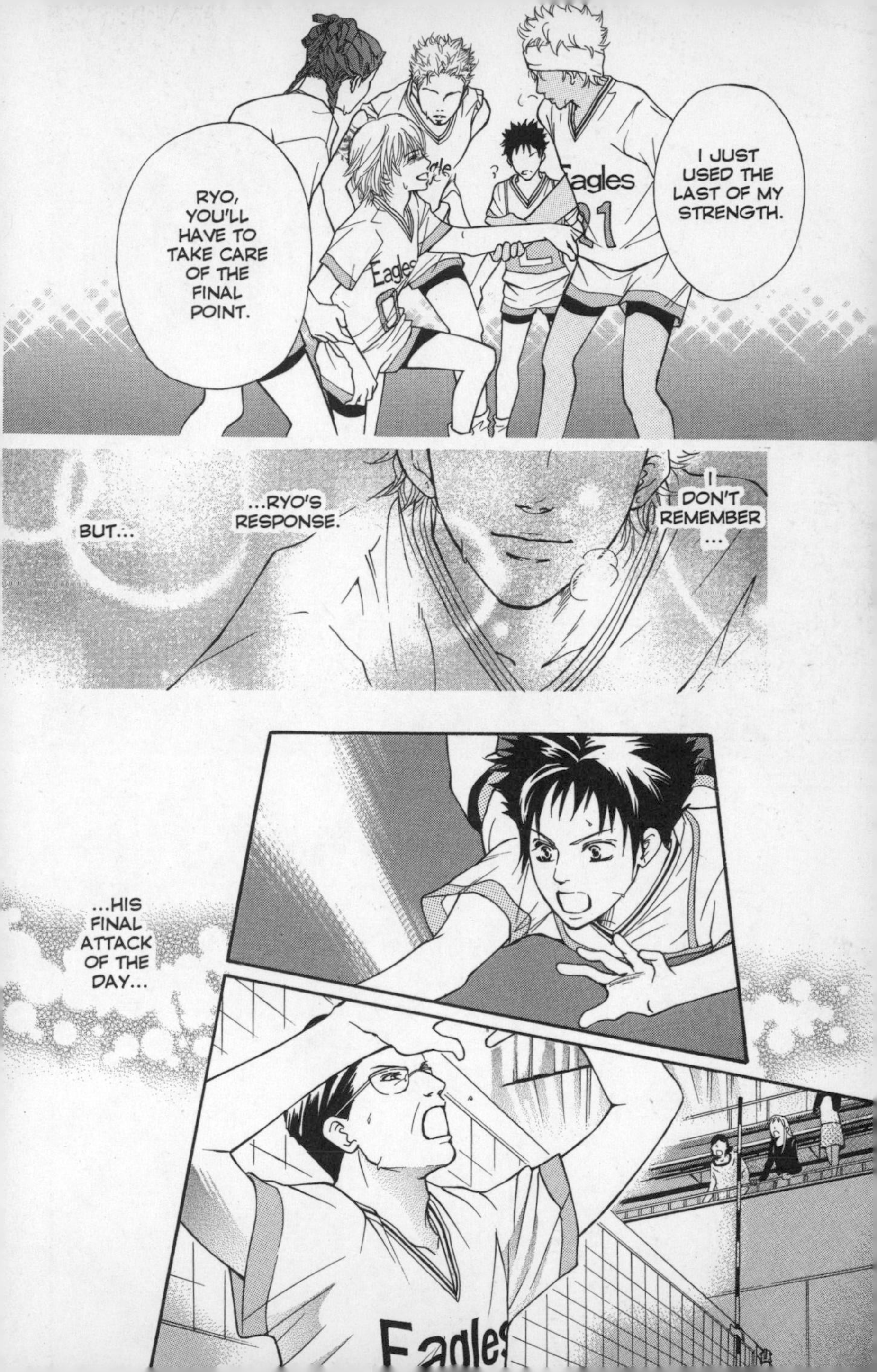
I JUST USED THE LAST OF MY STRENGTH.
RYO, YOU'LL HAVE TO TAKE CARE OF THE FINAL POINT.
I DON'T REMEMBER...
...RYO'S RESPONSE.
BUT...
...HIS FINAL ATTACK OF THE DAY...

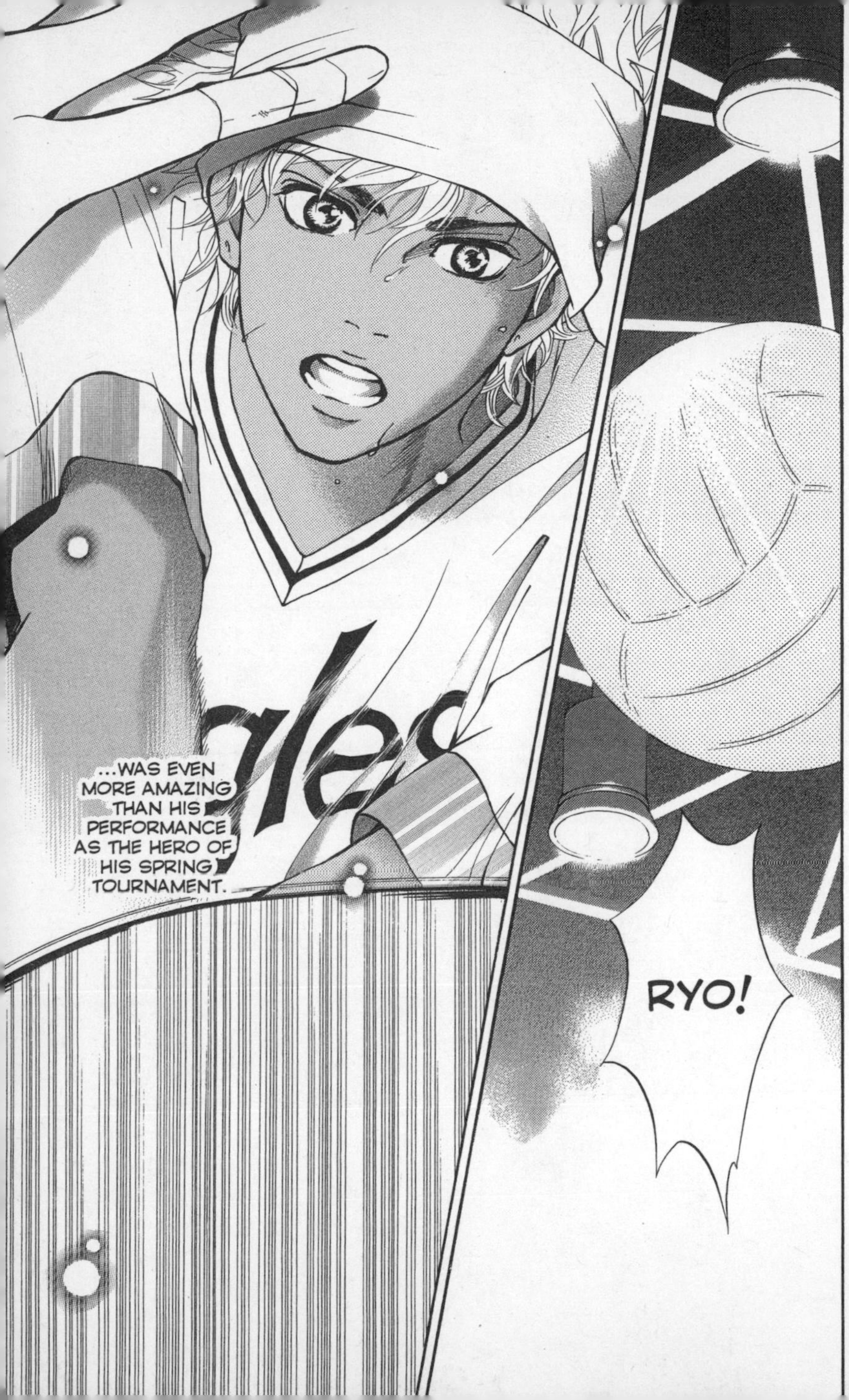
RYO!
...WAS EVEN MORE AMAZING THAN HIS PERFORMANCE AS THE HERO OF HIS SPRING TOURNAMENT.

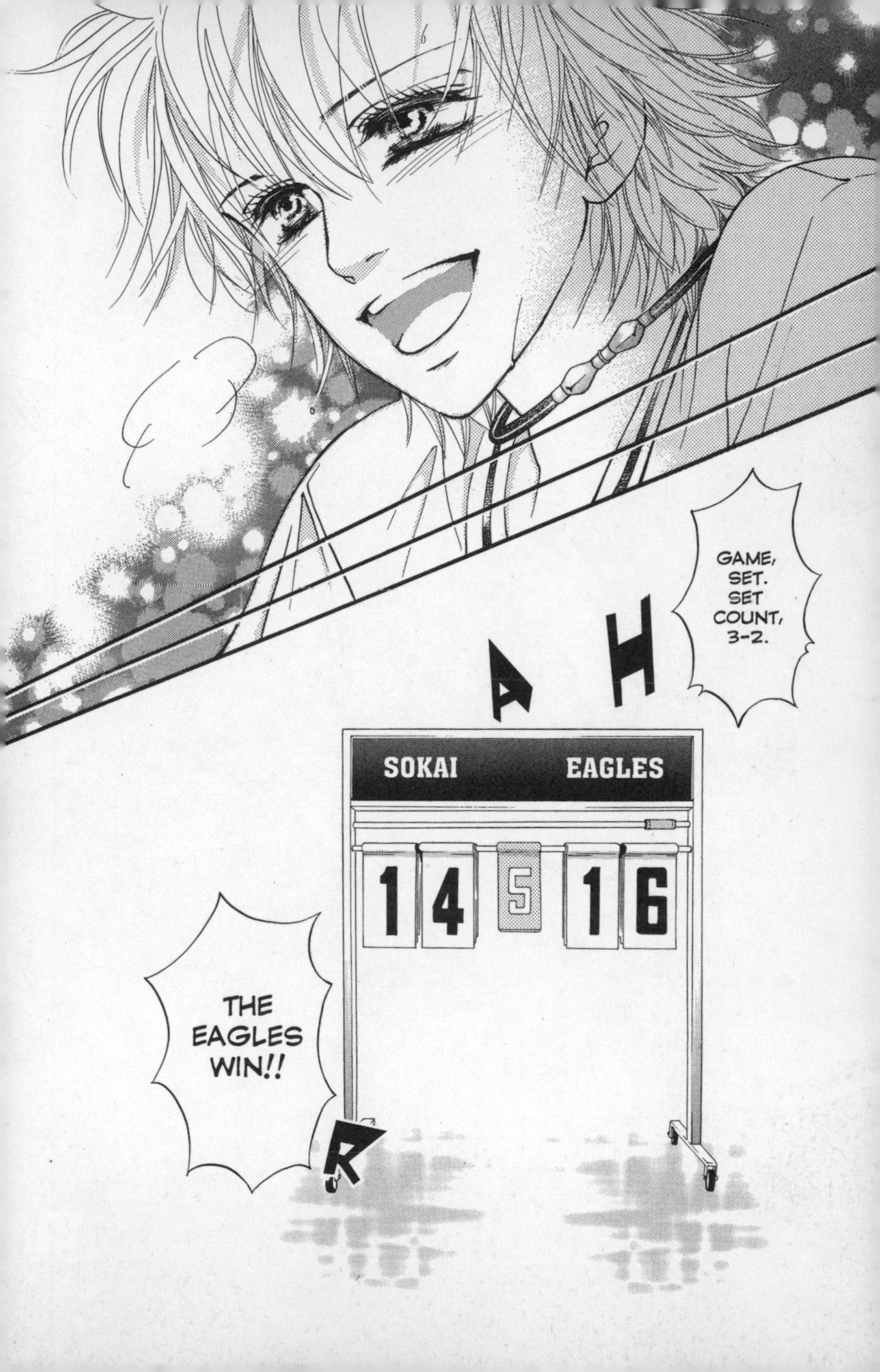
GAME, SET. SET COUNT, 3-2.
AH
SOKAI EAGLES
14 5 16
THE EAGLES WIN!!
R

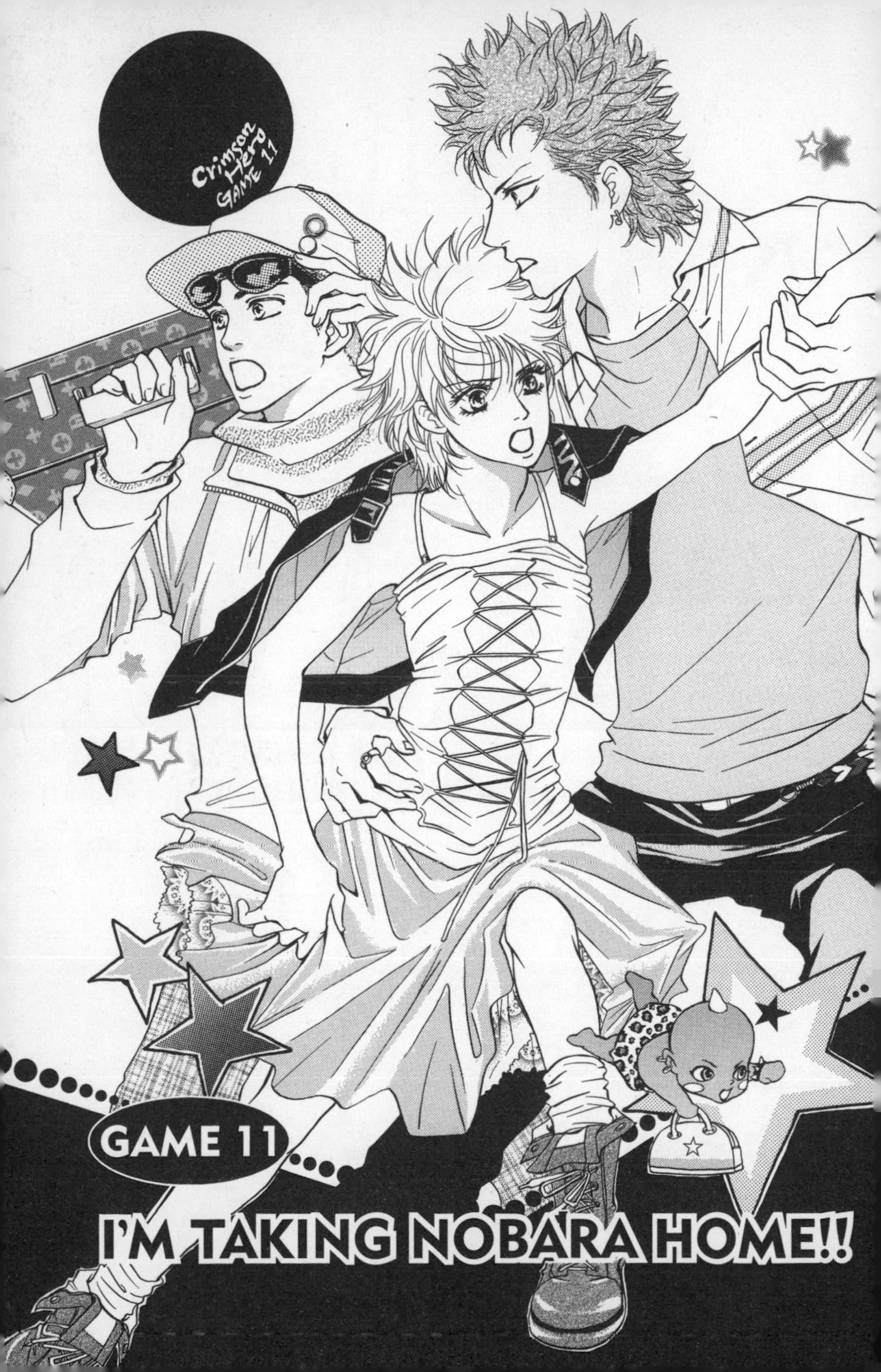
Crimson Hero GAME 11
GAME 11
I'M TAKING NOBARA HOME!!

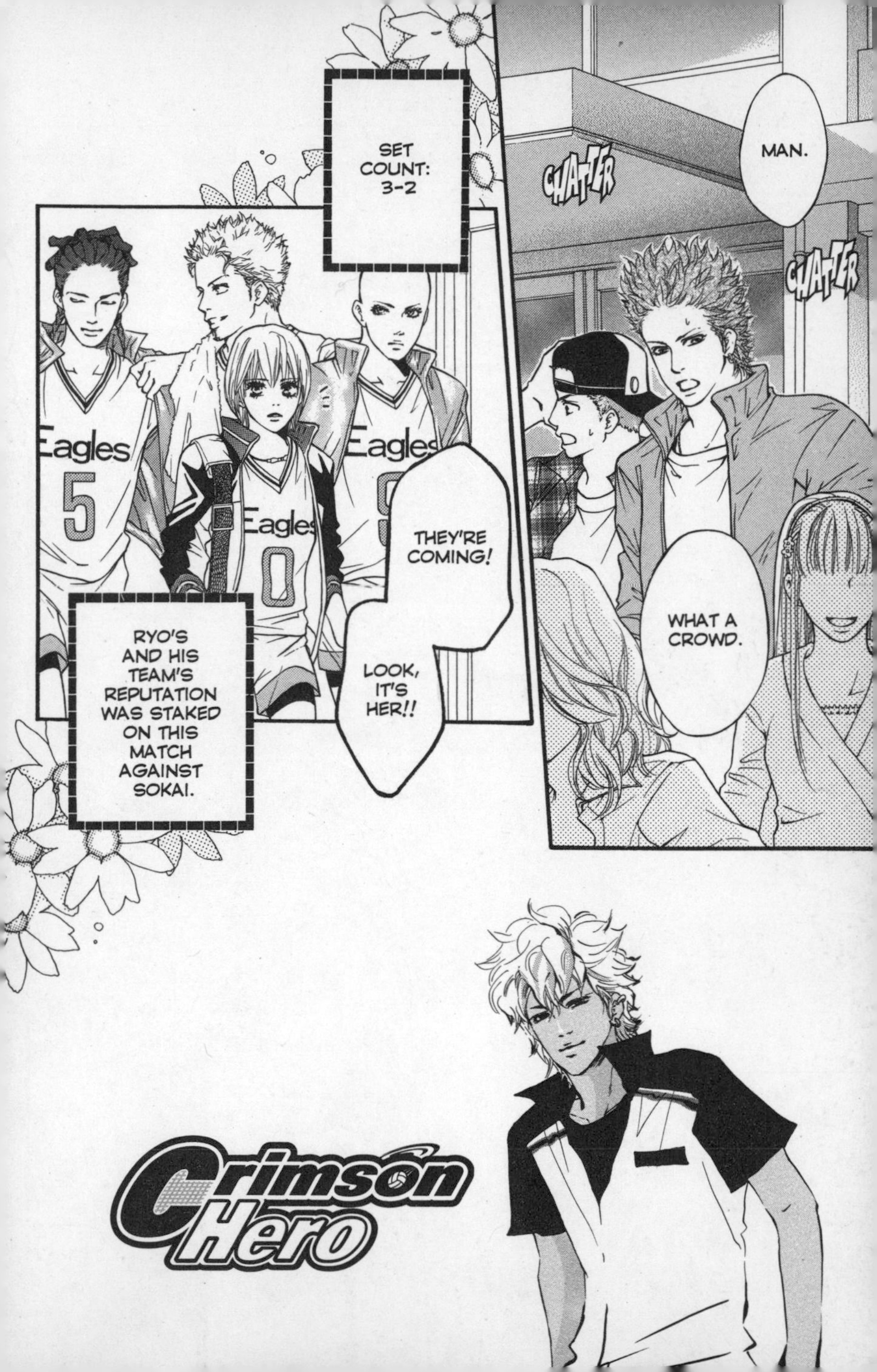
MAN.
CHATTER
CHATTER
WHAT A CROWD.
SET COUNT: 3-2
THEY'RE COMING!
LOOK, IT'S HER!!
RYO'S AND HIS TEAM'S REPUTATION WAS STAKED ON THIS MATCH AGAINST SOKAI.
Crimson Hero

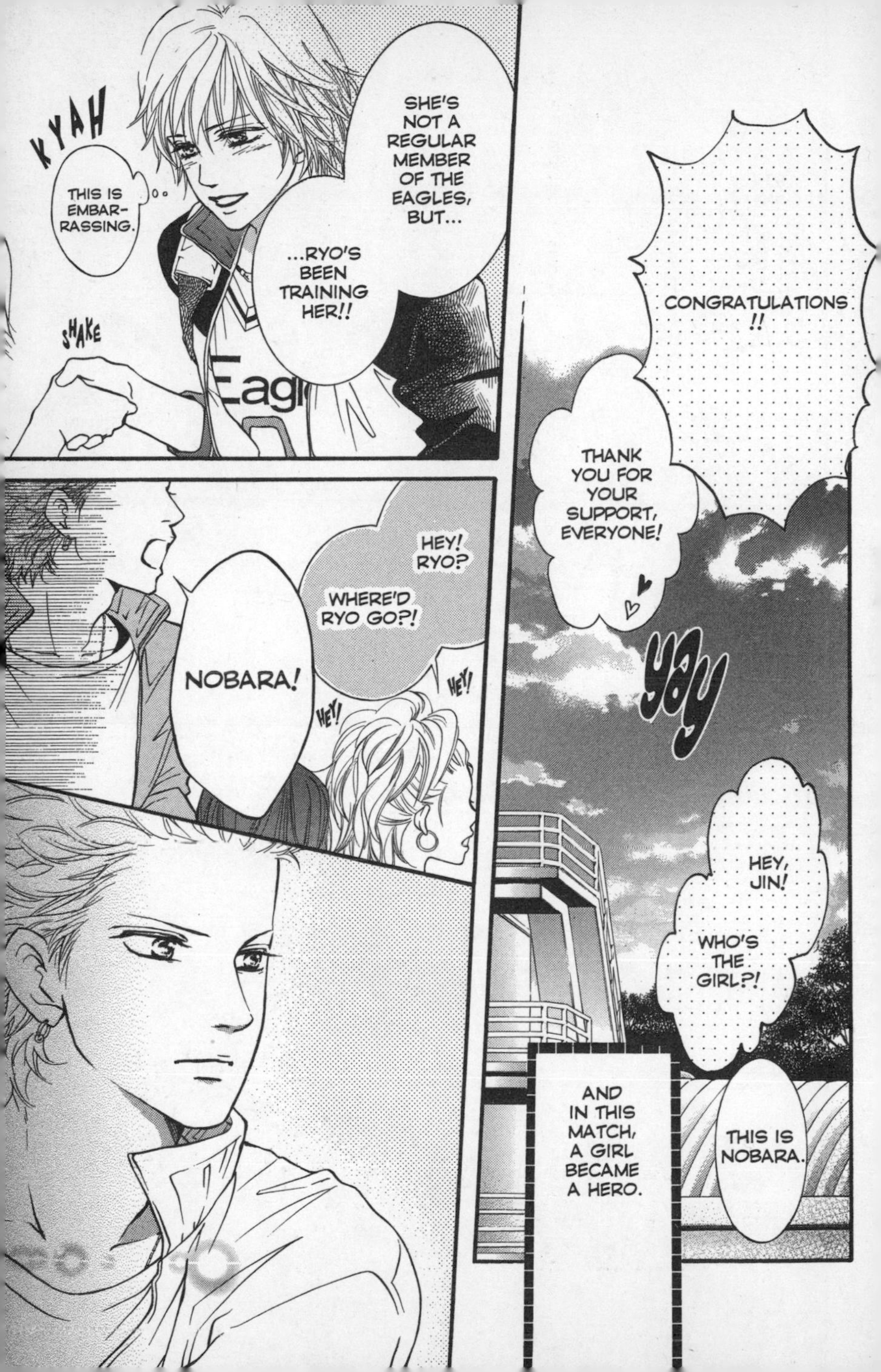
CONGRATULATIONS!!
THANK YOU FOR YOUR SUPPORT, EVERYONE!
YAY
HEY, JIN!
WHO'S THE GIRL?!
THIS IS NOBARA.
AND IN THIS MATCH, A GIRL BECAME A HERO.
SHE'S NOT A REGULAR MEMBER OF THE EAGLES, BUT...
...RYO'S BEEN TRAINING HER!!
KYAH
THIS IS EMBAR-RASSING.
SHAKE
Eagl
HEY! RYO?
WHERE'D RYO GO?!
HEY!
HEY!
NOBARA!

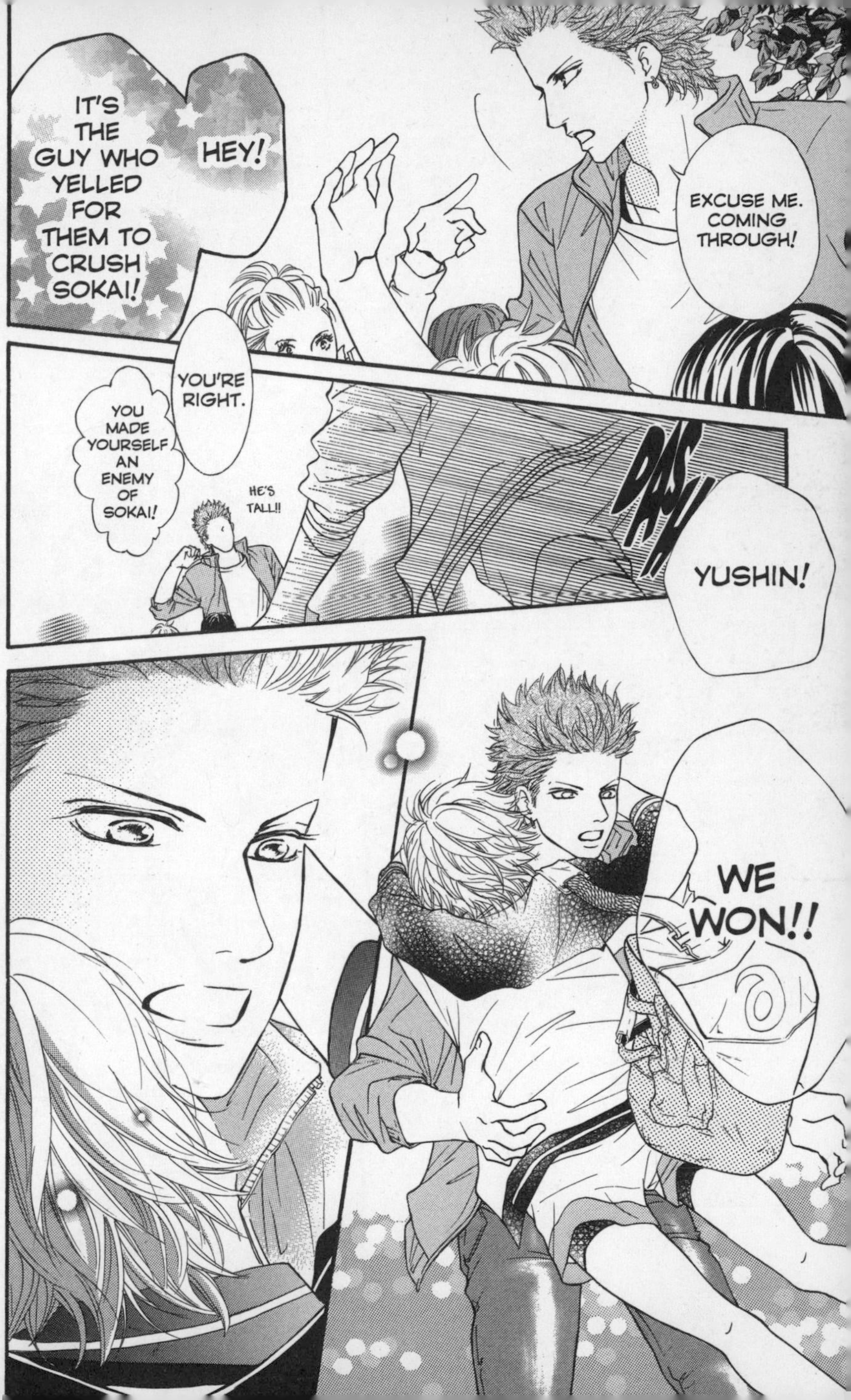
EXCUSE ME. COMING THROUGH!
HEY!
IT'S THE GUY WHO YELLED FOR THEM TO CRUSH SOKAI!
YOU'RE RIGHT.
DASH
YUSHIN!
HE'S TALL!!
YOU MADE YOURSELF AN ENEMY OF SOKAI!
WE WON!!

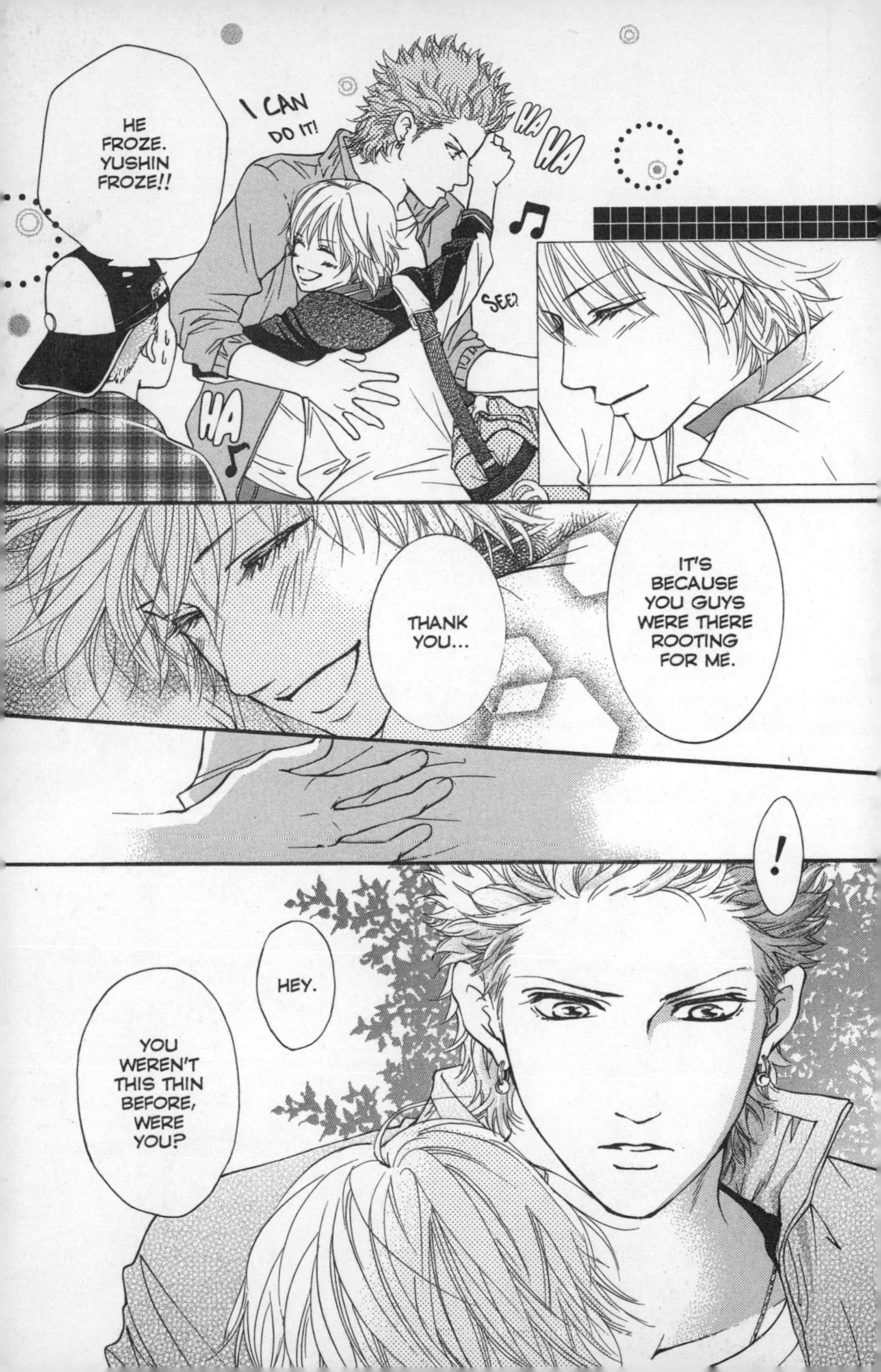
HA HA
I CAN DO IT!
HE FROZE. YUSHIN FROZE!!
SEE?
HA
IT'S BECAUSE YOU GUYS WERE THERE ROOTING FOR ME.
THANK YOU...
!
HEY.
YOU WEREN'T THIS THIN BEFORE, WERE YOU?

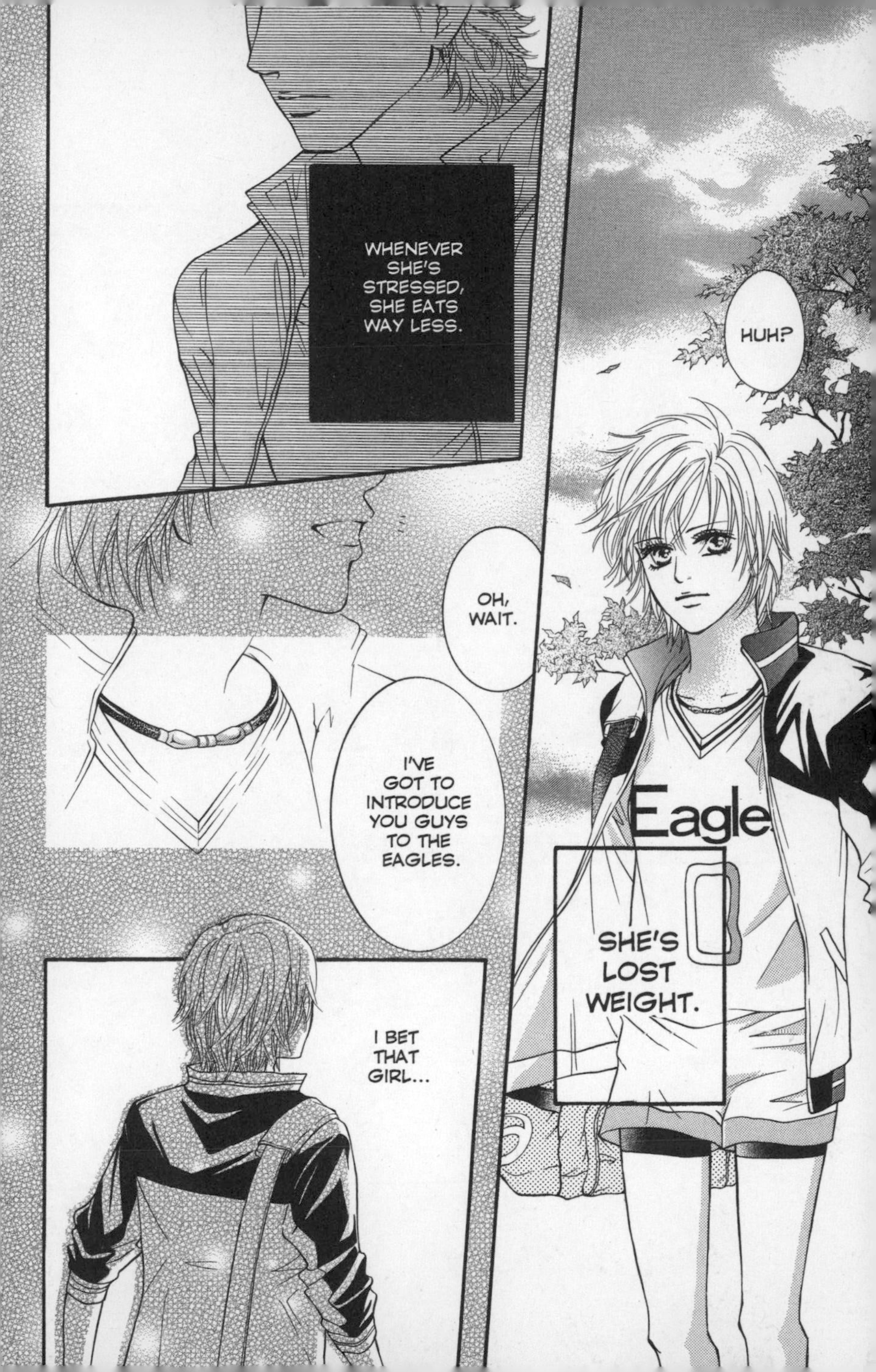
HUH?
SHE'S LOST WEIGHT.
WHENEVER SHE'S STRESSED, SHE EATS WAY LESS.
OH, WAIT.
I'VE GOT TO INTRODUCE YOU GUYS TO THE EAGLES.
I BET THAT GIRL...

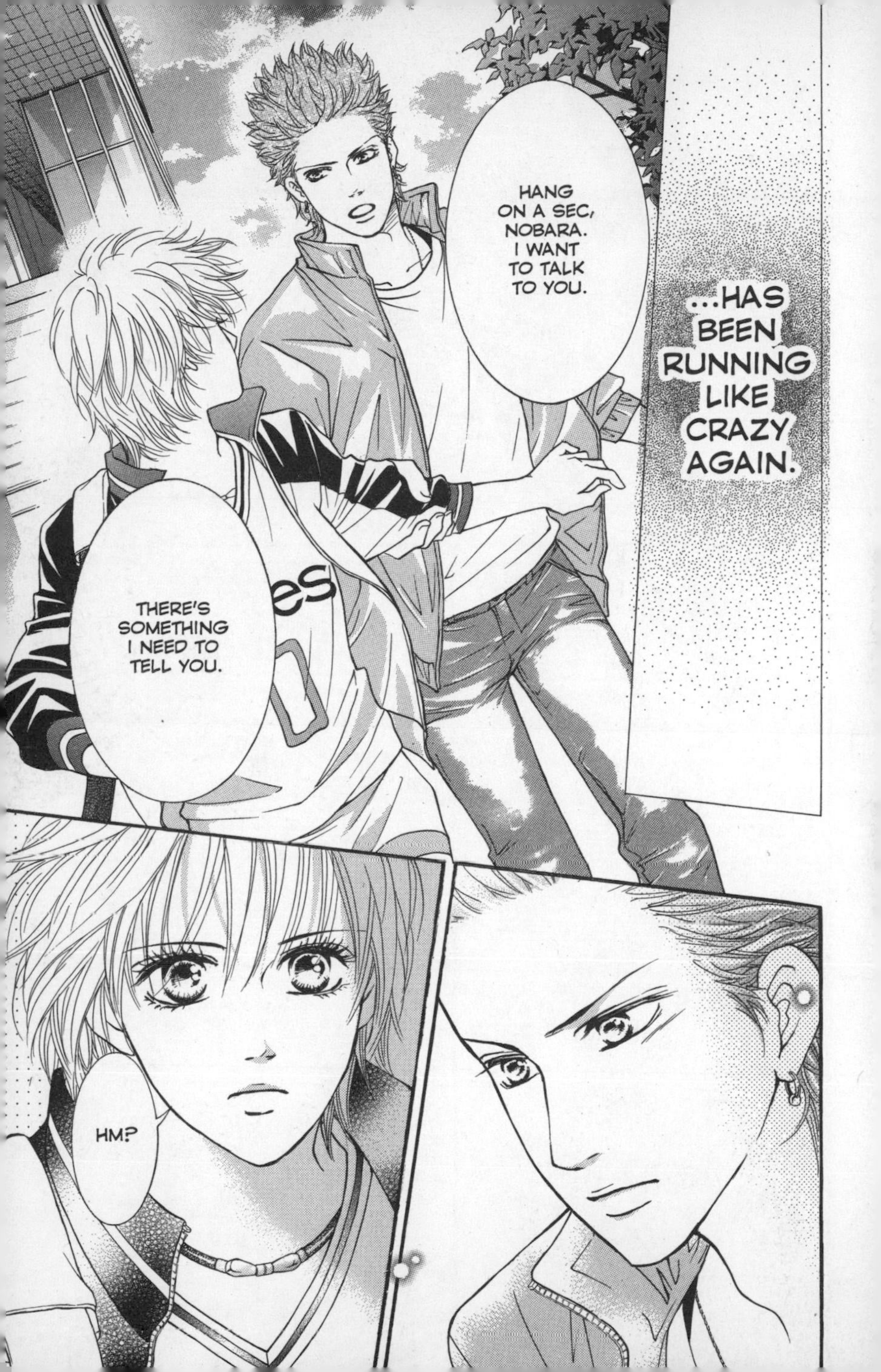
...HAS BEEN RUNNING LIKE CRAZY AGAIN.
HANG ON A SEC, NOBARA. I WANT TO TALK TO YOU.
THERE'S SOMETHING I NEED TO TELL YOU.
HM?

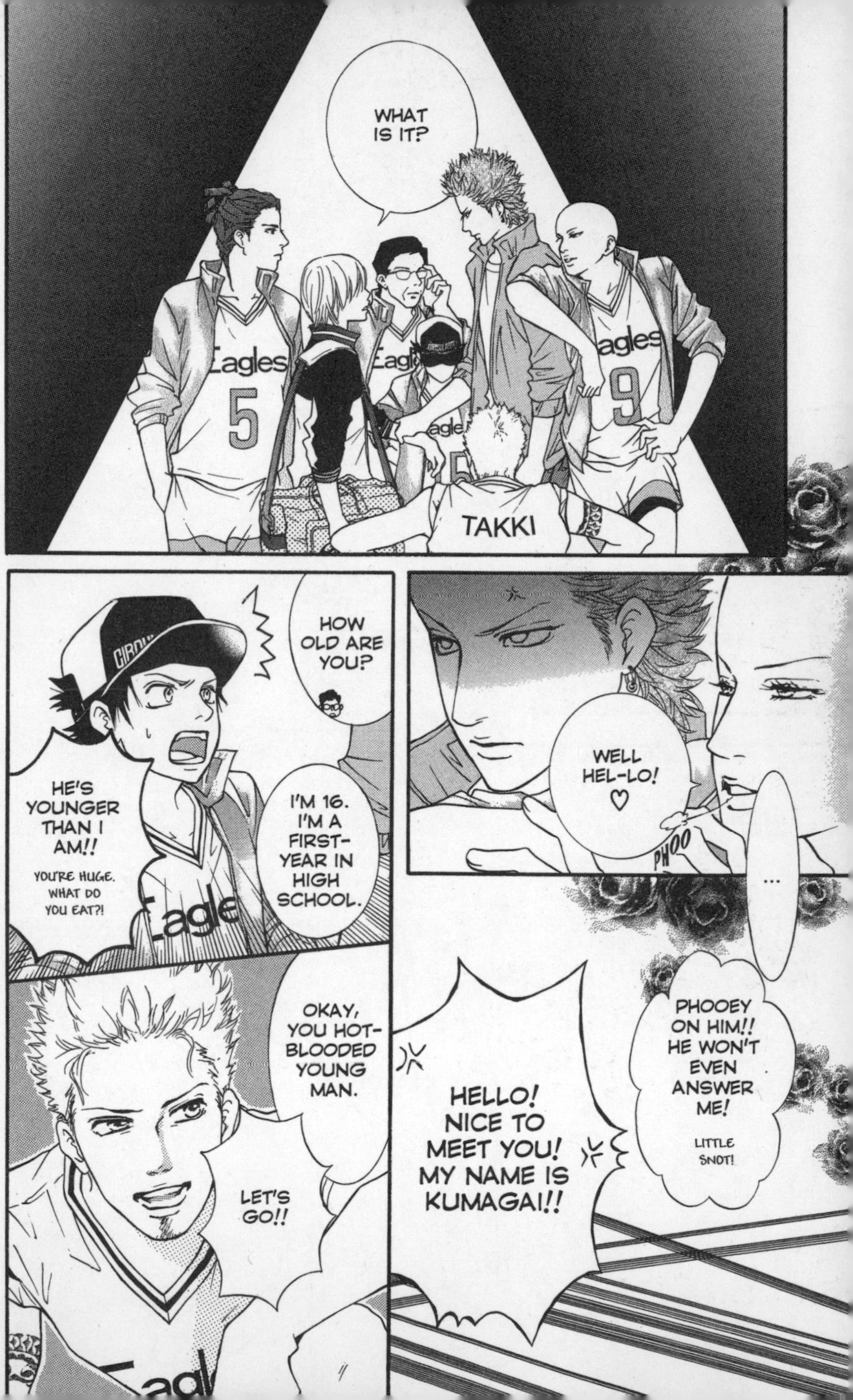
WHAT IS IT?
TAKKI
WELL HEL-LO! ♡
PHOO
...
HOW OLD ARE YOU?
I'M 16. I'M A FIRST-YEAR IN HIGH SCHOOL.
HE'S YOUNGER THAN I AM!!
YOU'RE HUGE. WHAT DO YOU EAT?!
PHOOEY ON HIM!! HE WON'T EVEN ANSWER ME!
LITTLE SNOT!
HELLO! NICE TO MEET YOU! MY NAME IS KUMAGAI!!
OKAY, YOU HOT-BLOODED YOUNG MAN.
LET'S GO!!

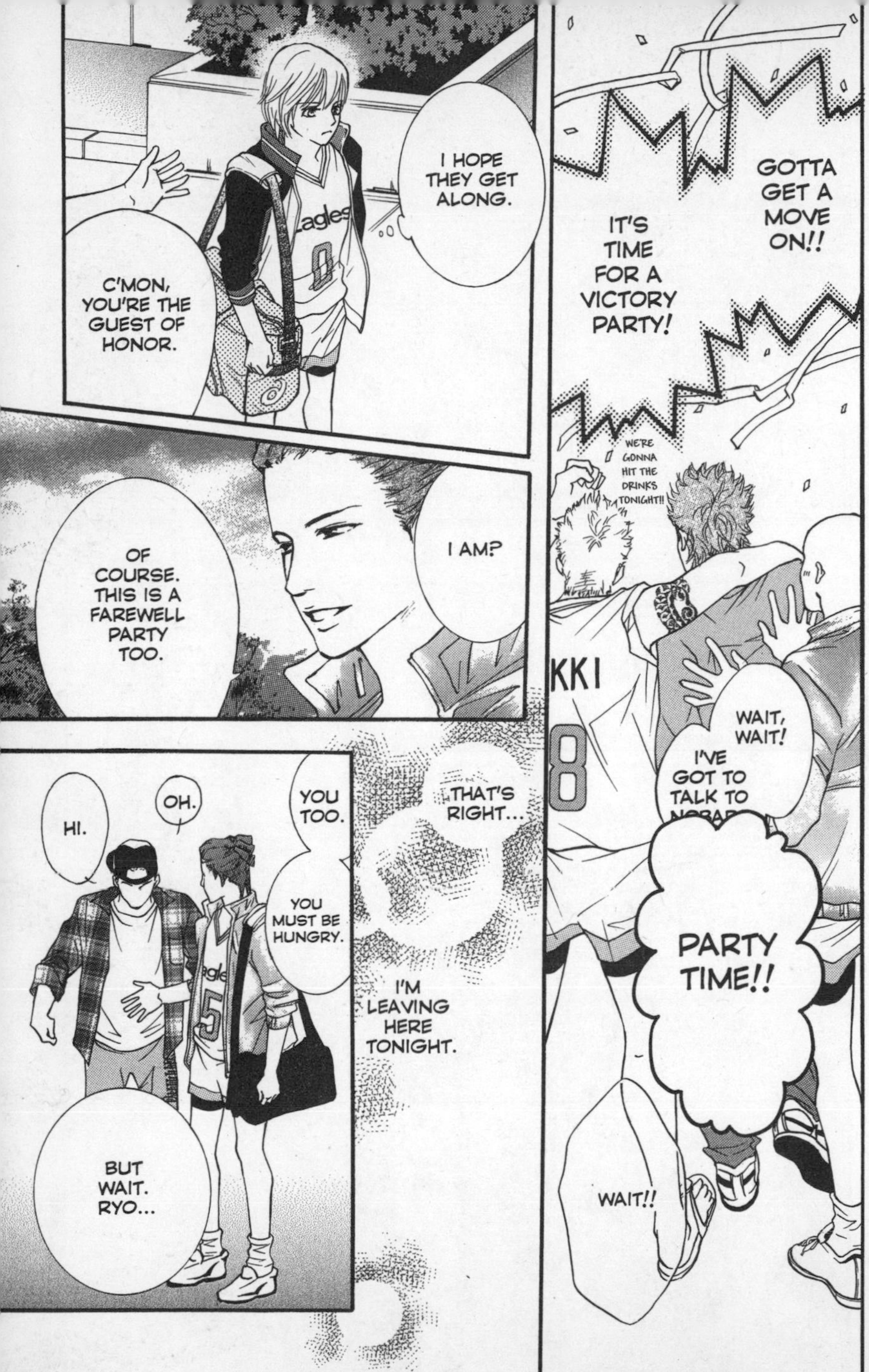
GOTTA GET A MOVE ON!!
IT'S TIME FOR A VICTORY PARTY!
WE'RE GONNA HIT THE DRINKS TONIGHT!!
WAIT, WAIT!
I'VE GOT TO TALK TO
PARTY TIME!!
WAIT!!
I HOPE THEY GET ALONG.
C'MON, YOU'RE THE GUEST OF HONOR.
I AM?
OF COURSE. THIS IS A FAREWELL PARTY TOO.
THAT'S RIGHT...
I'M LEAVING HERE TONIGHT.
YOU TOO.
OH.
HI.
YOU MUST BE HUNGRY.
BUT WAIT. RYO...

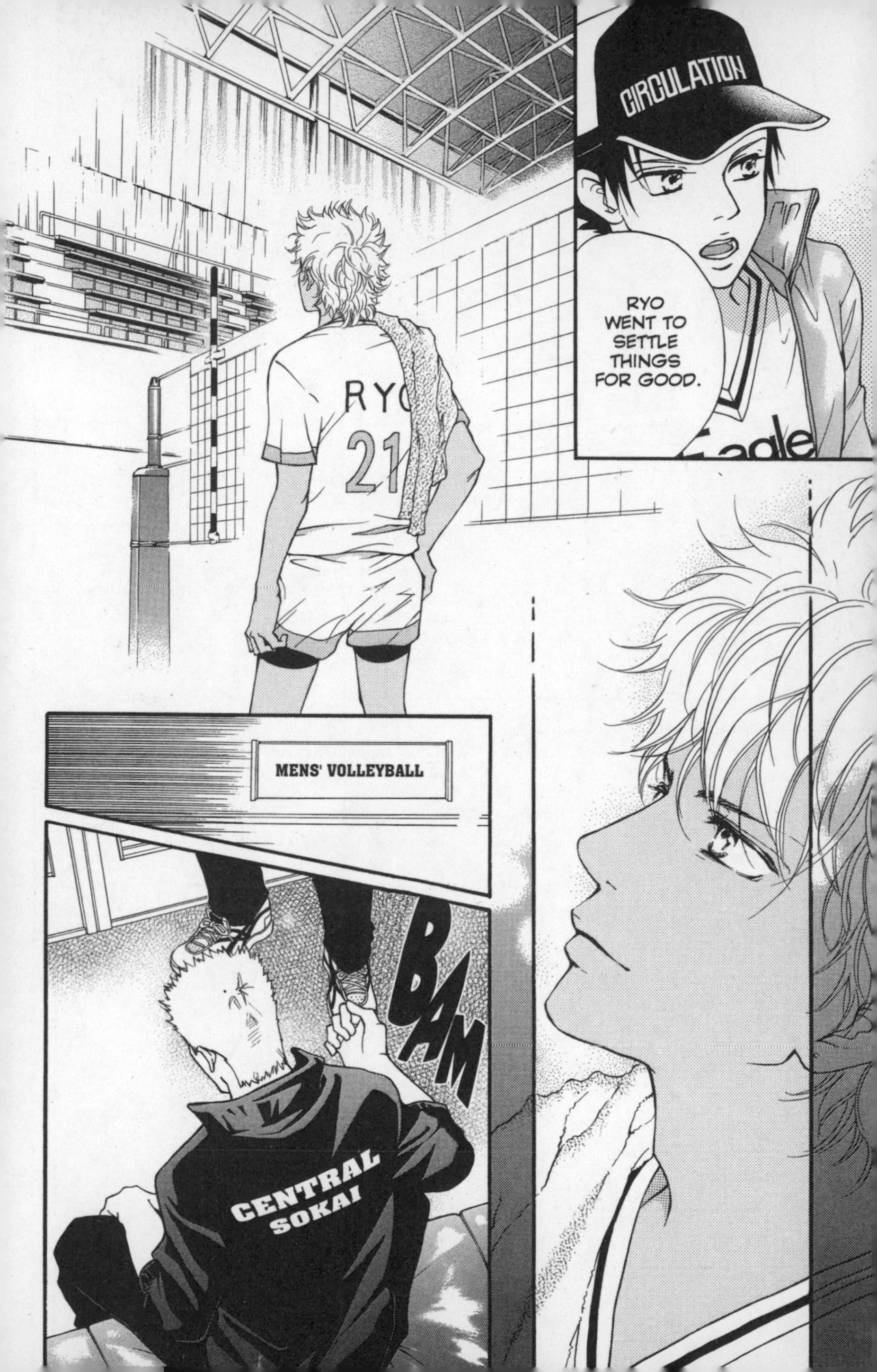
CIRCULATION
RYO WENT TO SETTLE THINGS FOR GOOD.
RYO
21
MENS' VOLLEYBALL
BAM
CENTRAL SOKAI

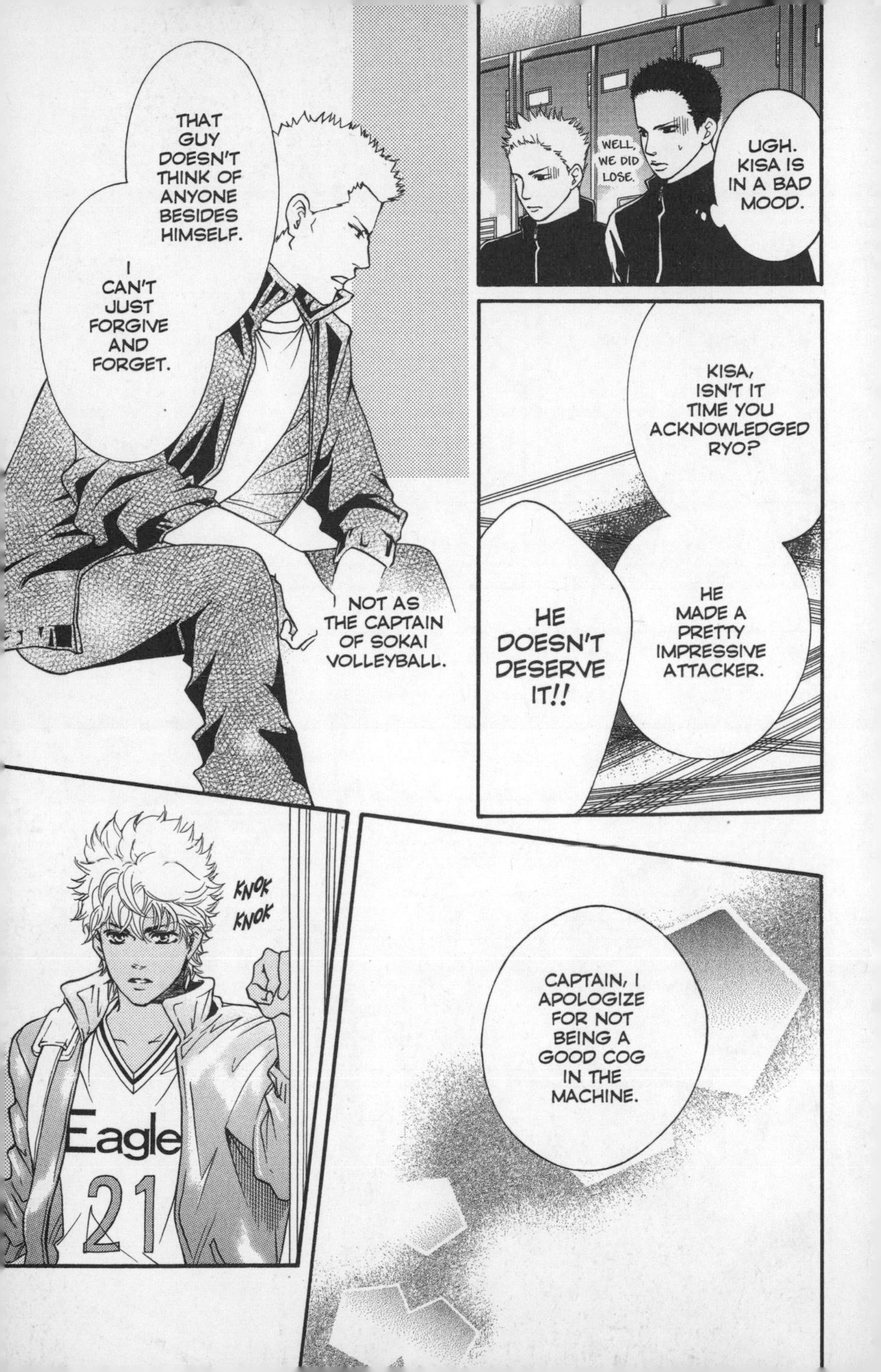
UGH. KISA IS IN A BAD MOOD.
WELL, WE DID LOSE.
KISA, ISN'T IT TIME YOU ACKNOWLEDGED RYO?
HE MADE A PRETTY IMPRESSIVE ATTACKER.
HE DOESN'T DESERVE IT!!
THAT GUY DOESN'T THINK OF ANYONE BESIDES HIMSELF.
I CAN'T JUST FORGIVE AND FORGET.
NOT AS THE CAPTAIN OF SOKAI VOLLEYBALL.
CAPTAIN, I APOLOGIZE FOR NOT BEING A GOOD COG IN THE MACHINE.
KNOK KNOK
Eagle
21

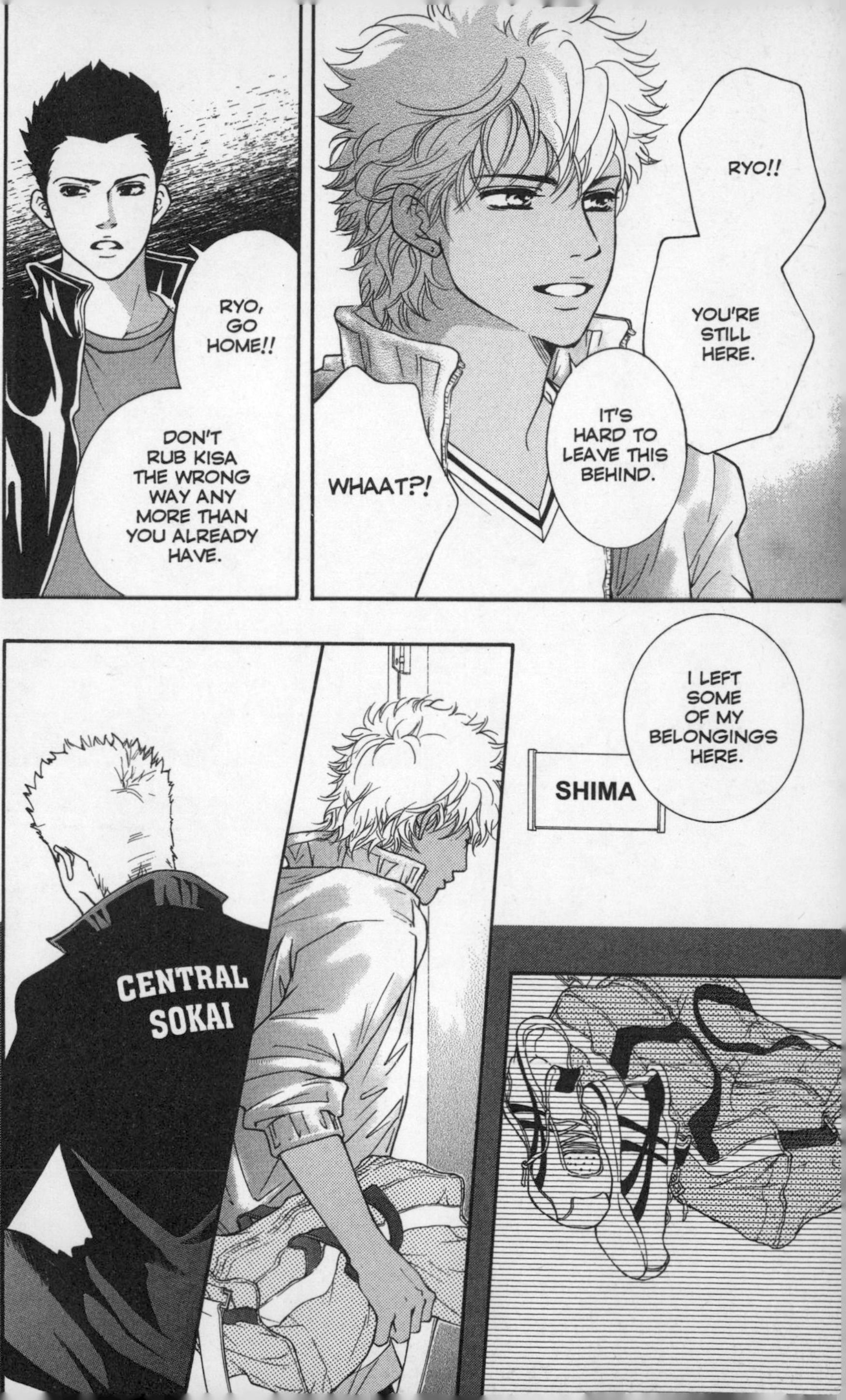
RYO!!
YOU'RE STILL HERE.
IT'S HARD TO LEAVE THIS BEHIND.
WHAAT?!
RYO, GO HOME!!
DON'T RUB KISA THE WRONG WAY ANY MORE THAN YOU ALREADY HAVE.
I LEFT SOME OF MY BELONGINGS HERE.
SHIMA
CENTRAL SOKAI

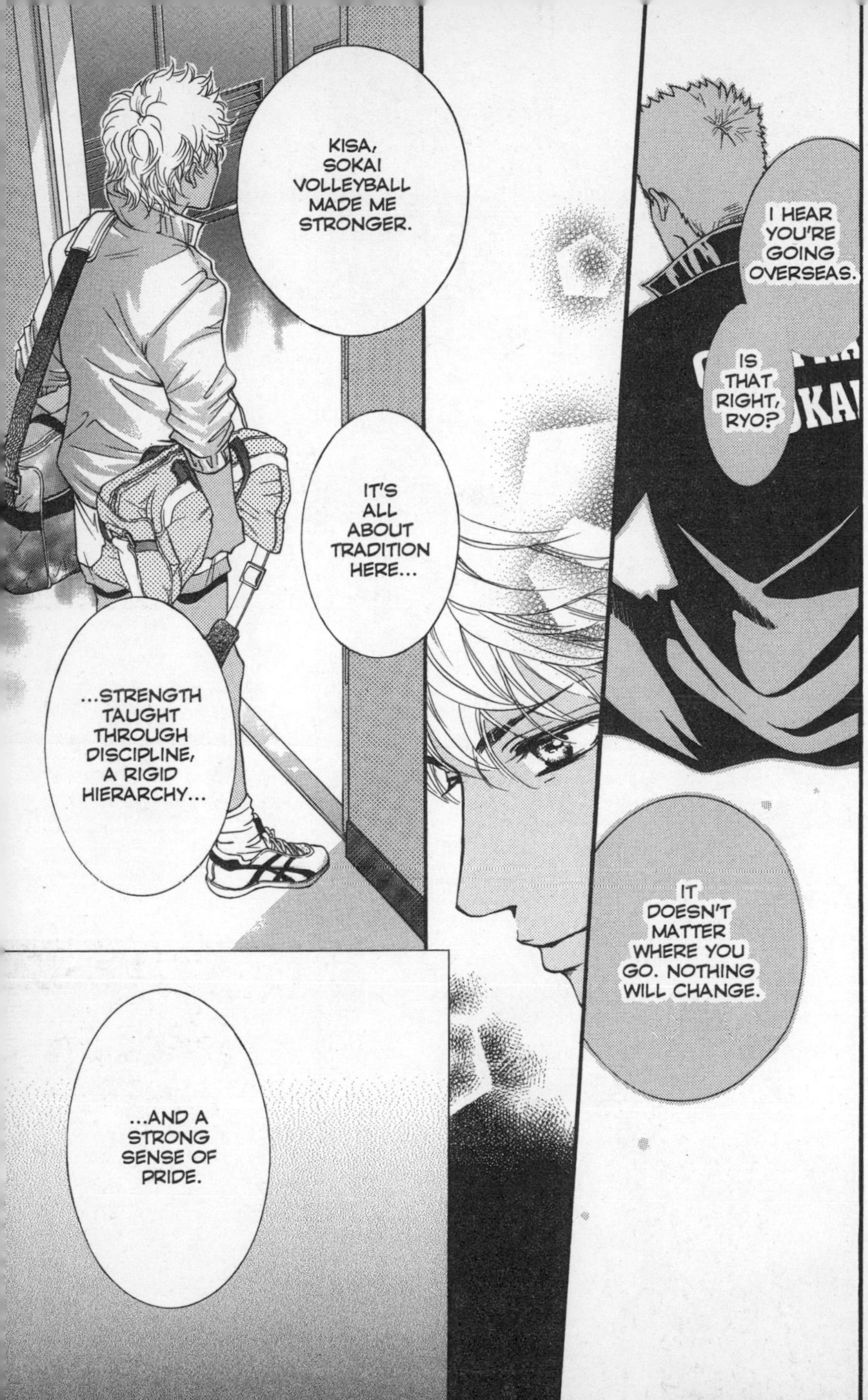
I HEAR YOU'RE GOING OVERSEAS.
IS THAT RIGHT, RYO?
IT DOESN'T MATTER WHERE YOU GO. NOTHING WILL CHANGE.
KISA, SOKAI VOLLEYBALL MADE ME STRONGER.
IT'S ALL ABOUT TRADITION HERE...
...STRENGTH TAUGHT THROUGH DISCIPLINE, A RIGID HIERARCHY...
...AND A STRONG SENSE OF PRIDE.

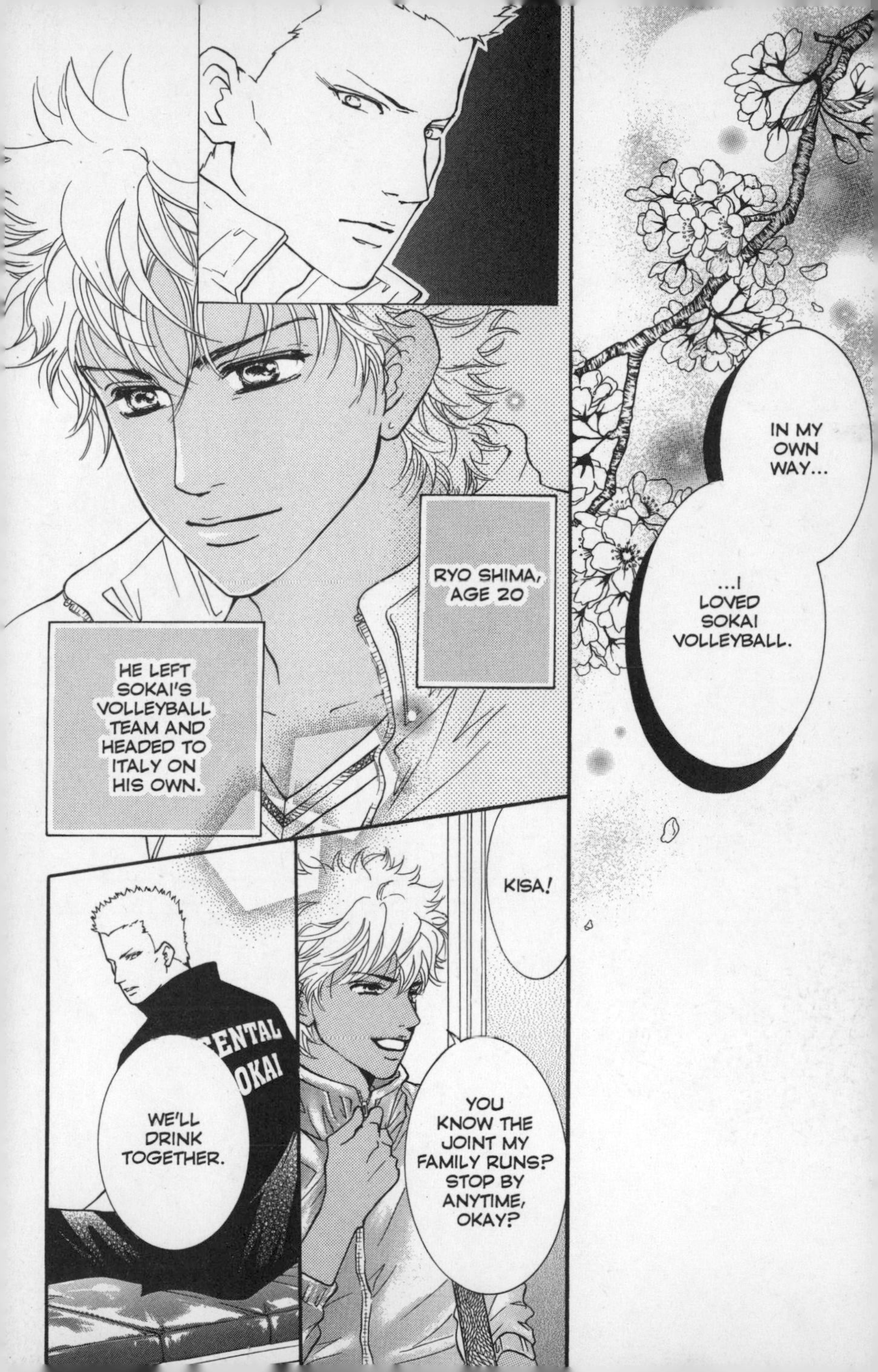
IN MY OWN WAY...
...I LOVED SOKAI VOLLEYBALL.
RYO SHIMA, AGE 20
HE LEFT SOKAI'S VOLLEYBALL TEAM AND HEADED TO ITALY ON HIS OWN.
KISA!
YOU KNOW THE JOINT MY FAMILY RUNS? STOP BY ANYTIME, OKAY?
WE'LL DRINK TOGETHER.

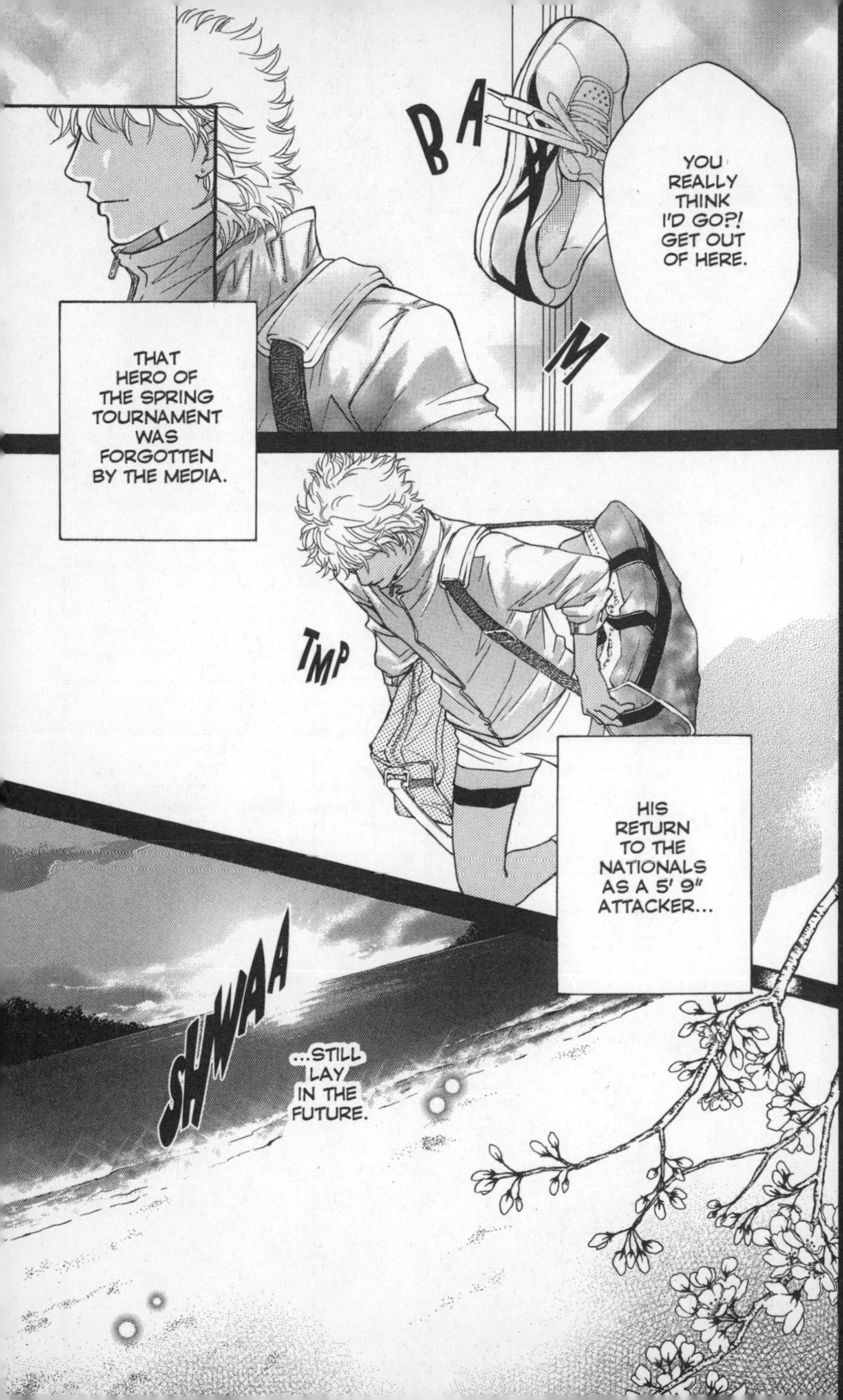
YOU REALLY THINK I'D GO?! GET OUT OF HERE.
BAM
THAT HERO OF THE SPRING TOURNAMENT WAS FORGOTTEN BY THE MEDIA.
TMP
HIS RETURN TO THE NATIONALS AS A 5' 9" ATTACKER...
SHWAA
...STILL LAY IN THE FUTURE.

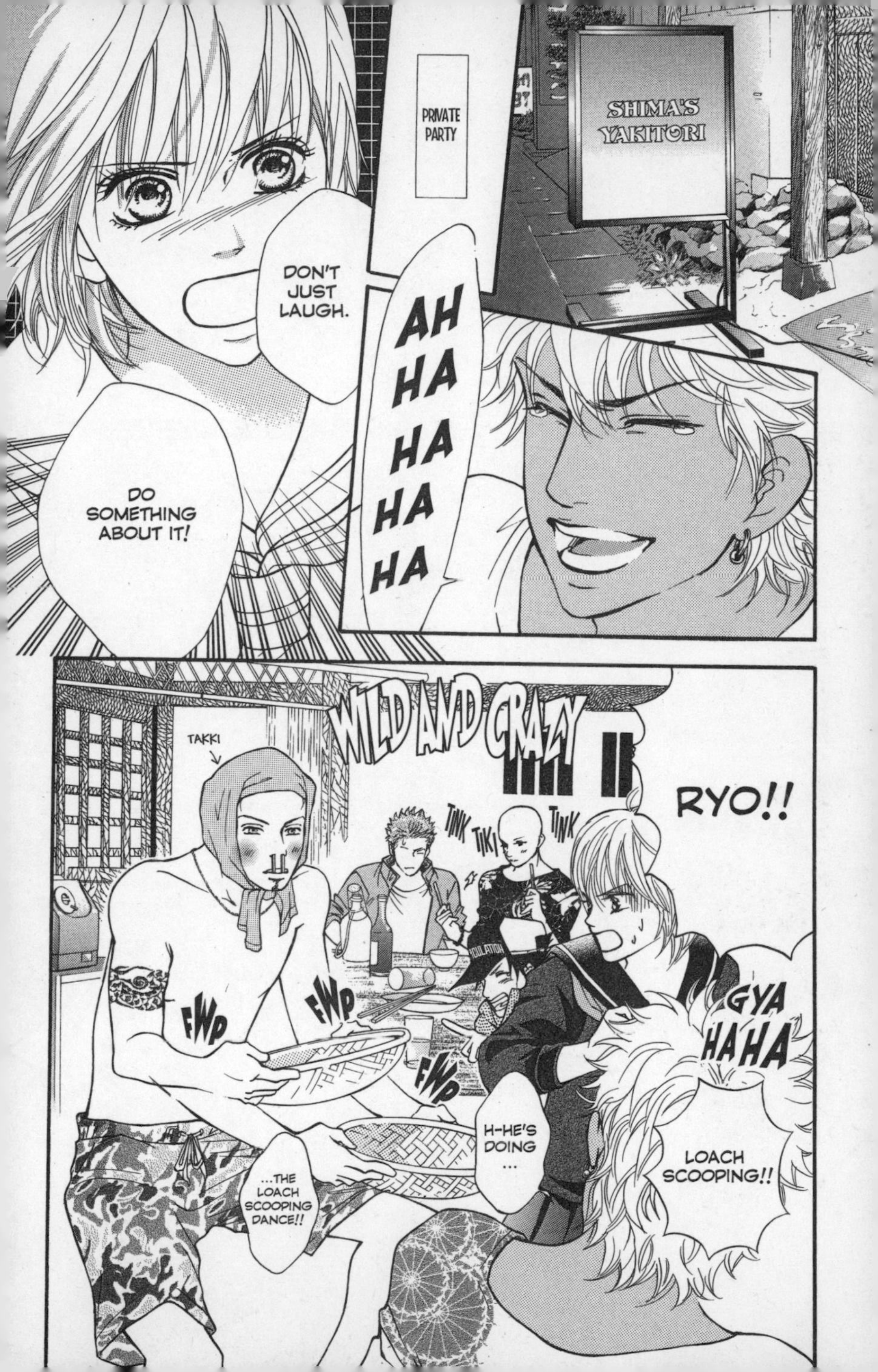
SHIMA'S YAKITORI
PRIVATE PARTY
AH HA HA HA HA HA
DON'T JUST LAUGH.
DO SOMETHING ABOUT IT!
RYO!!
WILD AND CRAZY
TINK TIKI TINK
TAKKI
GYA HAHA
LOACH SCOOPING!!
H-HE'S DOING...
FWP FWP FWP
...THE LOACH SCOOPING DANCE!!

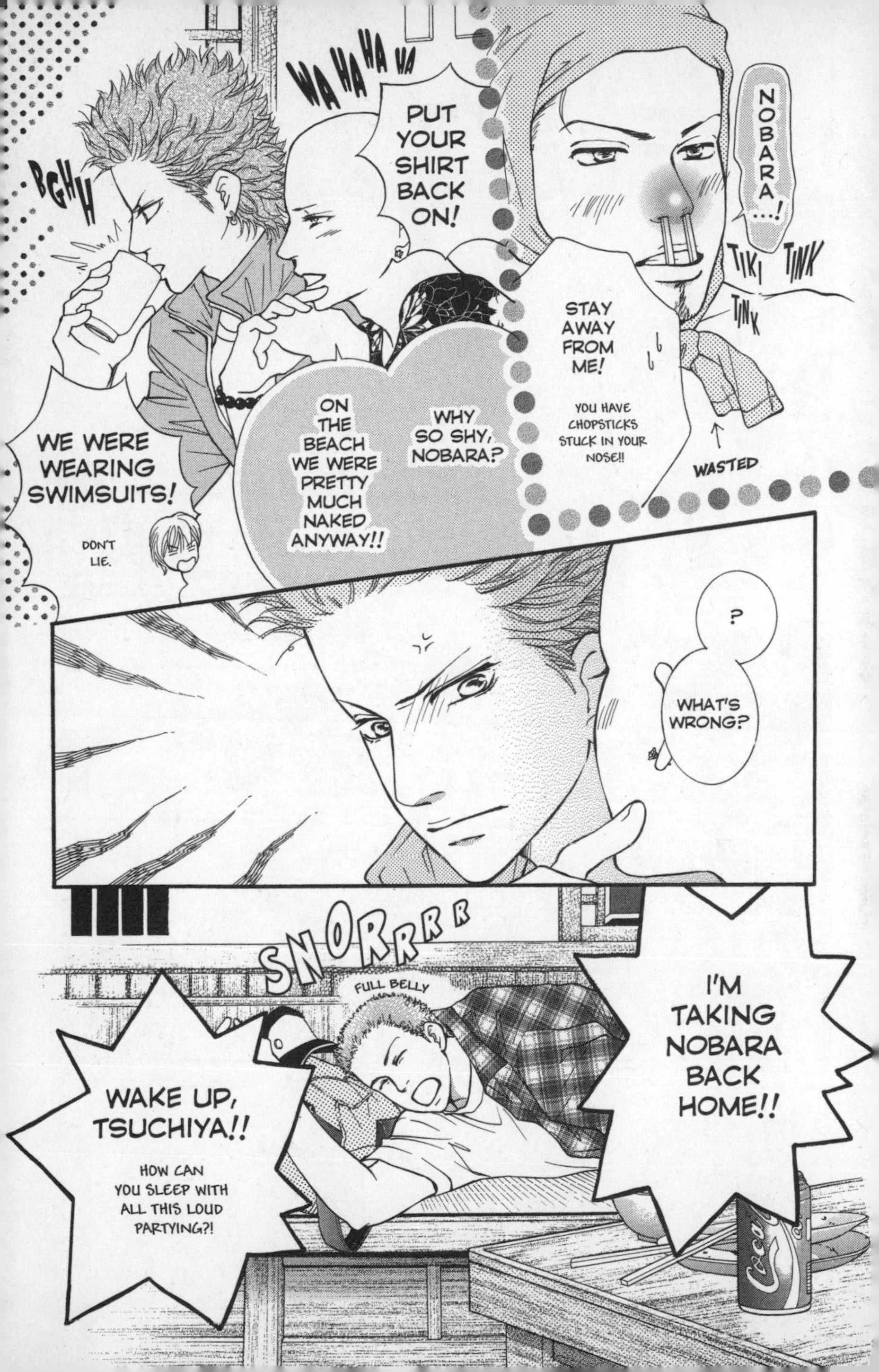
NOBARA ...!
TIKI TINK
TINK
STAY AWAY FROM ME!
YOU HAVE CHOPSTICKS STUCK IN YOUR NOSE!!
WASTED
WA HA HA HA
PUT YOUR SHIRT BACK ON!
WHY SO SHY, NOBARA?
ON THE BEACH WE WERE PRETTY MUCH NAKED ANYWAY!!
BGHH
WE WERE WEARING SWIMSUITS!
DON'T LIE.
?
WHAT'S WRONG?
I'M TAKING NOBARA BACK HOME!!
SNORRRRR
FULL BELLY
WAKE UP, TSUCHIYA!!
HOW CAN YOU SLEEP WITH ALL THIS LOUD PARTYING?!

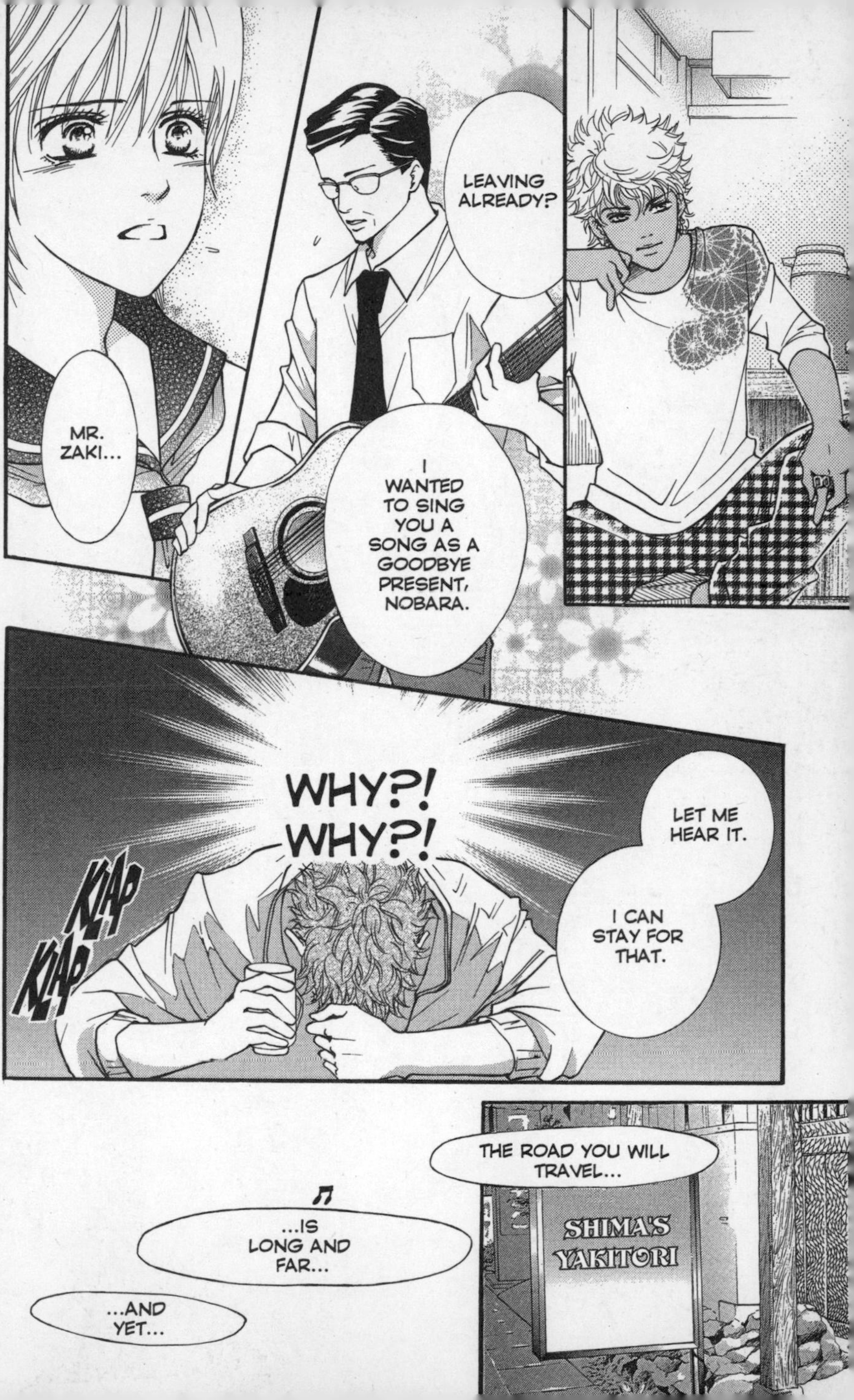
LEAVING ALREADY?
I WANTED TO SING YOU A SONG AS A GOODBYE PRESENT, NOBARA.
MR. ZAKI...
LET ME HEAR IT.
I CAN STAY FOR THAT.
WHY?! WHY?!
KLAP KLAP
THE ROAD YOU WILL TRAVEL...
SHIMA'S YAKITORI
...IS LONG AND FAR...
...AND YET...

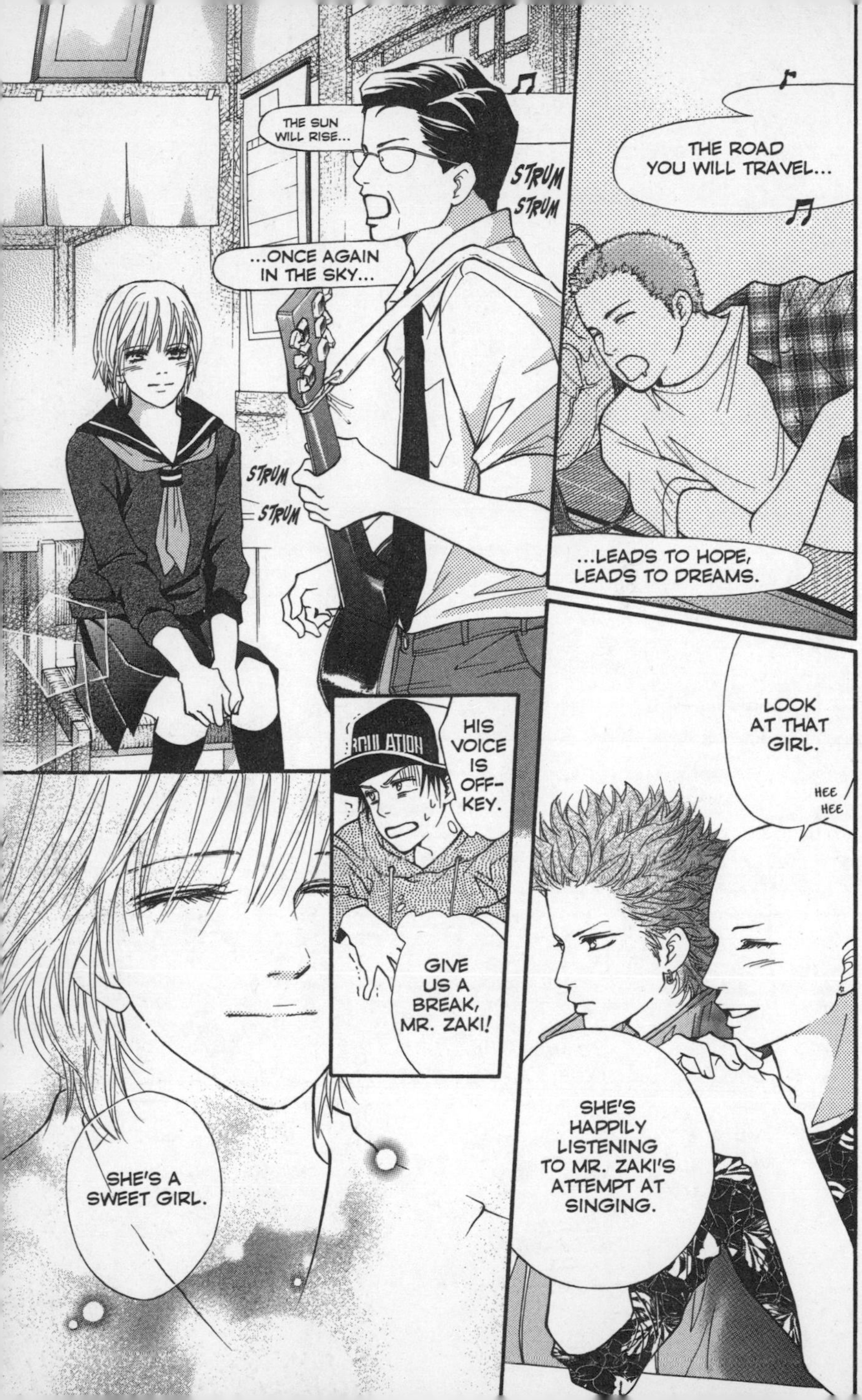
THE ROAD YOU WILL TRAVEL...
...LEADS TO HOPE, LEADS TO DREAMS.
THE SUN WILL RISE...
STRUM STRUM
...ONCE AGAIN IN THE SKY...
STRUM STRUM
LOOK AT THAT GIRL.
HEE HEE
SHE'S HAPPILY LISTENING TO MR. ZAKI'S ATTEMPT AT SINGING.
HIS VOICE IS OFF-KEY.
GIVE US A BREAK, MR. ZAKI!
SHE'S A SWEET GIRL.

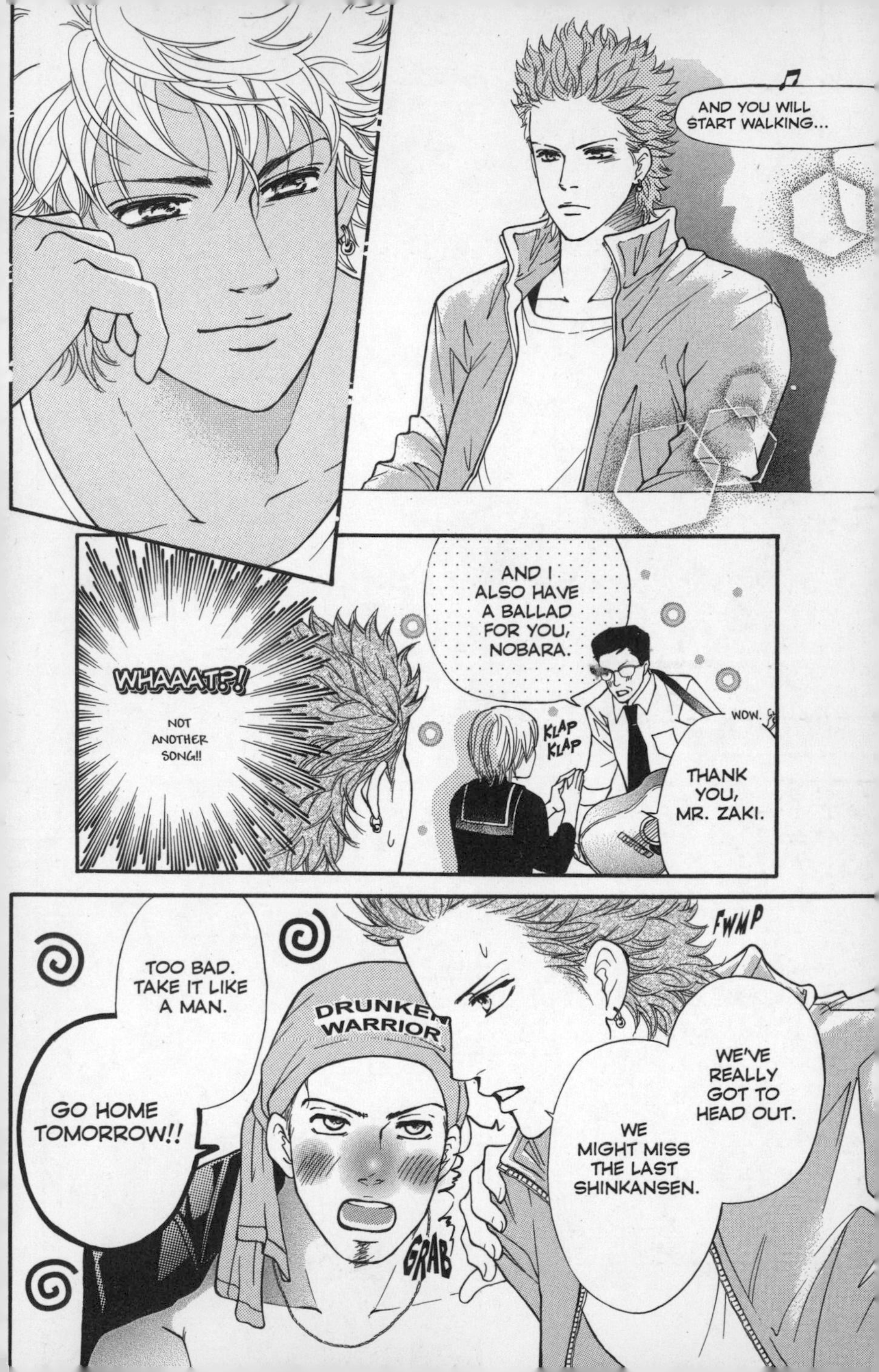
AND YOU WILL START WALKING...
AND I ALSO HAVE A BALLAD FOR YOU, NOBARA.
WOW.
THANK YOU, MR. ZAKI.
KLAP KLAP
WHAAAT?!
NOT ANOTHER SONG!!
FWMP
WE'VE REALLY GOT TO HEAD OUT.
WE MIGHT MISS THE LAST SHINKANSEN.
DRUNKEN WARRIOR
TOO BAD. TAKE IT LIKE A MAN.
GO HOME TOMORROW!!
GRAB

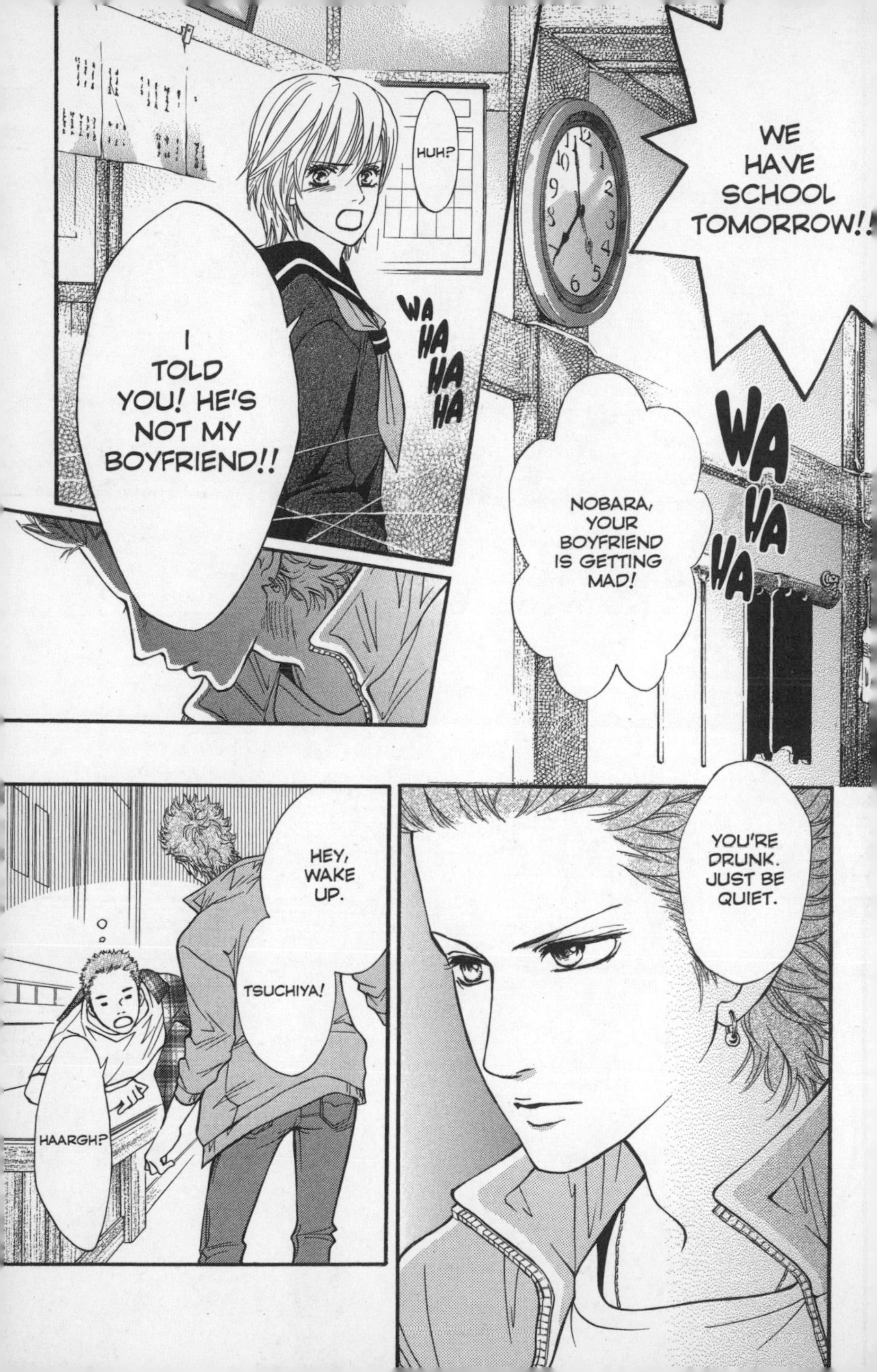
WE HAVE SCHOOL TOMORROW!!
WA HA HA
NOBARA, YOUR BOYFRIEND IS GETTING MAD!
HUH?
WA HA HA HA
I TOLD YOU! HE'S NOT MY BOYFRIEND!!
YOU'RE DRUNK. JUST BE QUIET.
HEY, WAKE UP.
TSUCHIYA!
HAARGH?

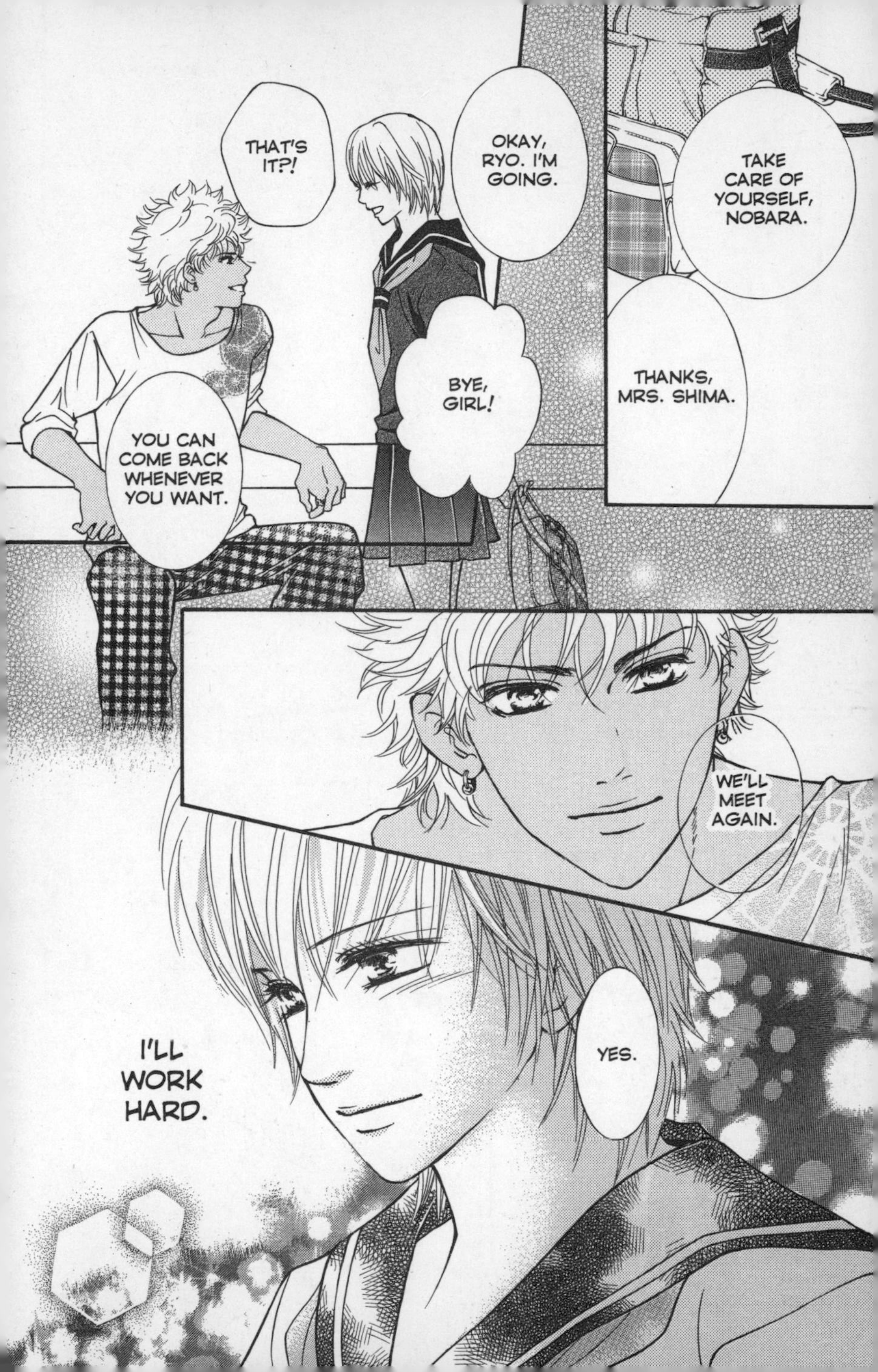
TAKE CARE OF YOURSELF, NOBARA.
THANKS, MRS. SHIMA.
OKAY, RYO. I'M GOING.
THAT'S IT?!
BYE, GIRL!
YOU CAN COME BACK WHENEVER YOU WANT.
WE'LL MEET AGAIN.
YES.
I'LL WORK HARD.

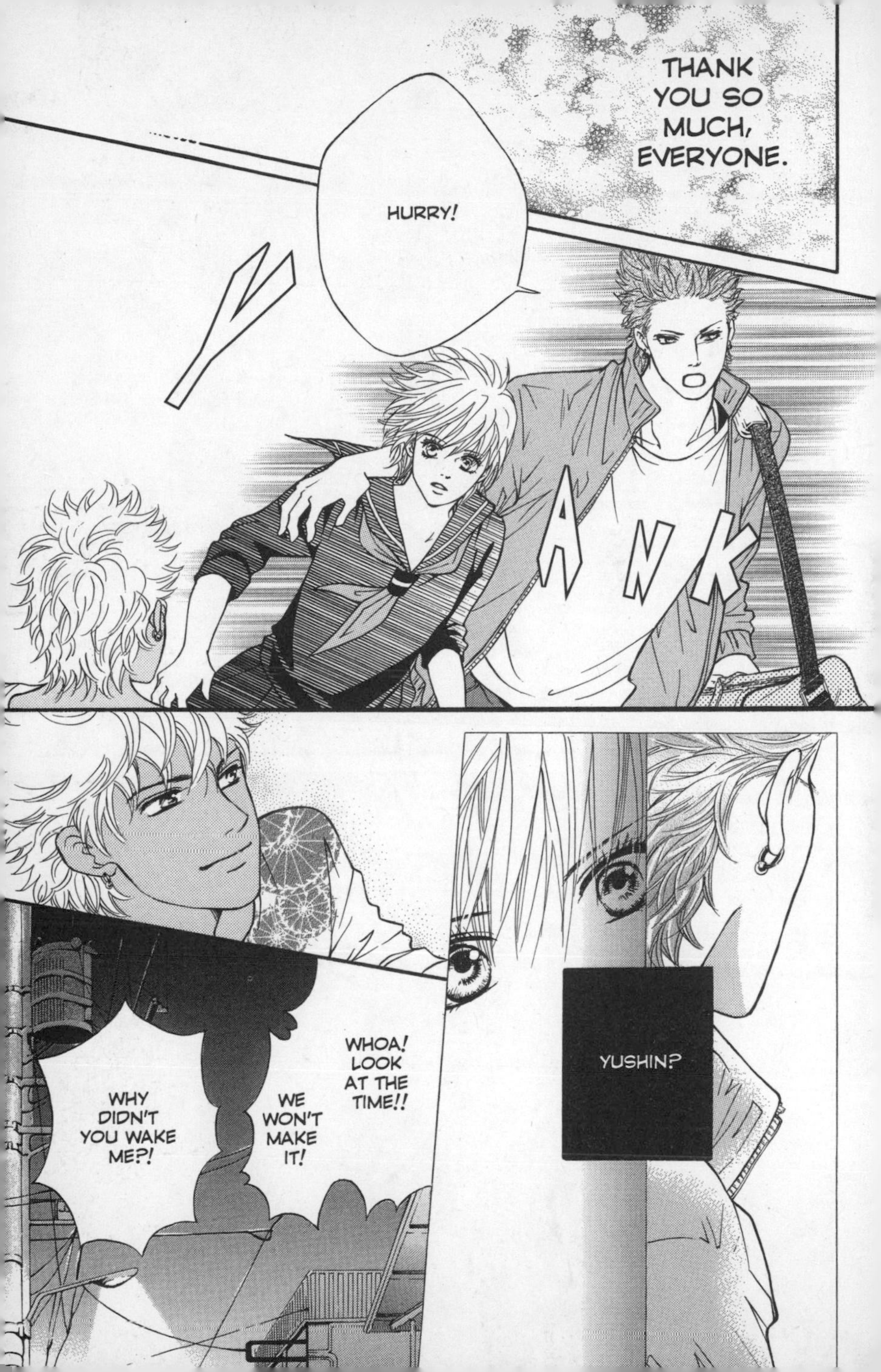
THANK YOU SO MUCH, EVERYONE.
HURRY!
YANK
YUSHIN?
WHOA! LOOK AT THE TIME!!
WE WON'T MAKE IT!
WHY DIDN'T YOU WAKE ME?!

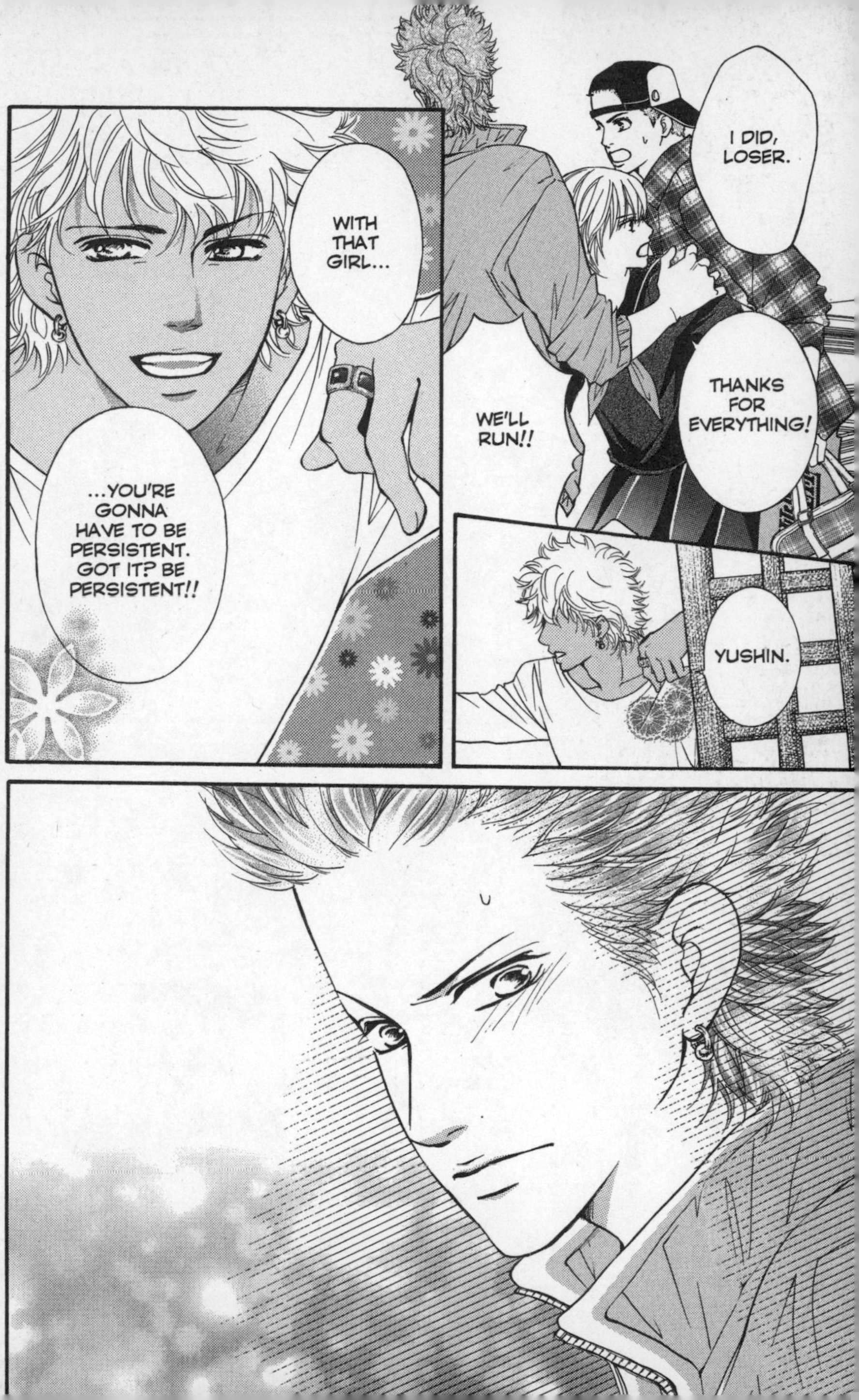
I DID, LOSER.
THANKS FOR EVERYTHING!
WE'LL RUN!!
YUSHIN.
WITH THAT GIRL...
...YOU'RE GONNA HAVE TO BE PERSISTENT. GOT IT? BE PERSISTENT!!

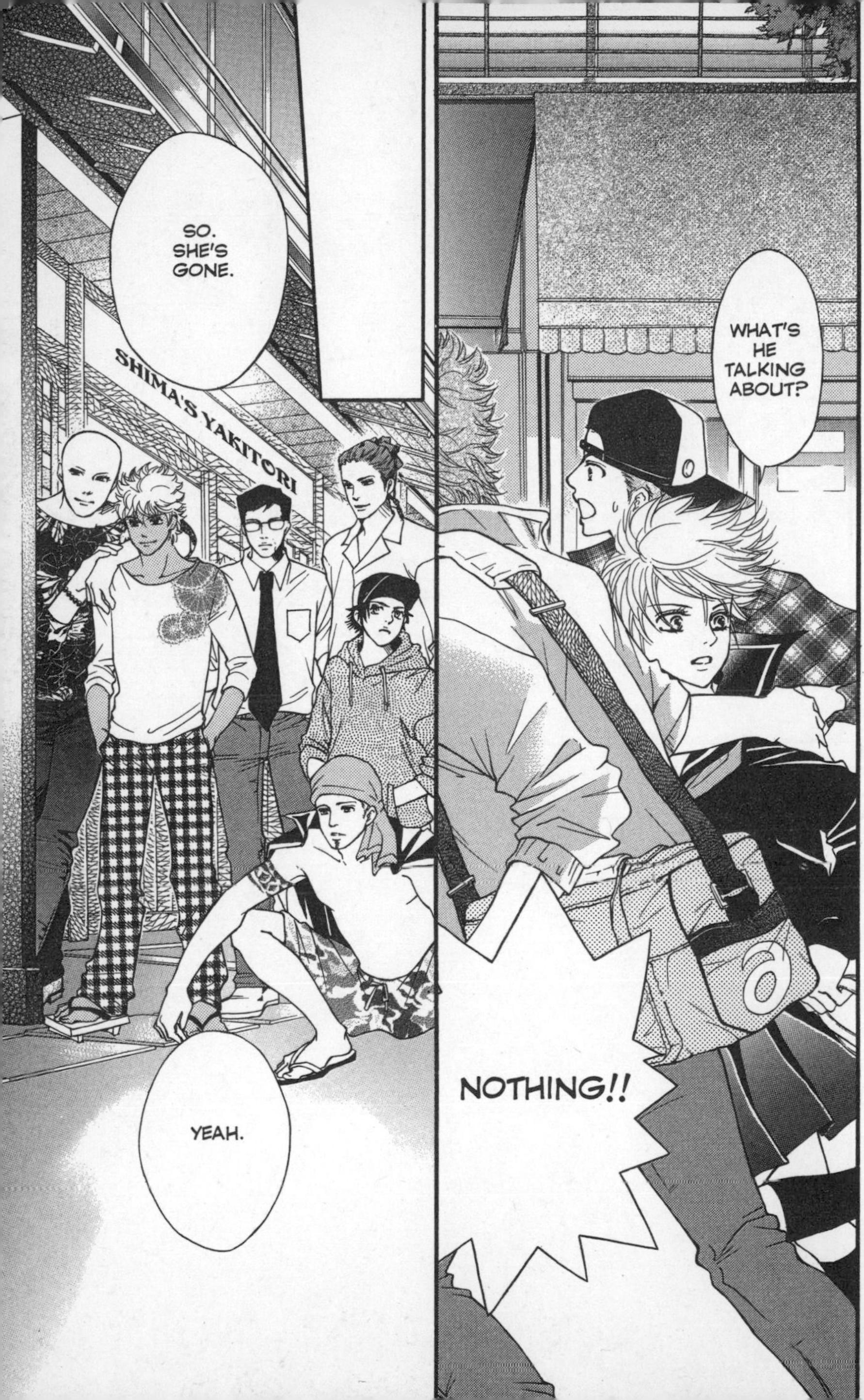
WHAT'S HE TALKING ABOUT?
NOTHING!!
SO. SHE'S GONE.
SHIMA'S YAKITORI
YEAH.

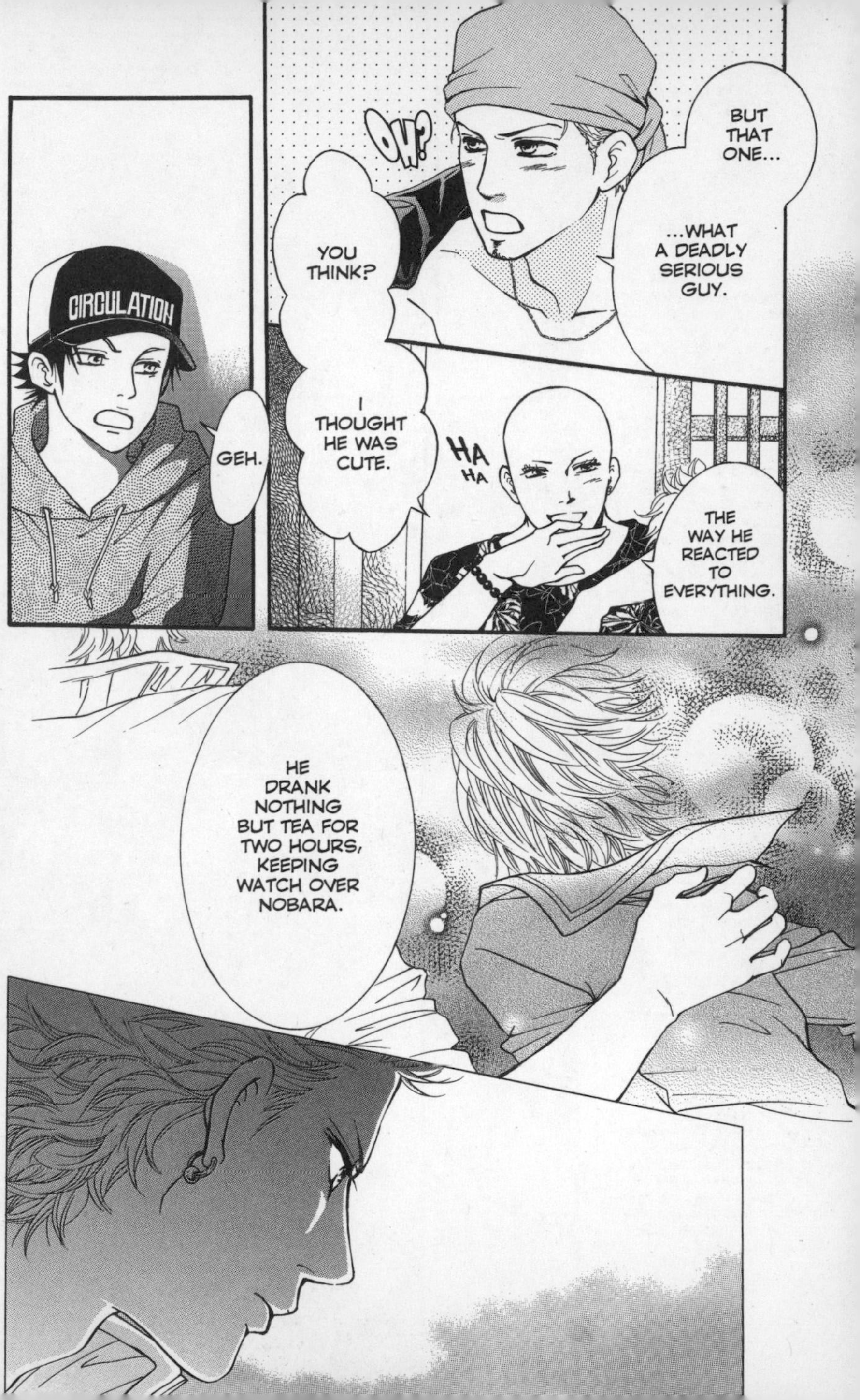
BUT THAT ONE...
...WHAT A DEADLY SERIOUS GUY.
OH?
YOU THINK?
I THOUGHT HE WAS CUTE.
HA HA
THE WAY HE REACTED TO EVERYTHING.
GEH.
HE DRANK NOTHING BUT TEA FOR TWO HOURS, KEEPING WATCH OVER NOBARA.

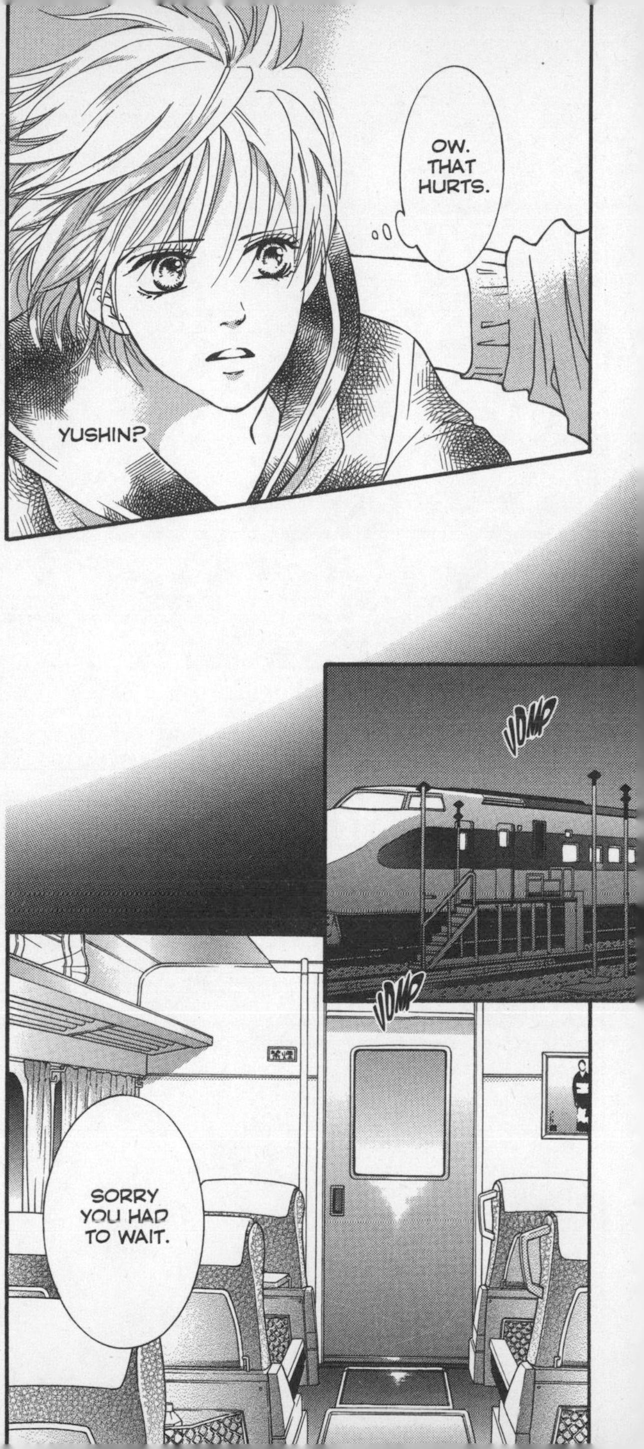
OW. THAT HURTS.
YUSHIN?
VOMP
VOMP
SORRY YOU HAD TO WAIT.

MITSUBA CLUB

VOL. 2

ROCK STAR

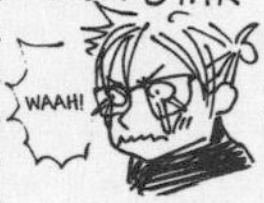
WAAH!

I'M NUMB FROM WATCHING A VIDEO OF AN IEMON (THE YELLOW MONKEY) CONCERT FOR THE FIRST TIME IN A WHILE. I'M WATCHING IT RIGHT NOW, AS I WRITE THIS. HOW MANY YEARS HAS IT BEEN SINCE THEY STOPPED PLAYING? FROM THE BOTTOM OF MY HEART: COME BACK!!! THEY'RE SO AWESOME IT MAKES ME CRY. THE VIDEO I HAVE IS *THE RED TAPE*. IT HAS YOSHII WITH LONG BLOND HAIR, BATHED IN PURPLE LIGHT, BELTING OUT "TENGOKU RYOKO." AND ANNIE'S GUITAR JUST NAILS IT. A WA WA WA...IT'S LIKE SOMEONE GRABBING ME BY THE COLLAR AND SHAKING ME.

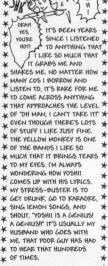

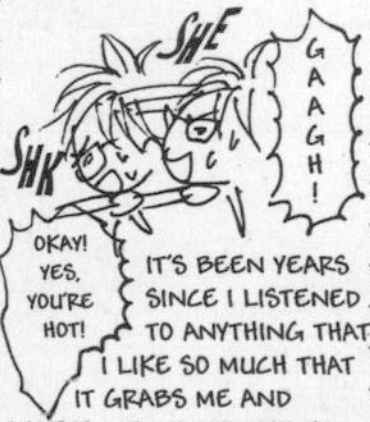
SHE
SHK
GAAGH!
OKAY! YES, YOU'RE HOT!

IT'S BEEN YEARS SINCE I LISTENED TO ANYTHING THAT I LIKE SO MUCH THAT IT GRABS ME AND SHAKES ME. NO MATTER HOW MANY CDS I BORROW AND LISTEN TO, IT'S RARE FOR ME TO COME ACROSS ANYTHING THAT APPROACHES THE LEVEL OF "OH MAN, I CAN'T TAKE IT!" EVEN THOUGH THERE'S LOTS OF STUFF I LIKE JUST FINE. THE YELLOW MONKEY IS ONE OF THE BANDS I LIKE SO MUCH THAT IT BRINGS TEARS TO MY EYES. I'M ALWAYS WONDERING HOW YOSHII COMES UP WITH HIS LYRICS. MY STRESS-BUSTER IS TO GET DRUNK, GO TO KARAOKE, SING IEMON SONGS, AND SHOUT, "YOSHII IS A GENIUS! A GENIUS!!" IT'S USUALLY MY HUSBAND WHO GOES WITH ME. THAT POOR GUY HAS HAD TO HEAR THAT HUNDREDS OF TIMES.

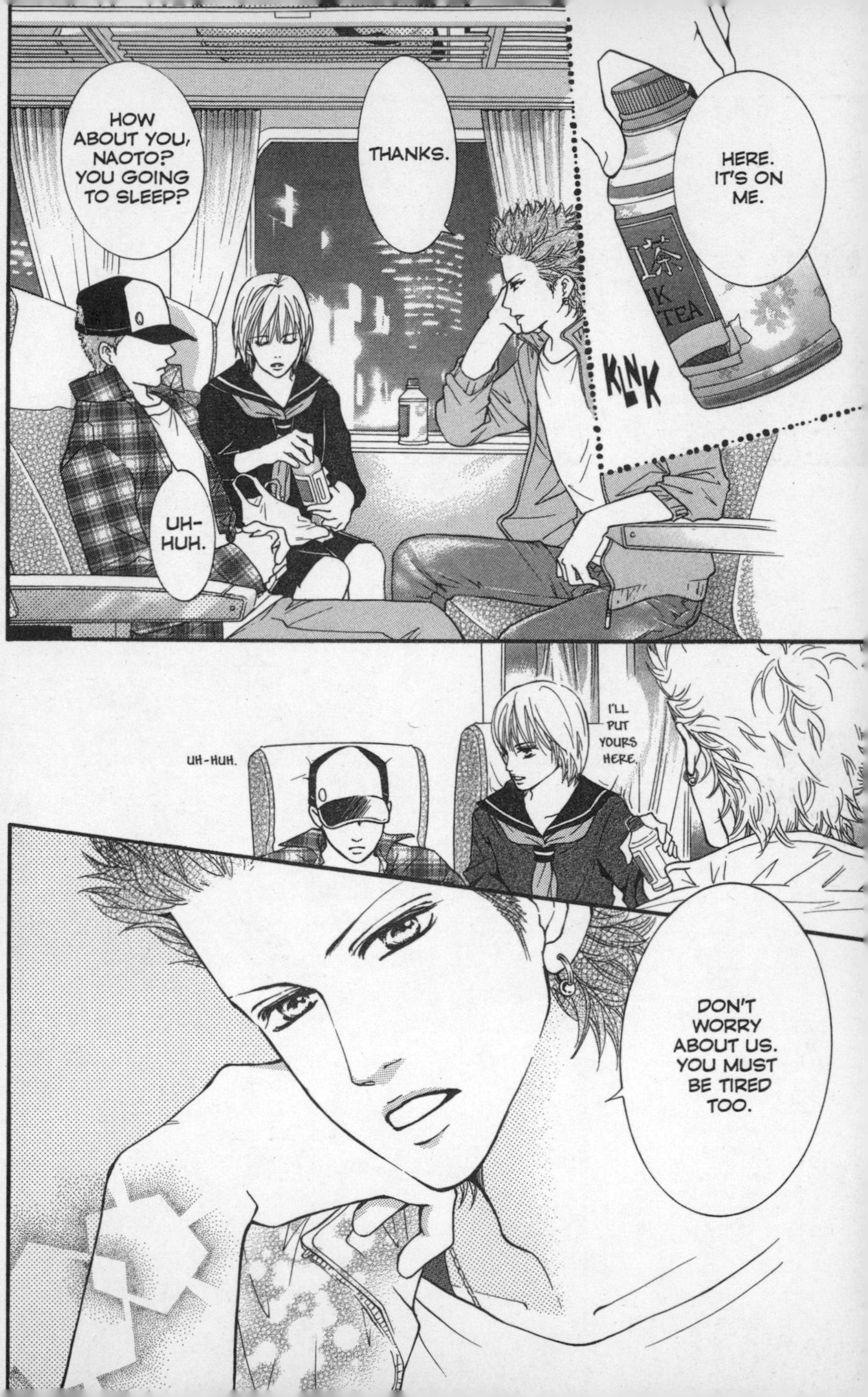
HERE. IT'S ON ME.
KLINK
THANKS.
HOW ABOUT YOU, NAOTO? YOU GOING TO SLEEP?
UH-HUH.
I'LL PUT YOURS HERE.
UH-HUH.
DON'T WORRY ABOUT US. YOU MUST BE TIRED TOO.

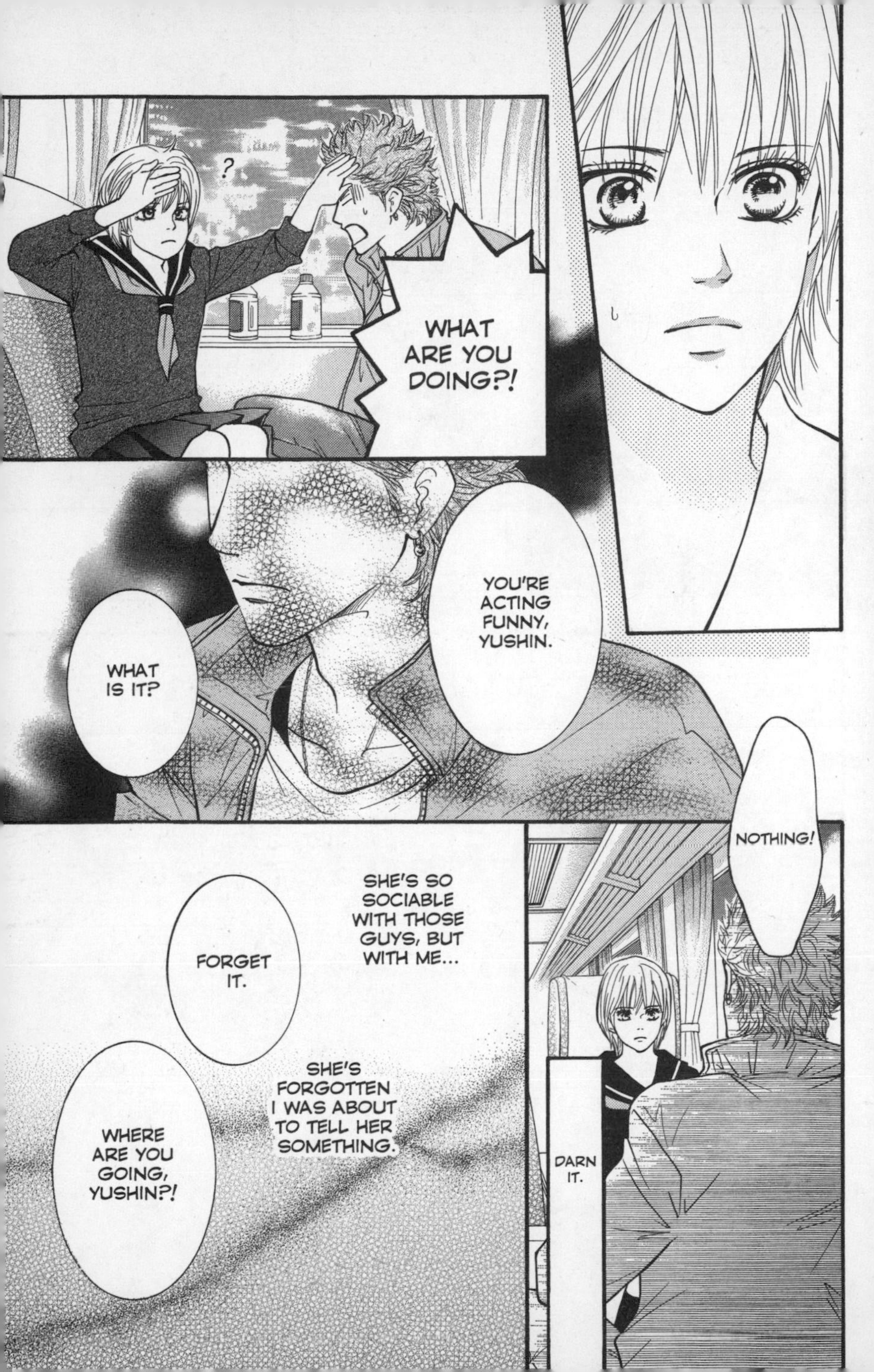
?
WHAT ARE YOU DOING?!
YOU'RE ACTING FUNNY, YUSHIN.
WHAT IS IT?
NOTHING!
DARN IT.
SHE'S SO SOCIABLE WITH THOSE GUYS, BUT WITH ME...
FORGET IT.
SHE'S FORGOTTEN I WAS ABOUT TO TELL HER SOMETHING.
WHERE ARE YOU GOING, YUSHIN?!

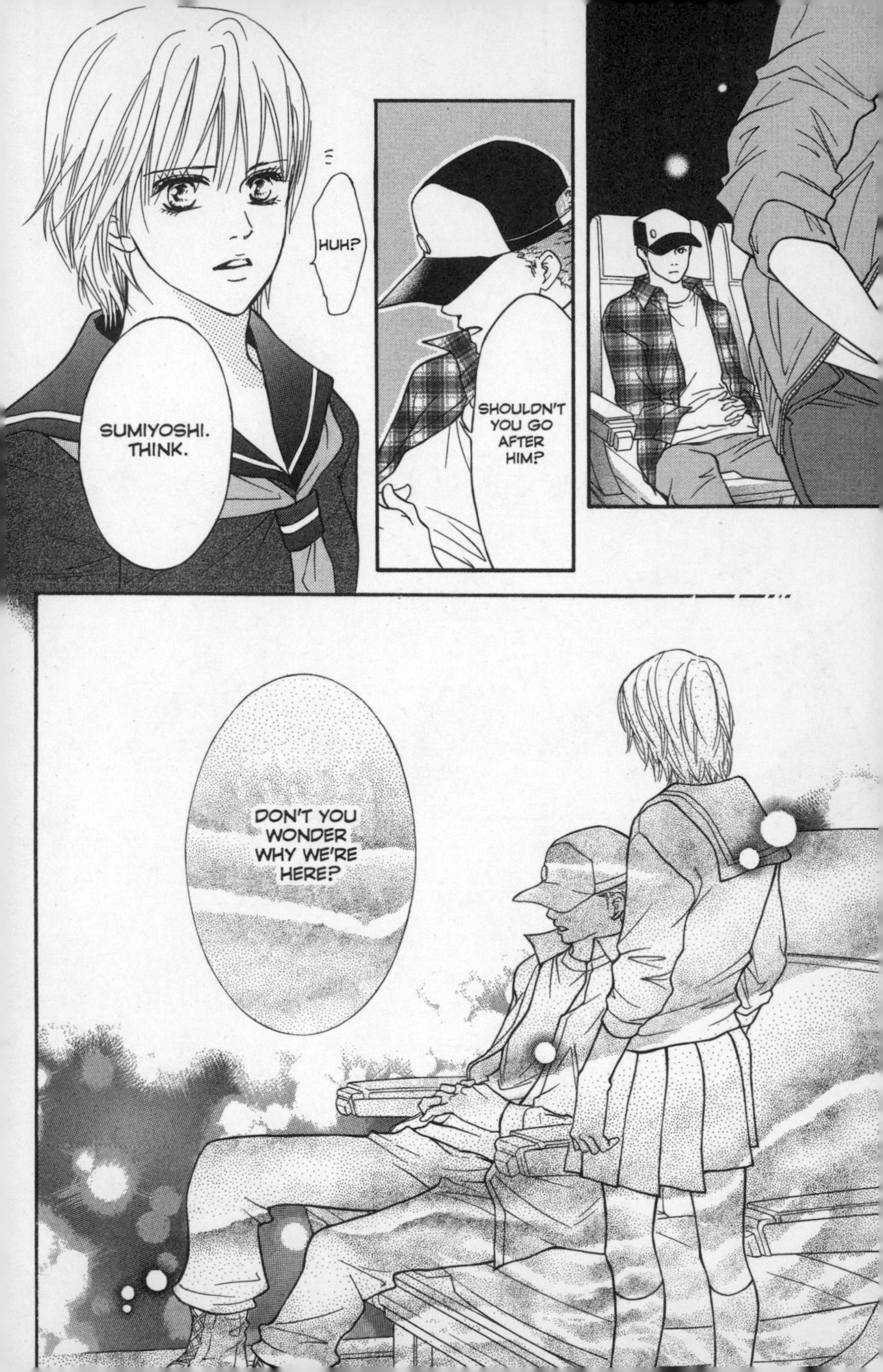
SHOULDN'T YOU GO AFTER HIM?
HUH?
SUMIYOSHI. THINK.
DON'T YOU WONDER WHY WE'RE HERE?

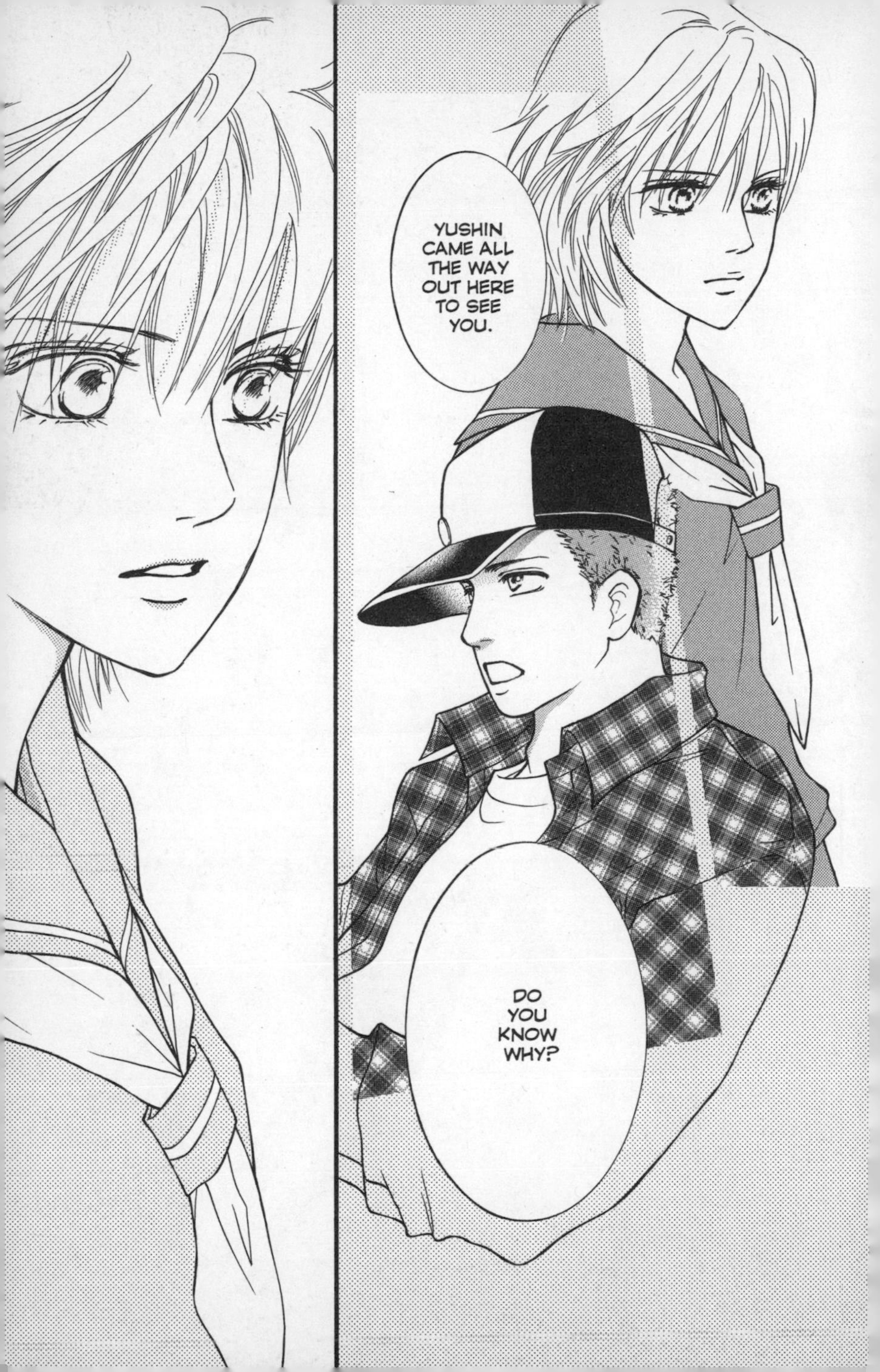
YUSHIN CAME ALL THE WAY OUT HERE TO SEE YOU.
DO YOU KNOW WHY?

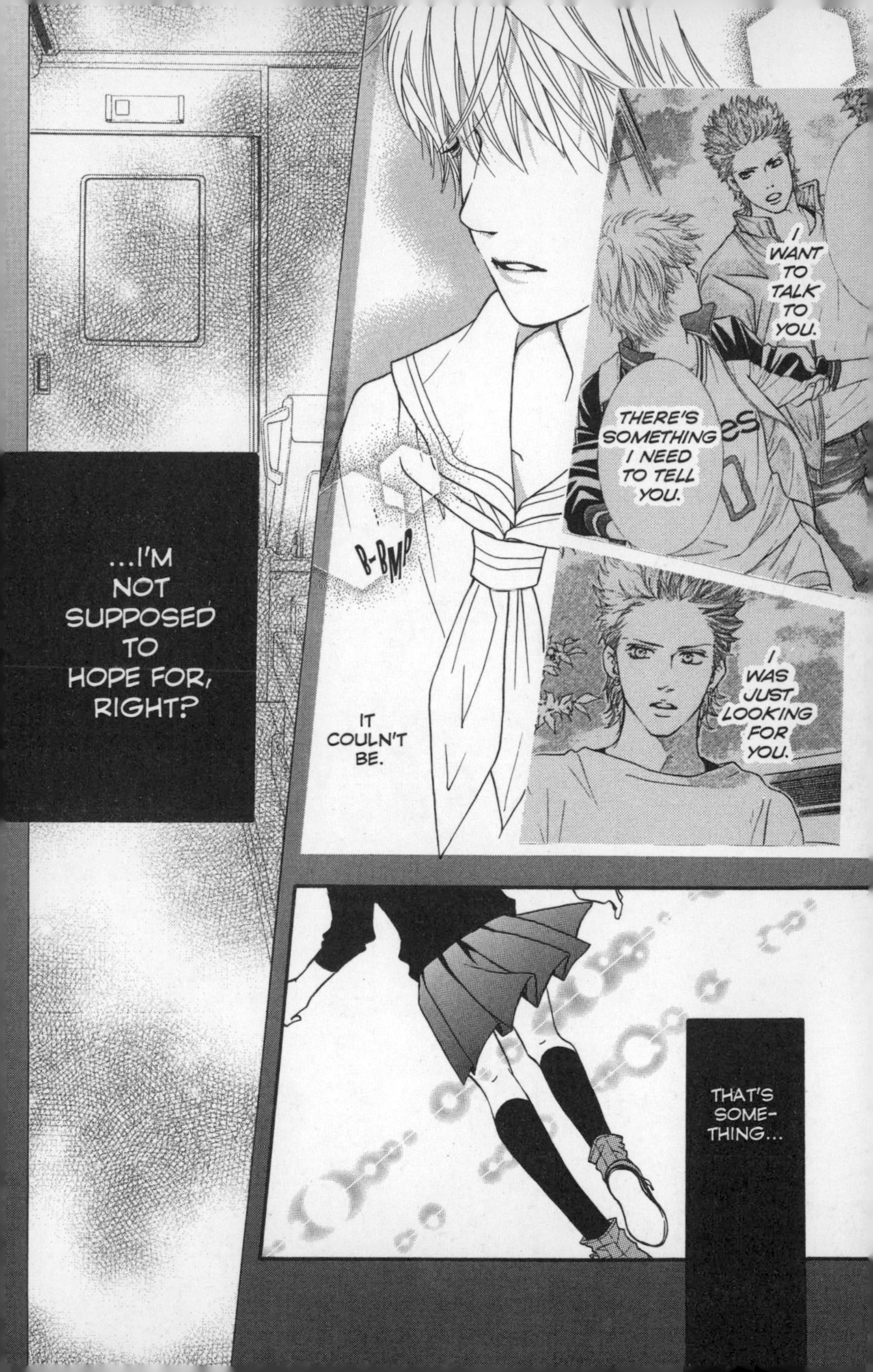
I WANT TO TALK TO YOU.
THERE'S SOMETHING I NEED TO TELL YOU.
I WAS JUST LOOKING FOR YOU.
B-BMP
IT COULN'T BE.
THAT'S SOME-THING...
...I'M NOT SUPPOSED TO HOPE FOR, RIGHT?

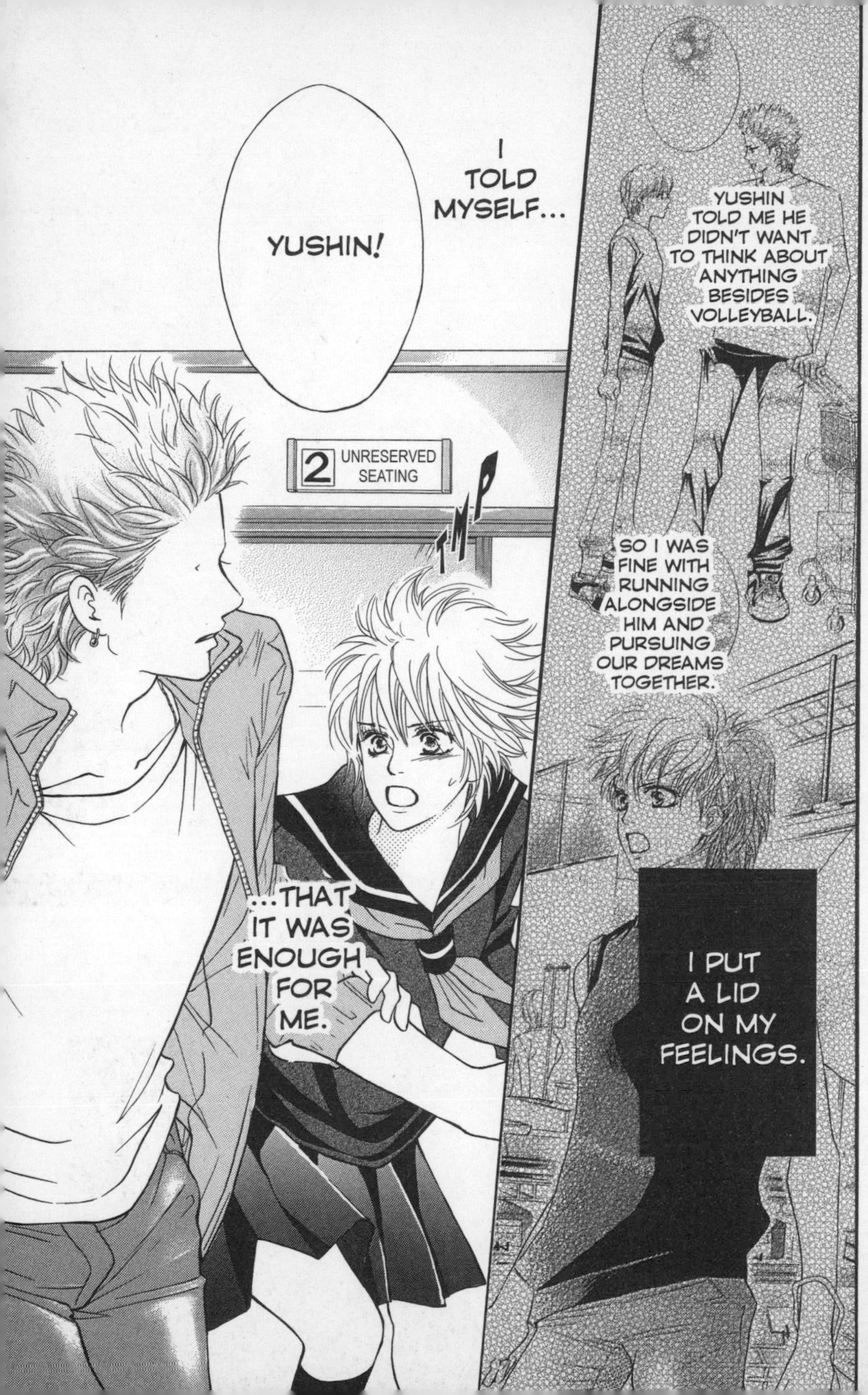
YUSHIN TOLD ME HE DIDN'T WANT TO THINK ABOUT ANYTHING BESIDES VOLLEYBALL.
SO I WAS FINE WITH RUNNING ALONGSIDE HIM AND PURSUING OUR DREAMS TOGETHER.
I PUT A LID ON MY FEELINGS.
I TOLD MYSELF...
YUSHIN!
2 UNRESERVED SEATING
TMP
...THAT IT WAS ENOUGH FOR ME.

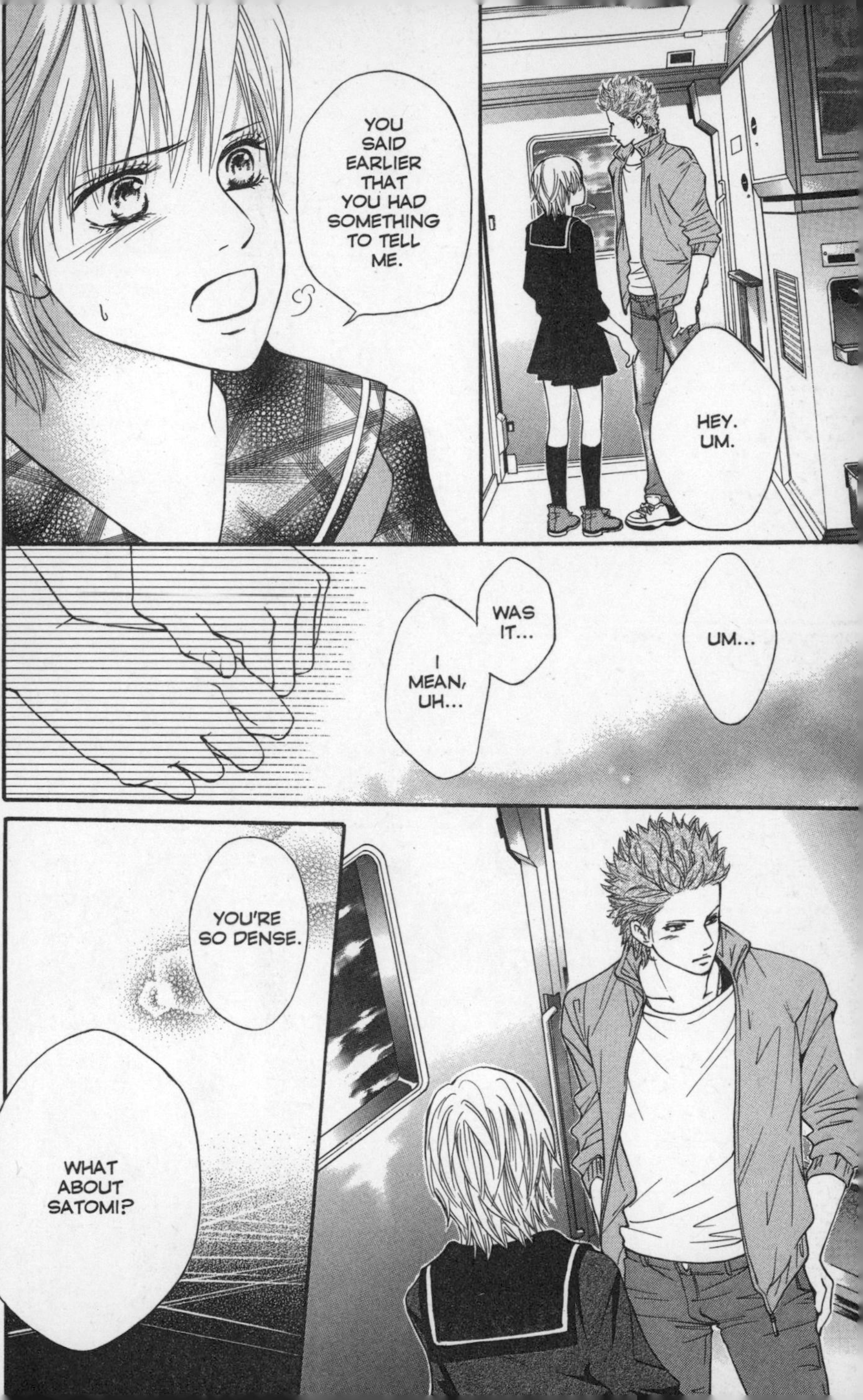
HEY. UM.
YOU SAID EARLIER THAT YOU HAD SOMETHING TO TELL ME.
UM...
WAS IT...
I MEAN, UH...
YOU'RE SO DENSE.
WHAT ABOUT SATOMI?

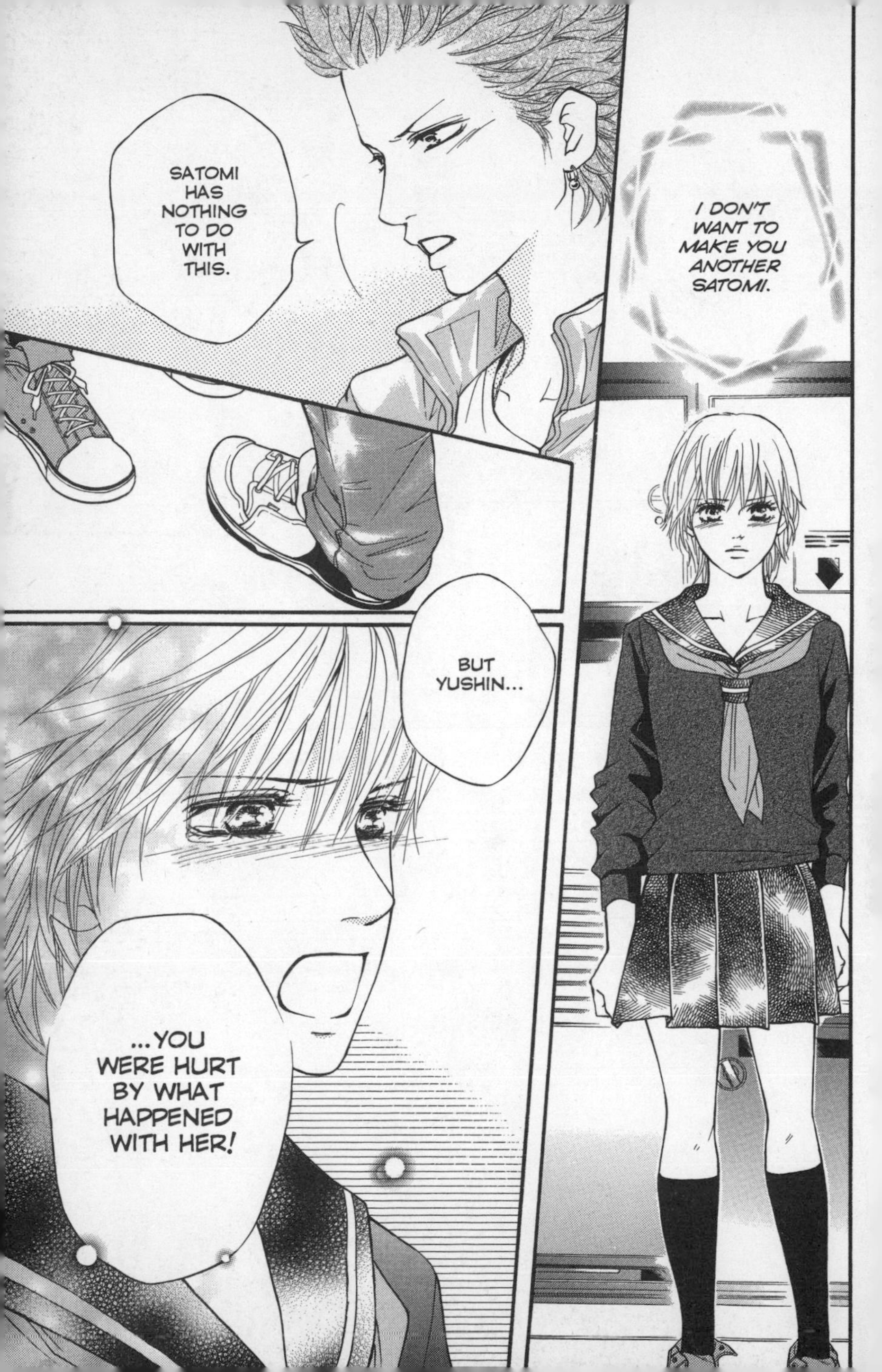
I DON'T WANT TO MAKE YOU ANOTHER SATOMI.
SATOMI HAS NOTHING TO DO WITH THIS.
BUT YUSHIN...
...YOU WERE HURT BY WHAT HAPPENED WITH HER!

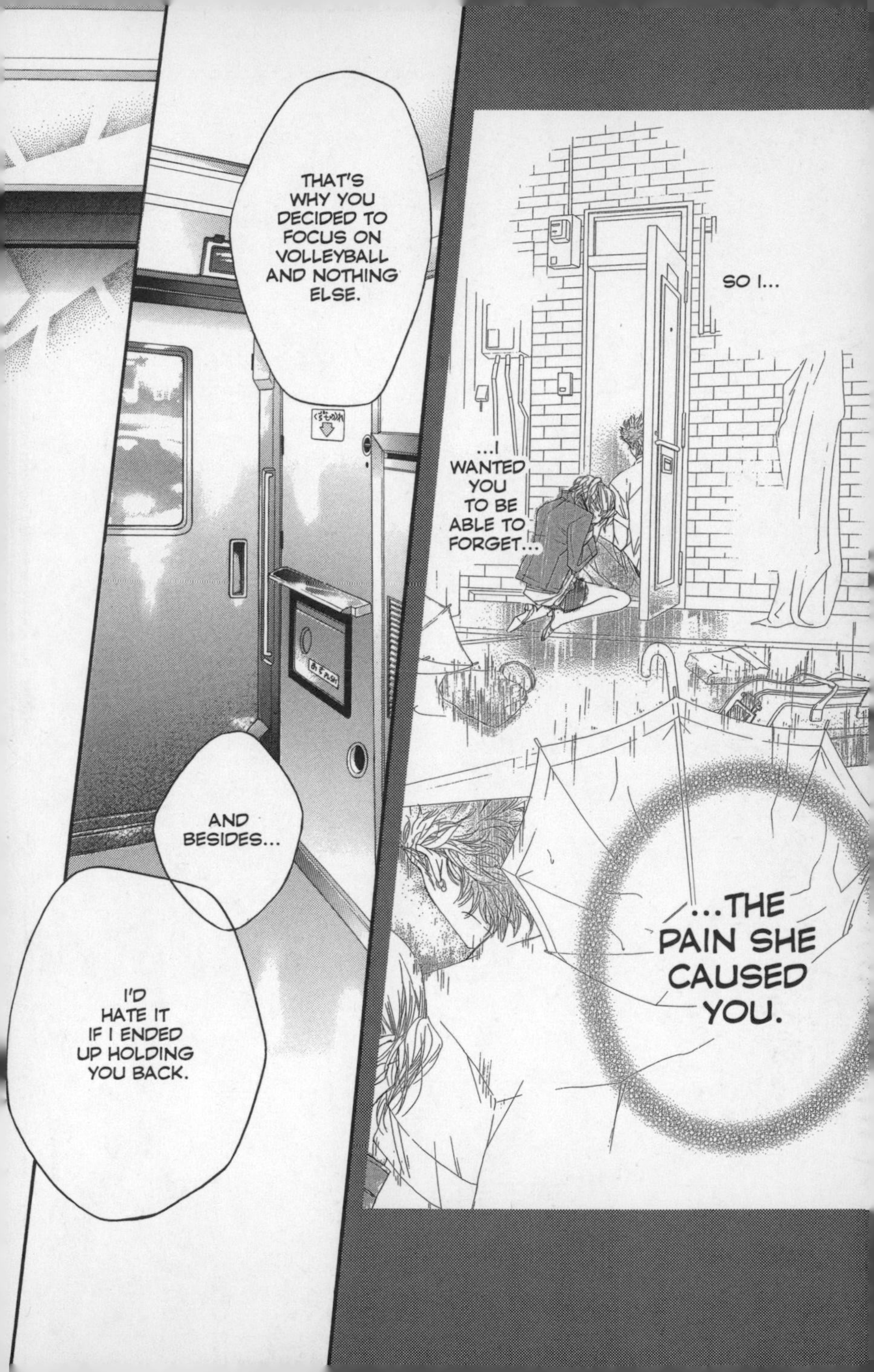
SO I...
...I WANTED YOU TO BE ABLE TO FORGET...
...THE PAIN SHE CAUSED YOU.
THAT'S WHY YOU DECIDED TO FOCUS ON VOLLEYBALL AND NOTHING ELSE.
AND BESIDES...
I'D HATE IT IF I ENDED UP HOLDING YOU BACK.

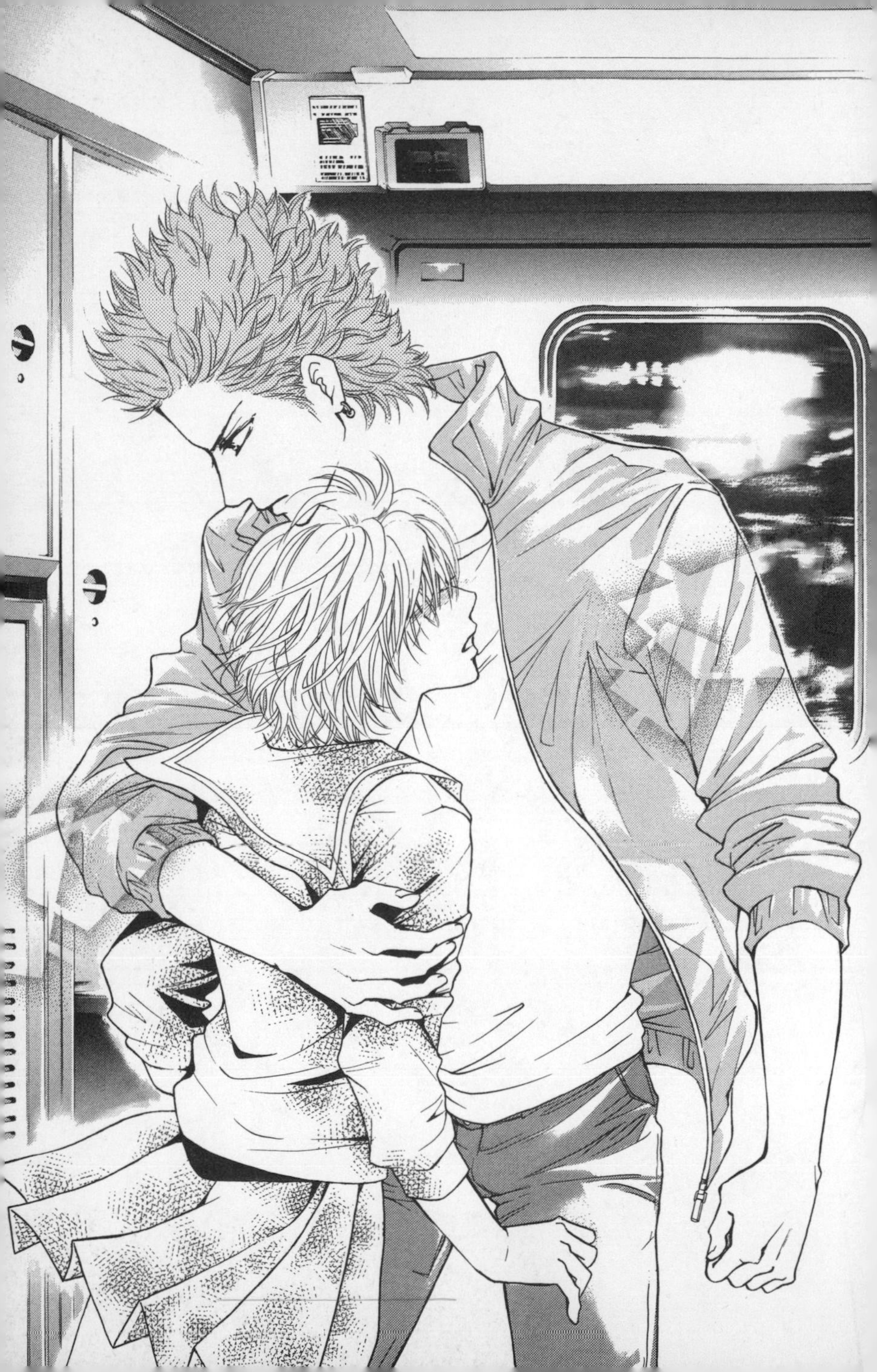

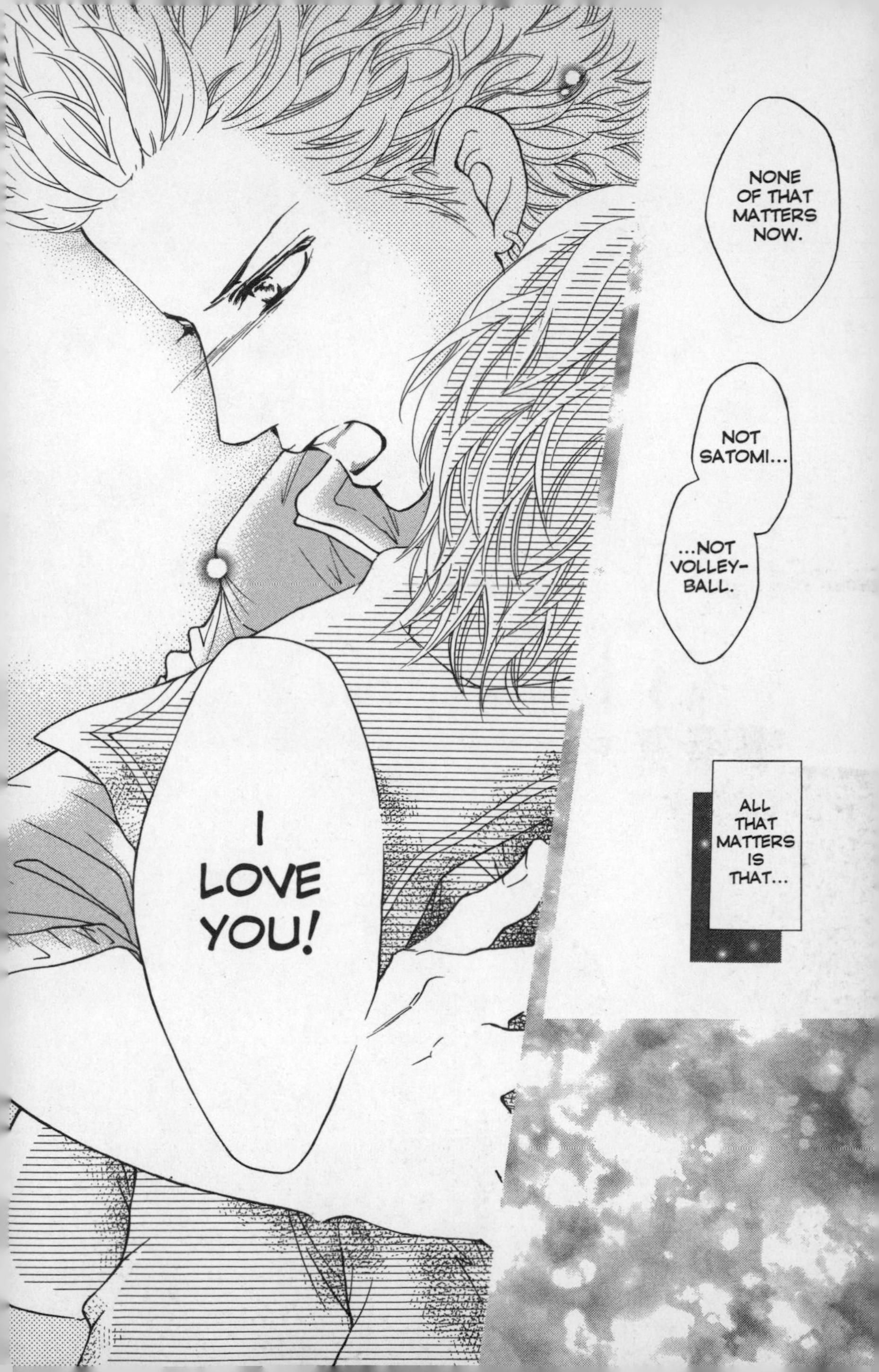
NONE OF THAT MATTERS NOW.
NOT SATOMI...
...NOT VOLLEY-BALL.
ALL THAT MATTERS IS THAT...
I LOVE YOU!

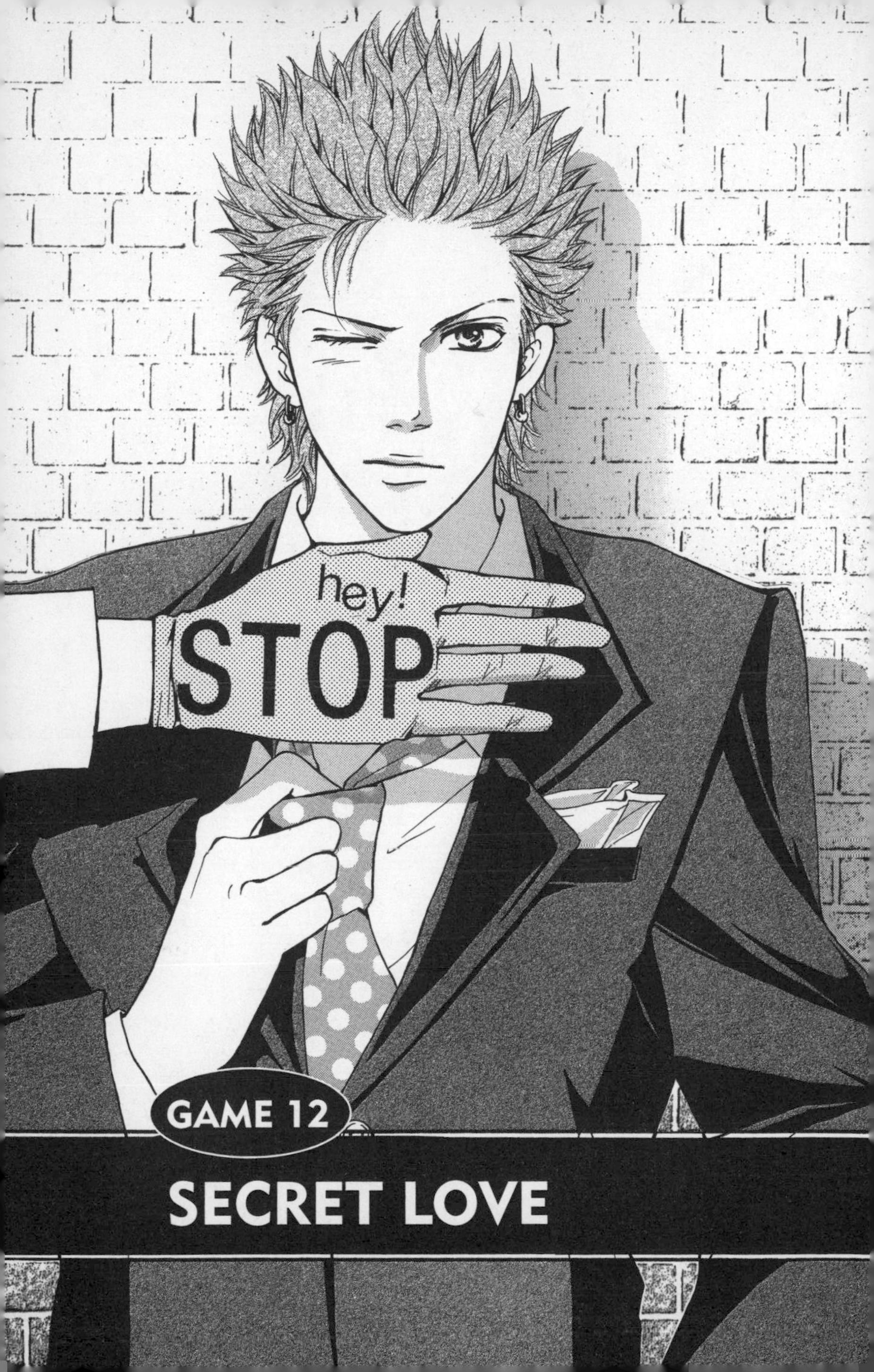
hey!
STOP
GAME 12
SECRET LOVE

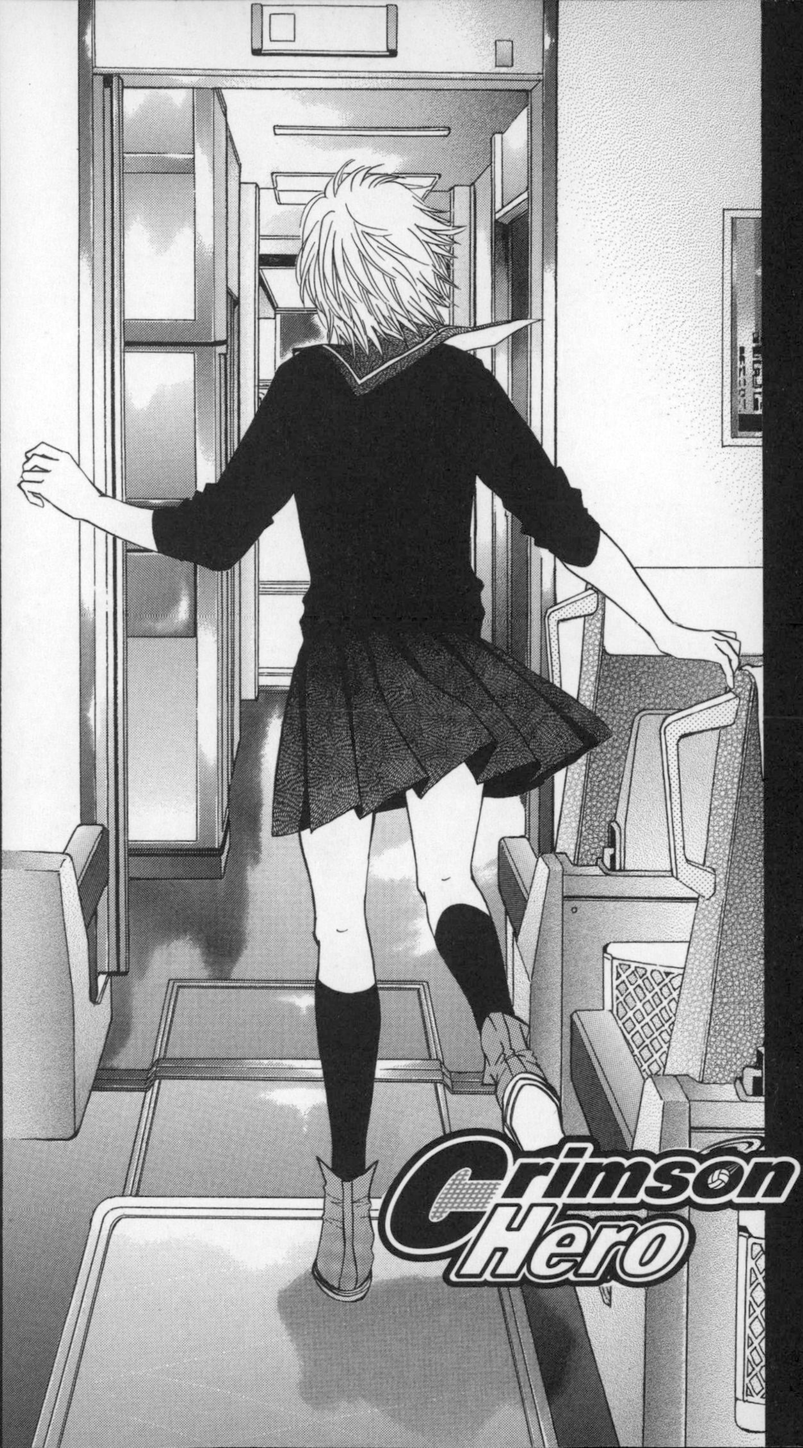
Crimson Hero

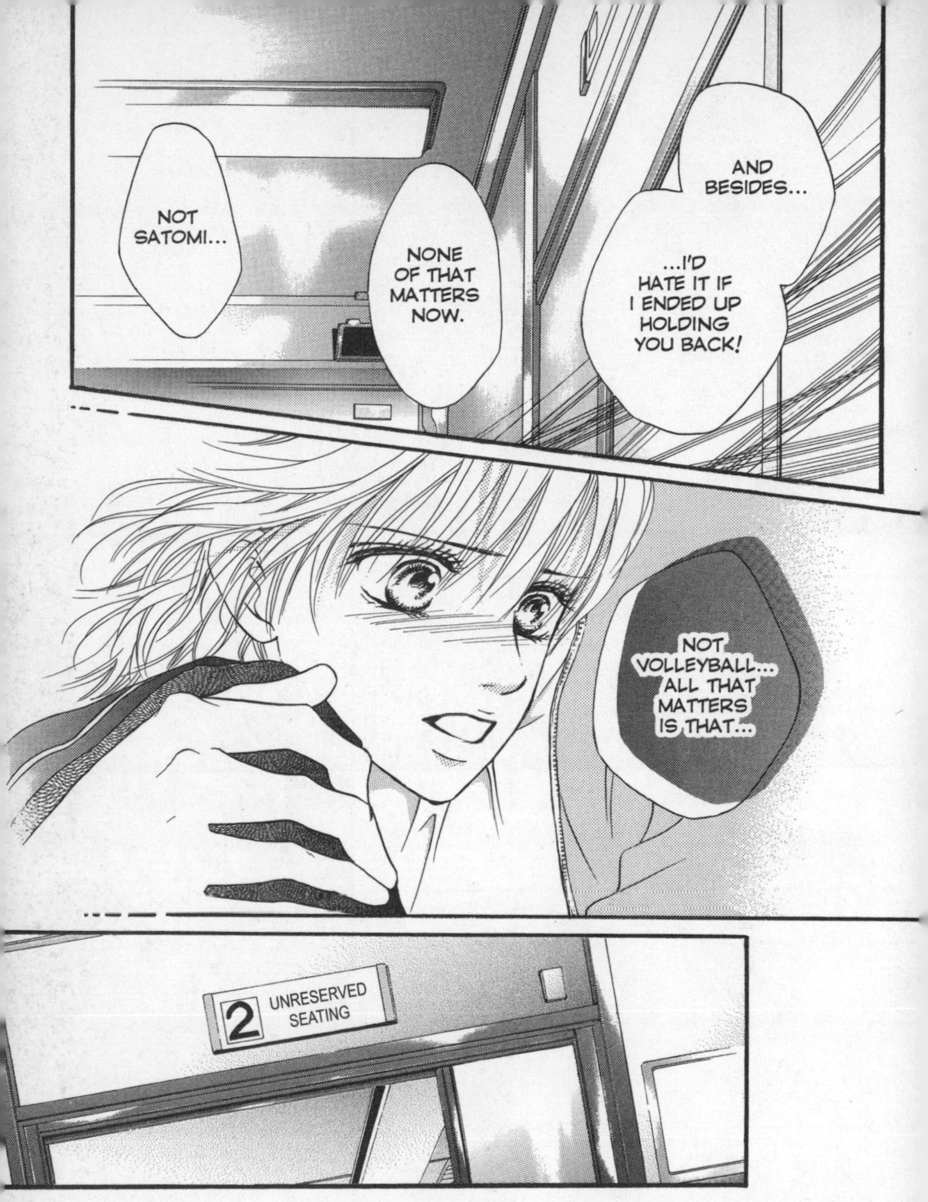
AND BESIDES...
...I'D HATE IT IF I ENDED UP HOLDING YOU BACK!
NONE OF THAT MATTERS NOW.
NOT SATOMI...
NOT VOLLEYBALL... ALL THAT MATTERS IS THAT...
2 UNRESERVED SEATING

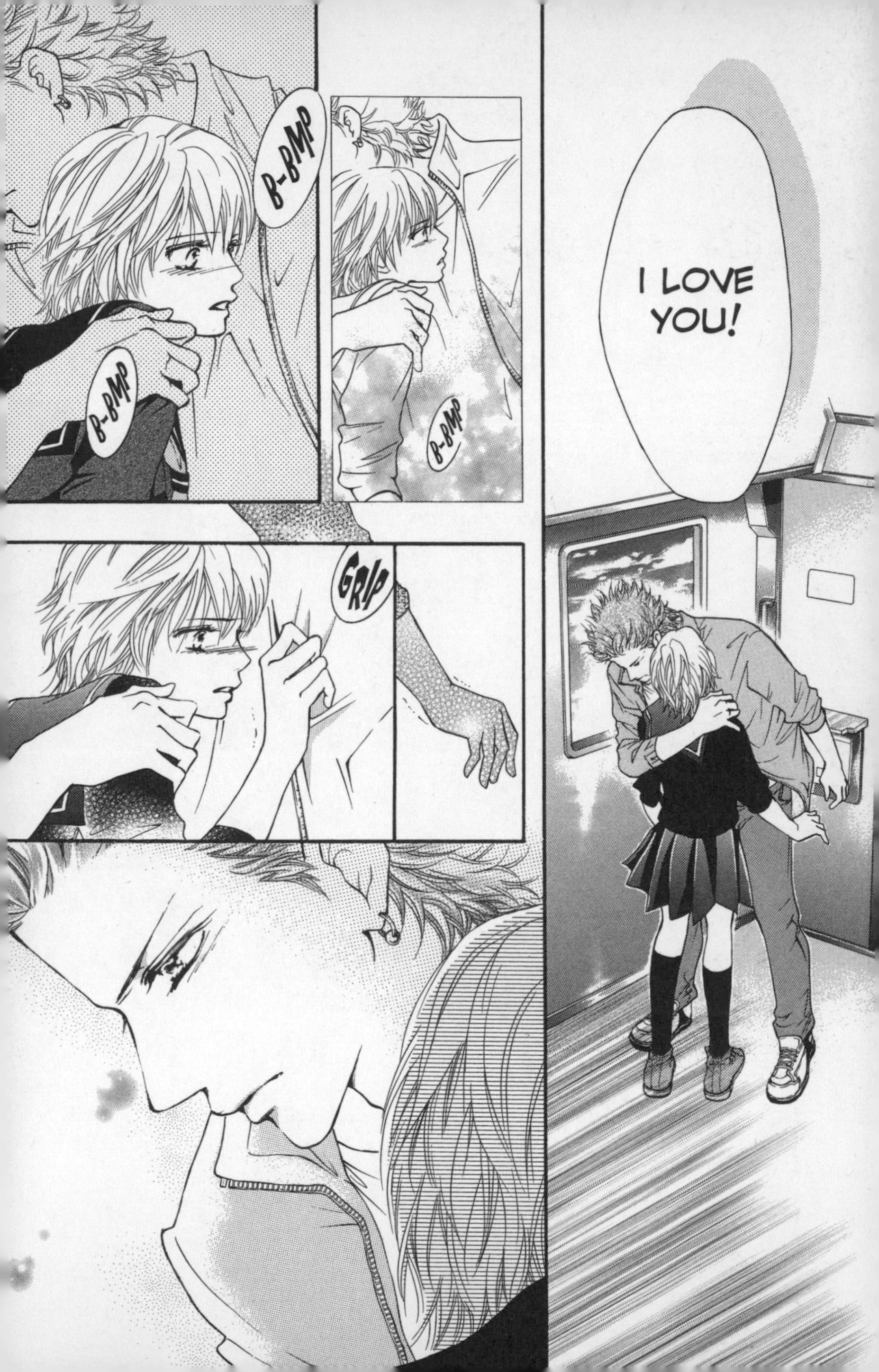
I LOVE YOU!
B-BMP
B-BMP
B-BMP
GRIP

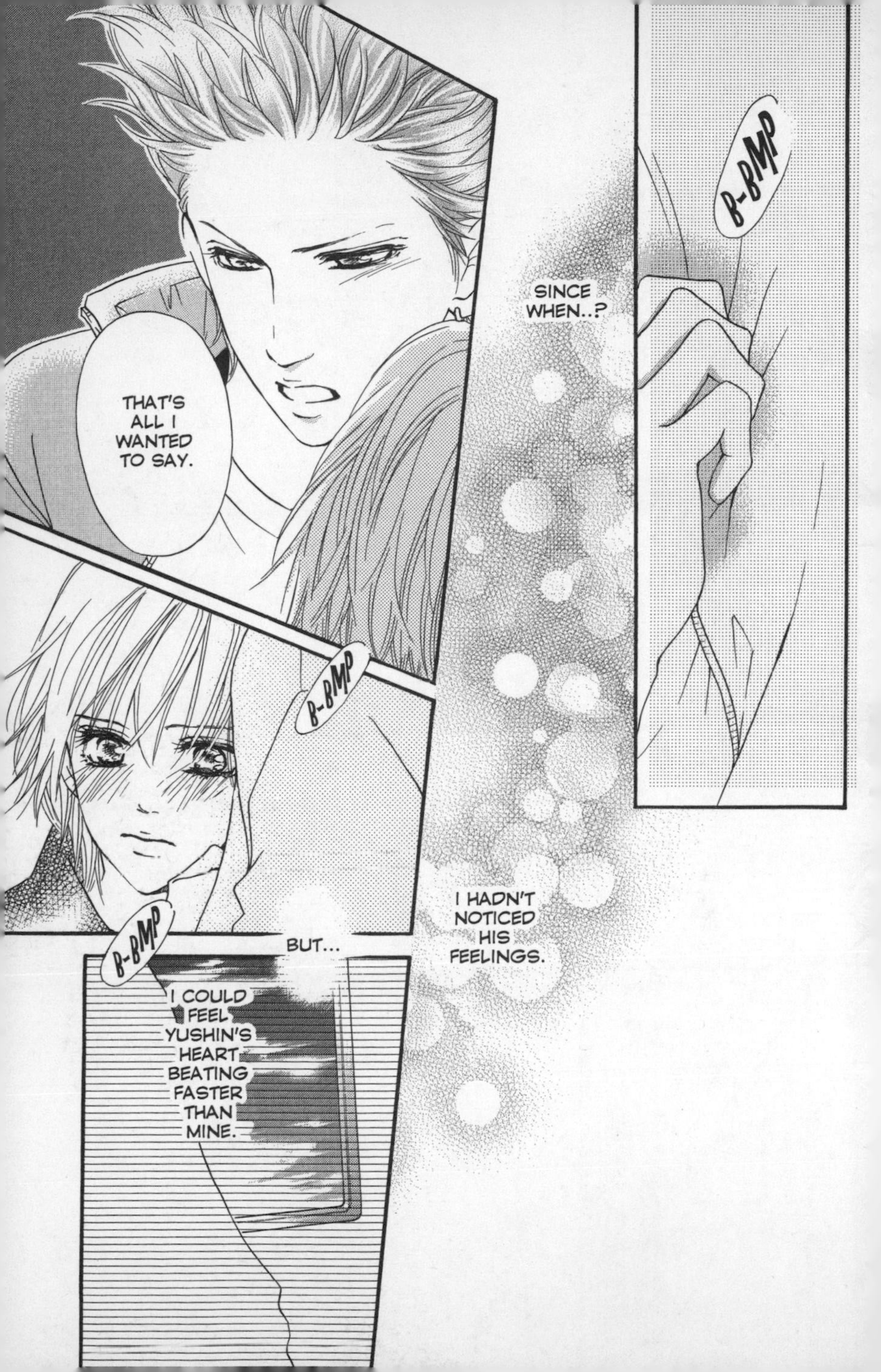
B-BMP
SINCE WHEN..?
THAT'S ALL I WANTED TO SAY.
B-BMP
I HADN'T NOTICED HIS FEELINGS.
B-BMP
BUT...
I COULD FEEL YUSHIN'S HEART BEATING FASTER THAN MINE.

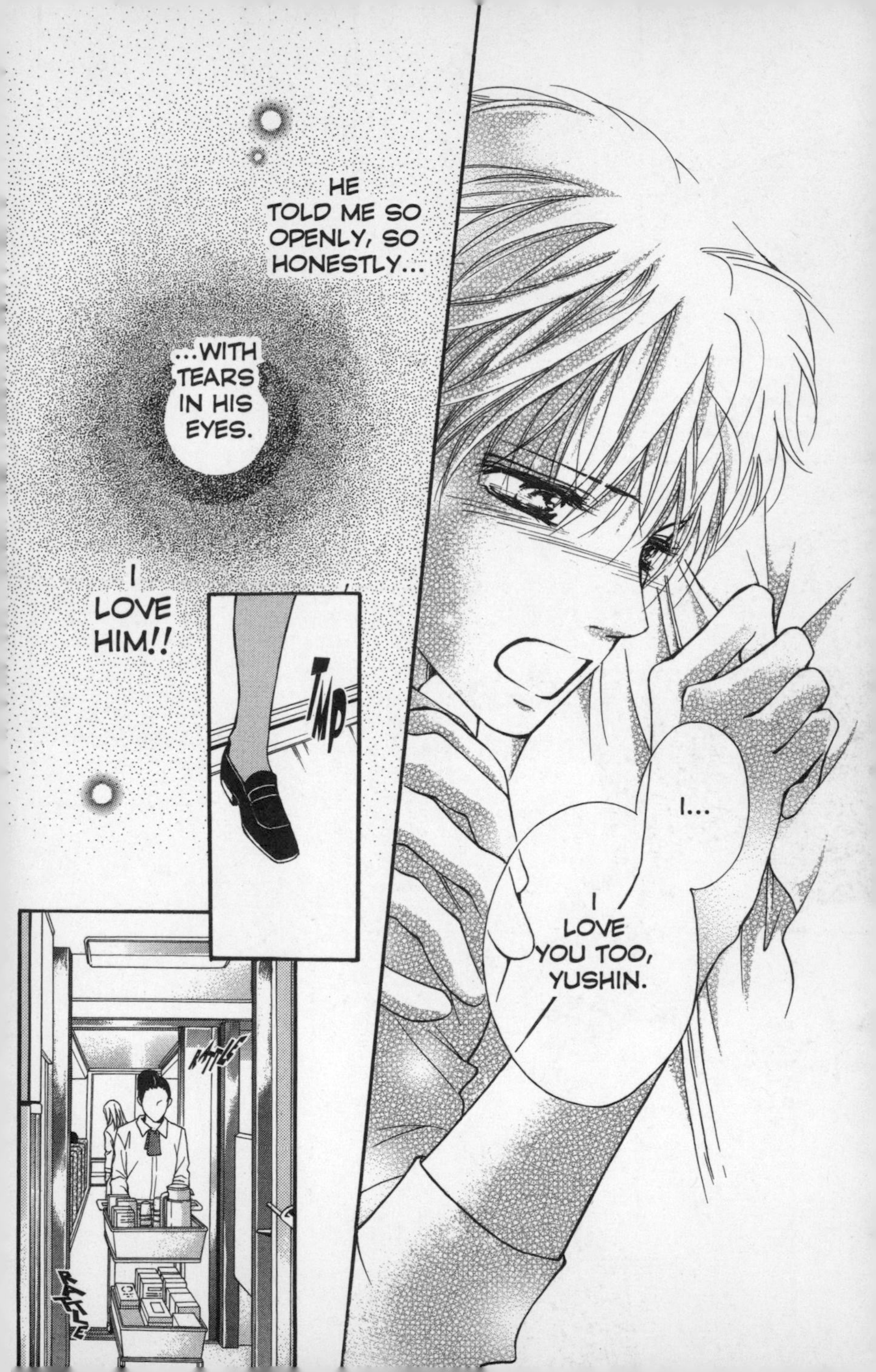
I...
I LOVE YOU TOO, YUSHIN.
HE TOLD ME SO OPENLY, SO HONESTLY...
...WITH TEARS IN HIS EYES.
I LOVE HIM!!
TMP
RATTLE
RATTLE

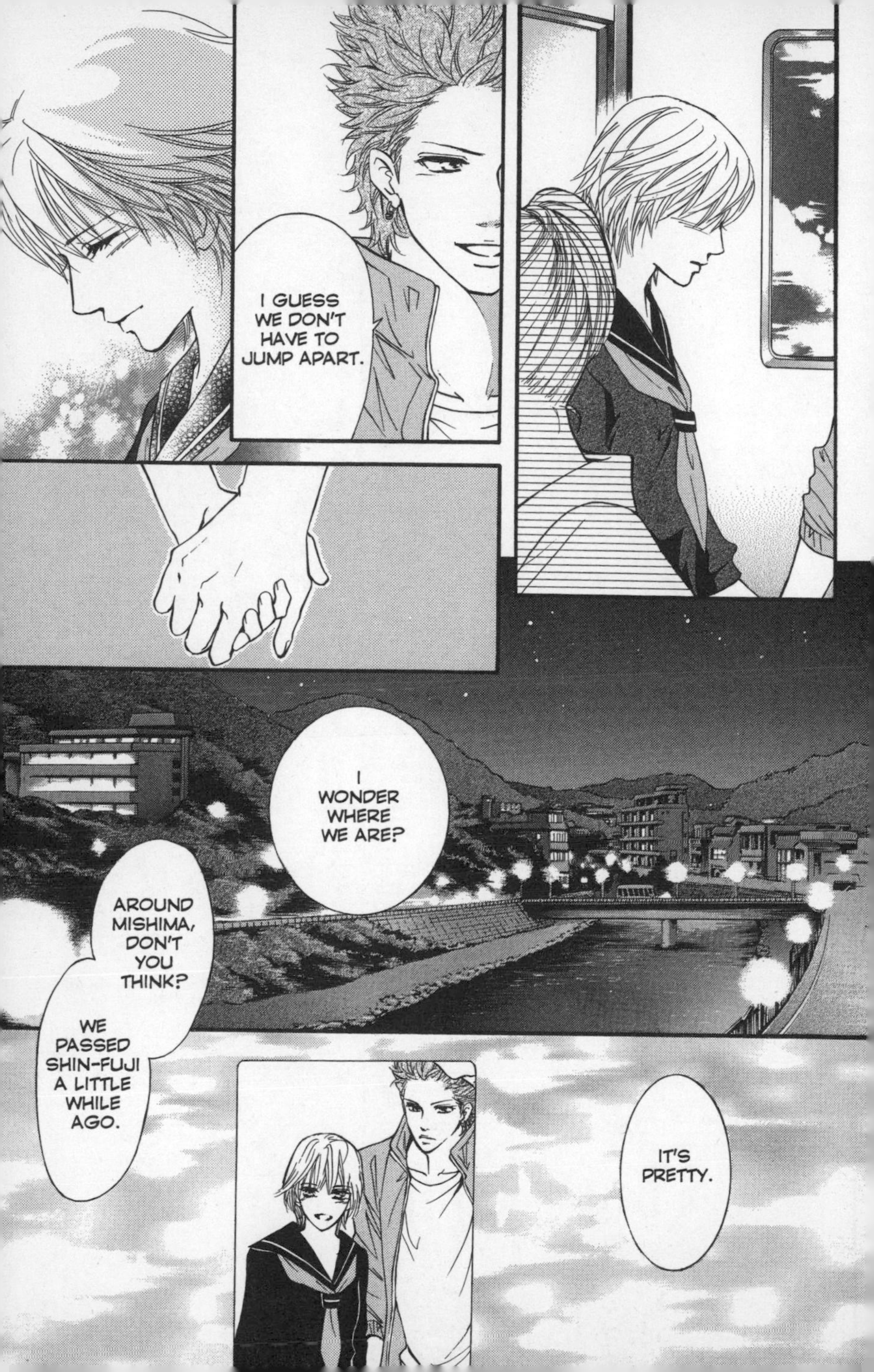
I GUESS WE DON'T HAVE TO JUMP APART.
I WONDER WHERE WE ARE?
AROUND MISHIMA, DON'T YOU THINK?
WE PASSED SHIN-FUJI A LITTLE WHILE AGO.
IT'S PRETTY.

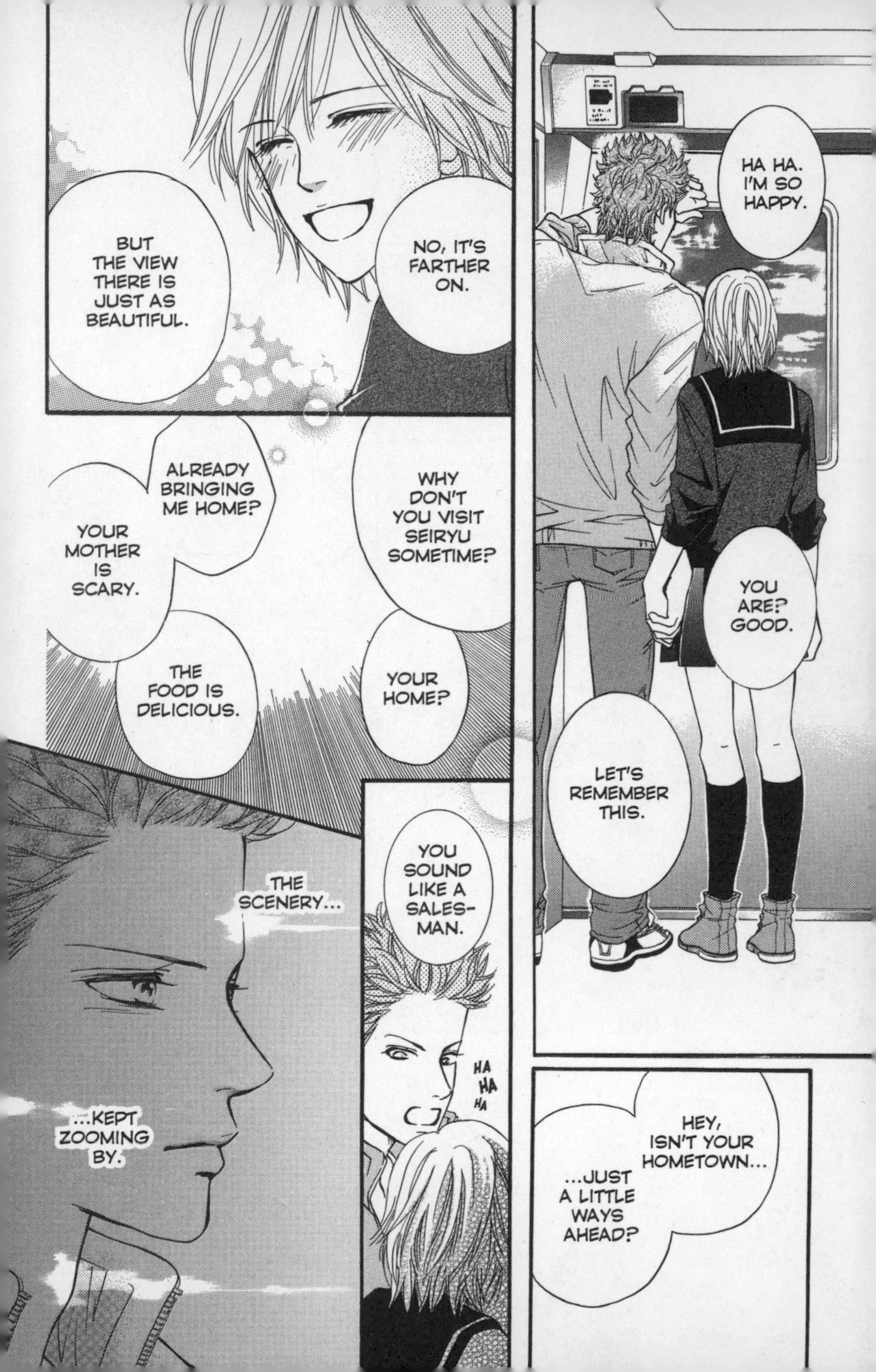
HA HA. I'M SO HAPPY.
YOU ARE? GOOD.
LET'S REMEMBER THIS.
HEY, ISN'T YOUR HOMETOWN...
...JUST A LITTLE WAYS AHEAD?
NO, IT'S FARTHER ON.
BUT THE VIEW THERE IS JUST AS BEAUTIFUL.
WHY DON'T YOU VISIT SEIRYU SOMETIME?
YOUR HOME?
ALREADY BRINGING ME HOME?
YOUR MOTHER IS SCARY.
THE FOOD IS DELICIOUS.
YOU SOUND LIKE A SALES-MAN.
HA HA HA
THE SCENERY...
...KEPT ZOOMING BY.

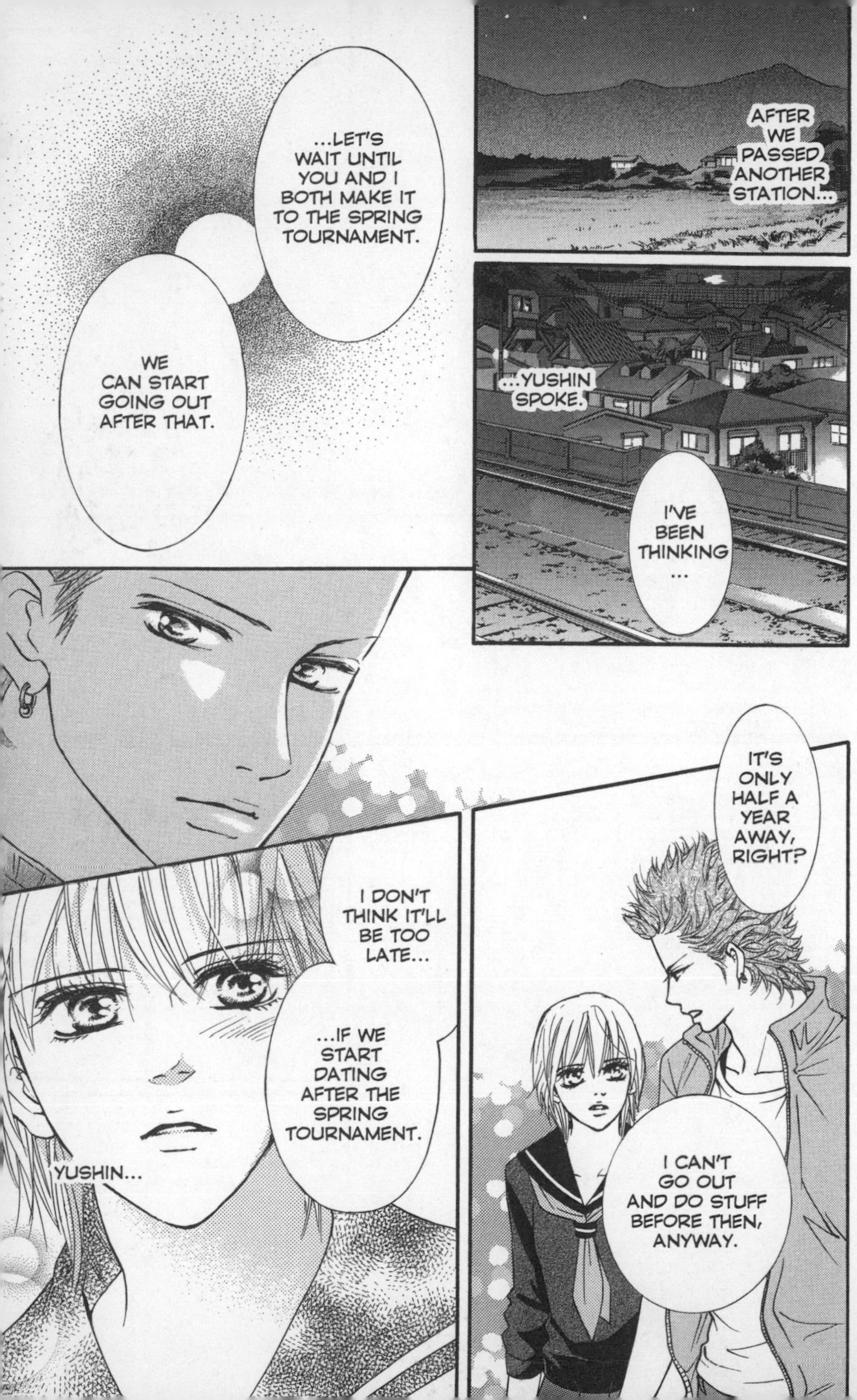
AFTER WE PASSED ANOTHER STATION...
...YUSHIN SPOKE.
I'VE BEEN THINKING...
...LET'S WAIT UNTIL YOU AND I BOTH MAKE IT TO THE SPRING TOURNAMENT.
WE CAN START GOING OUT AFTER THAT.
IT'S ONLY HALF A YEAR AWAY, RIGHT?
I CAN'T GO OUT AND DO STUFF BEFORE THEN, ANYWAY.
I DON'T THINK IT'LL BE TOO LATE...
...IF WE START DATING AFTER THE SPRING TOURNAMENT.
YUSHIN...

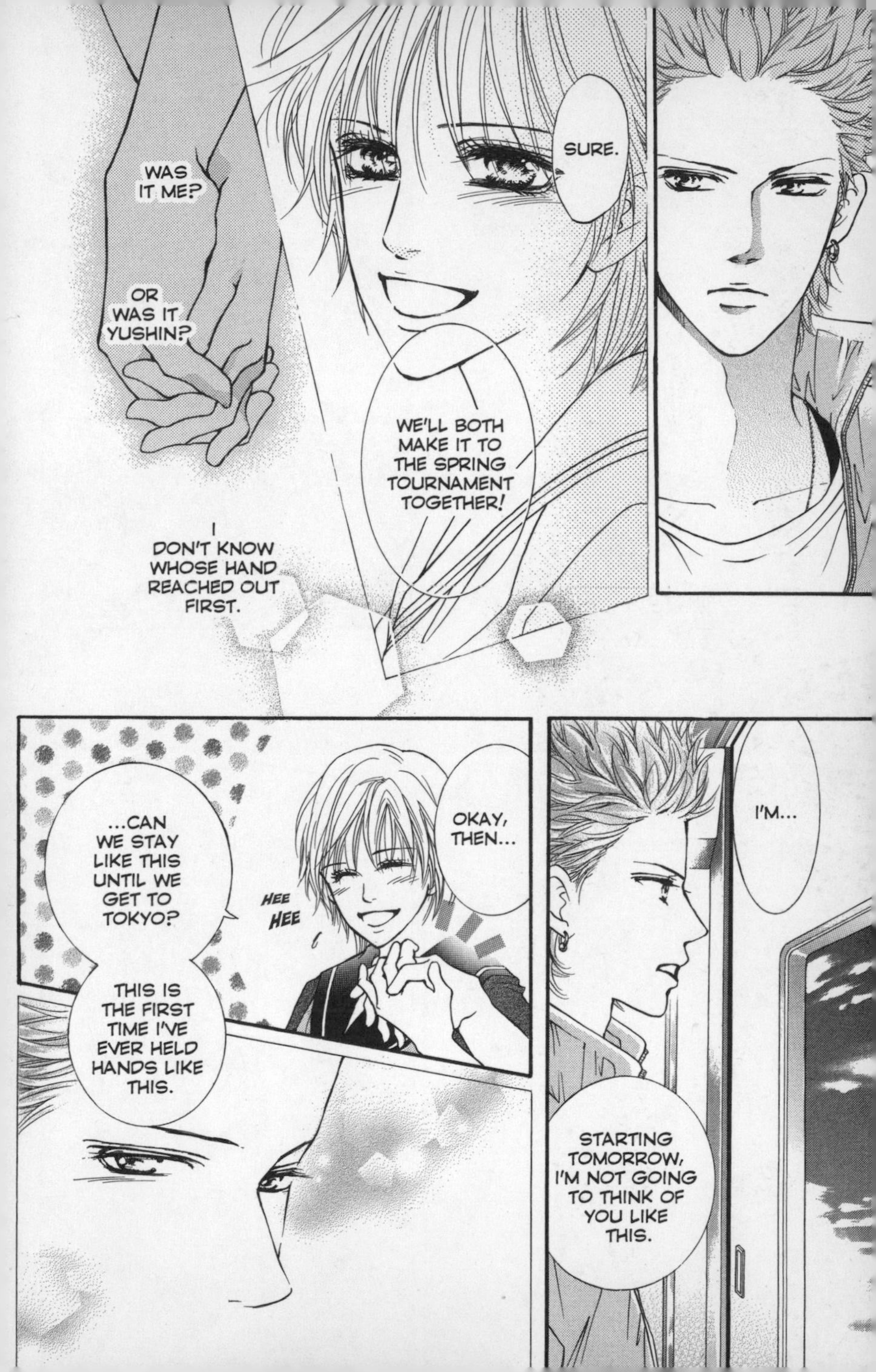
SURE.
WE'LL BOTH MAKE IT TO THE SPRING TOURNAMENT TOGETHER!
WAS IT ME?
OR WAS IT YUSHIN?
I DON'T KNOW WHOSE HAND REACHED OUT FIRST.
I'M...
STARTING TOMORROW, I'M NOT GOING TO THINK OF YOU LIKE THIS.
OKAY, THEN...
HEE HEE
...CAN WE STAY LIKE THIS UNTIL WE GET TO TOKYO?
THIS IS THE FIRST TIME I'VE EVER HELD HANDS LIKE THIS.

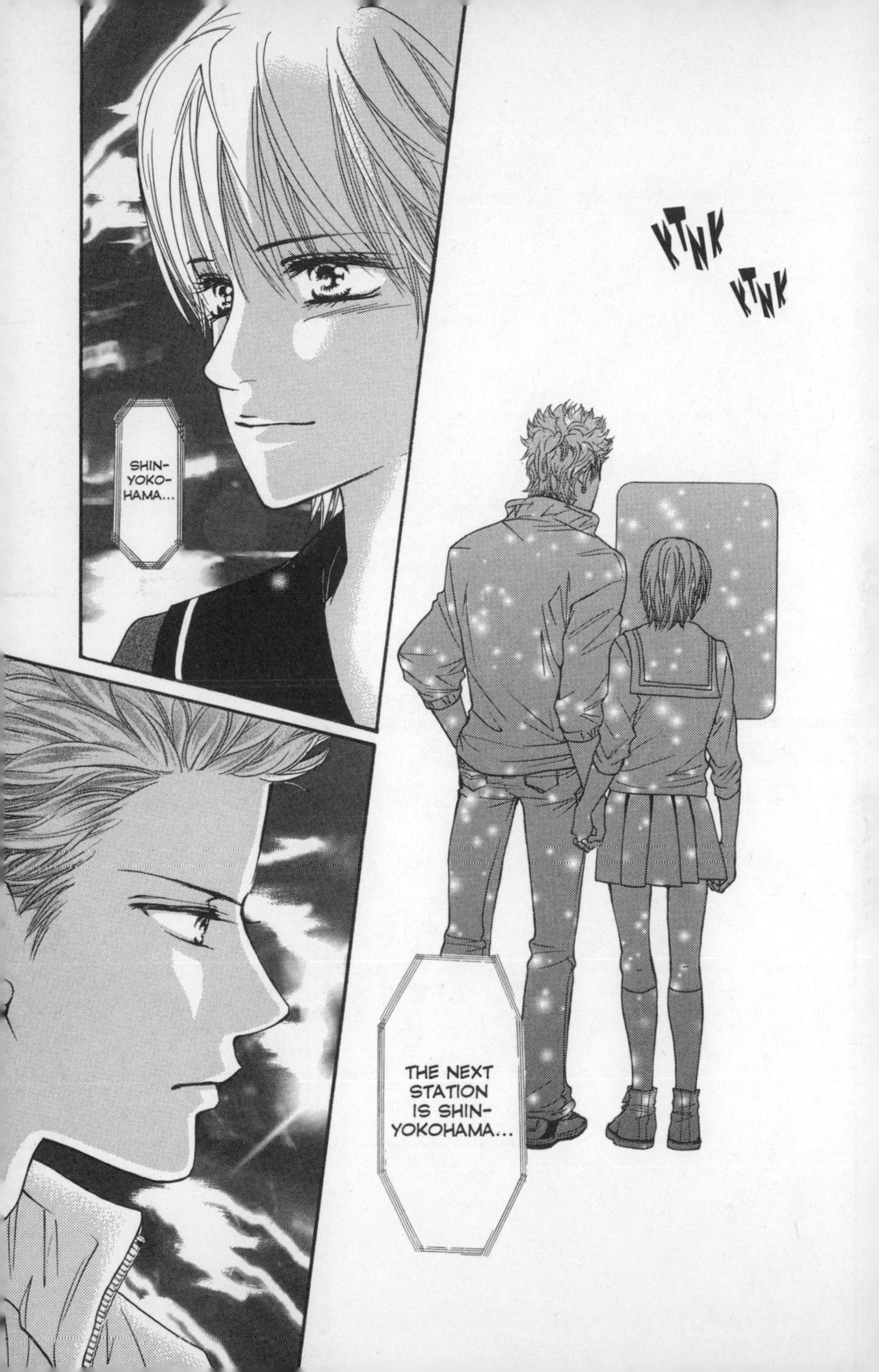
KTNK
KTNK
THE NEXT STATION IS SHIN-YOKOHAMA...
SHIN-YOKOHAMA...

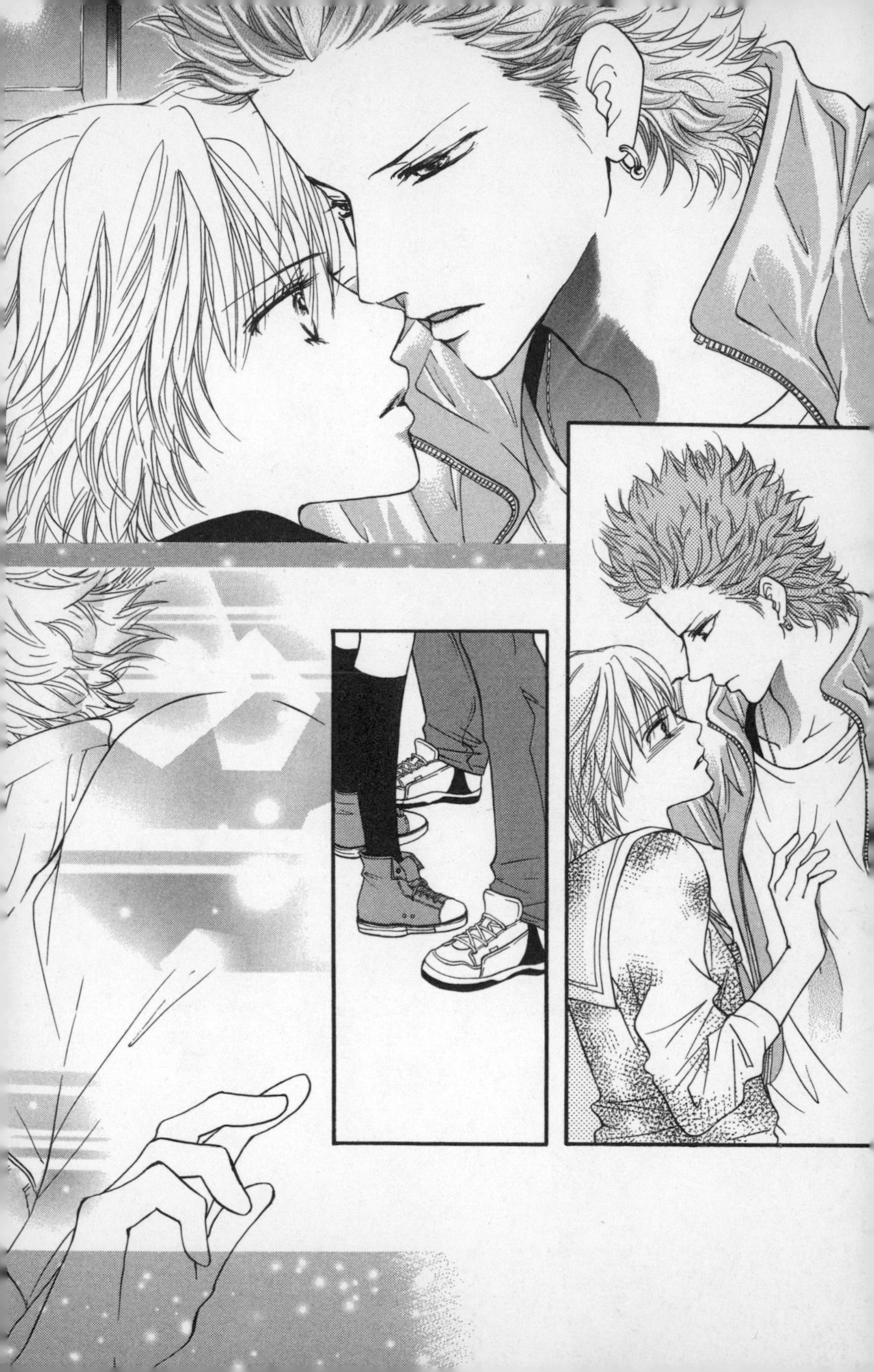

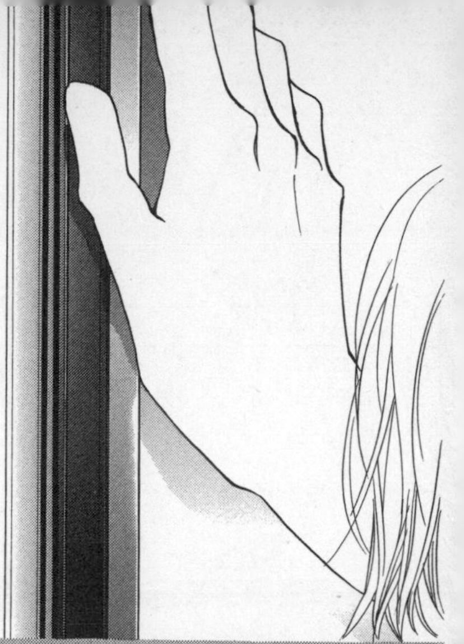
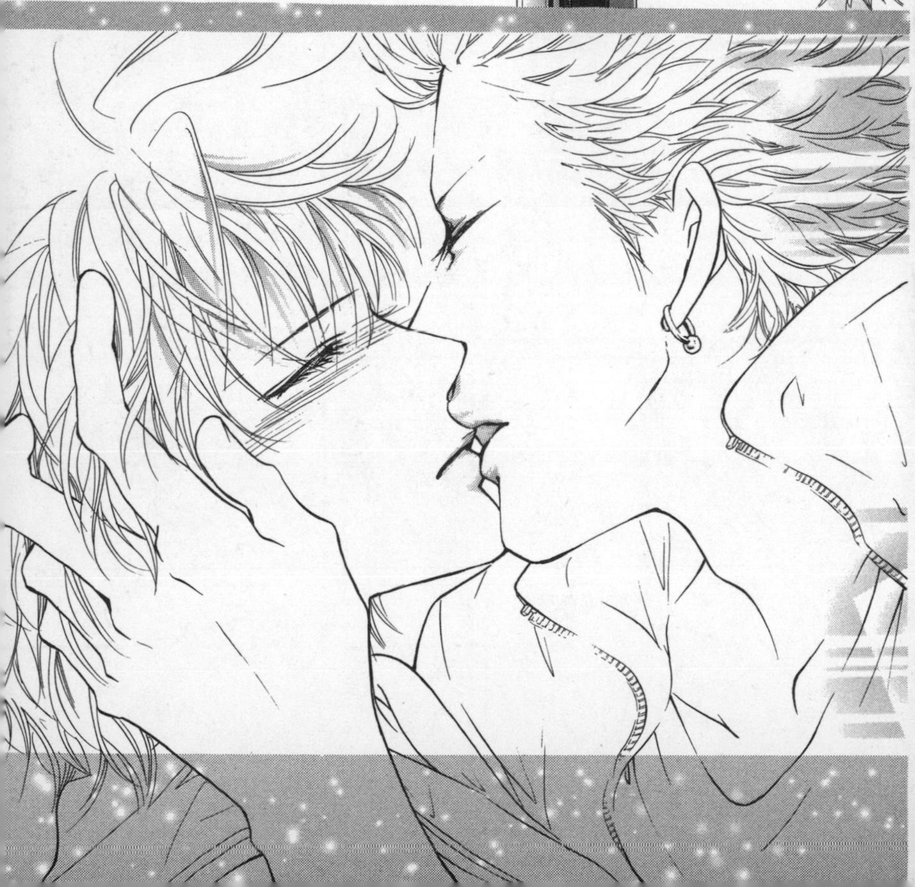

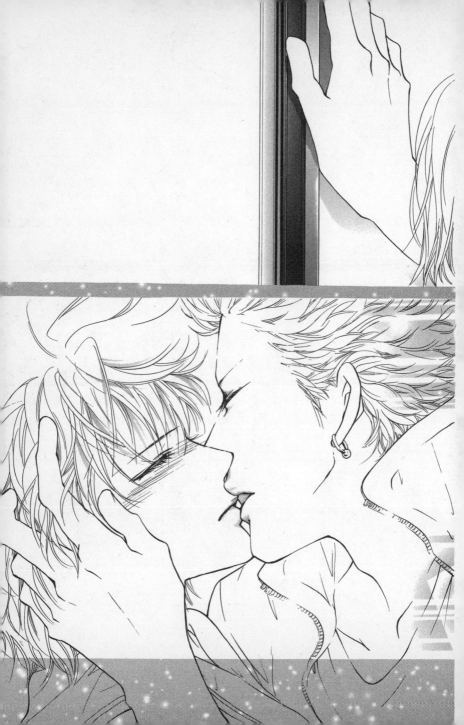

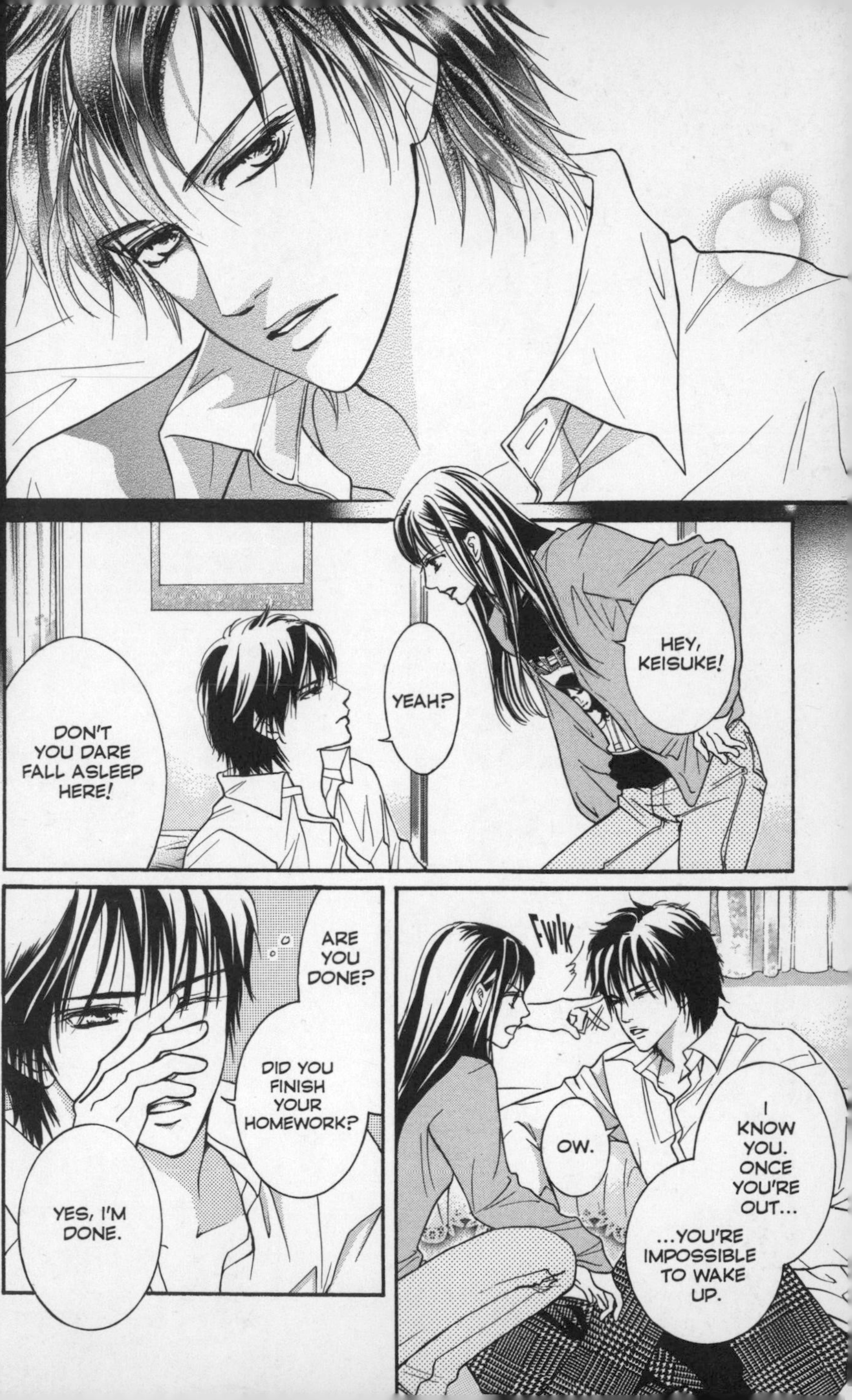
HEY, KEISUKE!
YEAH?
DON'T YOU DARE FALL ASLEEP HERE!
FWIK
I KNOW YOU. ONCE YOU'RE OUT...
...YOU'RE IMPOSSIBLE TO WAKE UP.
OW.
ARE YOU DONE?
DID YOU FINISH YOUR HOMEWORK?
YES, I'M DONE.

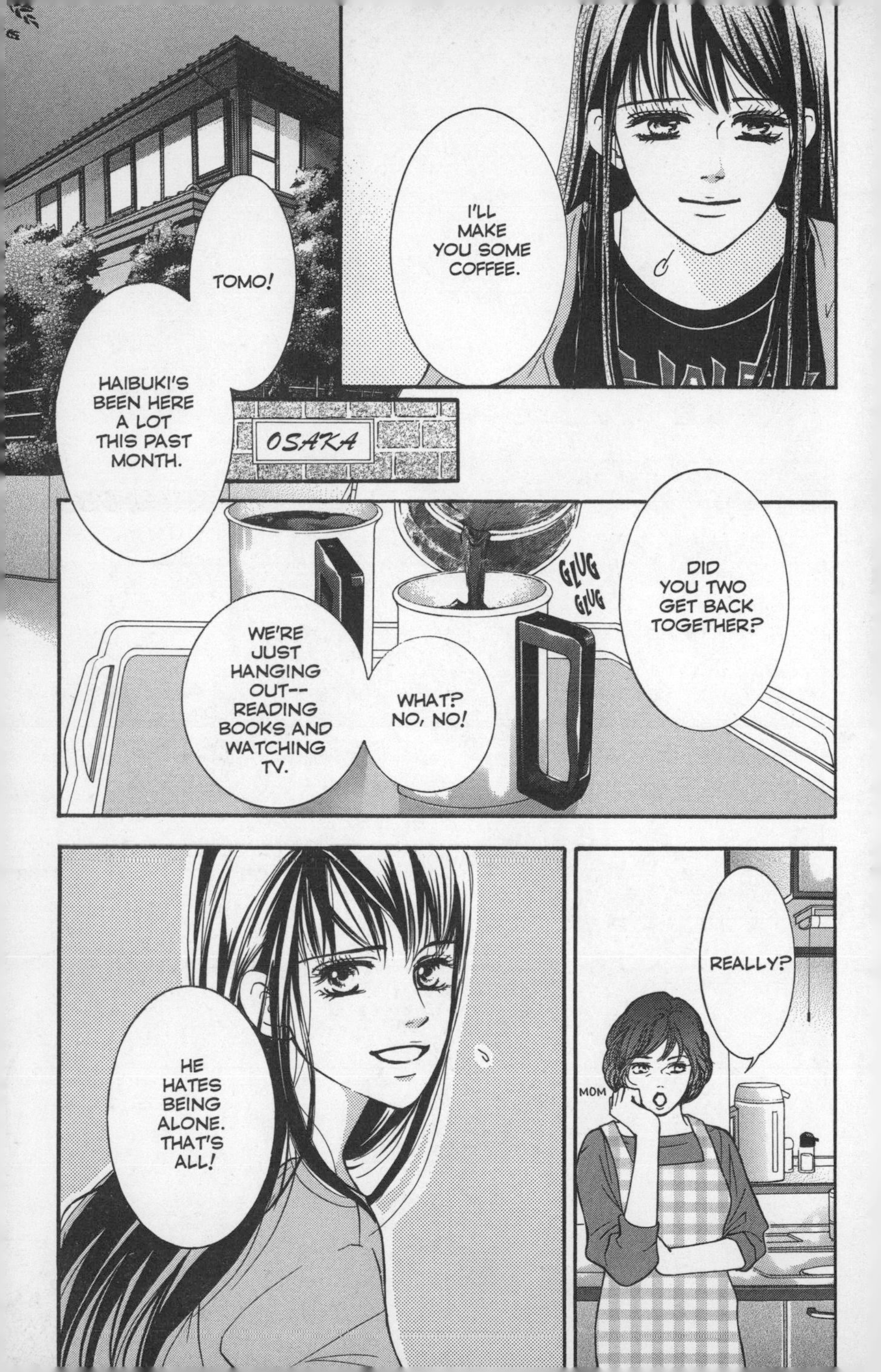
I'LL MAKE YOU SOME COFFEE.
TOMO!
HAIBUKI'S BEEN HERE A LOT THIS PAST MONTH.
OSAKA
GLUG GLUG
DID YOU TWO GET BACK TOGETHER?
WHAT? NO, NO!
WE'RE JUST HANGING OUT-- READING BOOKS AND WATCHING TV.
REALLY?
MOM
HE HATES BEING ALONE. THAT'S ALL!

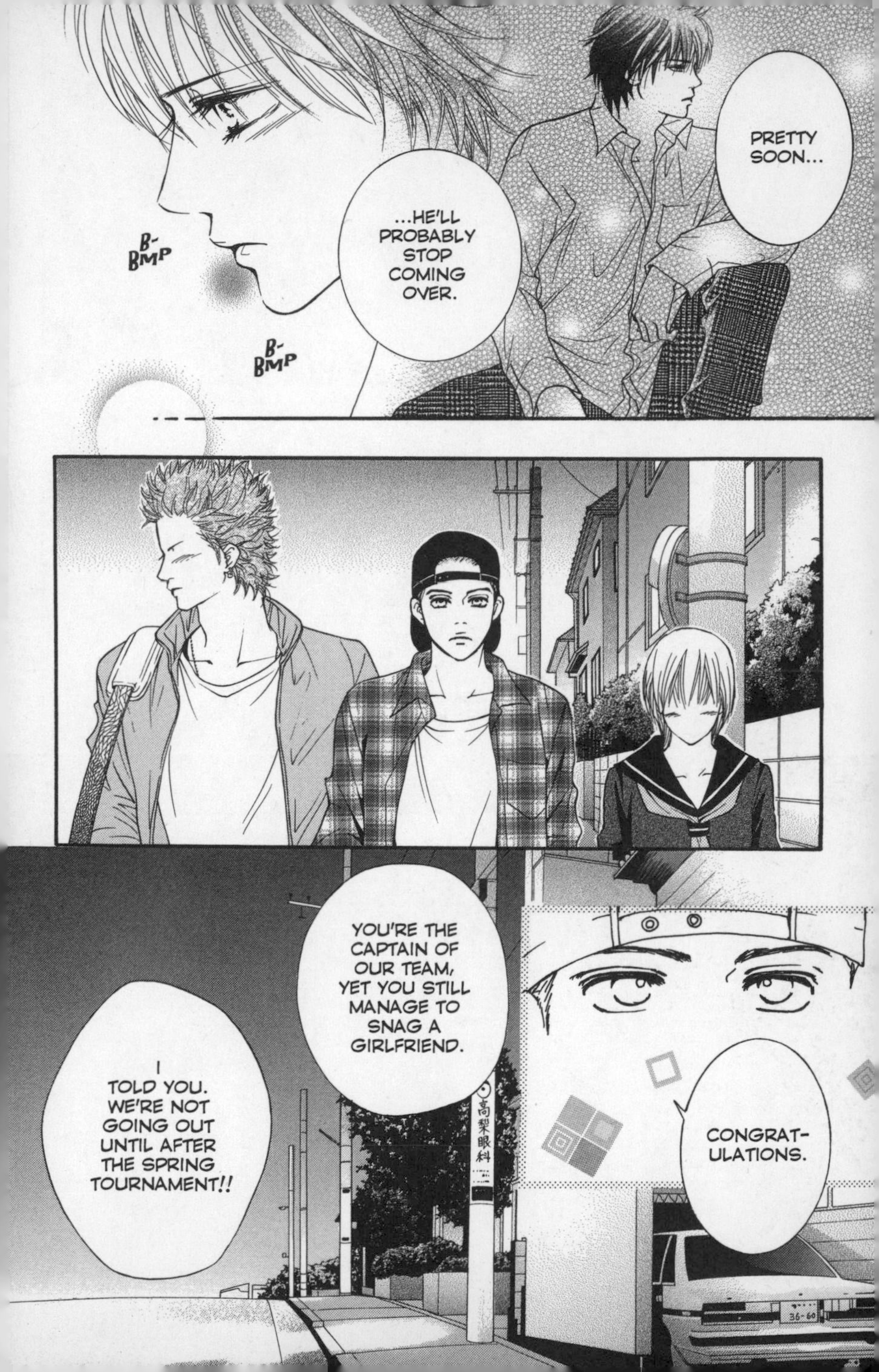
PRETTY SOON...
...HE'LL PROBABLY STOP COMING OVER.
B-BMP
B-BMP
CONGRAT-ULATIONS.
YOU'RE THE CAPTAIN OF OUR TEAM, YET YOU STILL MANAGE TO SNAG A GIRLFRIEND.
高梨眼科
I TOLD YOU. WE'RE NOT GOING OUT UNTIL AFTER THE SPRING TOURNAMENT!!

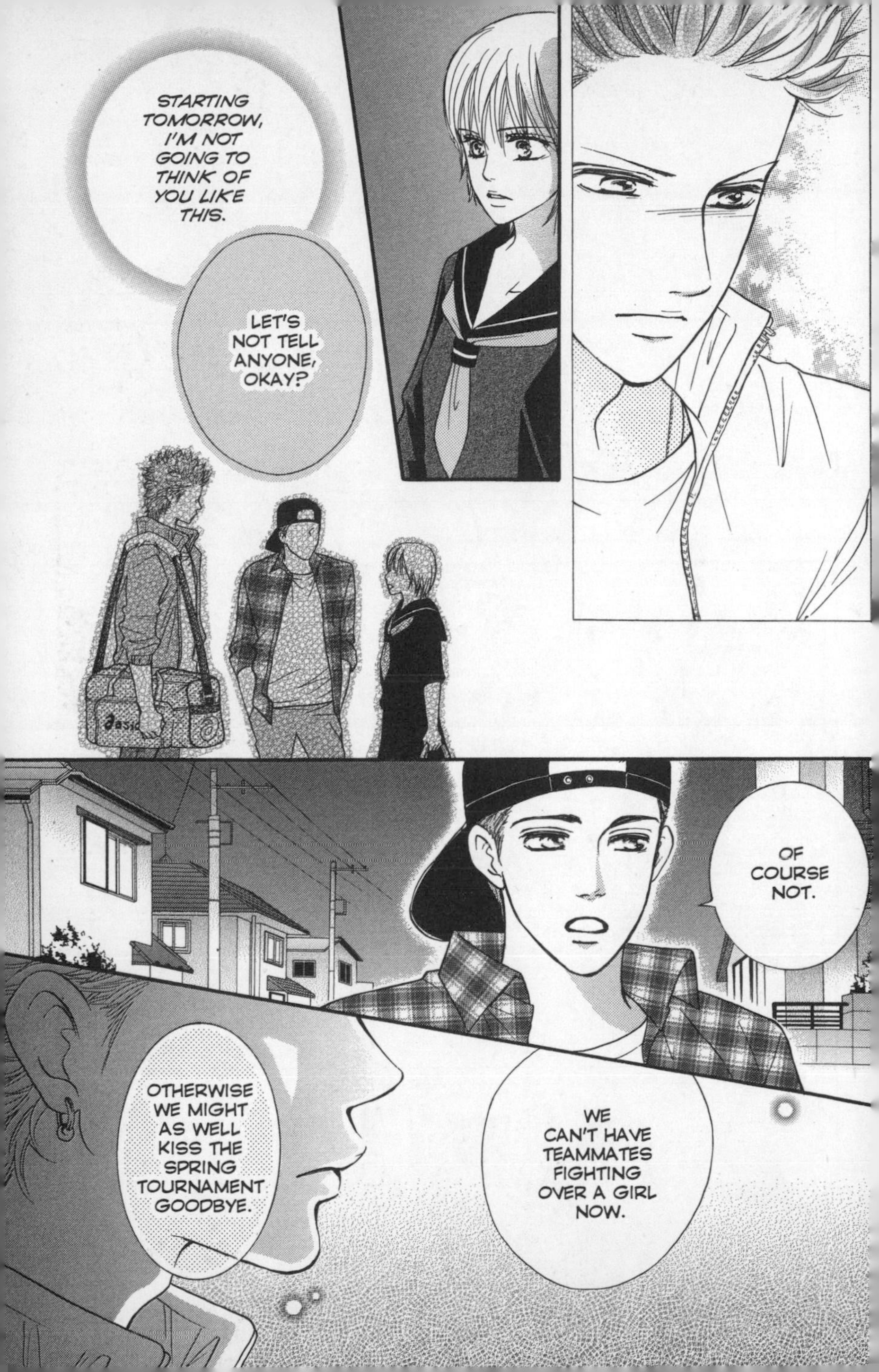
STARTING TOMORROW, I'M NOT GOING TO THINK OF YOU LIKE THIS.
LET'S NOT TELL ANYONE, OKAY?
OF COURSE NOT.
WE CAN'T HAVE TEAMMATES FIGHTING OVER A GIRL NOW.
OTHERWISE WE MIGHT AS WELL KISS THE SPRING TOURNAMENT GOODBYE.

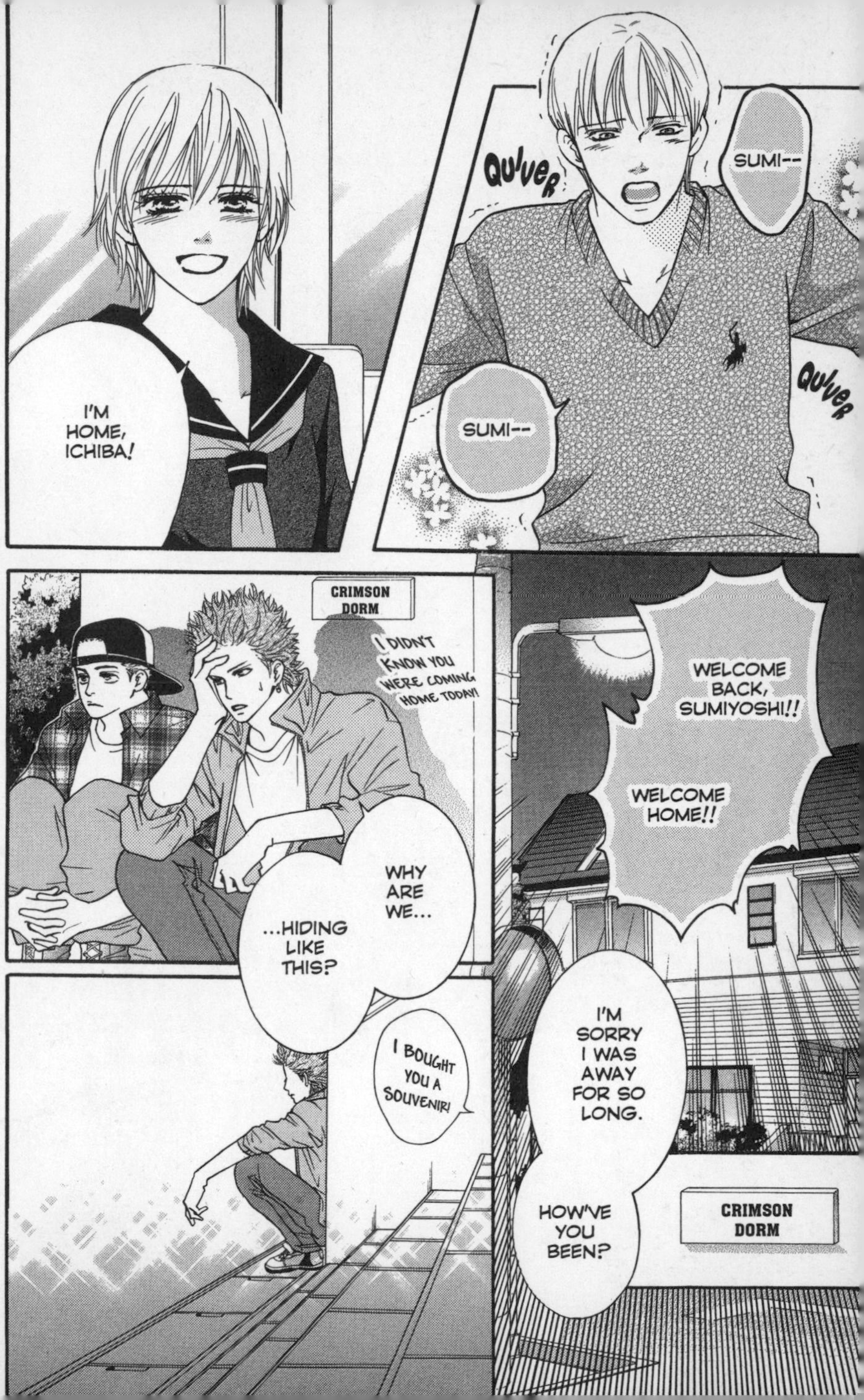
SUMI--
QUIVER
QUIVER
SUMI--
I'M HOME, ICHIBA!
WELCOME BACK, SUMIYOSHI!!
WELCOME HOME!!
CRIMSON DORM
I'M SORRY I WAS AWAY FOR SO LONG.
HOW'VE YOU BEEN?
CRIMSON DORM
I DIDN'T KNOW YOU WERE COMING HOME TODAY!
WHY ARE WE...
...HIDING LIKE THIS?
I BOUGHT YOU A SOUVENIR!

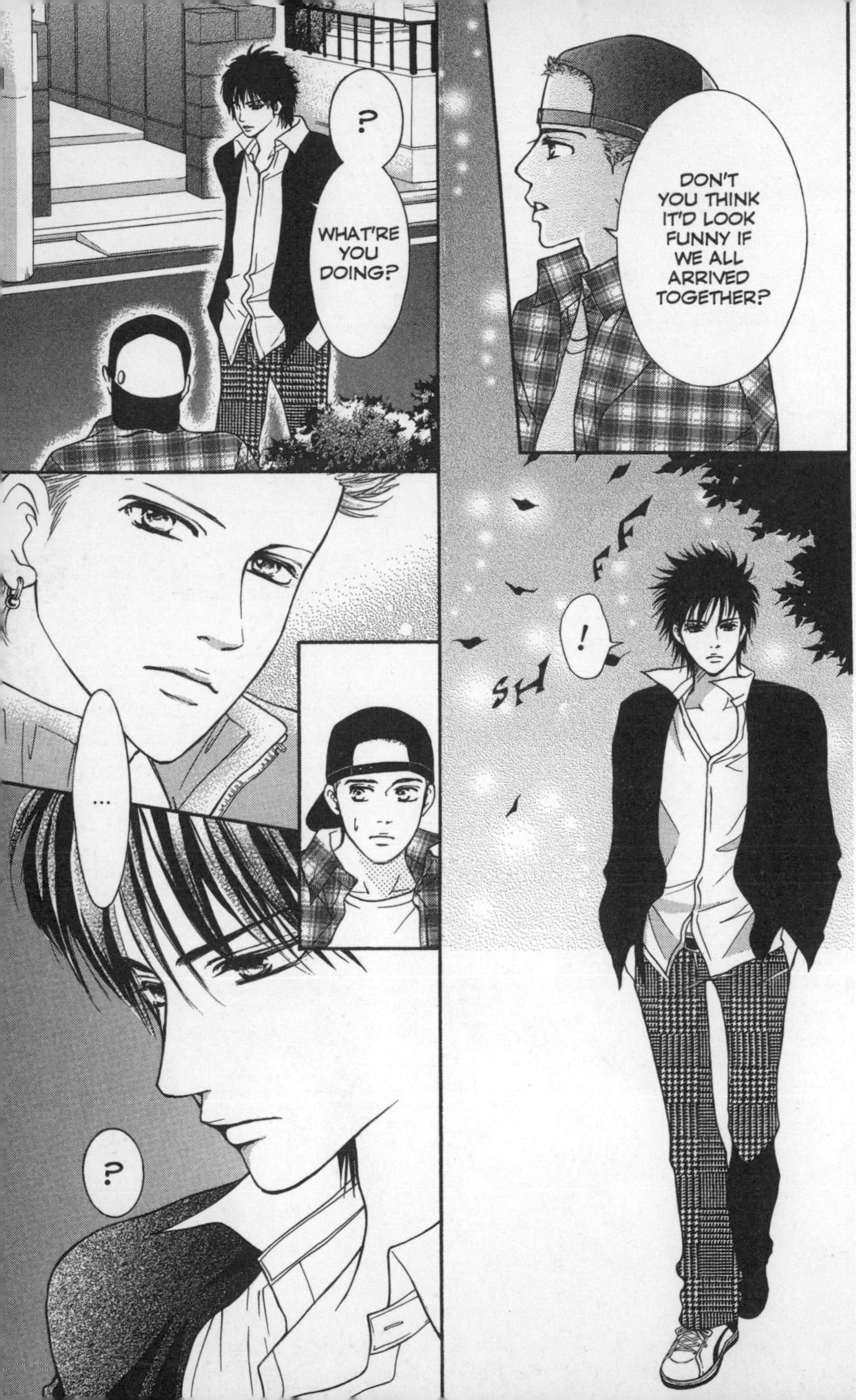
DON'T YOU THINK IT'D LOOK FUNNY IF WE ALL ARRIVED TOGETHER?
?
WHAT'RE YOU DOING?
!
SHFF
...
?

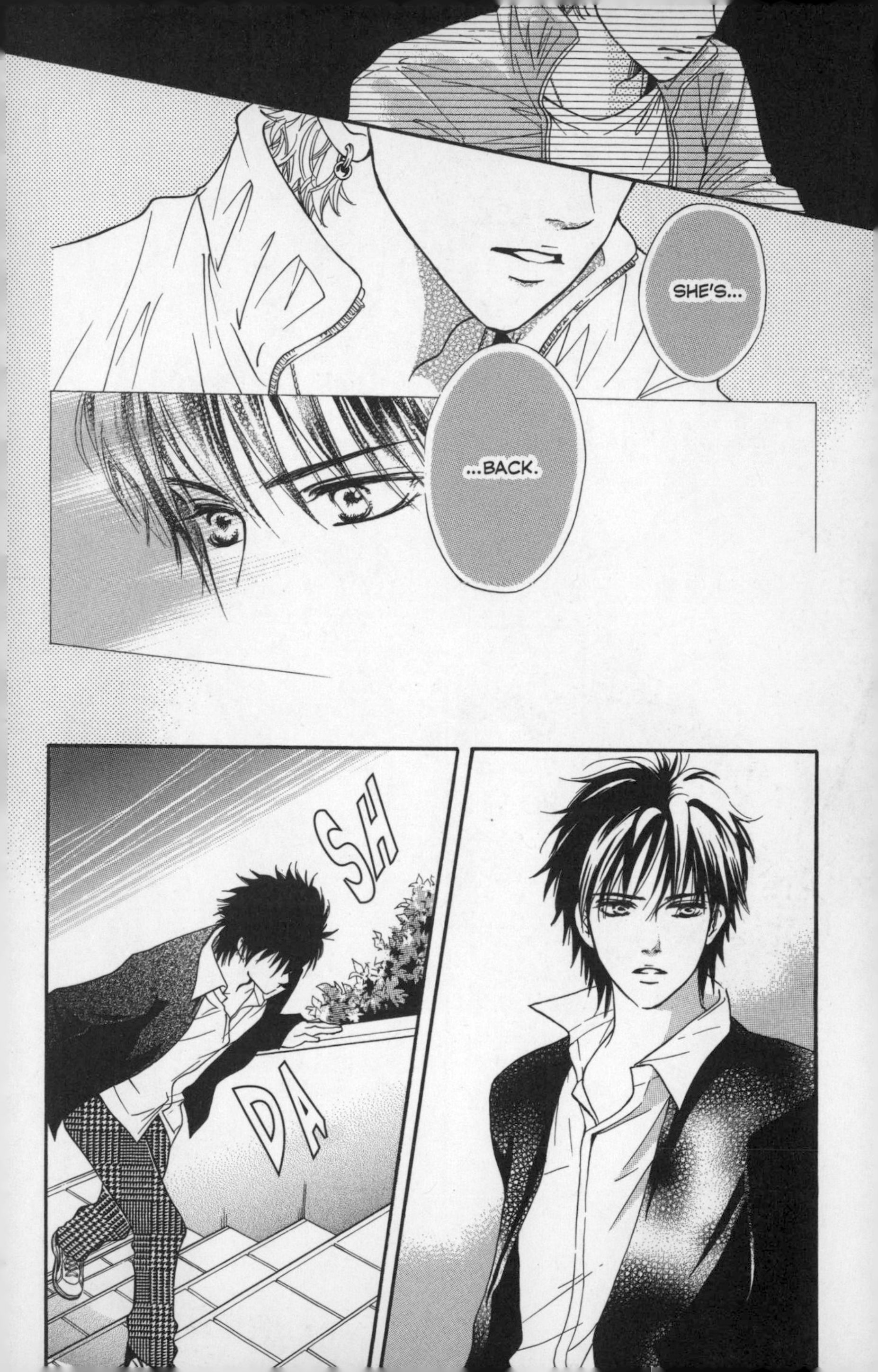
SHE'S...
...BACK.
DASH

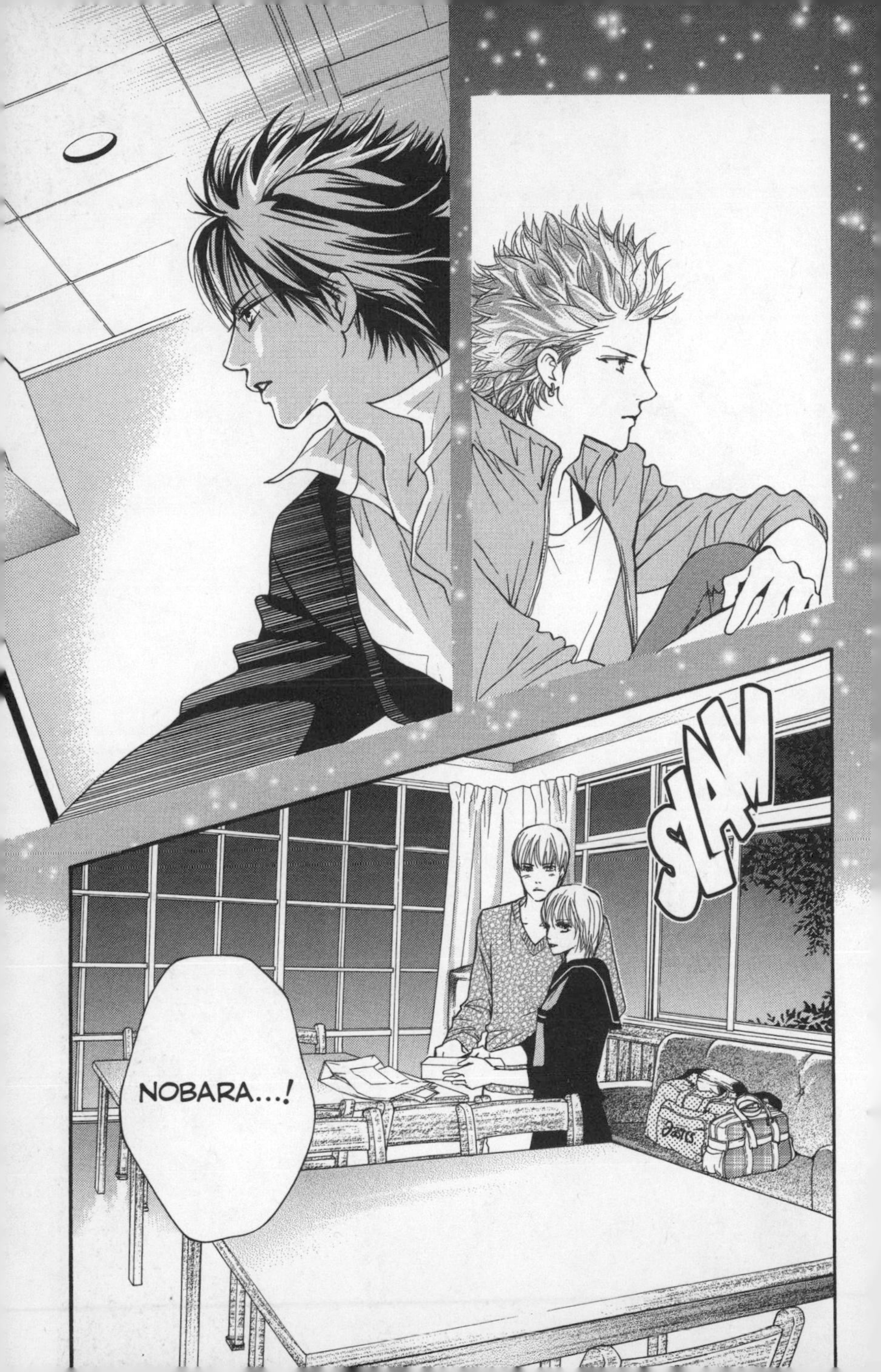
SLAM
NOBARA...!

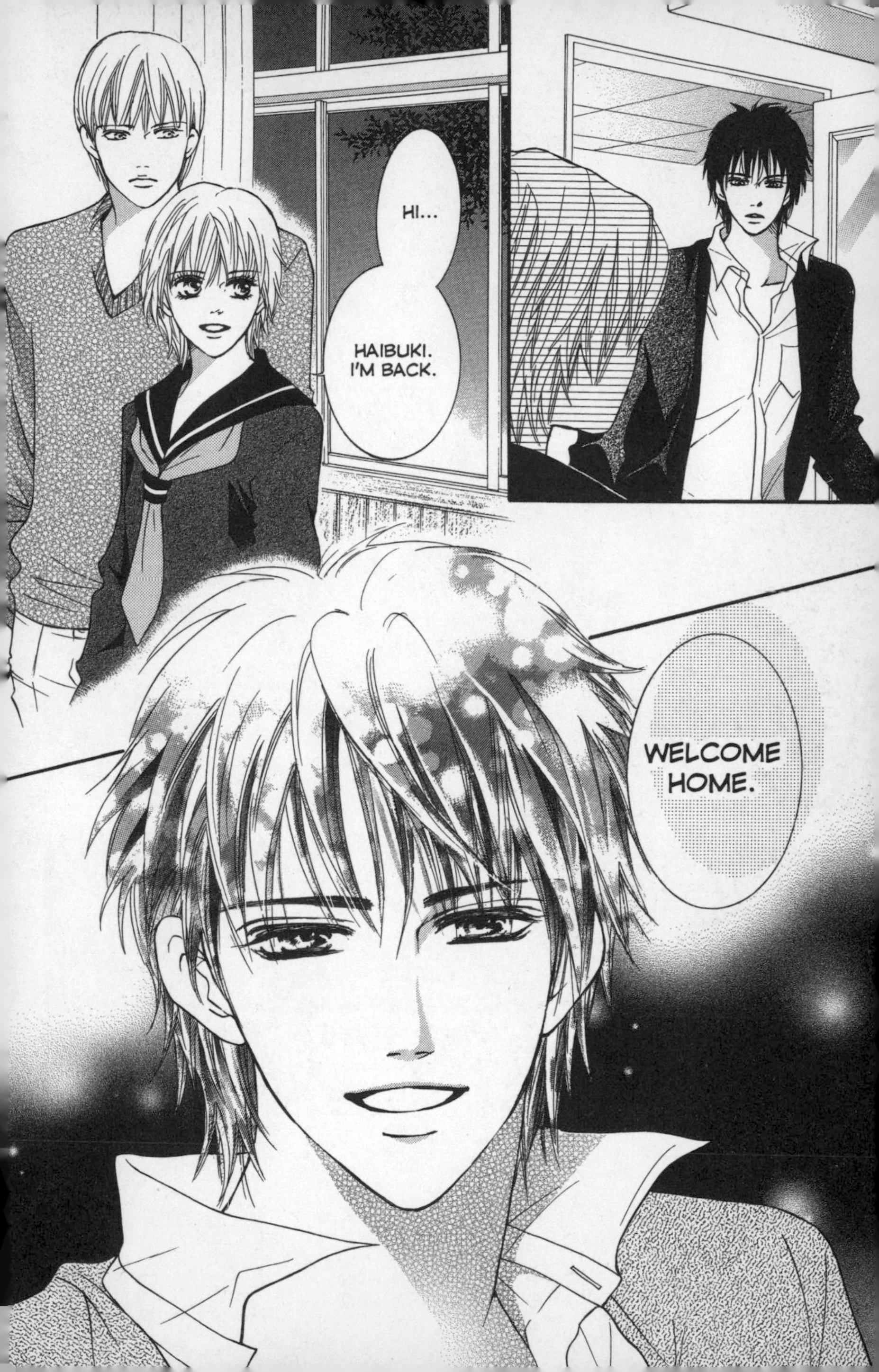
HI...
HAIBUKI. I'M BACK.
WELCOME HOME.

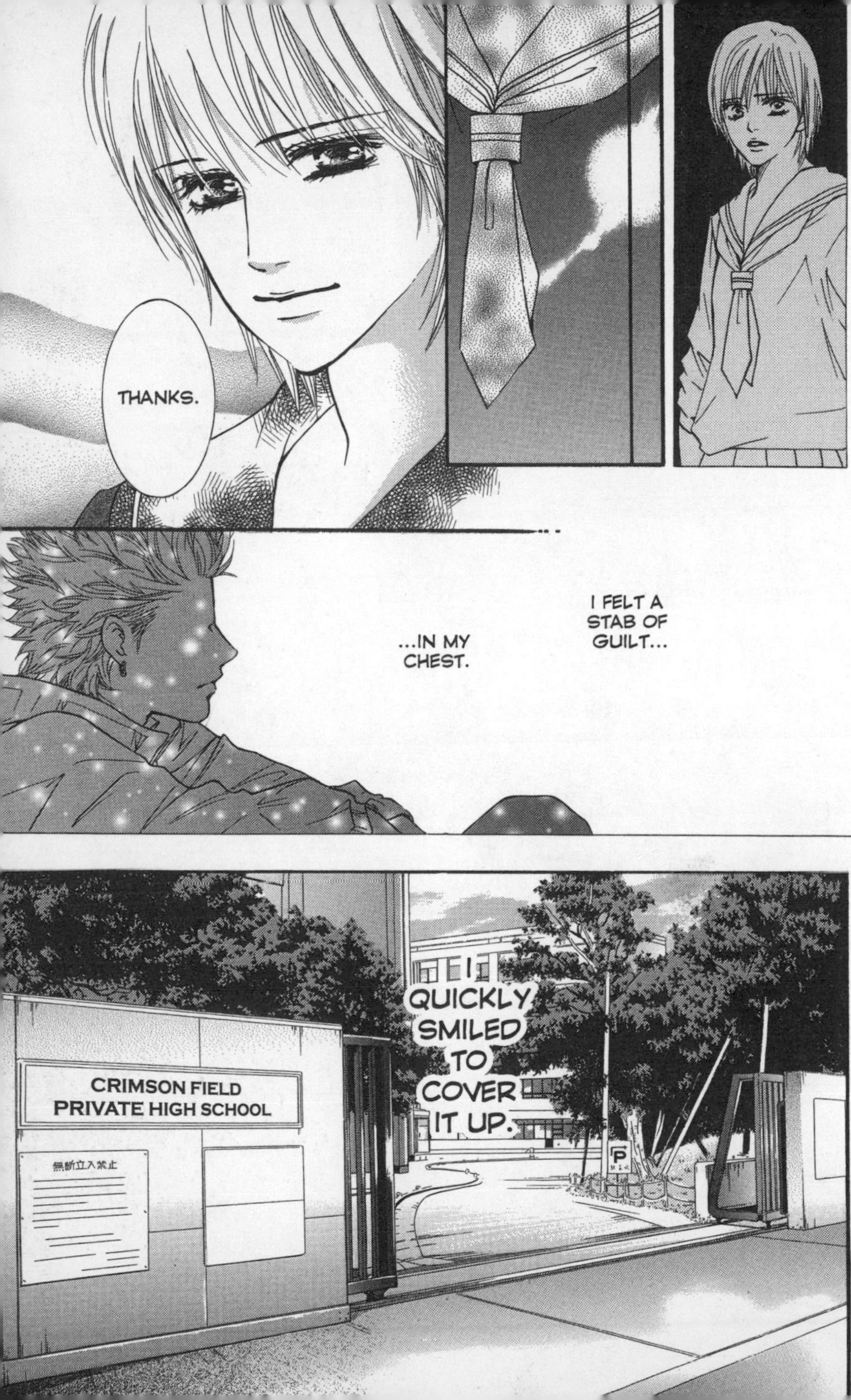
THANKS.
I FELT A STAB OF GUILT...
...IN MY CHEST.
I QUICKLY SMILED TO COVER IT UP.
CRIMSON FIELD PRIVATE HIGH SCHOOL
無断立入禁止

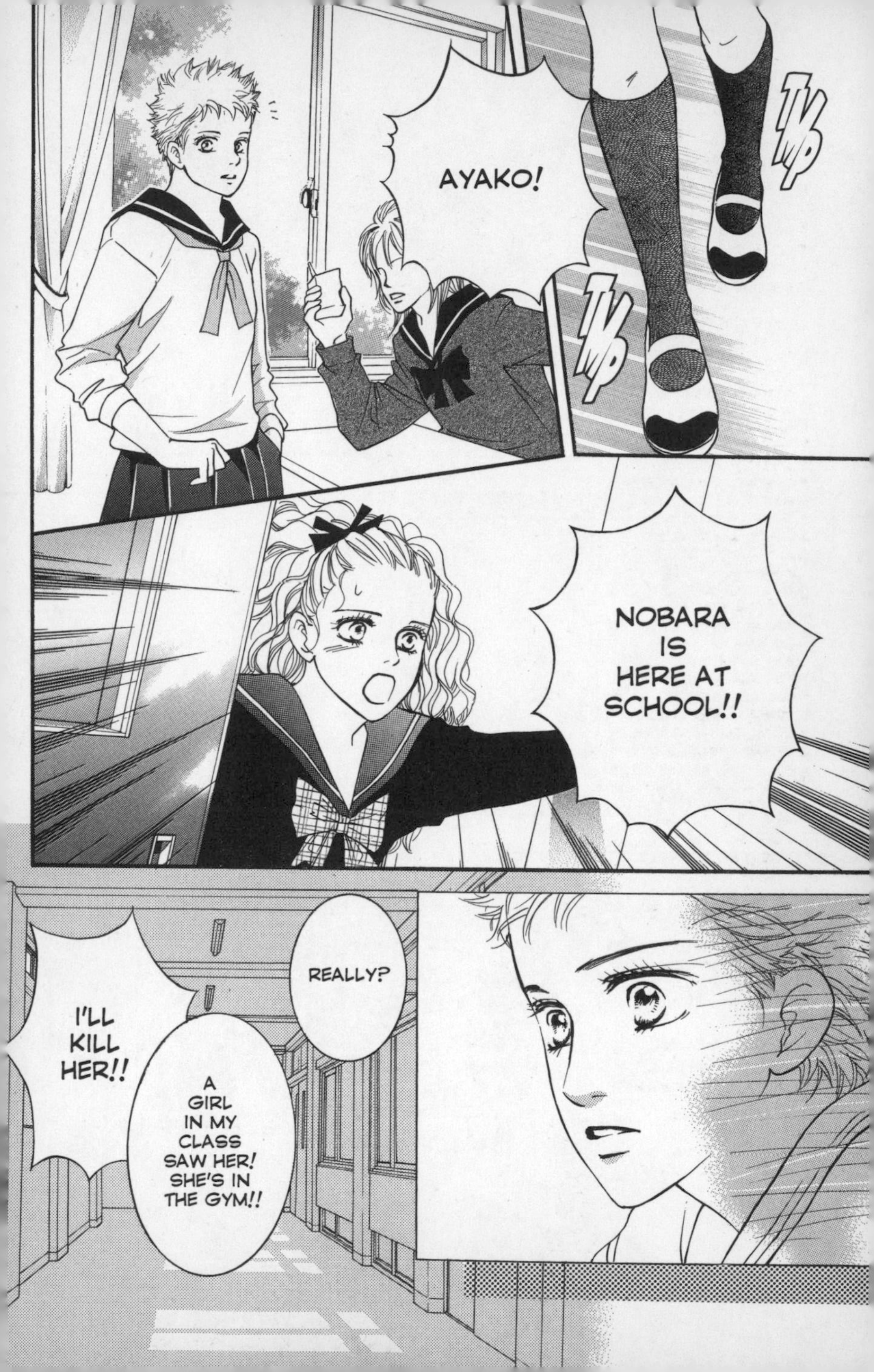
TMP
TMP
AYAKO!
NOBARA IS HERE AT SCHOOL!!
REALLY?
A GIRL IN MY CLASS SAW HER! SHE'S IN THE GYM!!
I'LL KILL HER!!

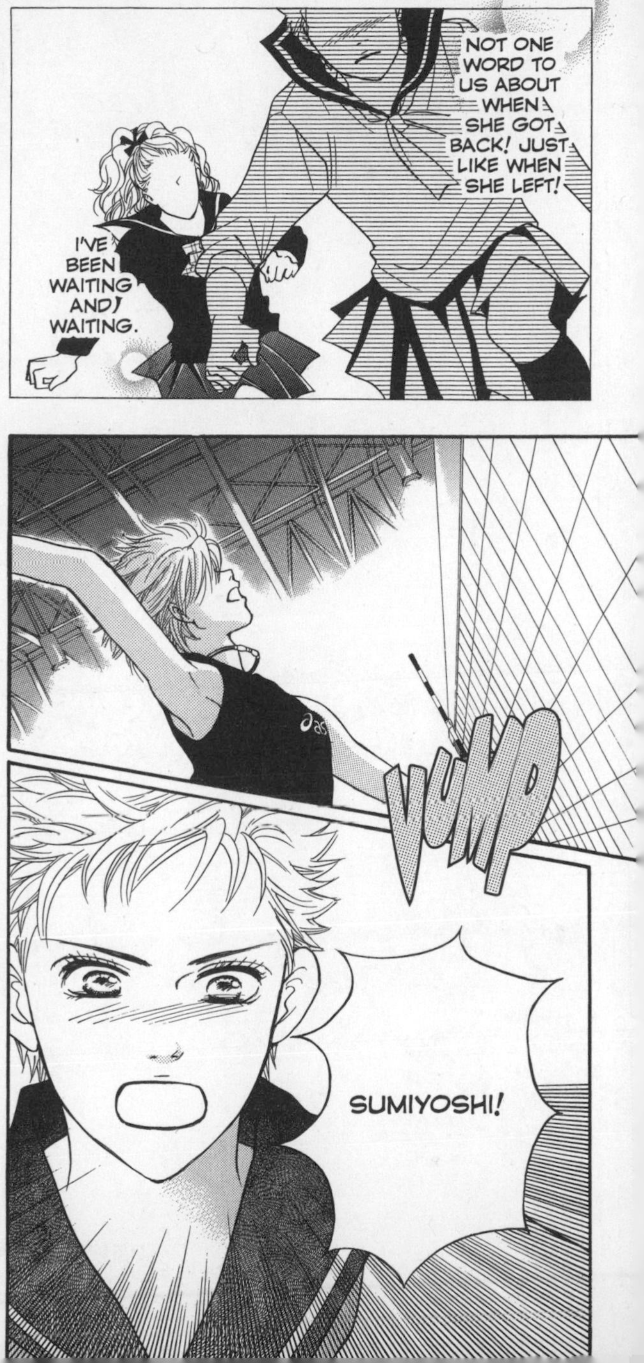
NOT ONE WORD TO US ABOUT WHEN SHE GOT BACK! JUST LIKE WHEN SHE LEFT!
I'VE BEEN WAITING AND WAITING.
VUMP
SUMIYOSHI!

MITSUBA CLUB

VoL. 3

LOSING WEIGHT IN 2006

SINCE I STARTED DRAWING MANGA EVERY MONTH, I'VE GAINED SEVEN KILOGRAMS. THAT'S ONE KILOGRAM EACH YEAR!!! NOT GOOD. AND IT'S NOT EVEN LIKE I'M THAT INTERESTED IN EATING. I'M SURROUNDED BY GOURMETS AND THEY'RE ALWAYS TALKING ABOUT THE SWEETS FROM THIS FAMOUS SHOP AND THE BAGELS FROM THAT OTHER FAMOUS SHOP. IT ALL GOES ABOVE MY HEAD. I DON'T HAVE A HIGHLY DEVELOPED SENSE OF TASTE. I LOVE THE KONNYAKU IN ODEN AND I LIKE TO EAT CHIKUWA STUFFED WITH CUCUMBER WITH SOME MAYO ON IT. OH, AND I LIKE MISO SOUP WITH CLAMS. I DON'T EAT A TON, SO WHY?! WHY ALL THIS JIGGLE? IT'S BECAUSE I NEVER MOVE!!! I KNOW, I KNOW!! IF YOU TOLD ME TO STAY PARKED ON THE SOFA ALL DAY, THAT'S WHAT I'D DO!!! I'M SORRY. I EVEN JOINED A GYM, BUT I NEVER GO. IT'S MONEY DOWN THE DRAIN. BUT LISTEN! THESE PAST TWO MONTHS I WAS WAY TOO BUSY TO GO! WHY AM I MAKING EXCUSES? THIS IS NOT GOOD. I HAVE TO MOTIVATE MYSELF TO MOVE AROUND MORE.

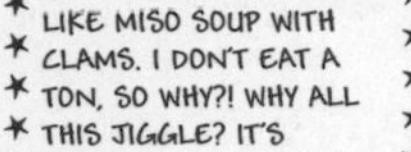
FWMP
FWMP

I MEAN, I'VE GOT TO START LIVING LIKE A HUMAN. SNIFF. I NEED A REALLY SCARY COACH TO MAKE ME GET UP IN THE MORNING. AAARRRRGH...!!!

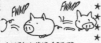

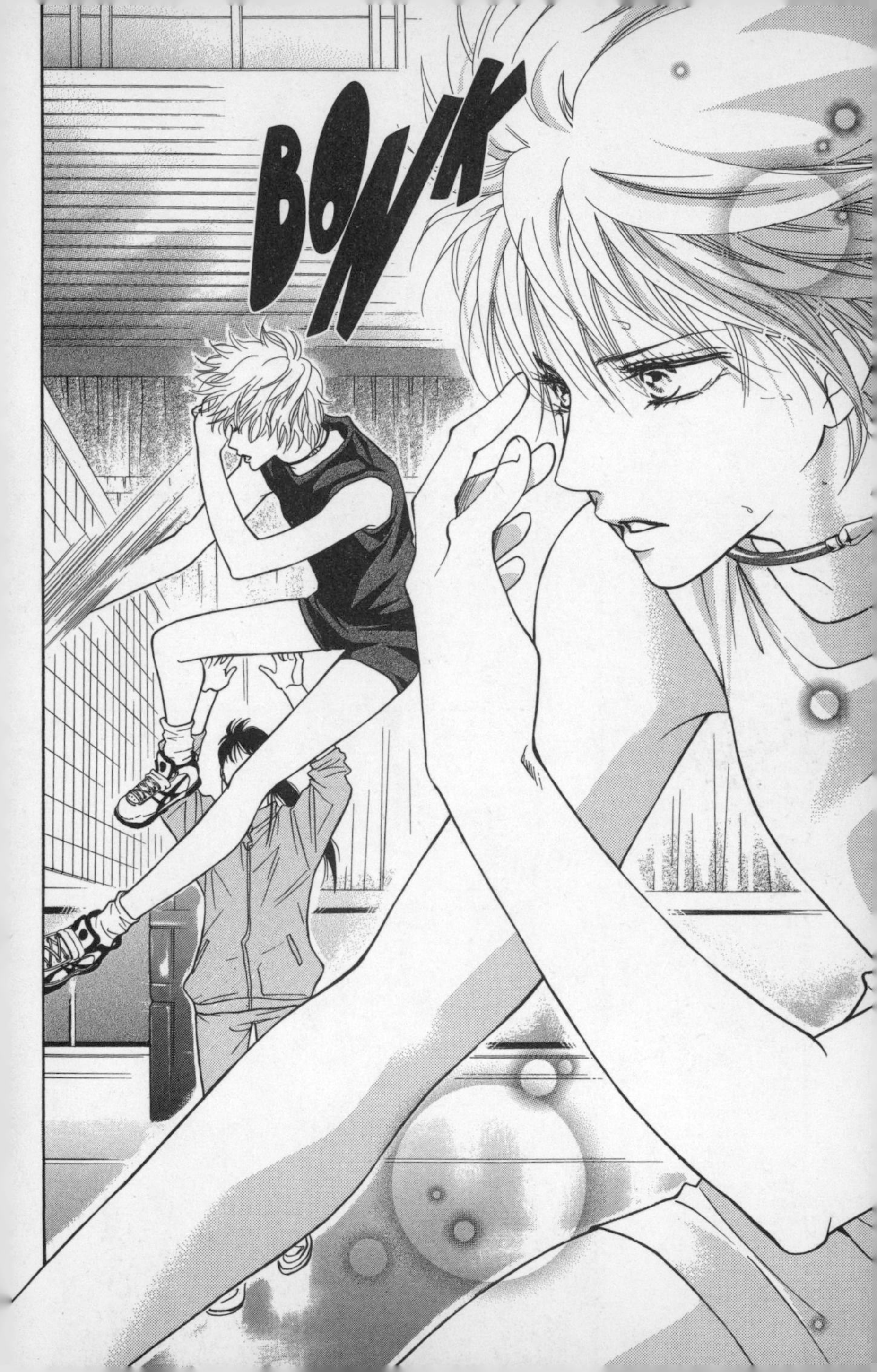
BONK

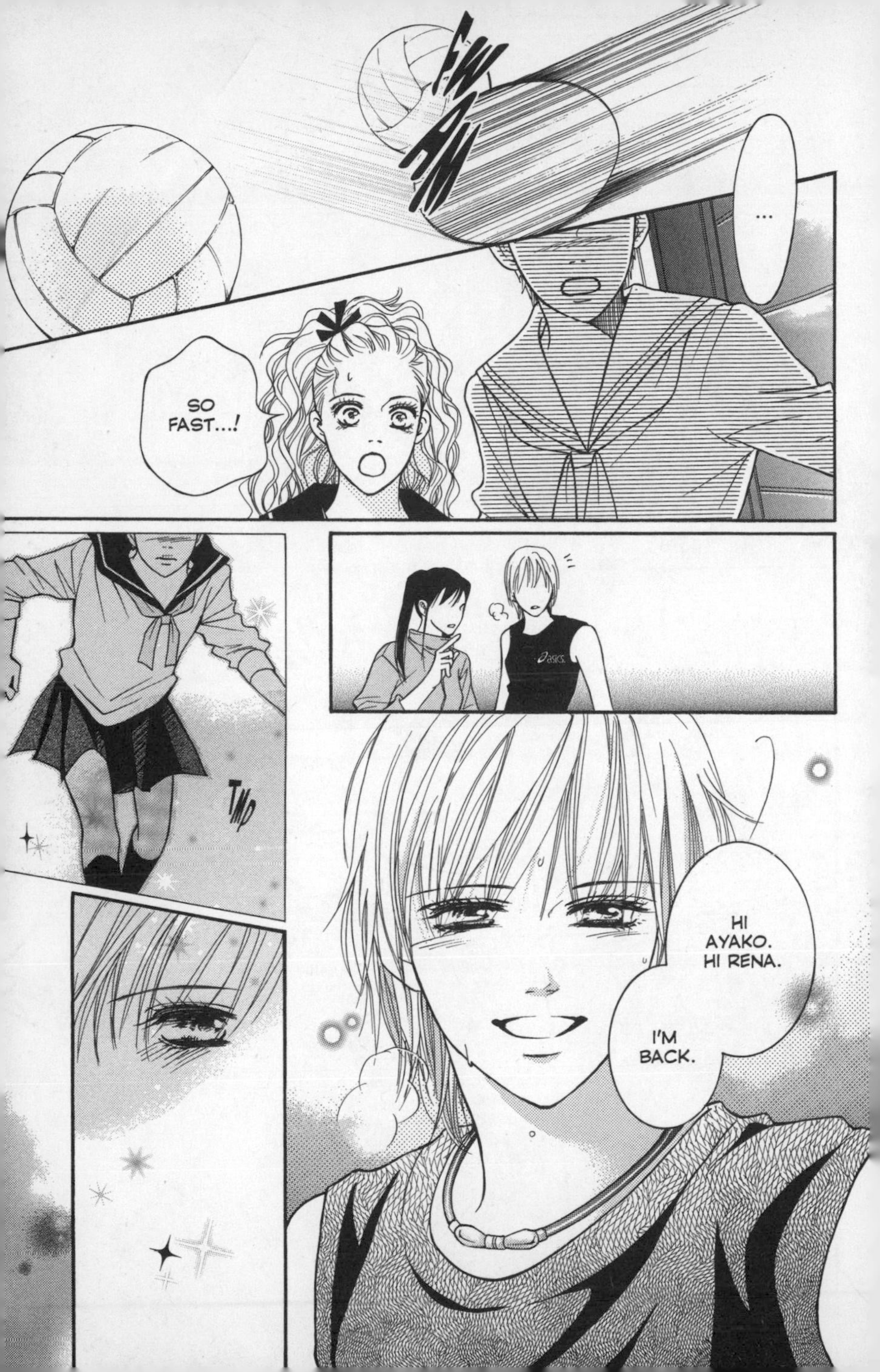
FWAM
...
SO FAST....!
TMP
HI AYAKO. HI RENA.
I'M BACK.

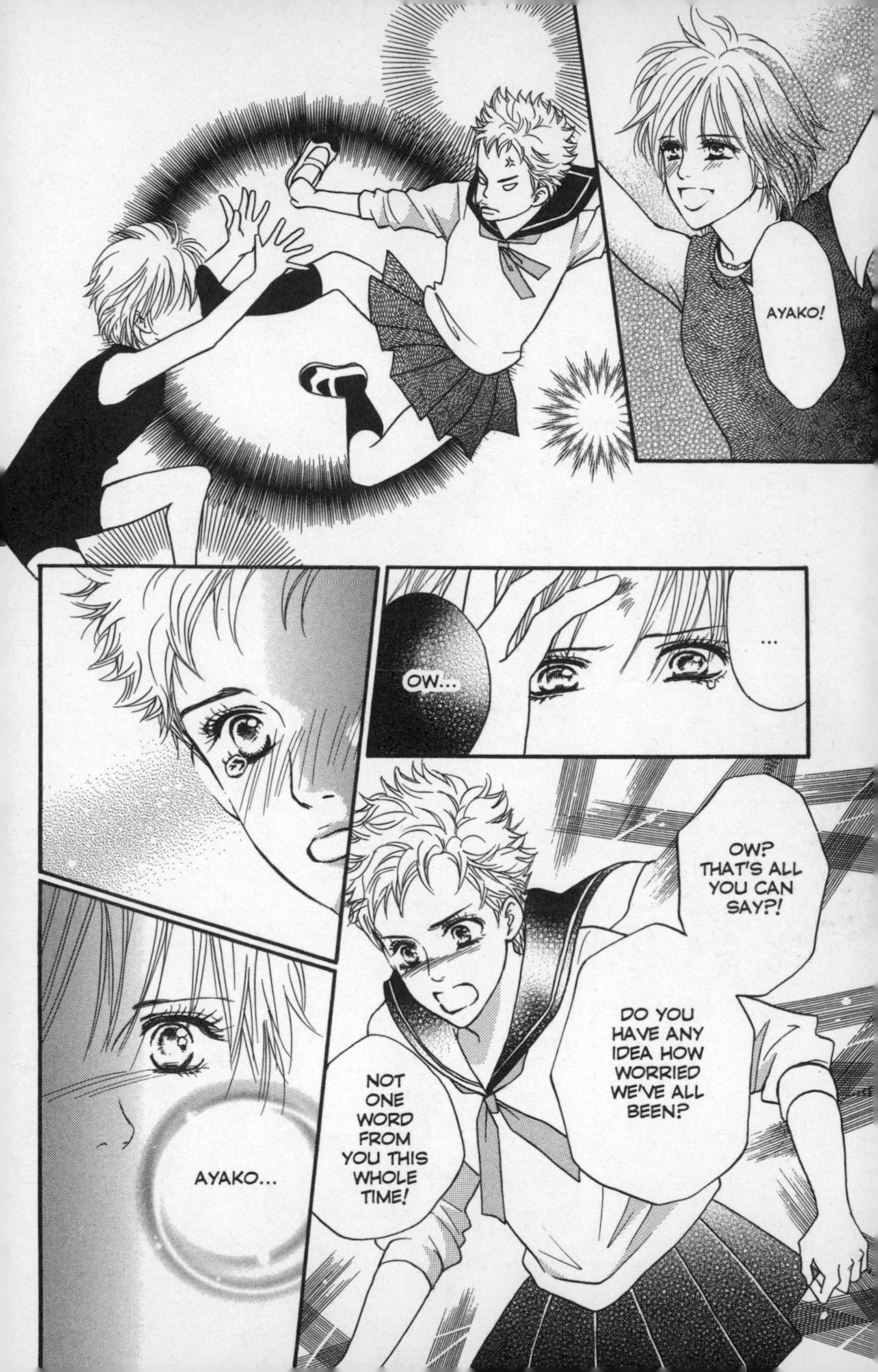
AYAKO!
...
OW...
OW? THAT'S ALL YOU CAN SAY?!
DO YOU HAVE ANY IDEA HOW WORRIED WE'VE ALL BEEN?
NOT ONE WORD FROM YOU THIS WHOLE TIME!
AYAKO...

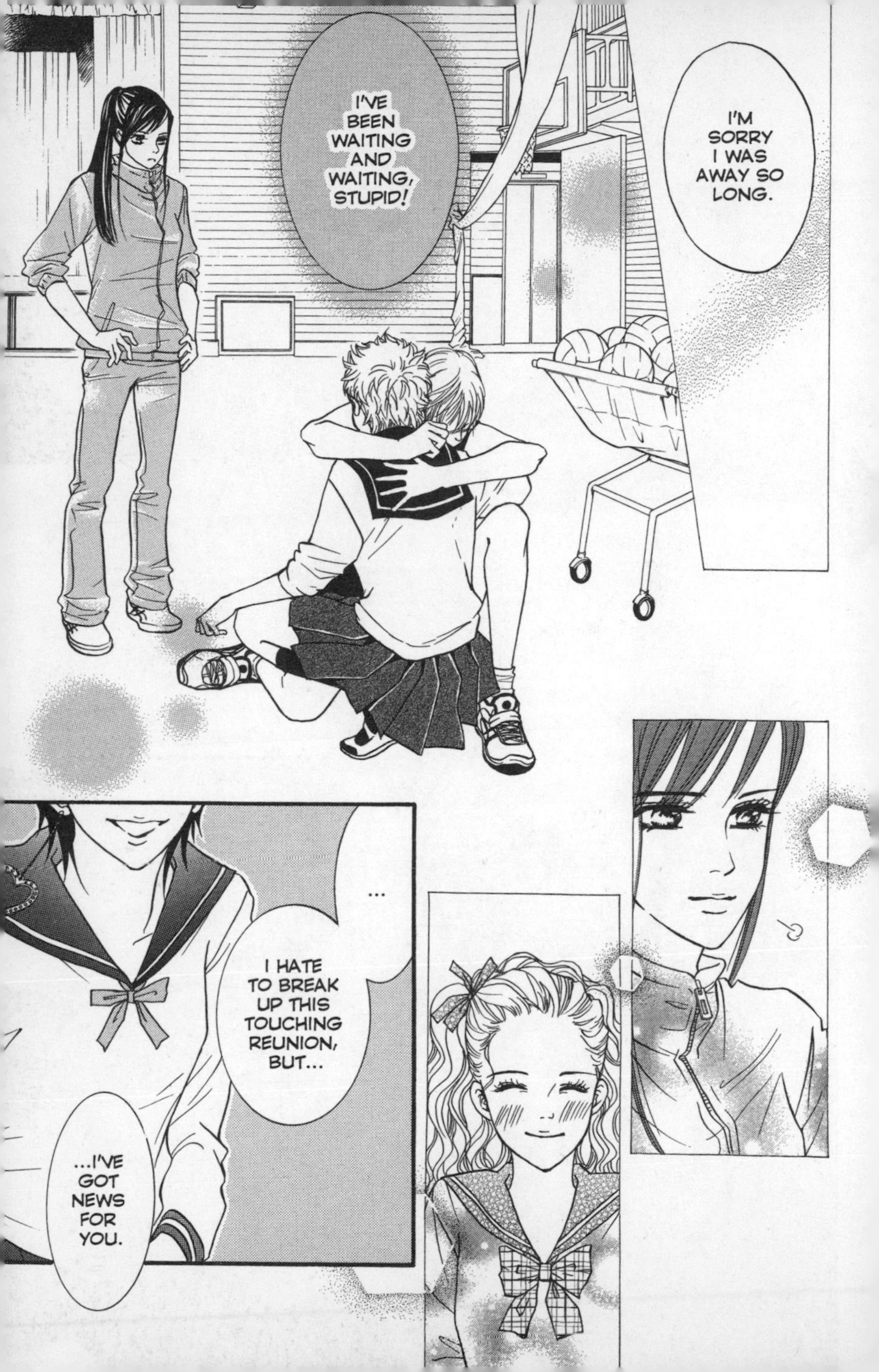
I'M SORRY I WAS AWAY SO LONG.
I'VE BEEN WAITING AND WAITING, STUPID!
...
I HATE TO BREAK UP THIS TOUCHING REUNION, BUT...
...I'VE GOT NEWS FOR YOU.

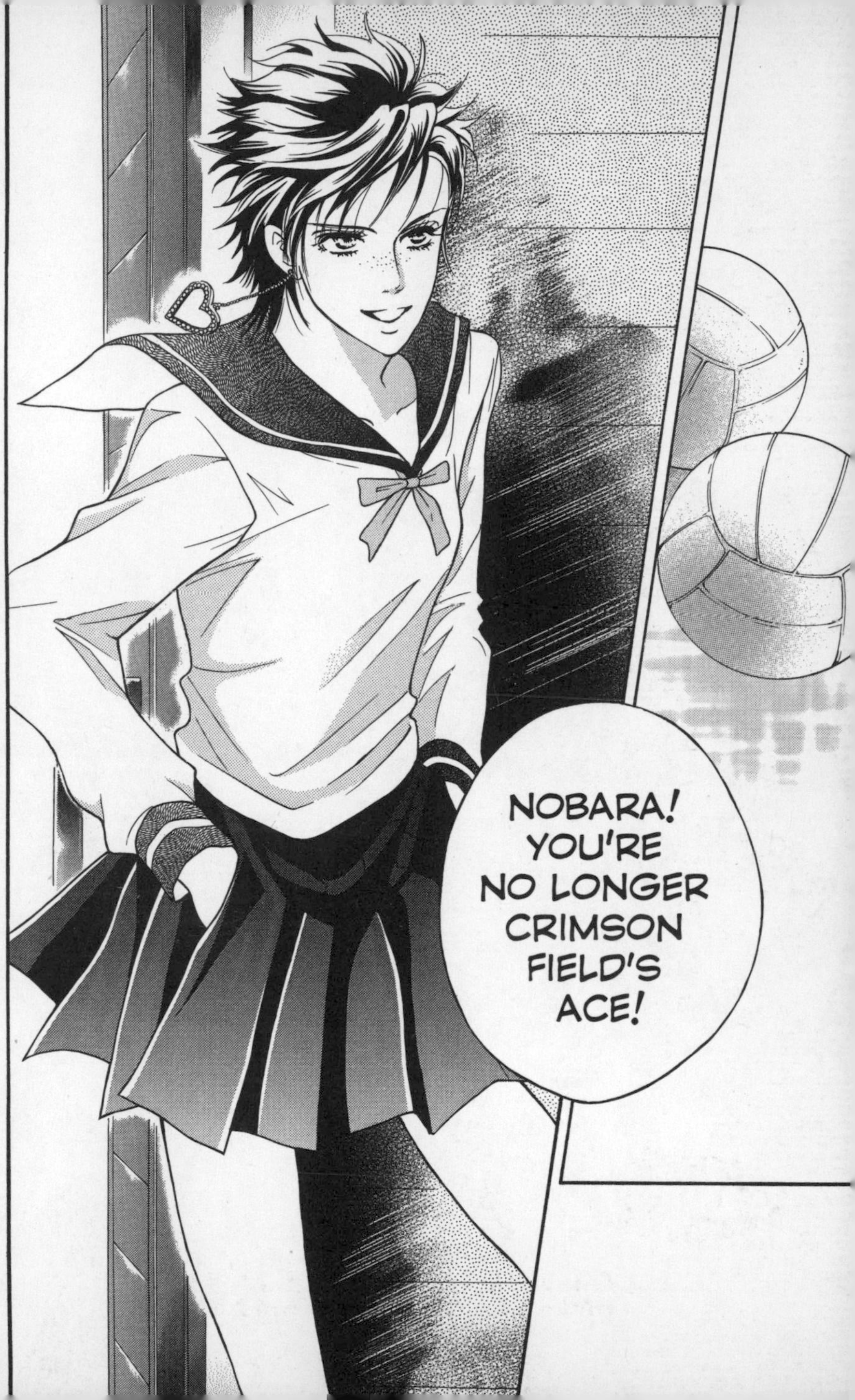
NOBARA! YOU'RE NO LONGER CRIMSON FIELD'S ACE!

NOBARA

KANA

MOCCHI

NEO

OPE

GAME 13

KANA'S FEELINGS

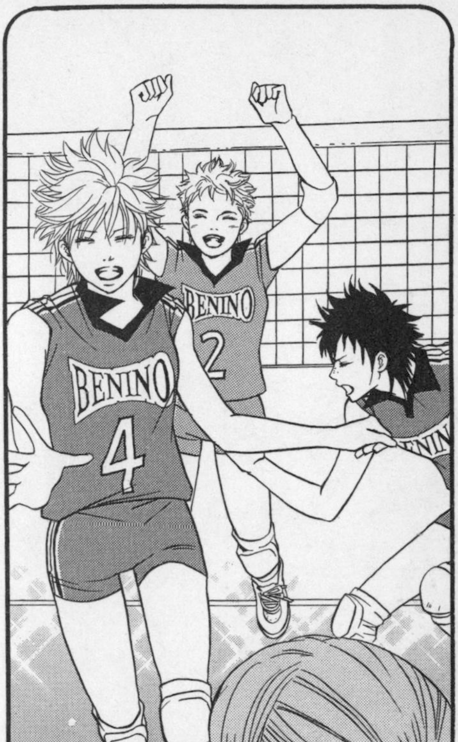
BENINO
2
BENINO
4
BENIN
VOLLEY
CLU

Crimson Hero

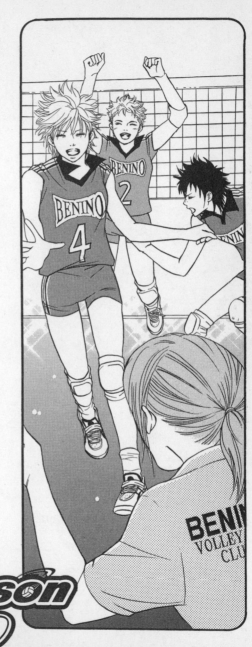

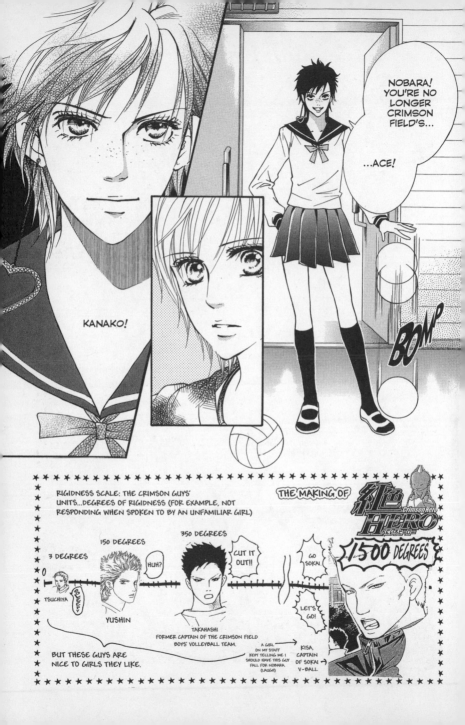

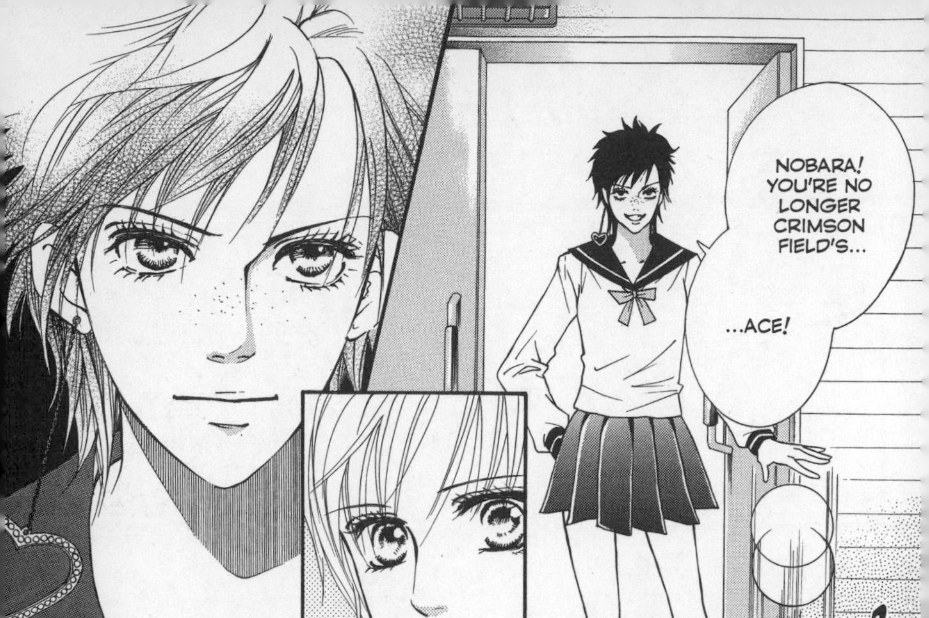
NOBARA! YOU'RE NO LONGER CRIMSON FIELD'S...
...ACE!
BOMP
KANAKO!

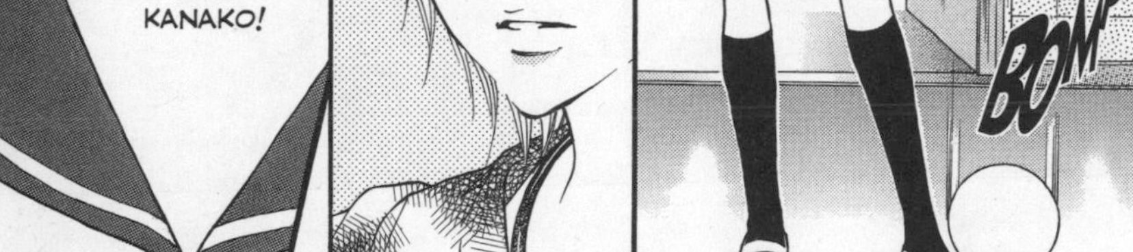
THE MAKING OF 紅色HERO Crimson Hero
RIGIDNESS SCALE: THE CRIMSON GUYS' UNITS...DEGREES OF RIGIDNESS (FOR EXAMPLE, NOT RESPONDING WHEN SPOKEN TO BY AN UNFAMILIAR GIRL)
1500 DEGREES
GO SOKAI.
LET'S GO!
350 DEGREES
CUT IT OUT!!
150 DEGREES
HUH?
3 DEGREES
0
SLEEPY
TSUCHIYA
YUSHIN
TAKAHASHI FORMER CAPTAIN OF THE CRIMSON FIELD BOYS' VOLLEYBALL TEAM.
KISA, CAPTAIN OF SOKAI V-BALL
A GIRL ON MY STAFF KEPT TELLING ME I SHOULD HAVE THIS GUY FALL FOR NOBARA (LAUGH)
BUT THESE GUYS ARE NICE TO GIRLS THEY LIKE.

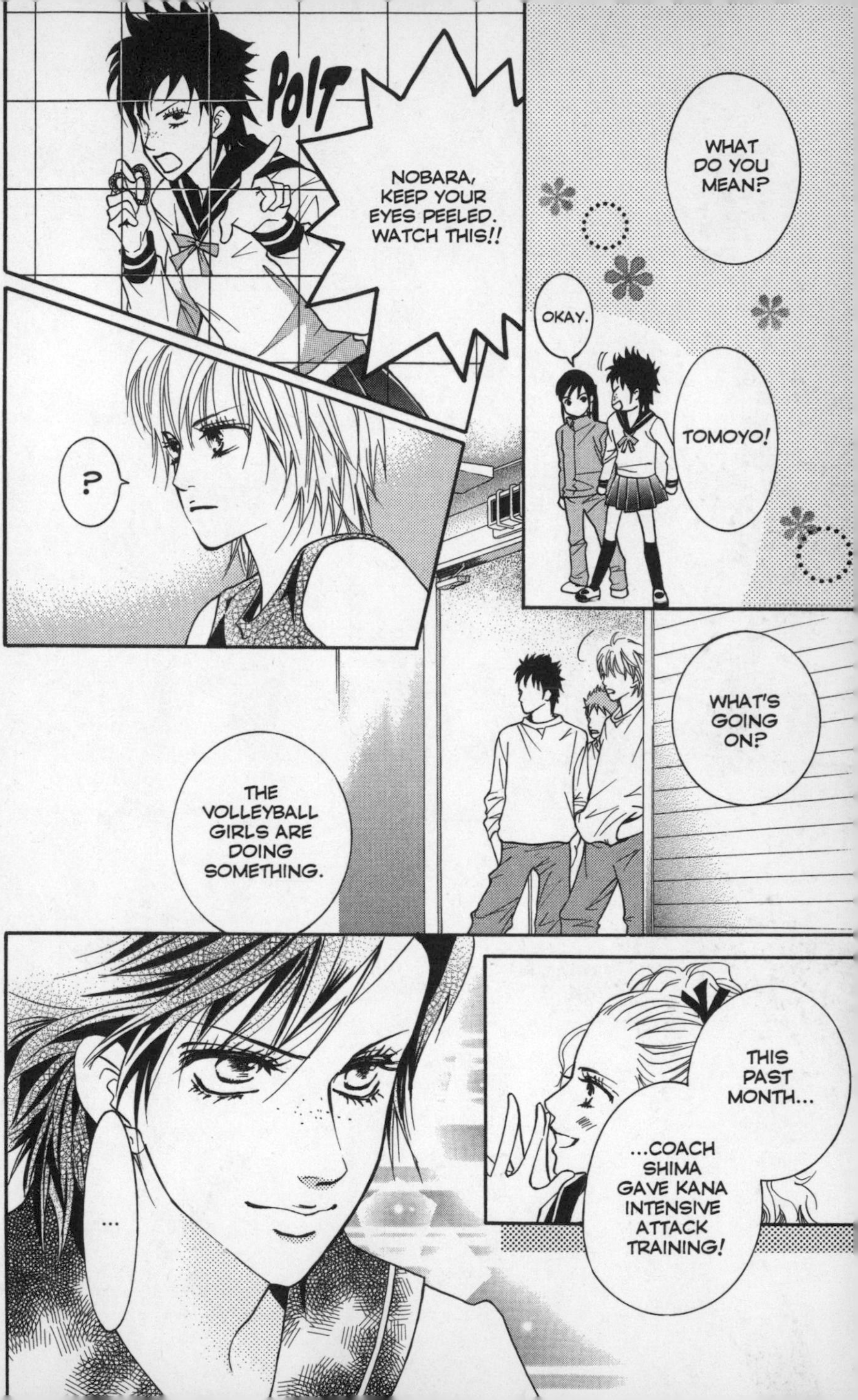
WHAT DO YOU MEAN?
OKAY.
TOMOYO!
POIT
NOBARA, KEEP YOUR EYES PEELED. WATCH THIS!!
?
WHAT'S GOING ON?
THE VOLLEYBALL GIRLS ARE DOING SOMETHING.
THIS PAST MONTH...
...COACH SHIMA GAVE KANA INTENSIVE ATTACK TRAINING!
...

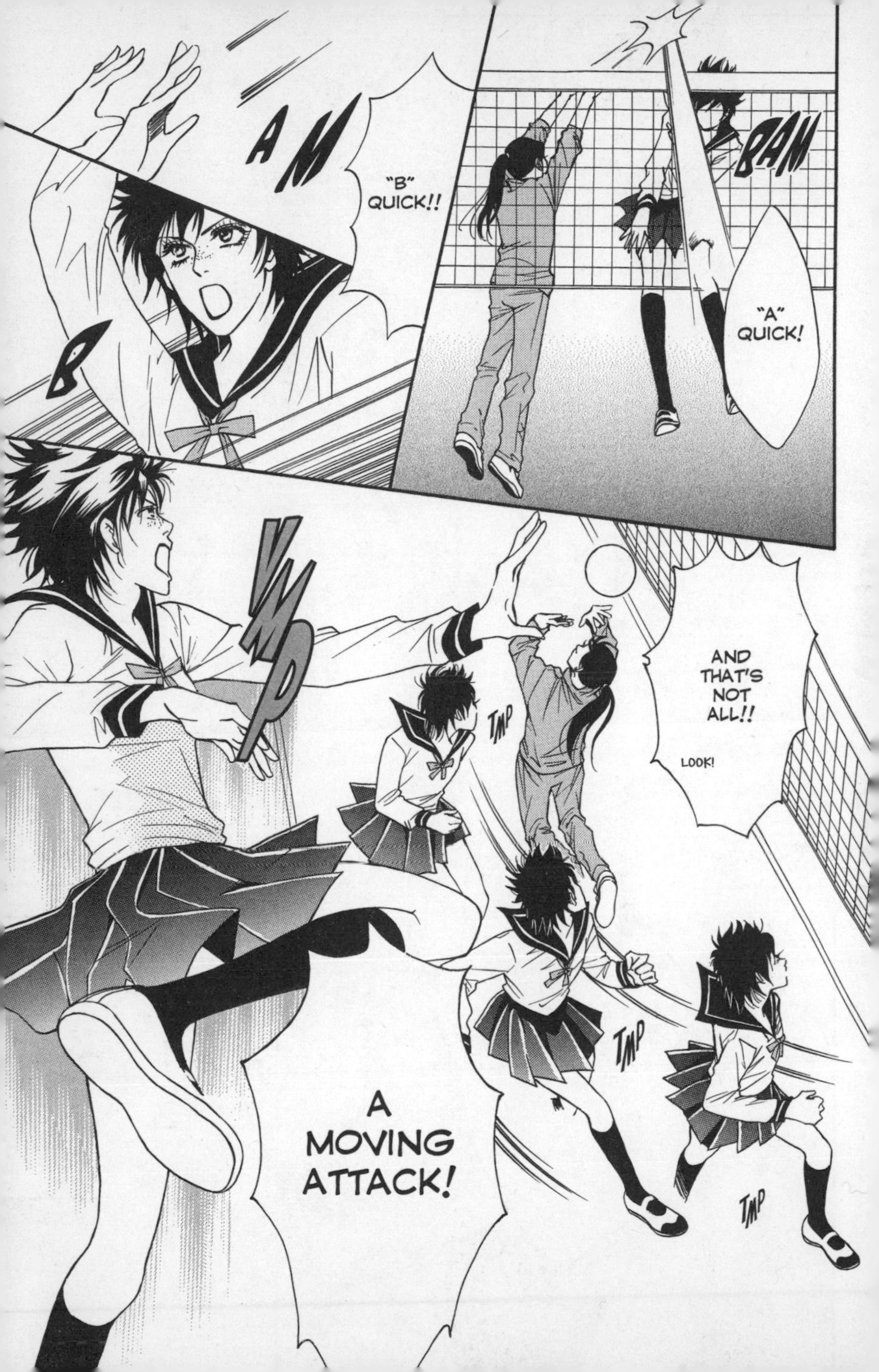
BAM
"A" QUICK!
"B" QUICK!!
BAM
AND THAT'S NOT ALL!!
LOOK!
TMP
TMP
TMP
A MOVING ATTACK!

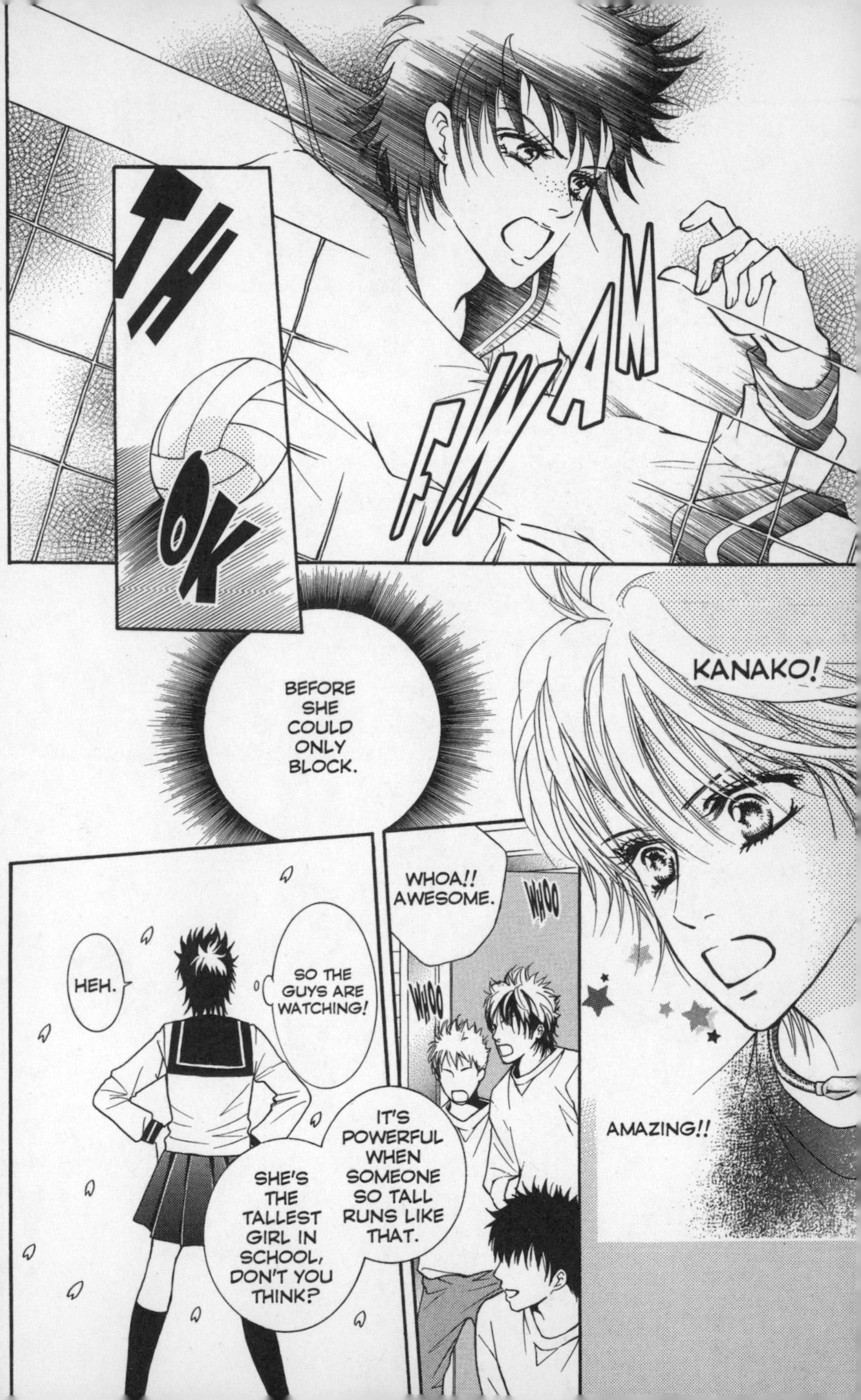
FWAM
THOK
KANAKO!
AMAZING!!
BEFORE SHE COULD ONLY BLOCK.
WHOA!! AWESOME.
WHOO
WHOO
IT'S POWERFUL WHEN SOMEONE SO TALL RUNS LIKE THAT.
SHE'S THE TALLEST GIRL IN SCHOOL, DON'T YOU THINK?
SO THE GUYS ARE WATCHING!
HEH.

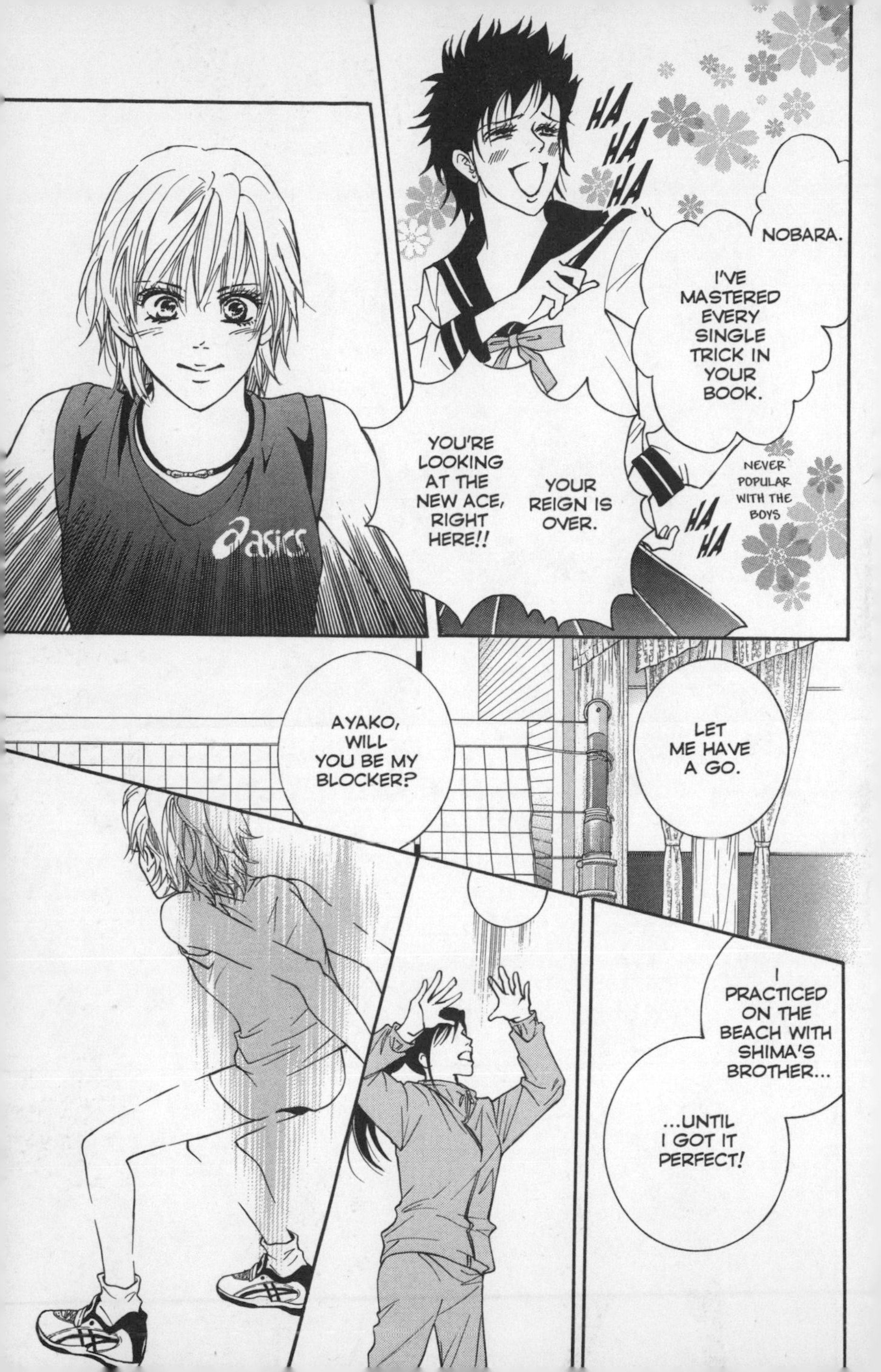
HA HA HA HA
NOBARA.
I'VE MASTERED EVERY SINGLE TRICK IN YOUR BOOK.
NEVER POPULAR WITH THE BOYS
HA HA
YOUR REIGN IS OVER.
YOU'RE LOOKING AT THE NEW ACE, RIGHT HERE!!
LET ME HAVE A GO.
AYAKO, WILL YOU BE MY BLOCKER?
I PRACTICED ON THE BEACH WITH SHIMA'S BROTHER...
...UNTIL I GOT IT PERFECT!

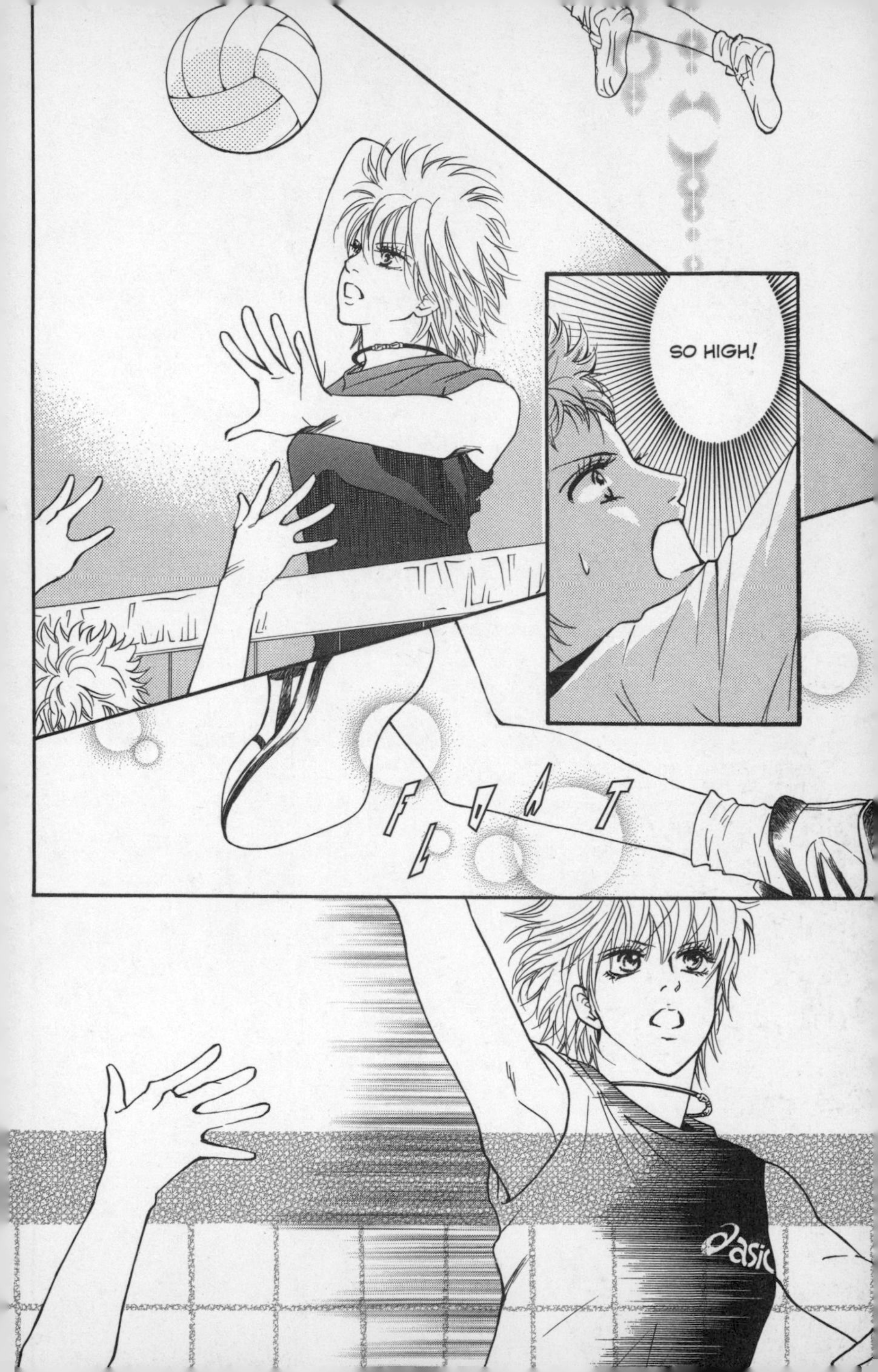
SO HIGH!
FLOAT

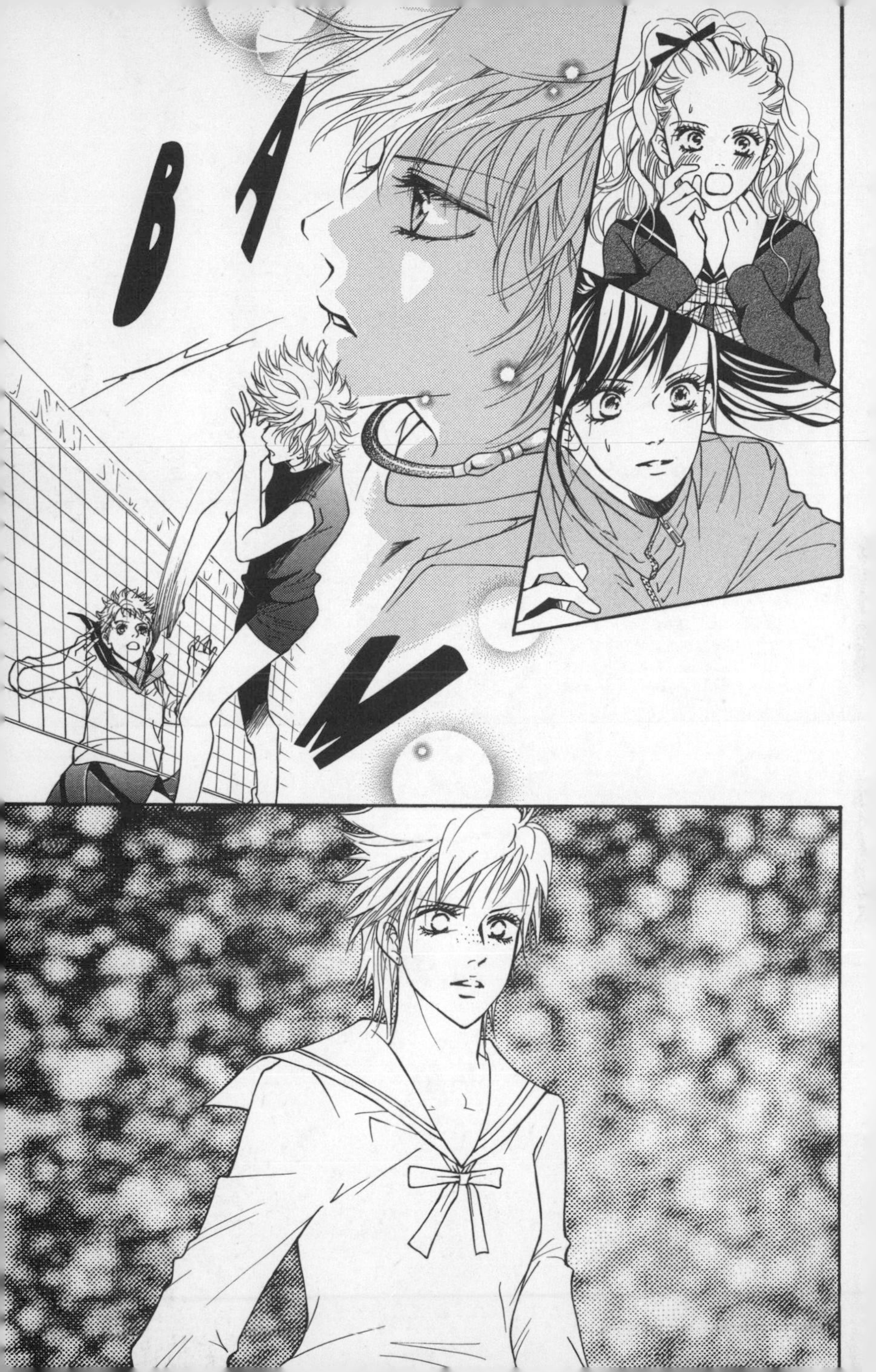
BAM

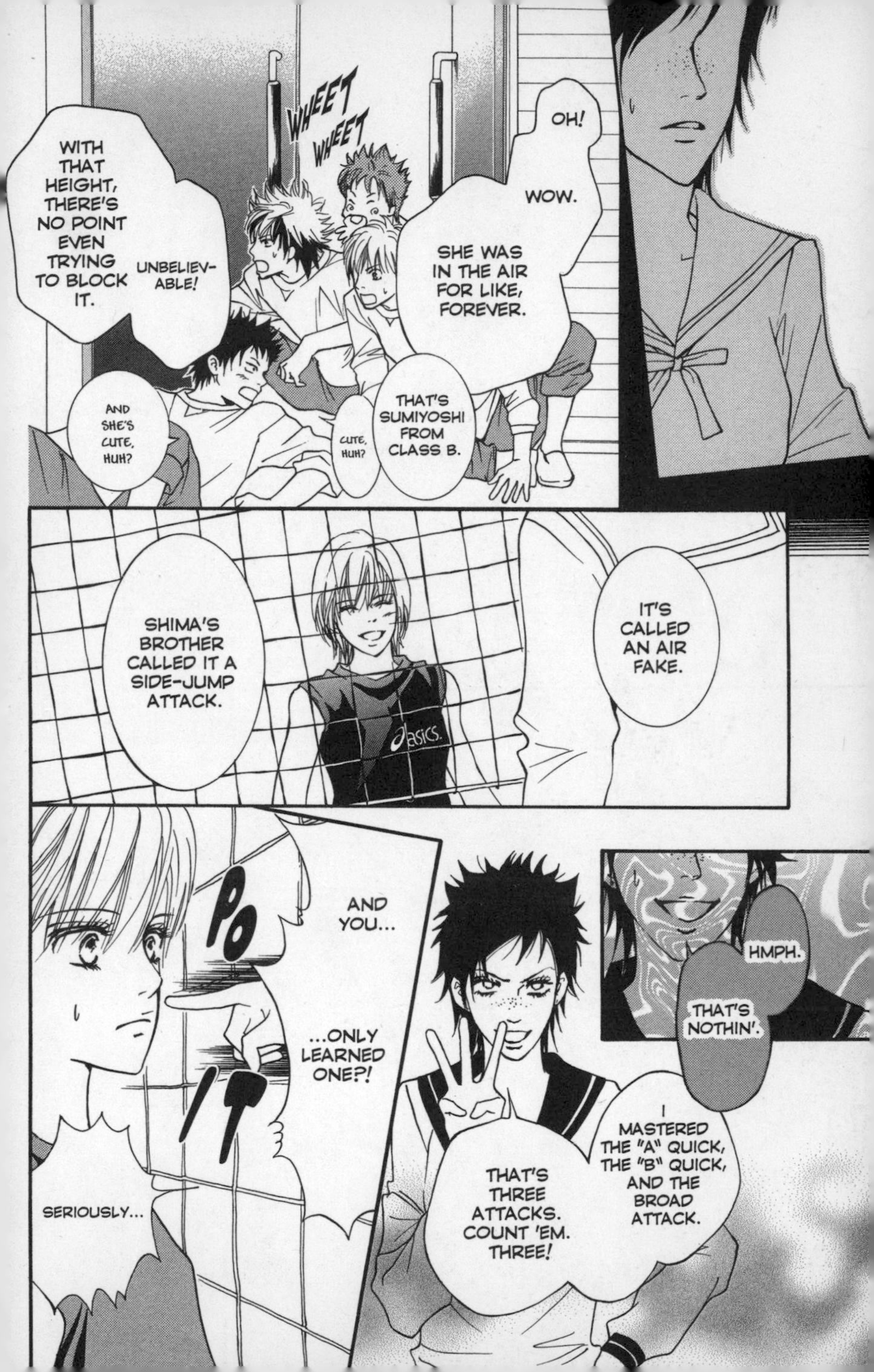
OH!
WOW.
SHE WAS IN THE AIR FOR LIKE, FOREVER.
WHEET WHEET
WITH THAT HEIGHT, THERE'S NO POINT EVEN TRYING TO BLOCK IT.
UNBELIEV-ABLE!
THAT'S SUMIYOSHI FROM CLASS B.
CUTE, HUH?
AND SHE'S CUTE, HUH?
IT'S CALLED AN AIR FAKE.
SHIMA'S BROTHER CALLED IT A SIDE-JUMP ATTACK.
HMPH.
THAT'S NOTHIN'.
I MASTERED THE "A" QUICK, THE "B" QUICK, AND THE BROAD ATTACK.
THAT'S THREE ATTACKS. COUNT 'EM. THREE!
AND YOU...
...ONLY LEARNED ONE?!
POIT
SERIOUSLY...

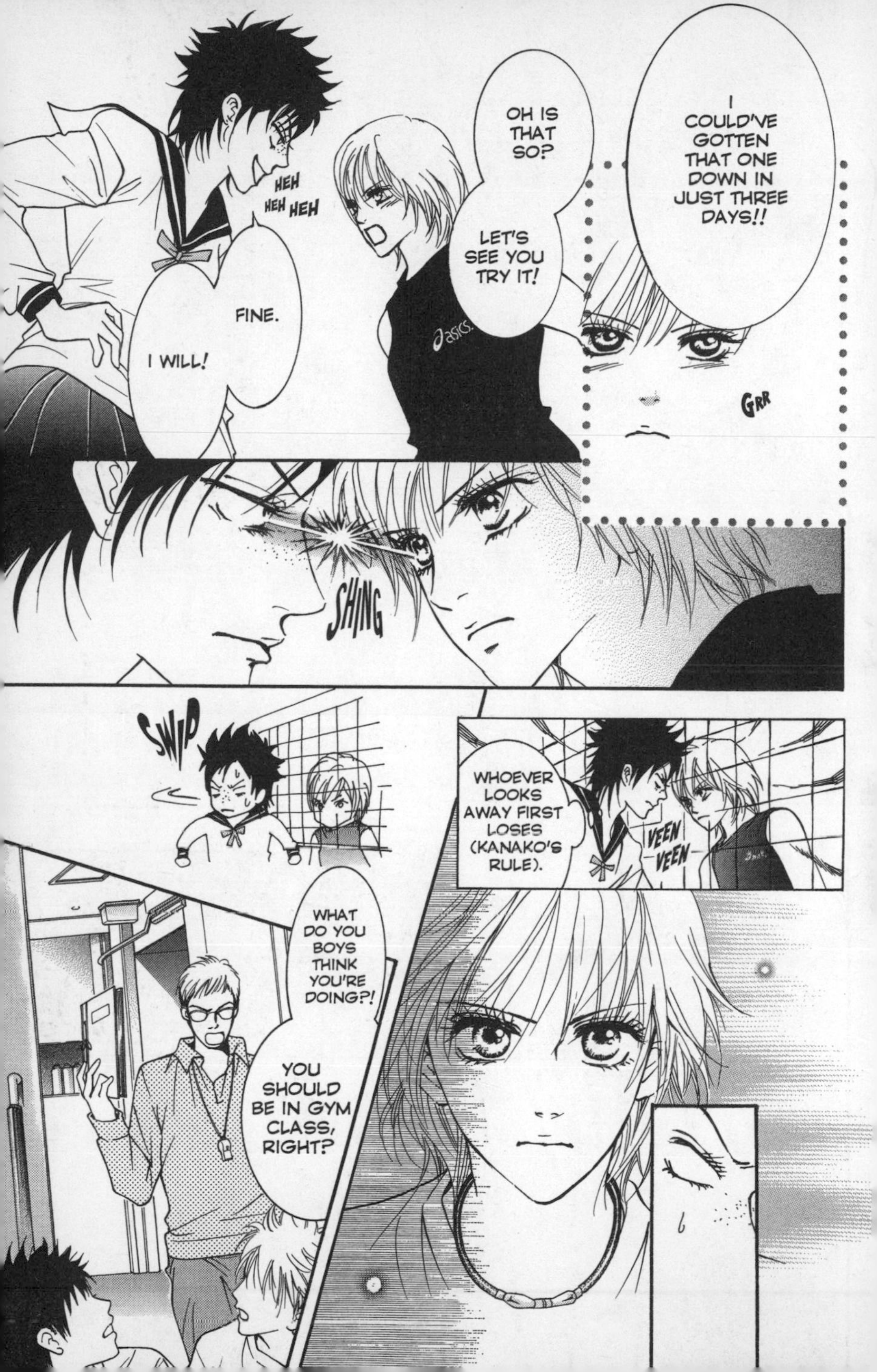
I COULD'VE GOTTEN THAT ONE DOWN IN JUST THREE DAYS!!
GRR
OH IS THAT SO?
LET'S SEE YOU TRY IT!
HEH HEH HEH
FINE.
I WILL!
SHING
WHOEVER LOOKS AWAY FIRST LOSES (KANAKO'S RULE).
VEEN VEEN
SWIP
WHAT DO YOU BOYS THINK YOU'RE DOING?!
YOU SHOULD BE IN GYM CLASS, RIGHT?

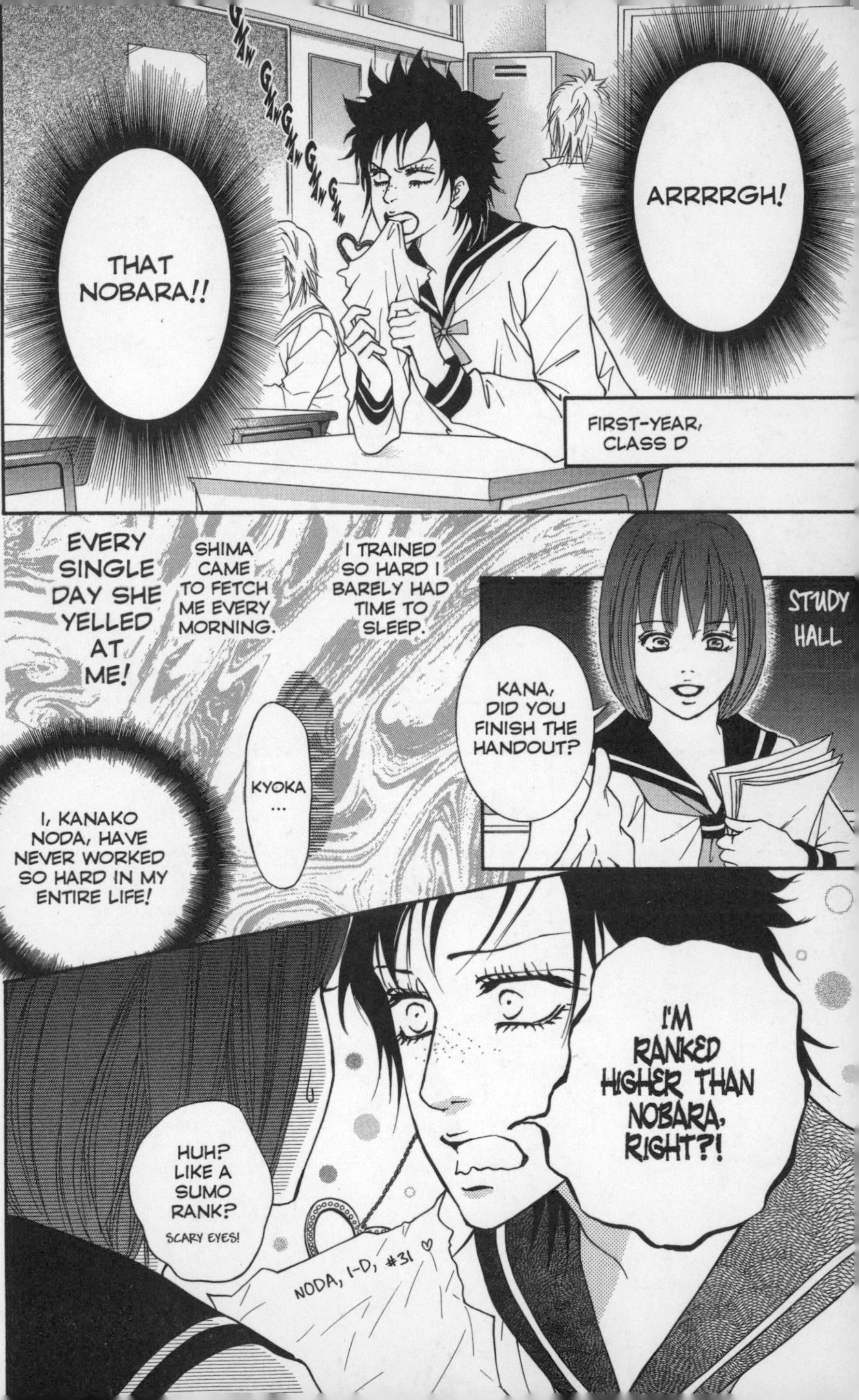
ARRRRGH!
FIRST-YEAR, CLASS D
THAT NOBARA!!
STUDY HALL
KANA, DID YOU FINISH THE HANDOUT?
I TRAINED SO HARD I BARELY HAD TIME TO SLEEP.
SHIMA CAME TO FETCH ME EVERY MORNING.
EVERY SINGLE DAY SHE YELLED AT ME!
KYOKA ...
I, KANAKO NODA, HAVE NEVER WORKED SO HARD IN MY ENTIRE LIFE!
I'M RANKED HIGHER THAN NOBARA, RIGHT?!
HUH? LIKE A SUMO RANK?
SCARY EYES!
NODA, 1-D, #31

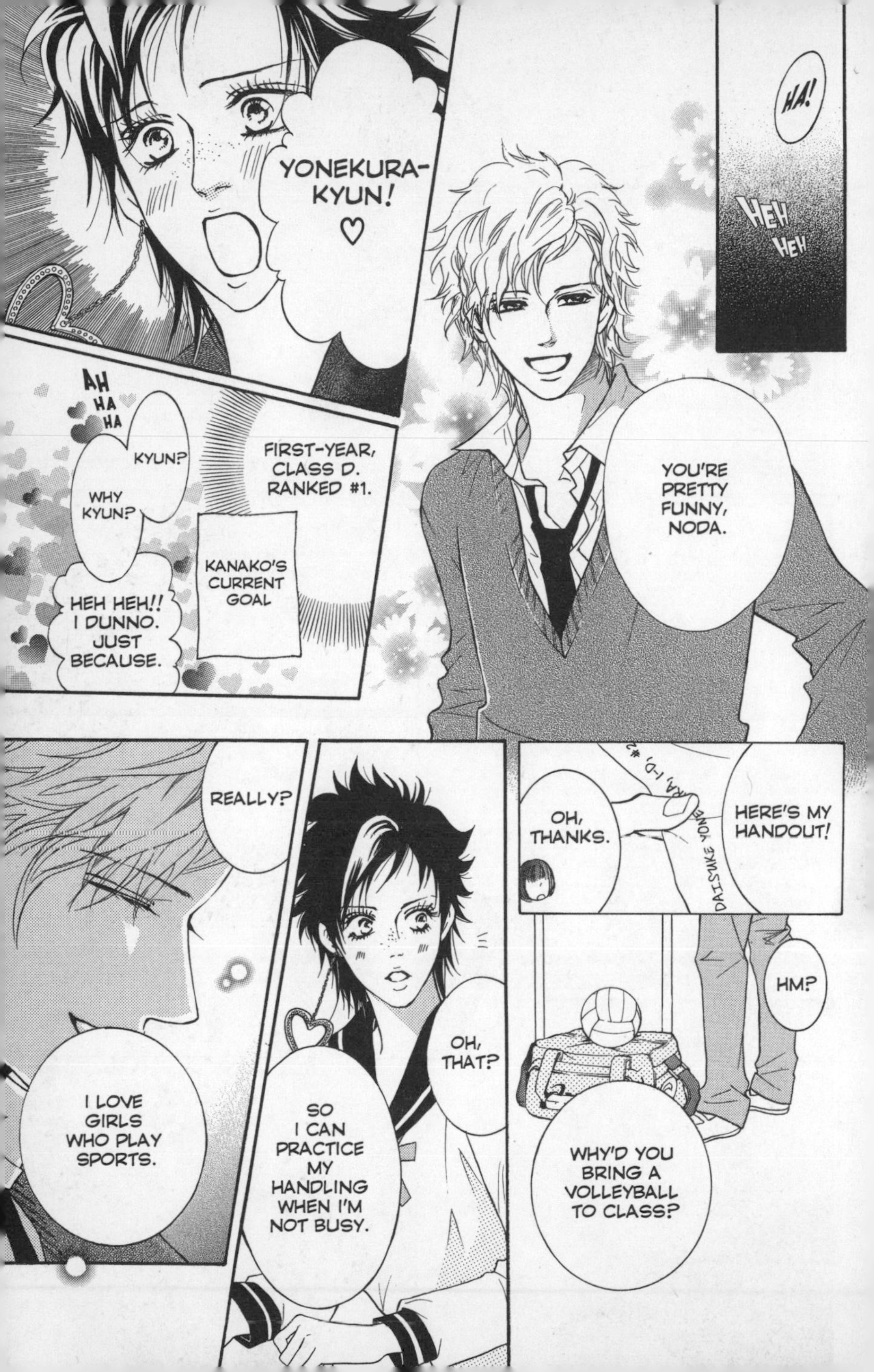
HA!
HEH HEH
YOU'RE PRETTY FUNNY, NODA.
YONEKURA-KYUN! ♡
AH HA HA
KYUN? WHY KYUN?
HEH HEH!! I DUNNO. JUST BECAUSE.
FIRST-YEAR, CLASS D. RANKED #1.
KANAKO'S CURRENT GOAL
HERE'S MY HANDOUT!
DAISUKE YONE
RA, 1-D, #2
OH, THANKS.
HM?
WHY'D YOU BRING A VOLLEYBALL TO CLASS?
OH, THAT?
SO I CAN PRACTICE MY HANDLING WHEN I'M NOT BUSY.
REALLY?
I LOVE GIRLS WHO PLAY SPORTS.

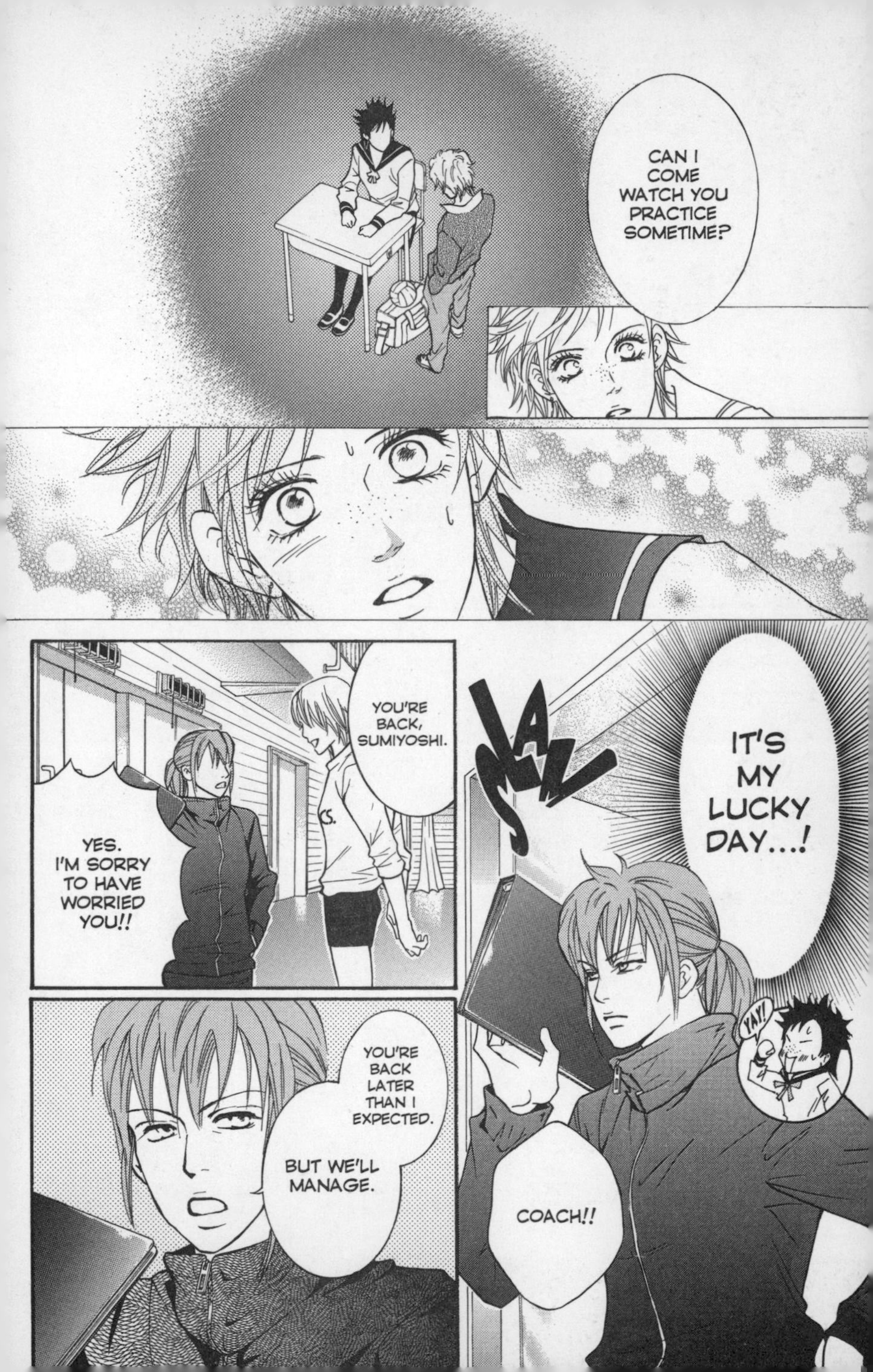
CAN I COME WATCH YOU PRACTICE SOMETIME?
SLAM
IT'S MY LUCKY DAY...!
YAY!
COACH!!
YOU'RE BACK, SUMIYOSHI.
YES. I'M SORRY TO HAVE WORRIED YOU!!
YOU'RE BACK LATER THAN I EXPECTED.
BUT WE'LL MANAGE.

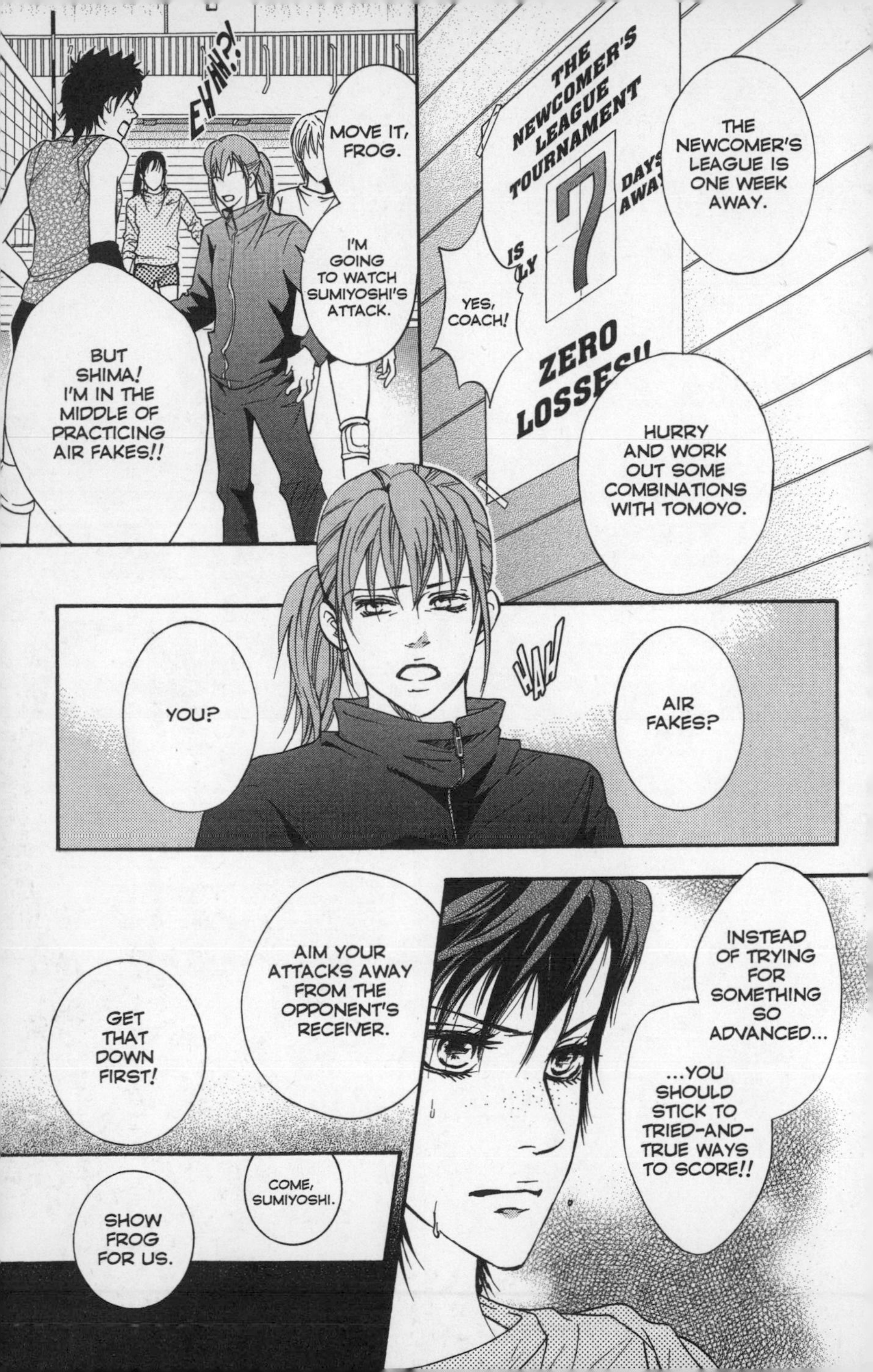

THE NEWCOMER'S LEAGUE TOURNAMENT
IS
LY
7
DAYS AWAY
ZERO
LOSSES
THE NEWCOMER'S LEAGUE IS ONE WEEK AWAY.
HURRY AND WORK OUT SOME COMBINATIONS WITH TOMOYO.
YES, COACH!
MOVE IT, FROG.
I'M GOING TO WATCH SUMIYOSHI'S ATTACK.
EHH?!
BUT SHIMA! I'M IN THE MIDDLE OF PRACTICING AIR FAKES!!
AIR FAKES?
YOU?
INSTEAD OF TRYING FOR SOMETHING SO ADVANCED...
...YOU SHOULD STICK TO TRIED-AND-TRUE WAYS TO SCORE!!
AIM YOUR ATTACKS AWAY FROM THE OPPONENT'S RECEIVER.
GET THAT DOWN FIRST!
COME, SUMIYOSHI.
SHOW FROG FOR US.

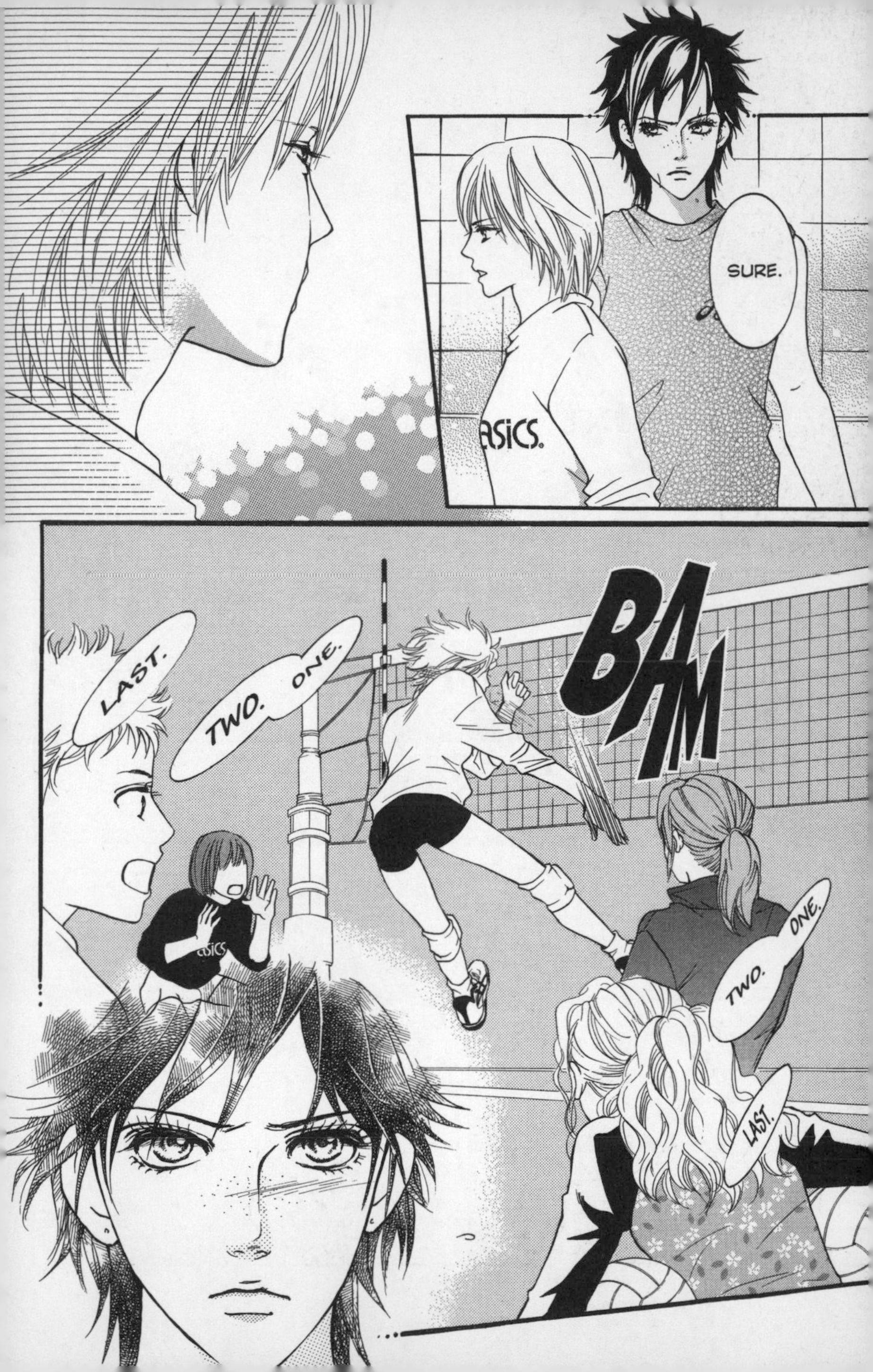
SURE.
ASICS.
BAM
TWO. ONE.
LAST.
TWO. ONE.
LAST.

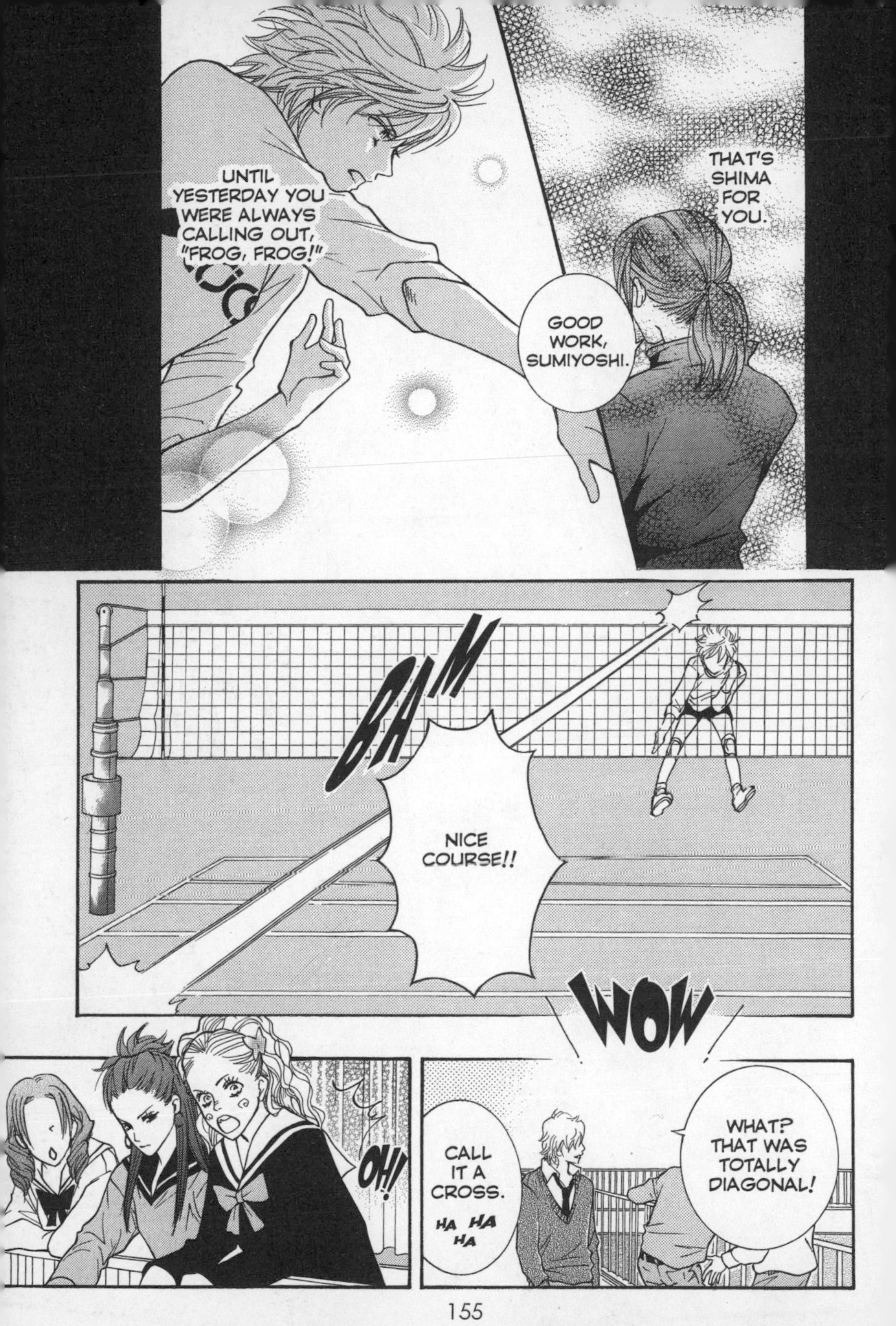
THAT'S SHIMA FOR YOU.
GOOD WORK, SUMIYOSHI.
UNTIL YESTERDAY YOU WERE ALWAYS CALLING OUT, "FROG, FROG!"
BAM
NICE COURSE!!
WOW
WHAT? THAT WAS TOTALLY DIAGONAL!
CALL IT A CROSS.
HA HA HA
OH!

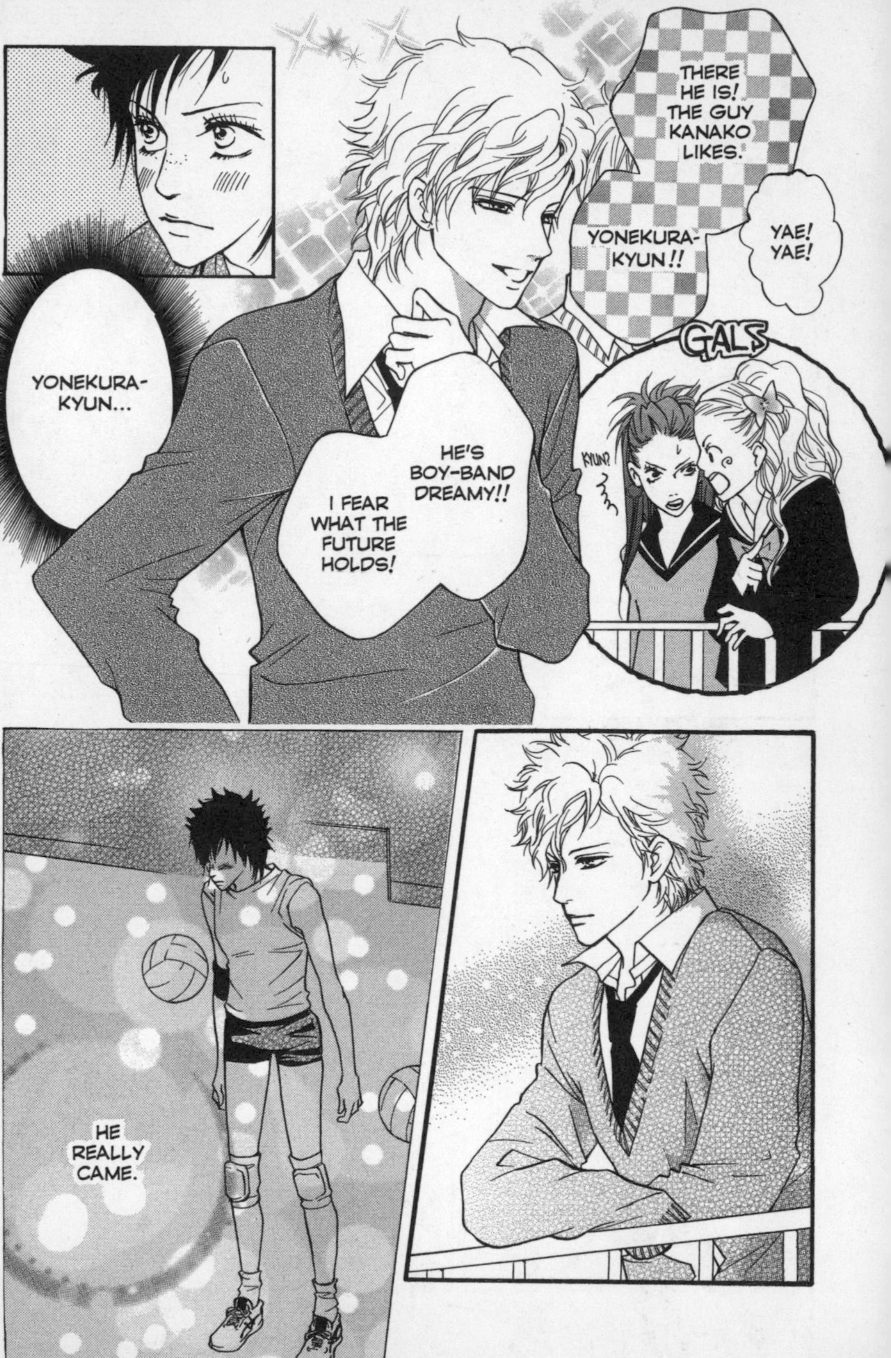
THERE HE IS! THE GUY KANAKO LIKES.
YAE! YAE!
YONEKURA-KYUN!!
GALS
KYUN?
HE'S BOY-BAND DREAMY!!
I FEAR WHAT THE FUTURE HOLDS!
YONEKURA-KYUN...
HE REALLY CAME.

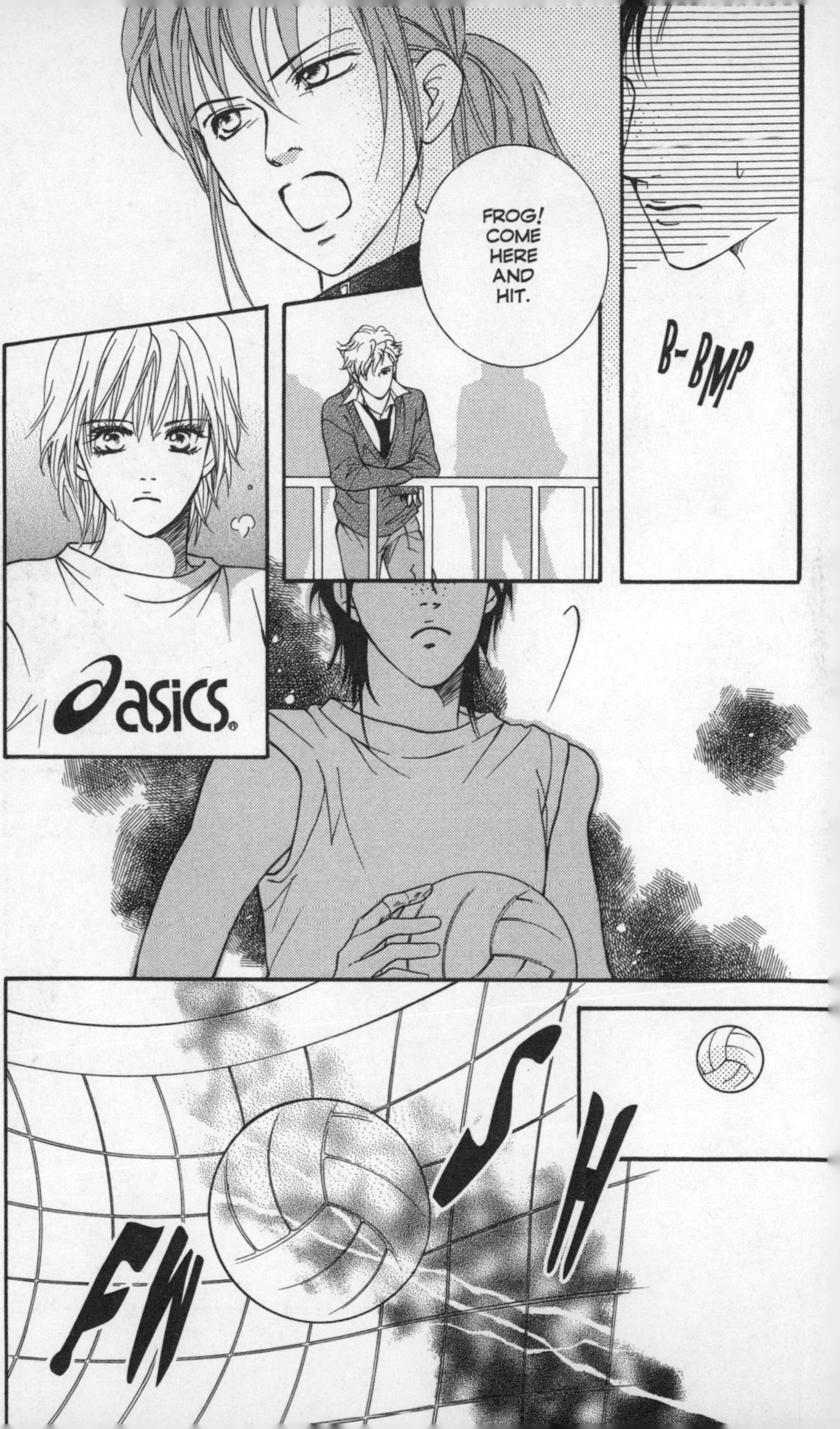
B-BMP
FROG! COME HERE AND HIT.
asics
FWSH

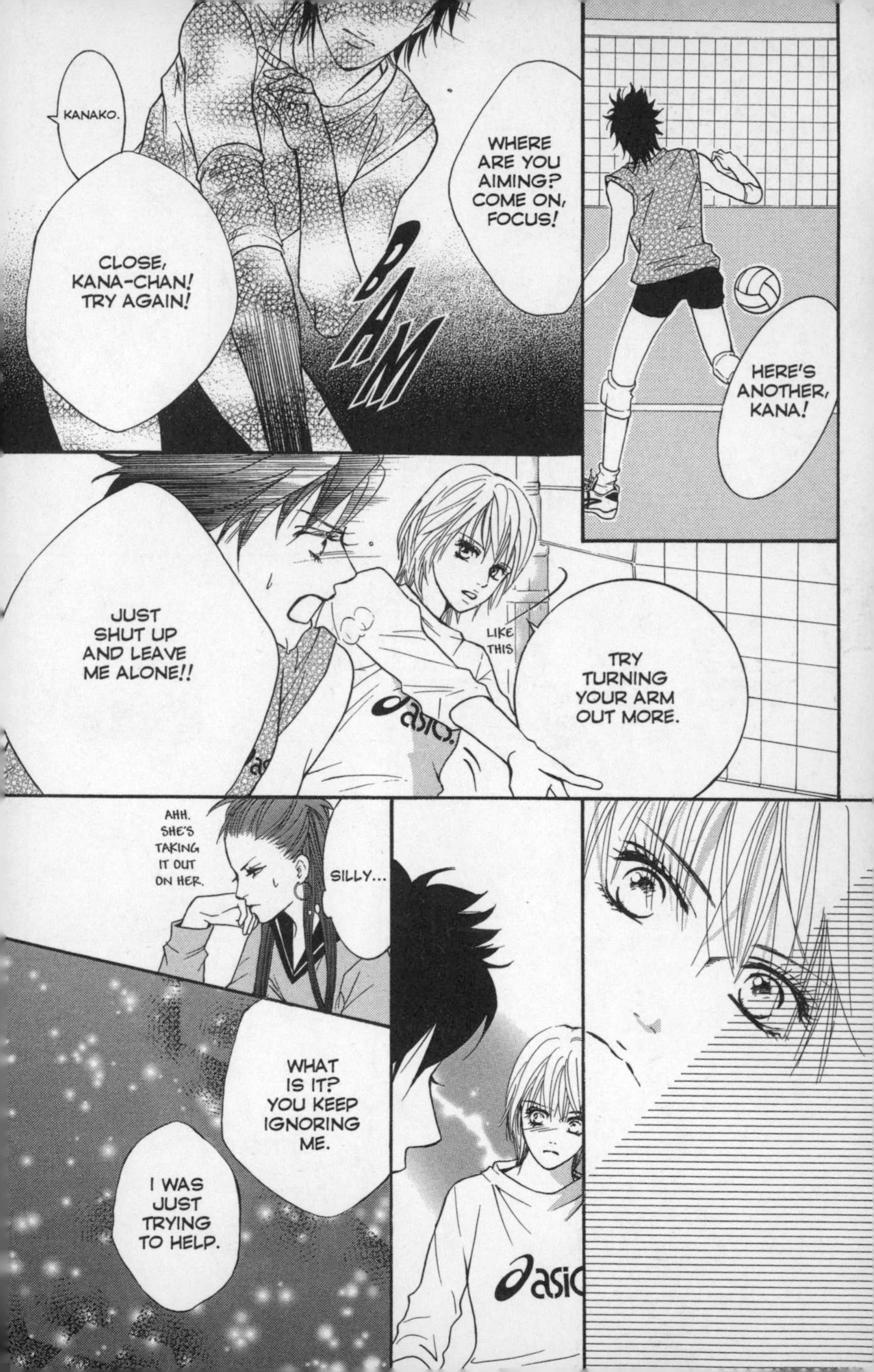
HERE'S ANOTHER, KANA!
WHERE ARE YOU AIMING? COME ON, FOCUS!
BAM
KANAKO.
CLOSE, KANA-CHAN! TRY AGAIN!
TRY TURNING YOUR ARM OUT MORE.
LIKE THIS
JUST SHUT UP AND LEAVE ME ALONE!!
SILLY...
AHH. SHE'S TAKING IT OUT ON HER.
WHAT IS IT? YOU KEEP IGNORING ME.
I WAS JUST TRYING TO HELP.

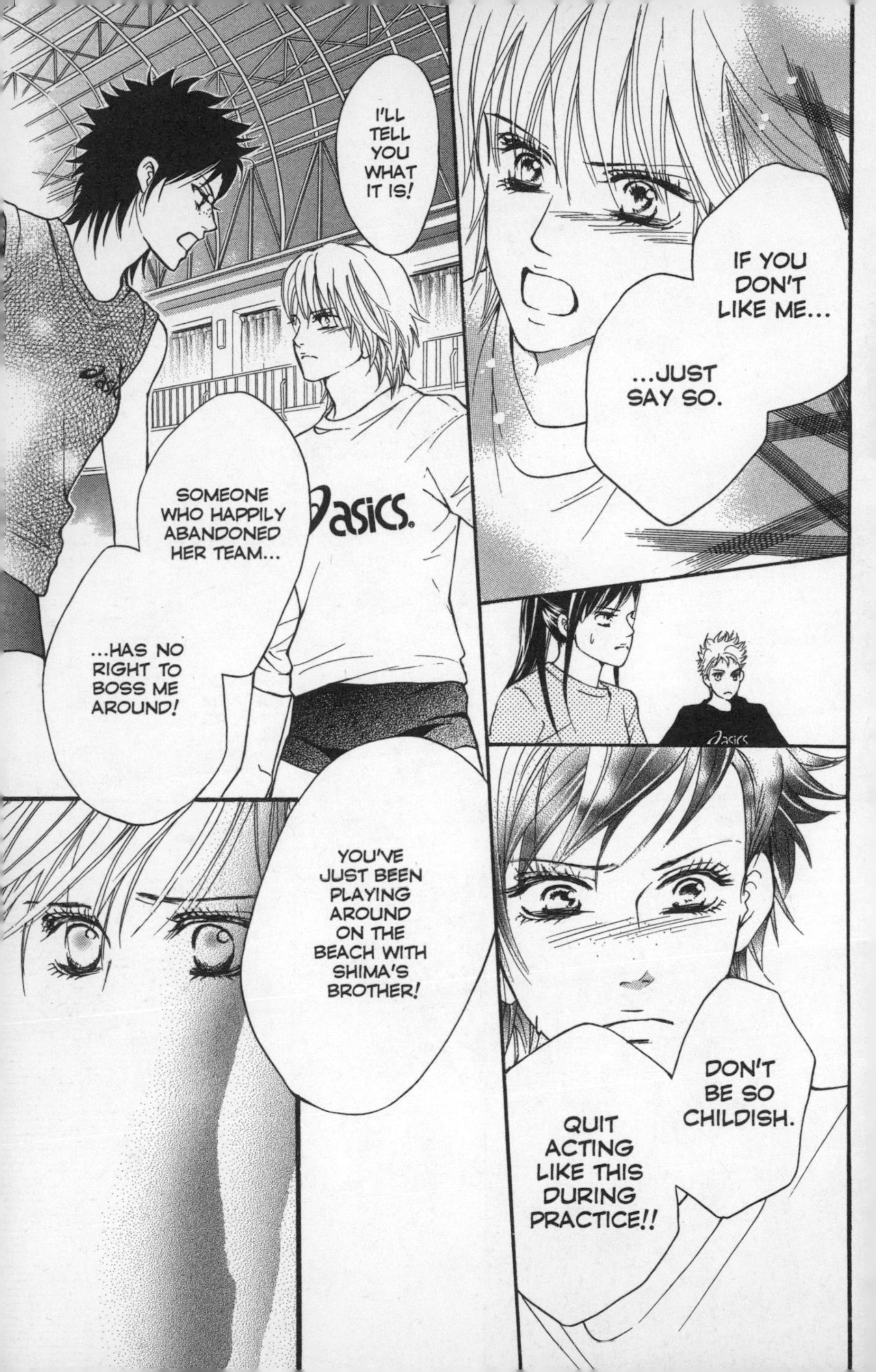
IF YOU DON'T LIKE ME...
...JUST SAY SO.
I'LL TELL YOU WHAT IT IS!
SOMEONE WHO HAPPILY ABANDONED HER TEAM...
...HAS NO RIGHT TO BOSS ME AROUND!
DON'T BE SO CHILDISH.
QUIT ACTING LIKE THIS DURING PRACTICE!!
YOU'VE JUST BEEN PLAYING AROUND ON THE BEACH WITH SHIMA'S BROTHER!

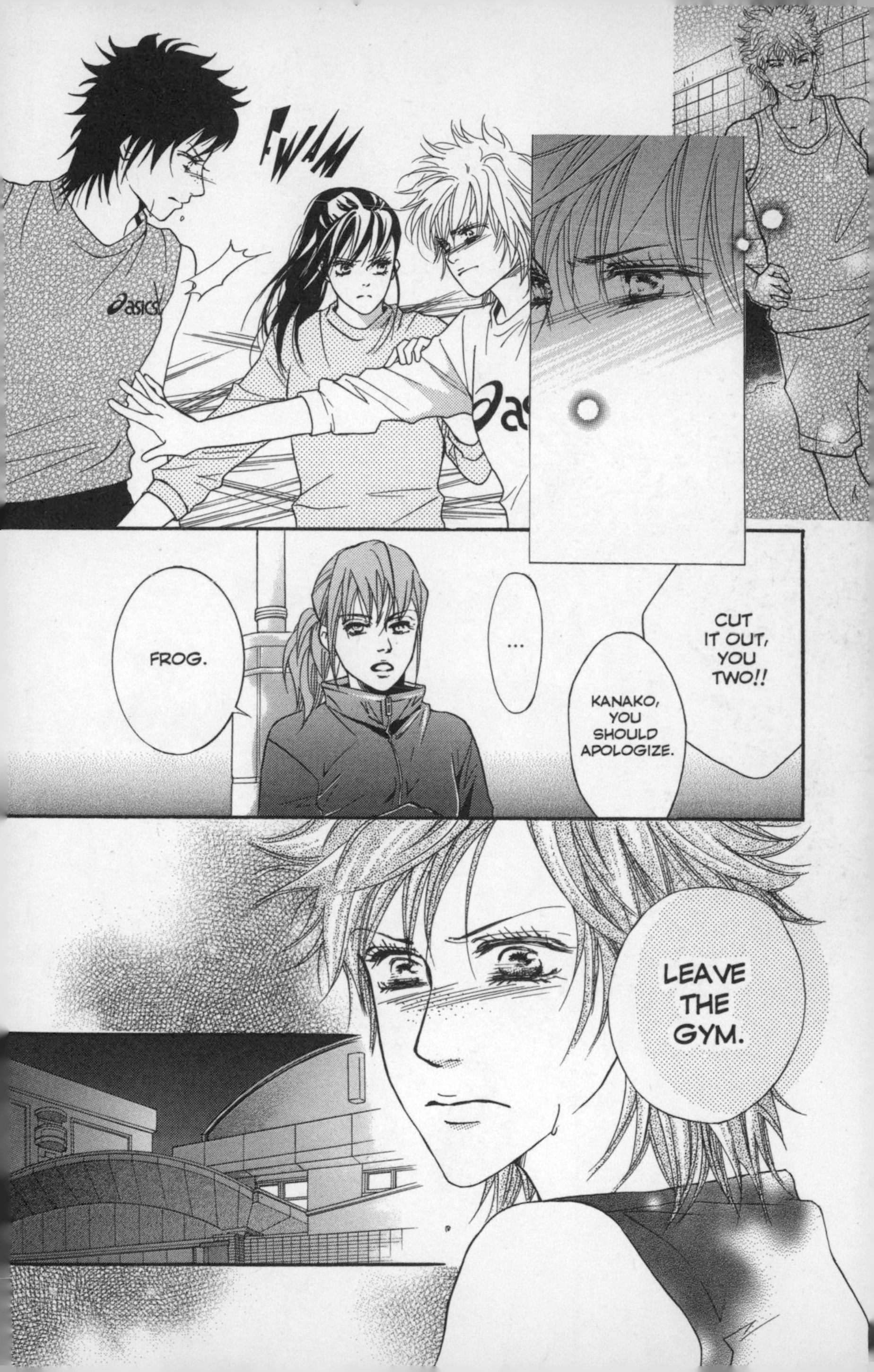
FWAM
CUT IT OUT, YOU TWO!!
KANAKO, YOU SHOULD APOLOGIZE.
...
FROG.
LEAVE THE GYM.

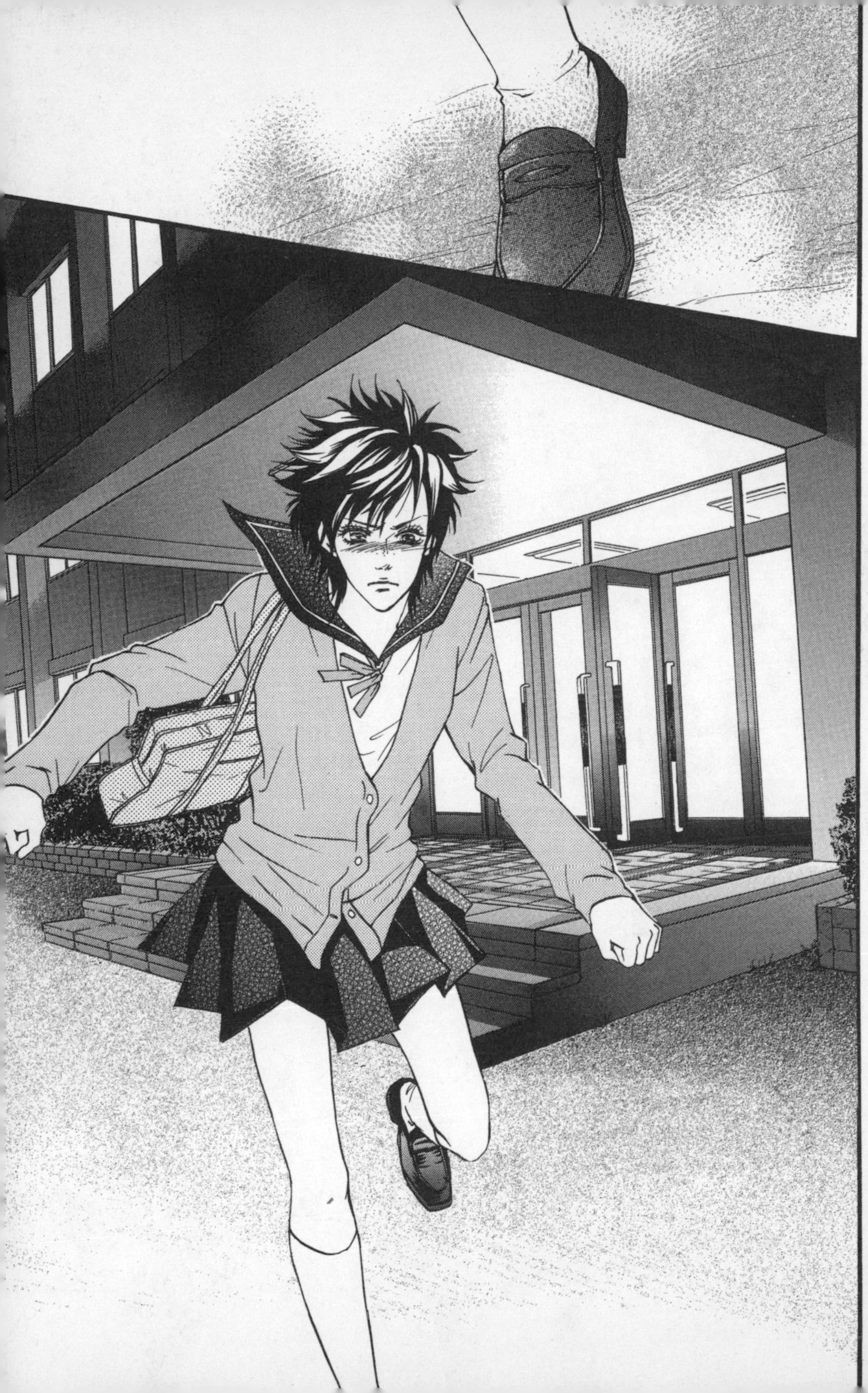

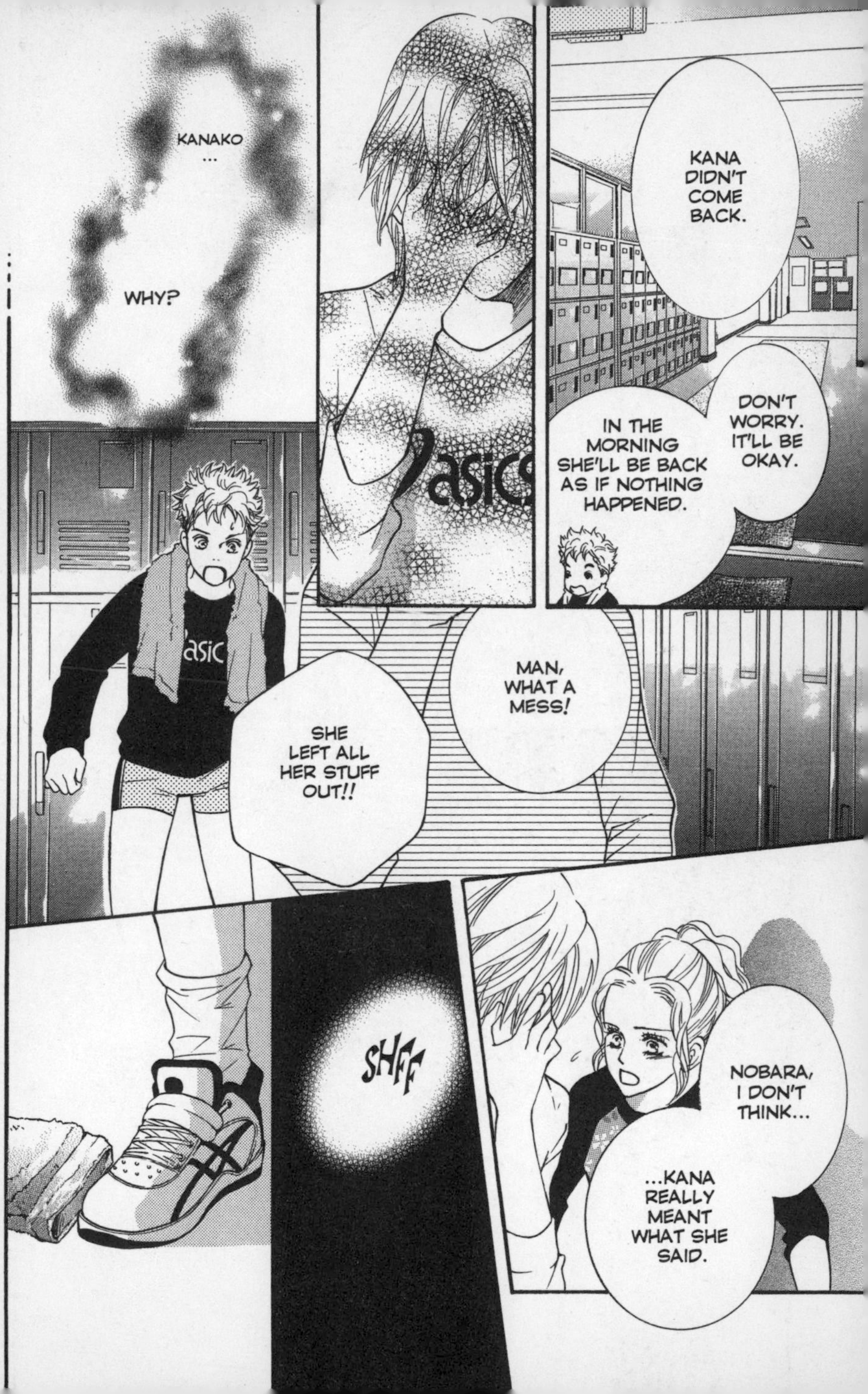
KANA DIDN'T COME BACK.
DON'T WORRY. IT'LL BE OKAY.
IN THE MORNING SHE'LL BE BACK AS IF NOTHING HAPPENED.
KANAKO ...
WHY?
MAN, WHAT A MESS!
SHE LEFT ALL HER STUFF OUT!!
NOBARA, I DON'T THINK...
...KANA REALLY MEANT WHAT SHE SAID.
SHFF

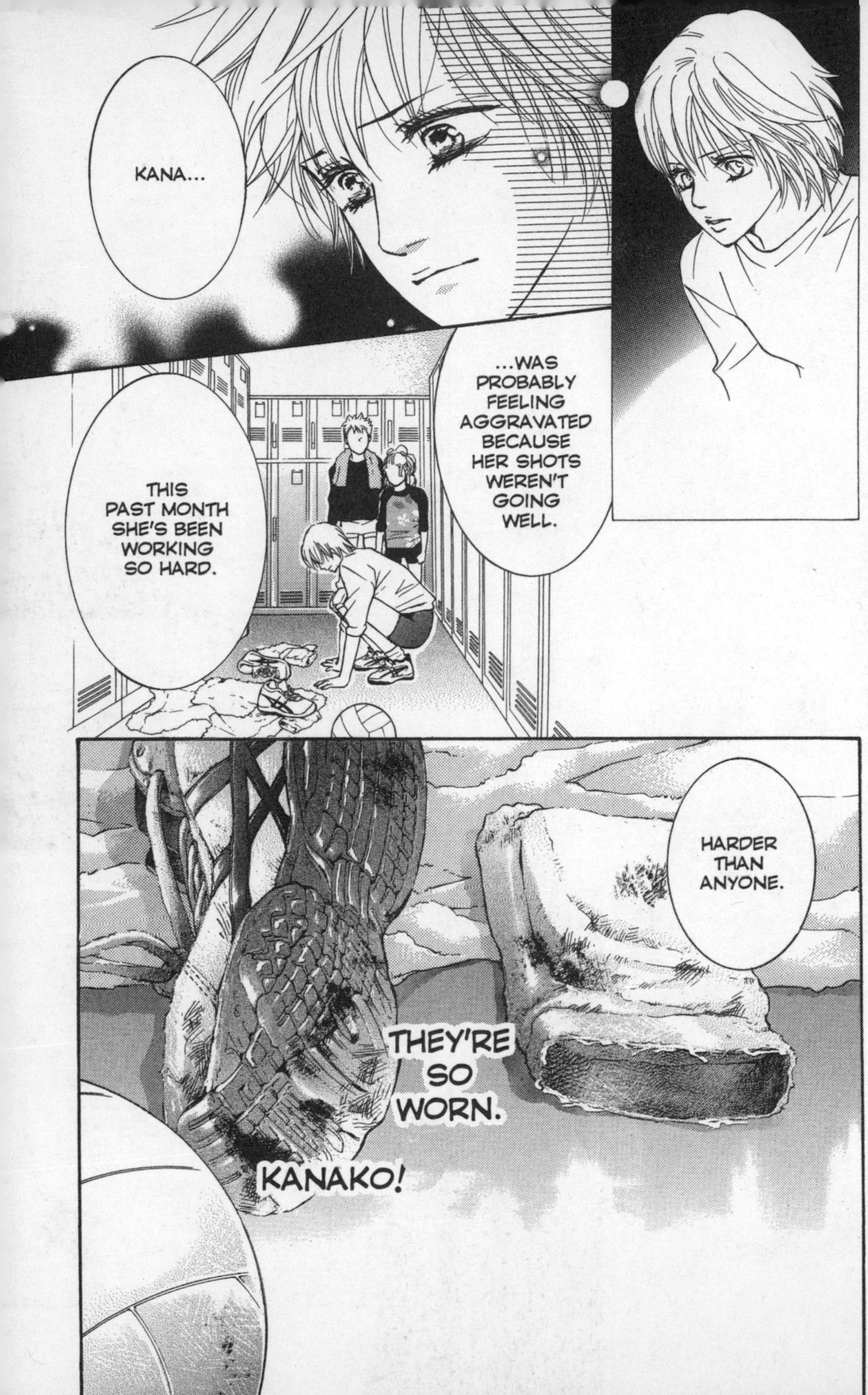
KANA...
...WAS PROBABLY FEELING AGGRAVATED BECAUSE HER SHOTS WEREN'T GOING WELL.
THIS PAST MONTH SHE'S BEEN WORKING SO HARD.
HARDER THAN ANYONE.
THEY'RE SO WORN.
KANAKO!

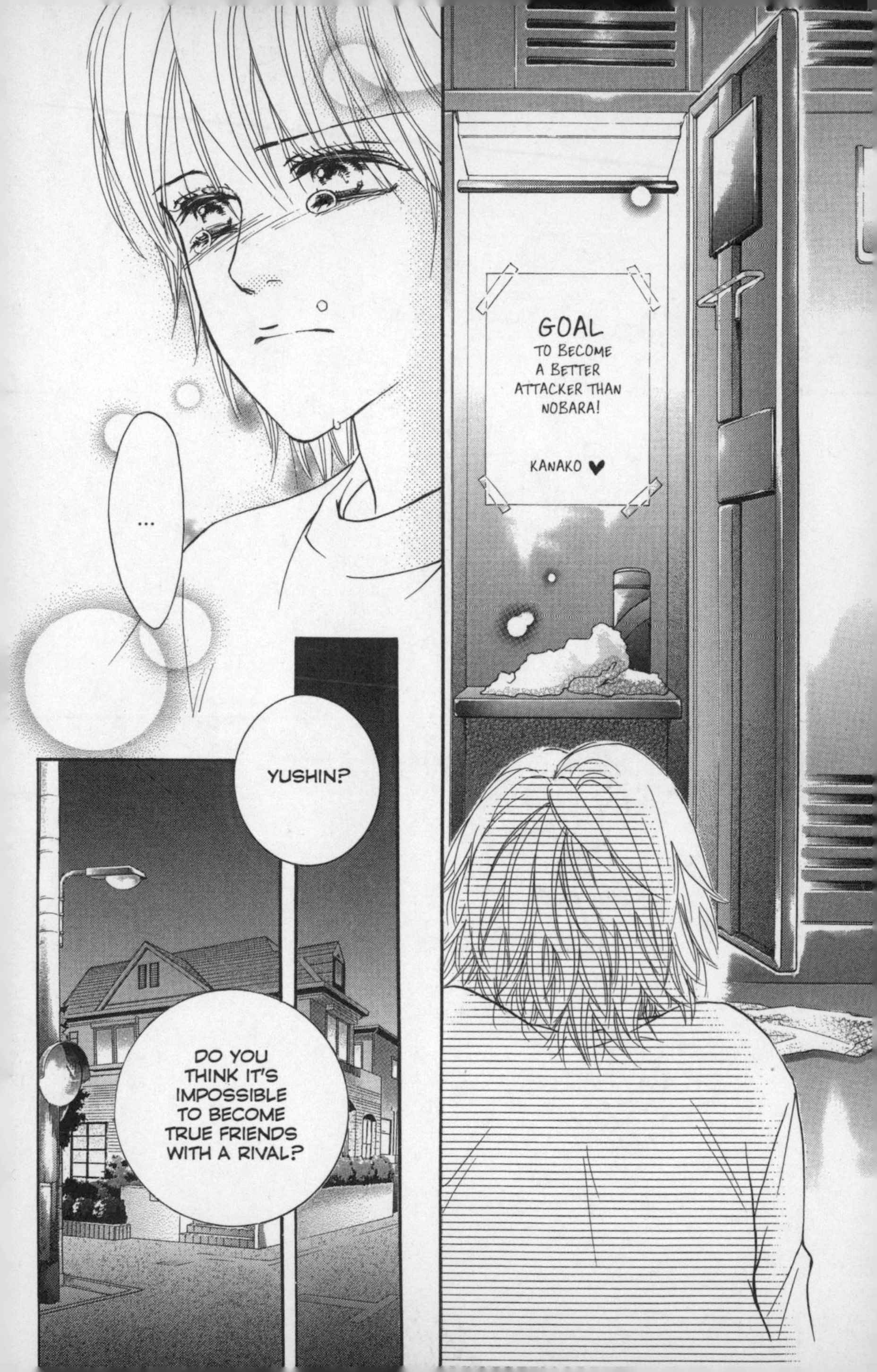
GOAL
TO BECOME A BETTER ATTACKER THAN NOBARA!
KANAKO ♥
...
YUSHIN?
DO YOU THINK IT'S IMPOSSIBLE TO BECOME TRUE FRIENDS WITH A RIVAL?

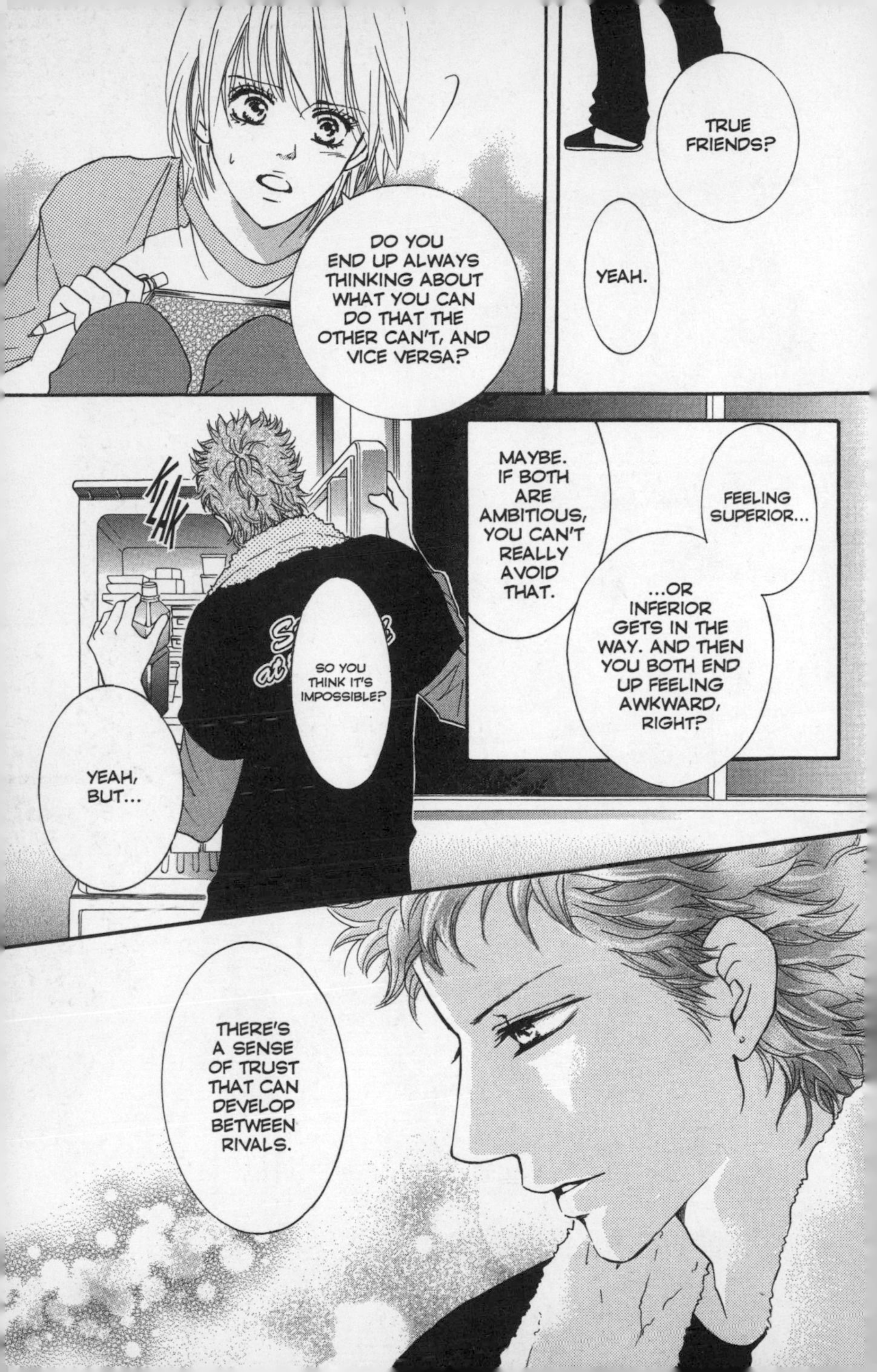
TRUE FRIENDS?
YEAH.
DO YOU END UP ALWAYS THINKING ABOUT WHAT YOU CAN DO THAT THE OTHER CAN'T, AND VICE VERSA?
MAYBE. IF BOTH ARE AMBITIOUS, YOU CAN'T REALLY AVOID THAT.
FEELING SUPERIOR...
...OR INFERIOR GETS IN THE WAY. AND THEN YOU BOTH END UP FEELING AWKWARD, RIGHT?
KLAK
SO YOU THINK IT'S IMPOSSIBLE?
YEAH, BUT...
THERE'S A SENSE OF TRUST THAT CAN DEVELOP BETWEEN RIVALS.

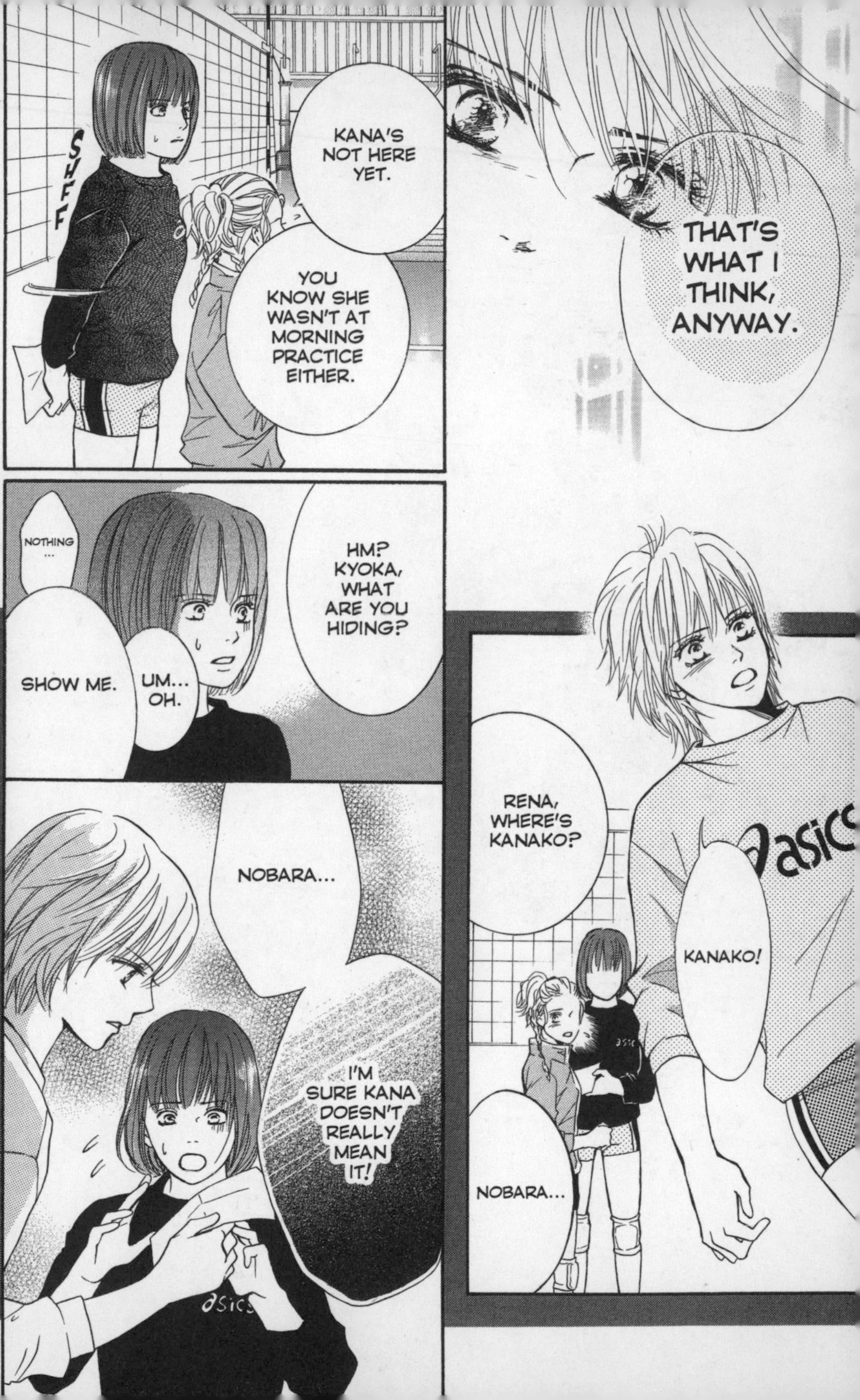
THAT'S WHAT I THINK, ANYWAY.
KANA'S NOT HERE YET.
YOU KNOW SHE WASN'T AT MORNING PRACTICE EITHER.
SHFF
RENA, WHERE'S KANAKO?
KANAKO!
NOBARA...
HM? KYOKA, WHAT ARE YOU HIDING?
UM... OH.
NOTHING...
SHOW ME.
NOBARA...
I'M SURE KANA DOESN'T REALLY MEAN IT!

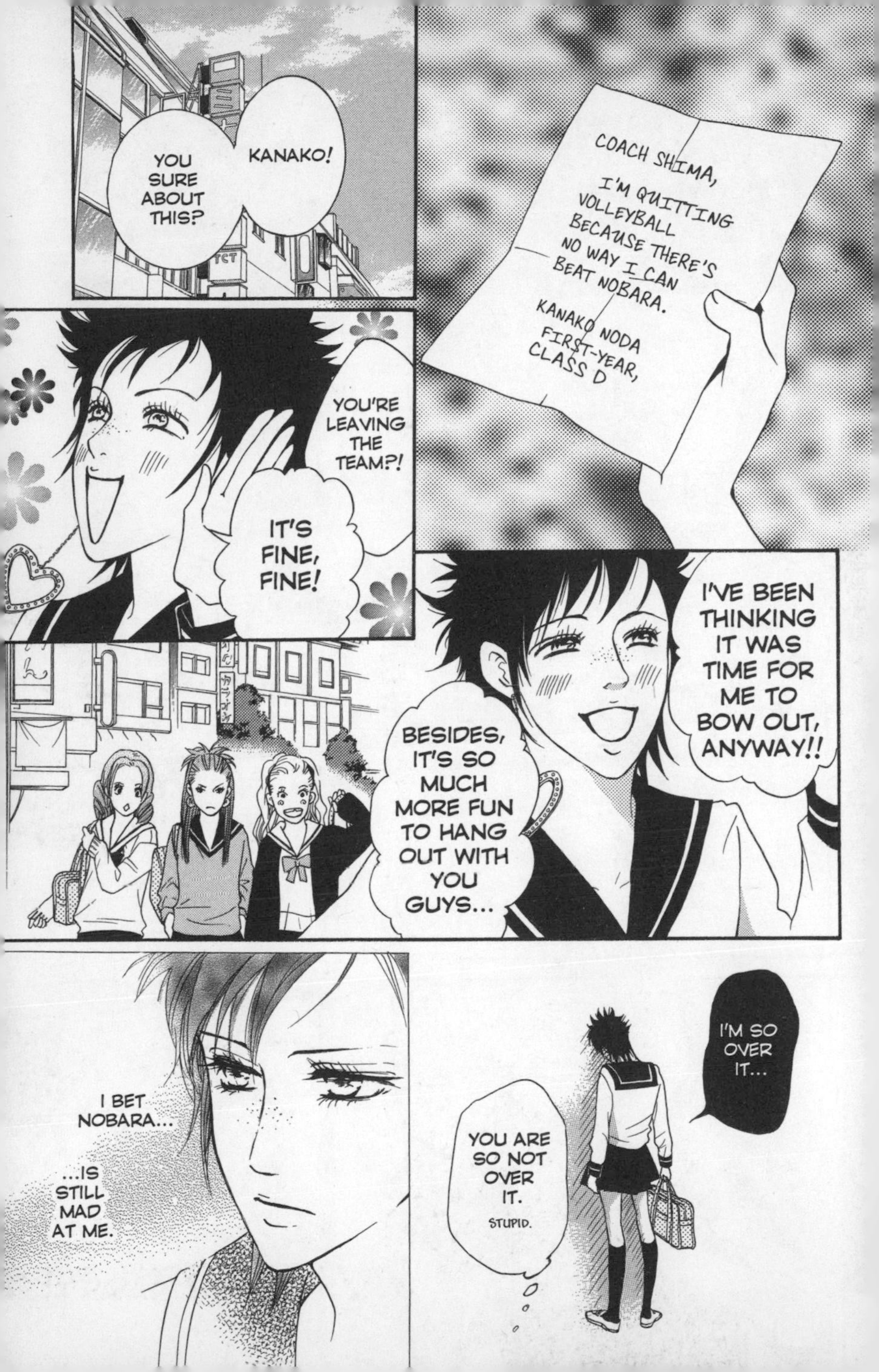
COACH SHIMA,
I'M QUITTING VOLLEYBALL BECAUSE THERE'S NO WAY I CAN BEAT NOBARA.
KANAKO NODA
FIRST-YEAR, CLASS D
KANAKO!
YOU SURE ABOUT THIS?
YOU'RE LEAVING THE TEAM?!
IT'S FINE, FINE!
I'VE BEEN THINKING IT WAS TIME FOR ME TO BOW OUT, ANYWAY!!
BESIDES, IT'S SO MUCH MORE FUN TO HANG OUT WITH YOU GUYS...
I'M SO OVER IT...
YOU ARE SO NOT OVER IT.
STUPID.
I BET NOBARA...
...IS STILL MAD AT ME.

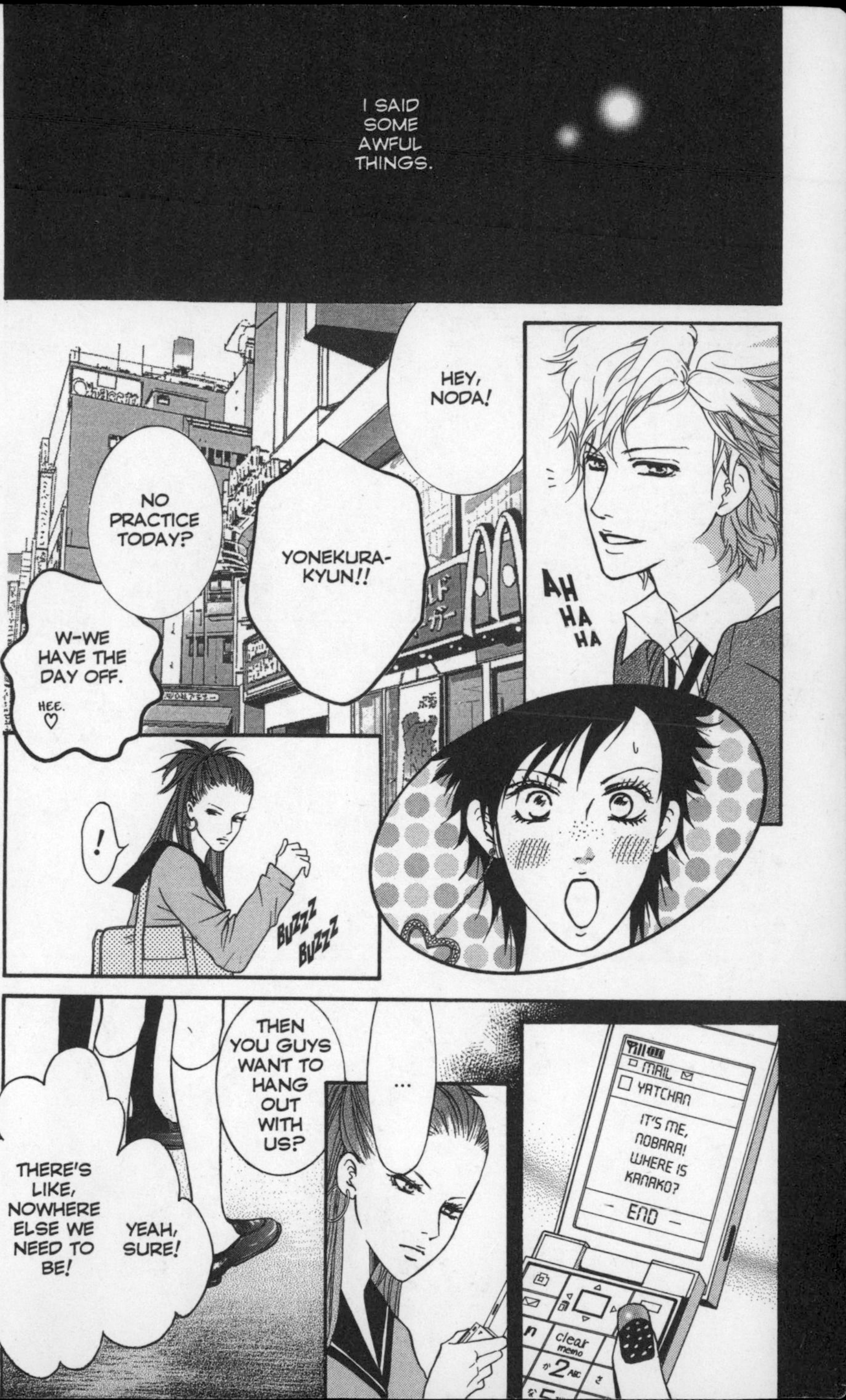
I SAID SOME AWFUL THINGS.
HEY, NODA!
AH HA HA
YONEKURA-KYUN!!
NO PRACTICE TODAY?
W-WE HAVE THE DAY OFF.
HEE. ♡
!
BUZZZ BUZZZ
MAIL
YATCHAN
IT'S ME, NOBARA! WHERE IS KANAKO?
- END -
...
THEN YOU GUYS WANT TO HANG OUT WITH US?
YEAH, SURE!
THERE'S LIKE, NOWHERE ELSE WE NEED TO BE!

MITSUBA CLUB

VoL.4

WELL, IT'S ABOUT TIME TO SAY FAREWELL AGAIN. THIS TIME I KEPT WRITING ABOUT IRRELEVANT THINGS. SORRY. I'LL WRITE MORE NEXT TIME. BIG THANKS TO ALL OF YOU WHO WROTE LETTERS. I READ THEM ALL. I LOVE YOU ALL. I'M SORRY I CAN'T ANSWER THEM. JUST KNOW THAT I DO READ EVERY ONE. AND THANKS TO THOSE OF YOU WHO EMAILED ME ON MY BIRTHDAY. YOU EVEN WORRY ABOUT MY HEALTH. I'M DOING WELL, THANKS. I'LL STILL KEEP DRAWING MANGA. LOTS OF MANGA. RECENTLY I'VE GOTTEN TOTALLY HOOKED ON SUPER SENTO BATHS. I OFTEN GO TO ONE WHERE YOU LIE DOWN ON TOP OF ROCKS. IT'S LIKE NAKED HEAVEN. ALL OF A SUDDEN I NOTICE THAT I'VE BEEN SLEEPING FOR HALF AN HOUR, NAKED. (OBVIOUSLY.) OOOH, BUT I STILL LONG TO GO TO A REAL HOT SPRING.

A KAPPA! A KAPPA!

SO, EVERYONE, PLEASE BE KIND TO ME AND WRITE LETTERS. THEY ARE MY SOURCE OF ENERGY. AND TELL ME WHAT'S BEEN HAPPENING AT YOUR SCHOOL TOO.

— ADDRESS LETTERS TO: —

CRIMSON HERO EDITOR
VIZ MEDIA LLC
P.O. BOX 77010
SAN FRANCISCO, CA 94107

OH YEAH! *THE DEVIL MAY EXIST* IS NOW GOING TO BE AIRED IN JAPAN!

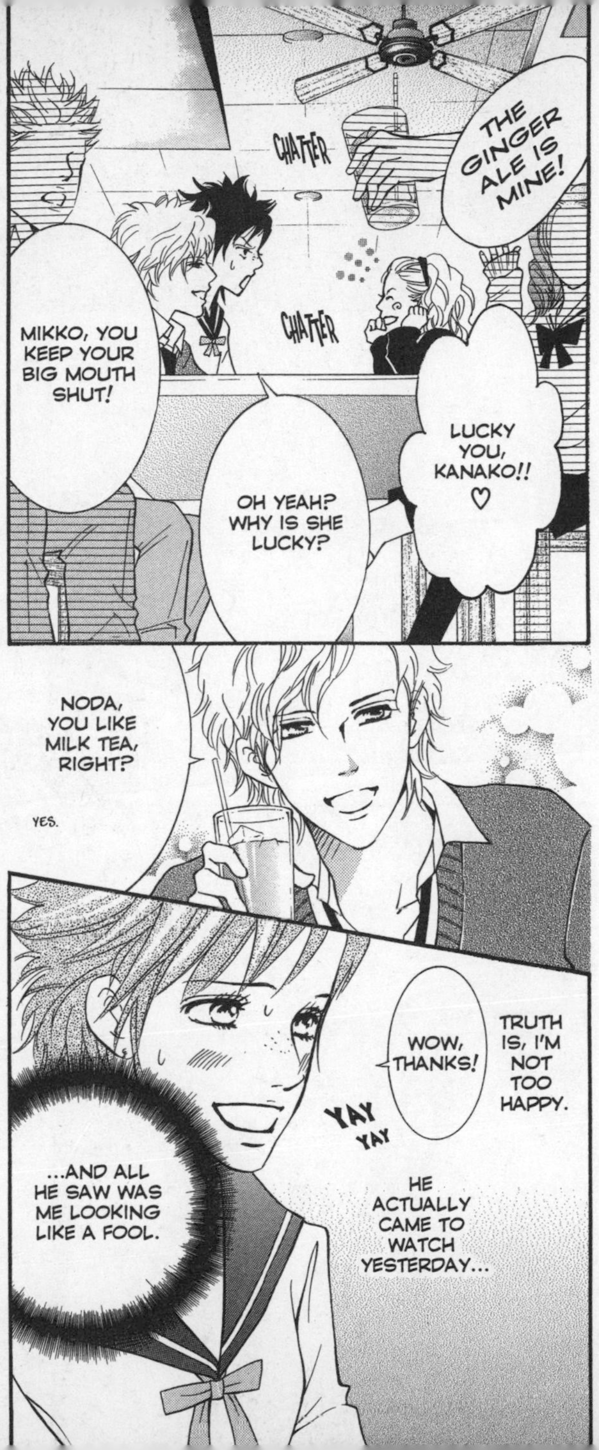
THE GINGER ALE IS MINE!
CHATTER
CHATTER
LUCKY YOU, KANAKO!! ♡
OH YEAH? WHY IS SHE LUCKY?
MIKKO, YOU KEEP YOUR BIG MOUTH SHUT!
NODA, YOU LIKE MILK TEA, RIGHT?
YES.
TRUTH IS, I'M NOT TOO HAPPY.
WOW, THANKS!
YAY YAY
HE ACTUALLY CAME TO WATCH YESTERDAY...
...AND ALL HE SAW WAS ME LOOKING LIKE A FOOL.

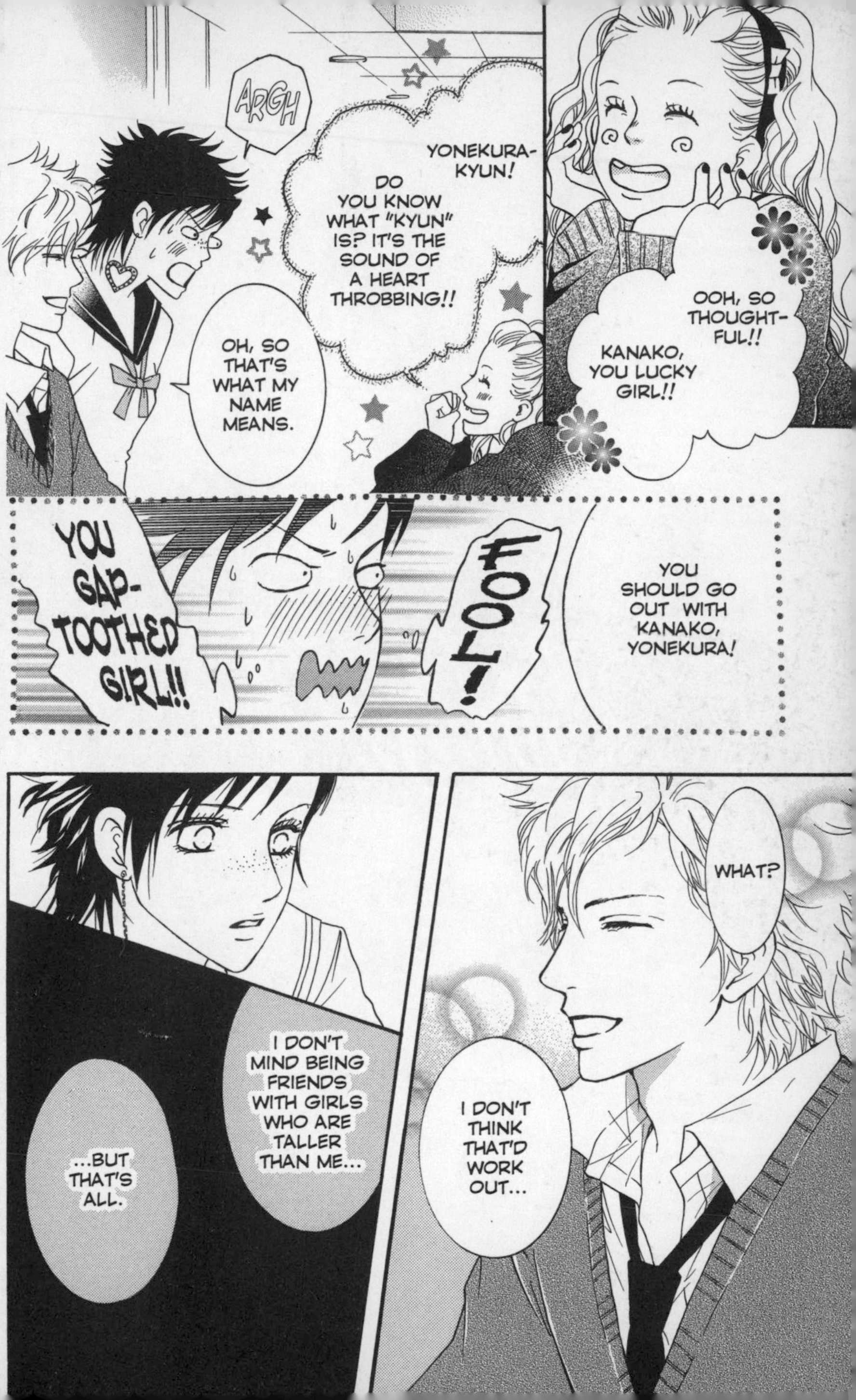
OOH, SO THOUGHTFUL!!
KANAKO, YOU LUCKY GIRL!!
YONEKURA-KYUN!
DO YOU KNOW WHAT "KYUN" IS? IT'S THE SOUND OF A HEART THROBBING!!
ARGH
OH, SO THAT'S WHAT MY NAME MEANS.
YOU SHOULD GO OUT WITH KANAKO, YONEKURA!
FOOL!
YOU GAP-TOOTHED GIRL!!
WHAT?
I DON'T THINK THAT'D WORK OUT...
I DON'T MIND BEING FRIENDS WITH GIRLS WHO ARE TALLER THAN ME...
...BUT THAT'S ALL.

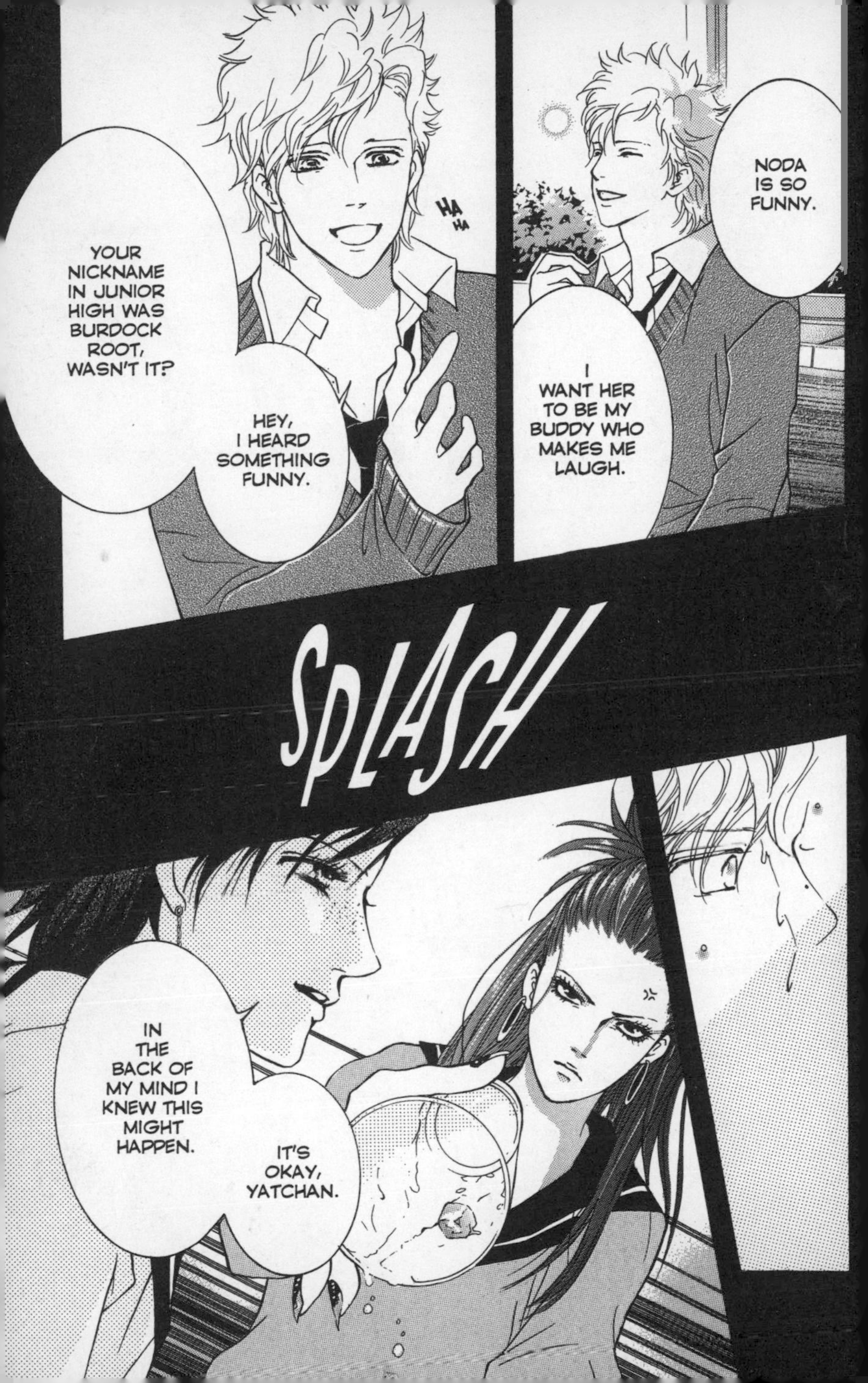
NODA IS SO FUNNY.
I WANT HER TO BE MY BUDDY WHO MAKES ME LAUGH.
HA HA
HEY, I HEARD SOMETHING FUNNY.
YOUR NICKNAME IN JUNIOR HIGH WAS BURDOCK ROOT, WASN'T IT?
SPLASH
IN THE BACK OF MY MIND I KNEW THIS MIGHT HAPPEN.
IT'S OKAY, YATCHAN.

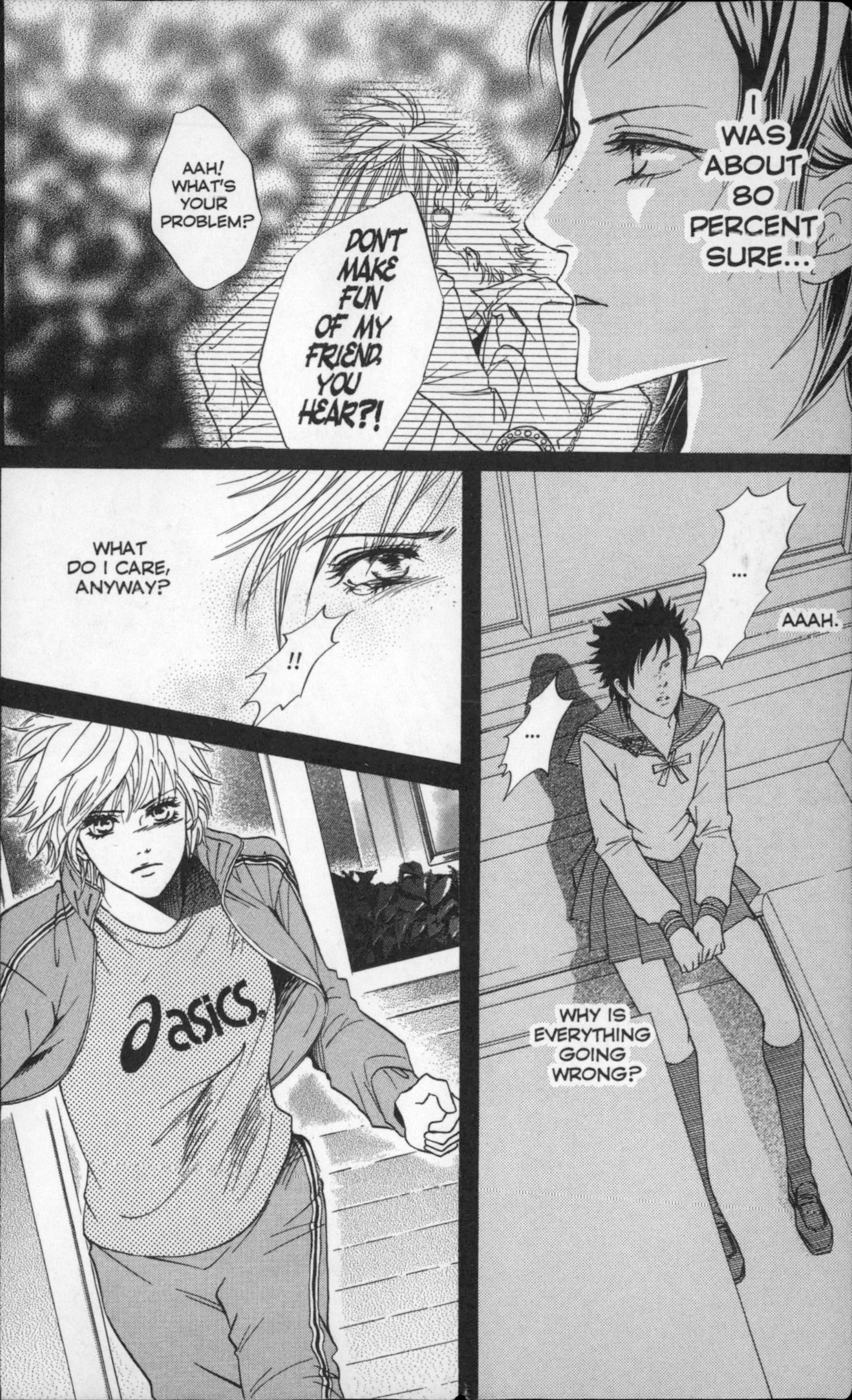
I WAS ABOUT 80 PERCENT SURE...
DON'T MAKE FUN OF MY FRIEND, YOU HEAR?!
AAH! WHAT'S YOUR PROBLEM?
...
AAAH.
...
WHY IS EVERYTHING GOING WRONG?
WHAT DO I CARE, ANYWAY?
!!

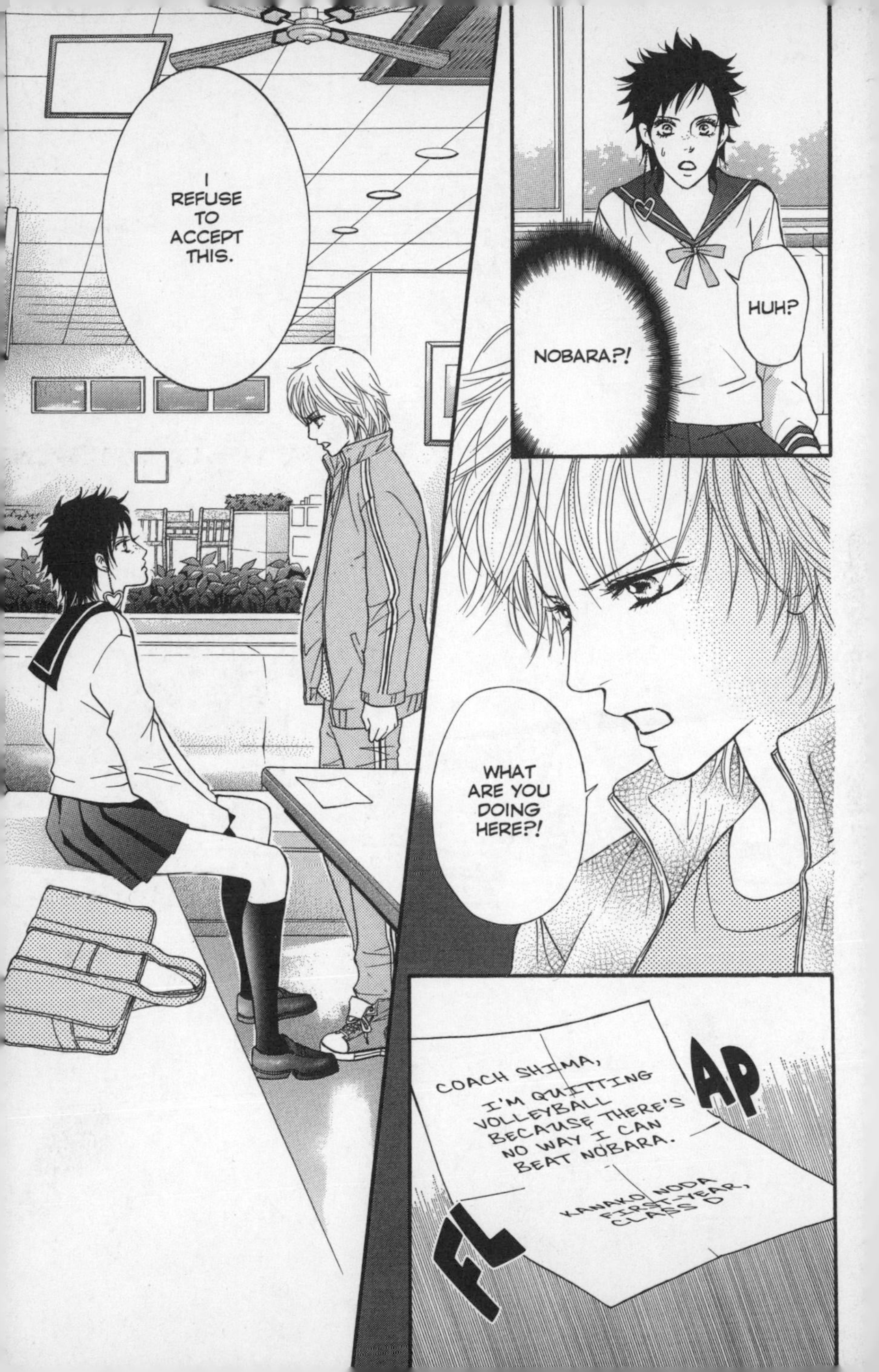
HUH?
NOBARA?!
WHAT ARE YOU DOING HERE?!
FLAP
COACH SHIMA,
I'M QUITTING VOLLEYBALL BECAUSE THERE'S NO WAY I CAN BEAT NOBARA.
KANAKO NODA
FIRST-YEAR, CLASS D
I REFUSE TO ACCEPT THIS.

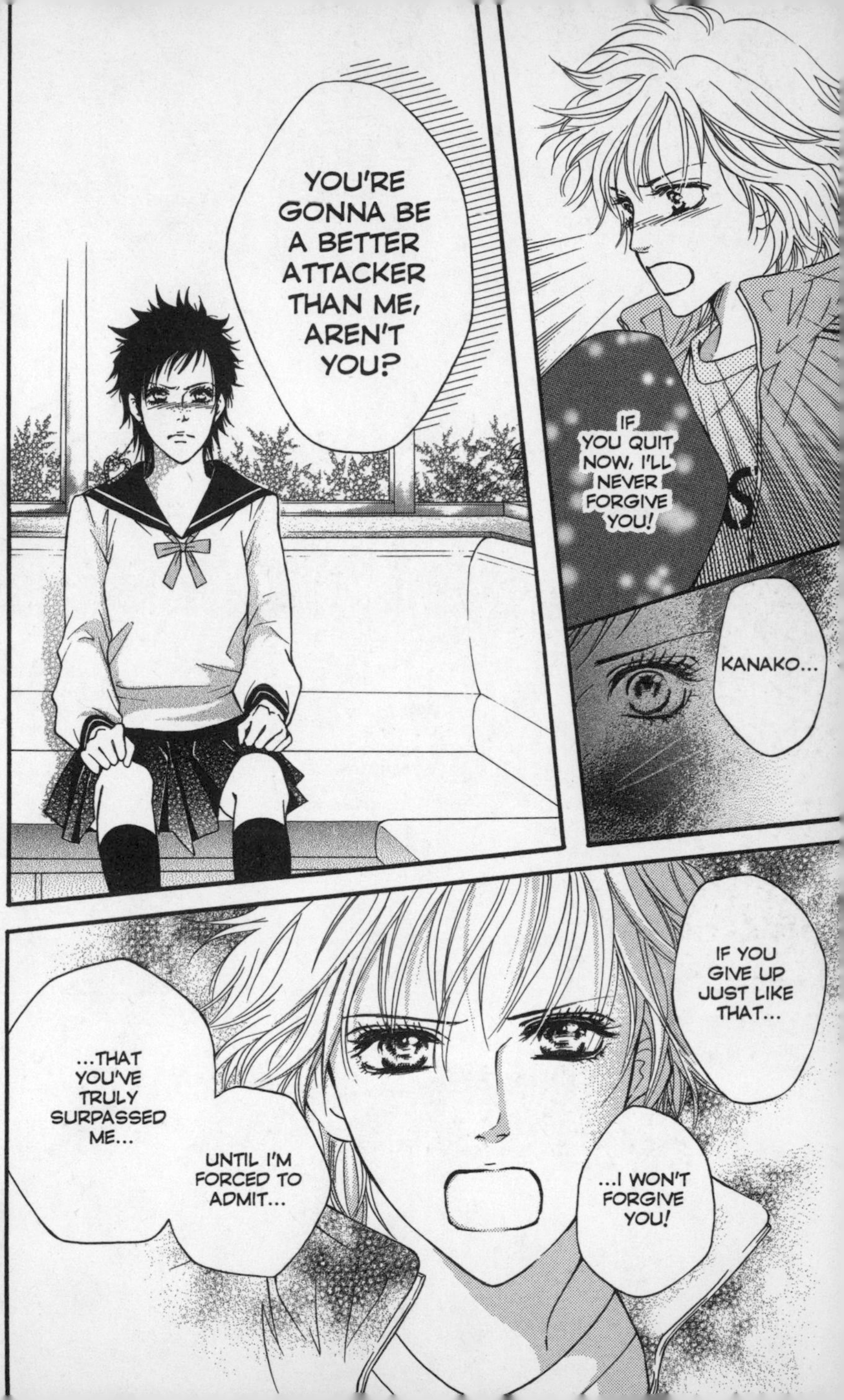
IF YOU QUIT NOW, I'LL NEVER FORGIVE YOU!
KANAKO...
YOU'RE GONNA BE A BETTER ATTACKER THAN ME, AREN'T YOU?
IF YOU GIVE UP JUST LIKE THAT...
...I WON'T FORGIVE YOU!
UNTIL I'M FORCED TO ADMIT...
...THAT YOU'VE TRULY SURPASSED ME...

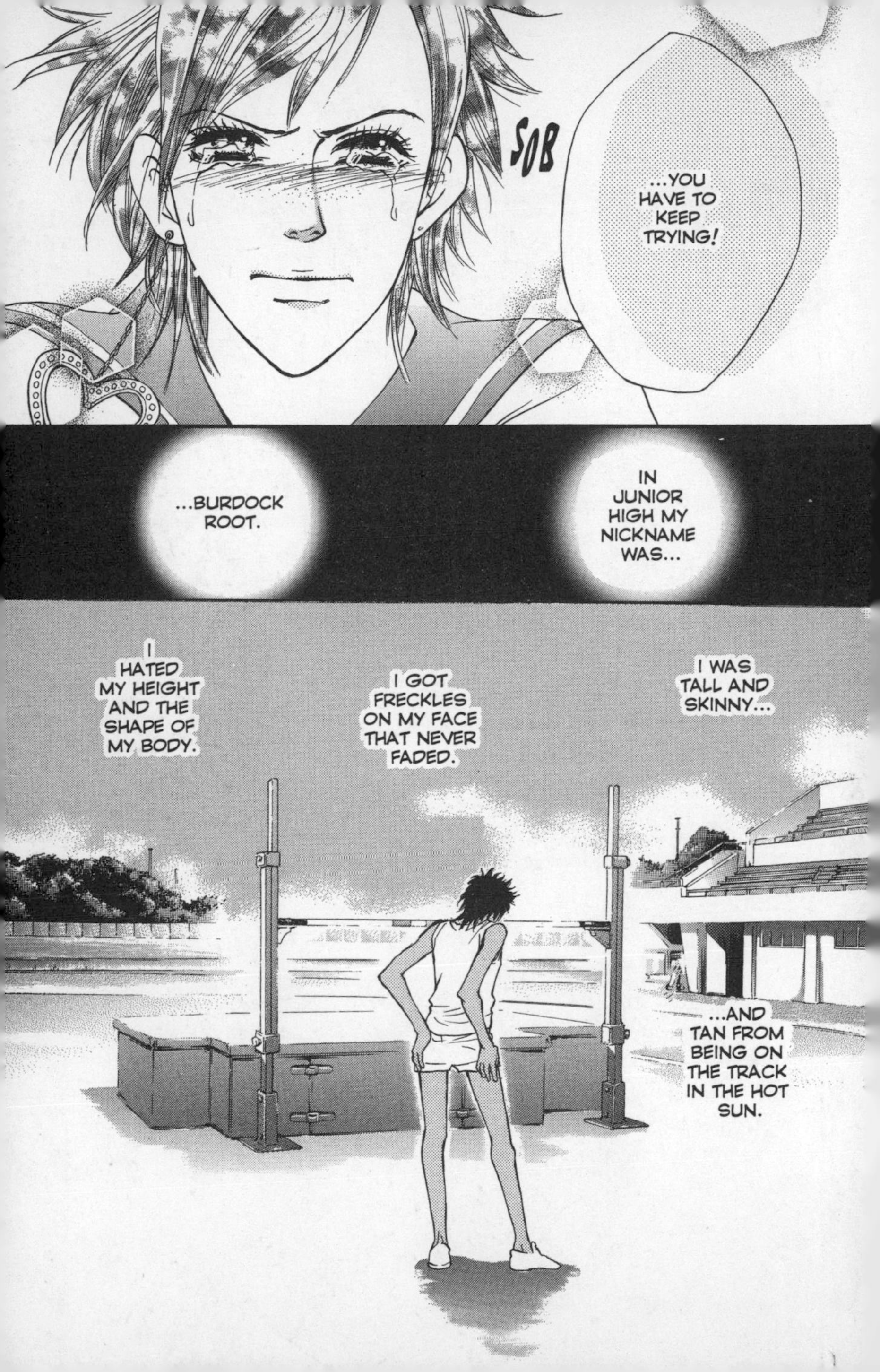
...YOU HAVE TO KEEP TRYING!
SOB
IN JUNIOR HIGH MY NICKNAME WAS...
...BURDOCK ROOT.
I WAS TALL AND SKINNY...
...AND TAN FROM BEING ON THE TRACK IN THE HOT SUN.
I GOT FRECKLES ON MY FACE THAT NEVER FADED.
I HATED MY HEIGHT AND THE SHAPE OF MY BODY.

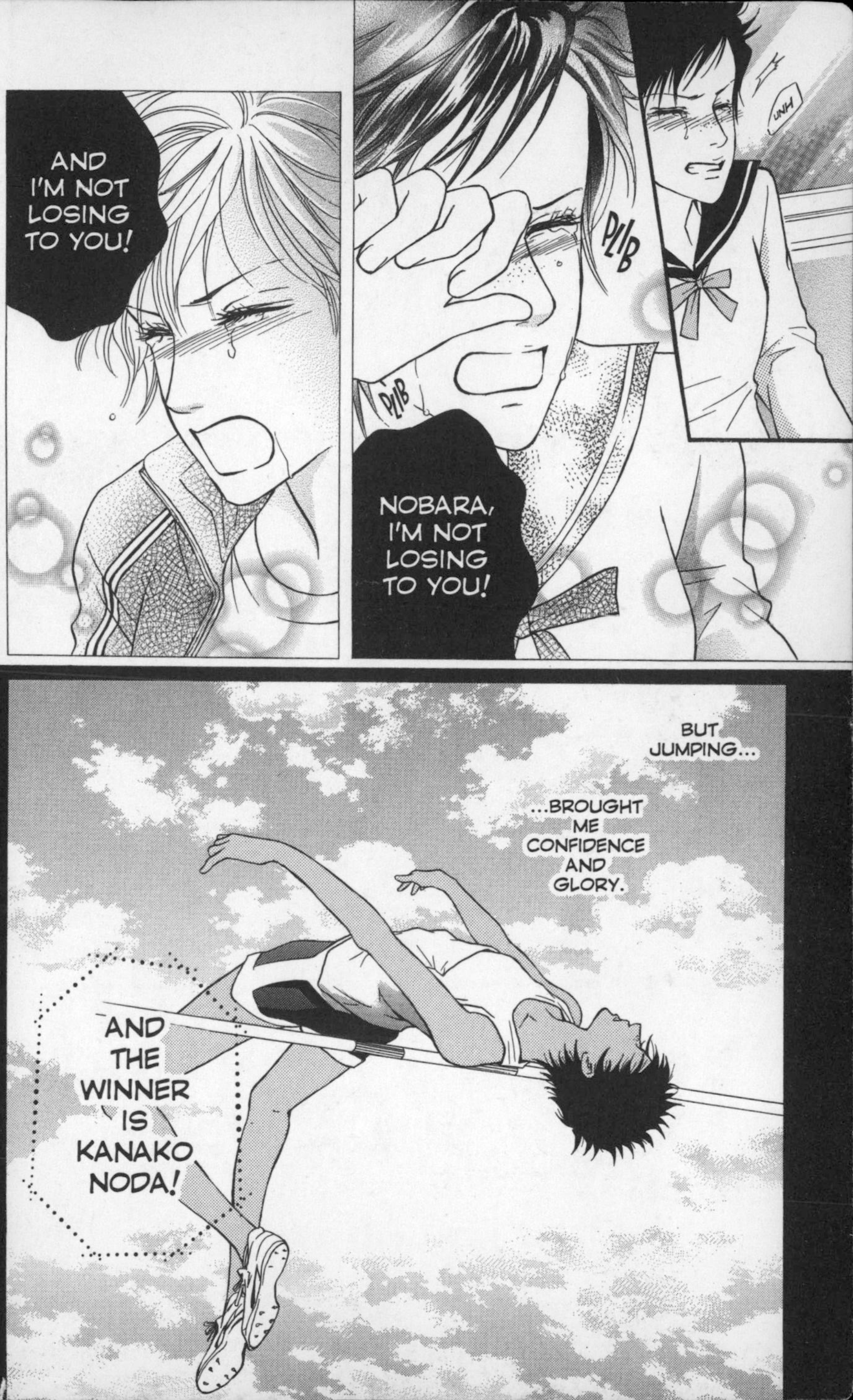
UNH
PLIB
PLIB
NOBARA, I'M NOT LOSING TO YOU!
AND I'M NOT LOSING TO YOU!
BUT JUMPING...
...BROUGHT ME CONFIDENCE AND GLORY.
AND THE WINNER IS KANAKO NODA!

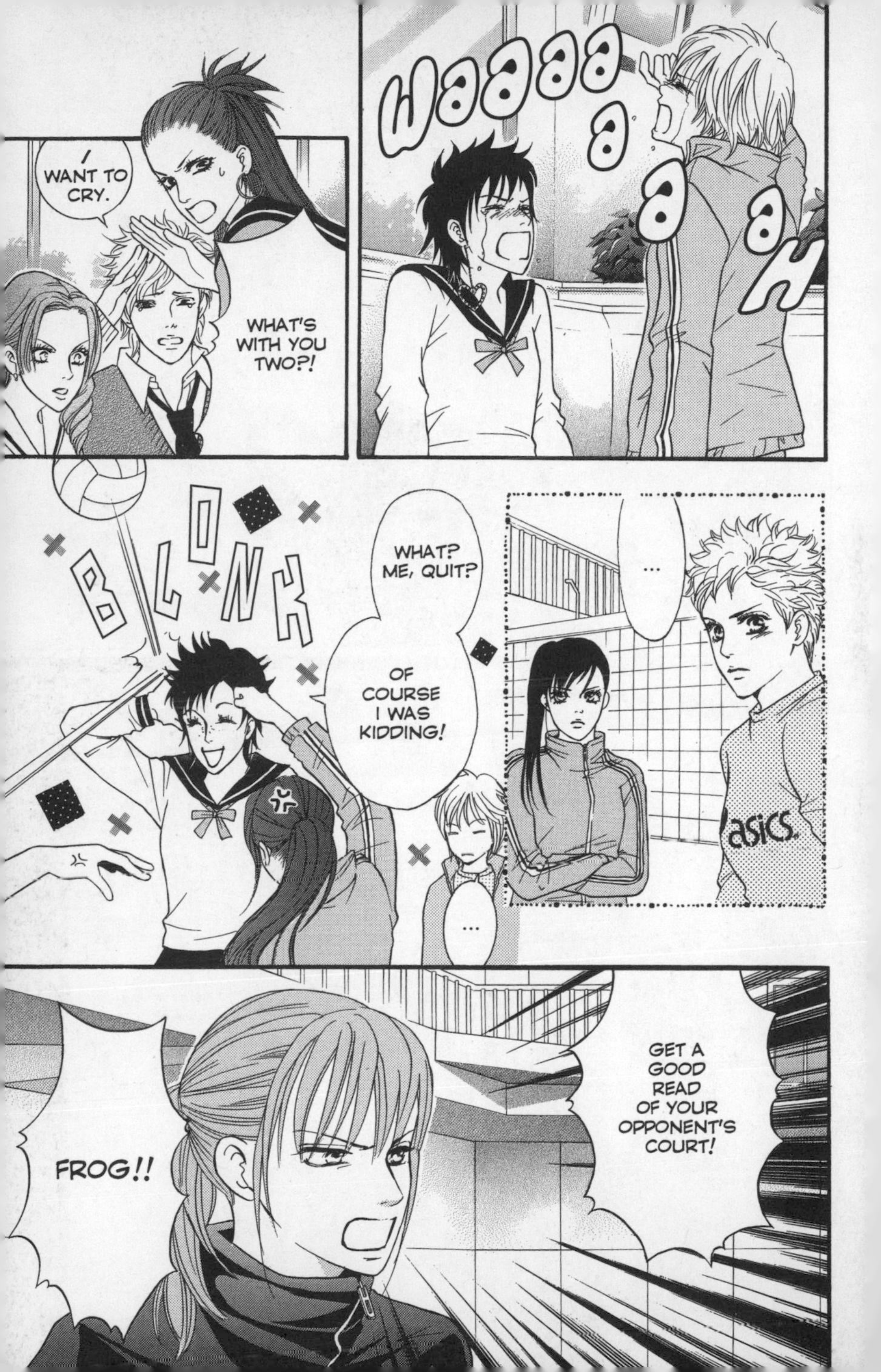
WAAAAAAAH
I WANT TO CRY.
WHAT'S WITH YOU TWO?!
...
WHAT? ME, QUIT?
OF COURSE I WAS KIDDING!
BLONK
...
GET A GOOD READ OF YOUR OPPONENT'S COURT!
FROG!!

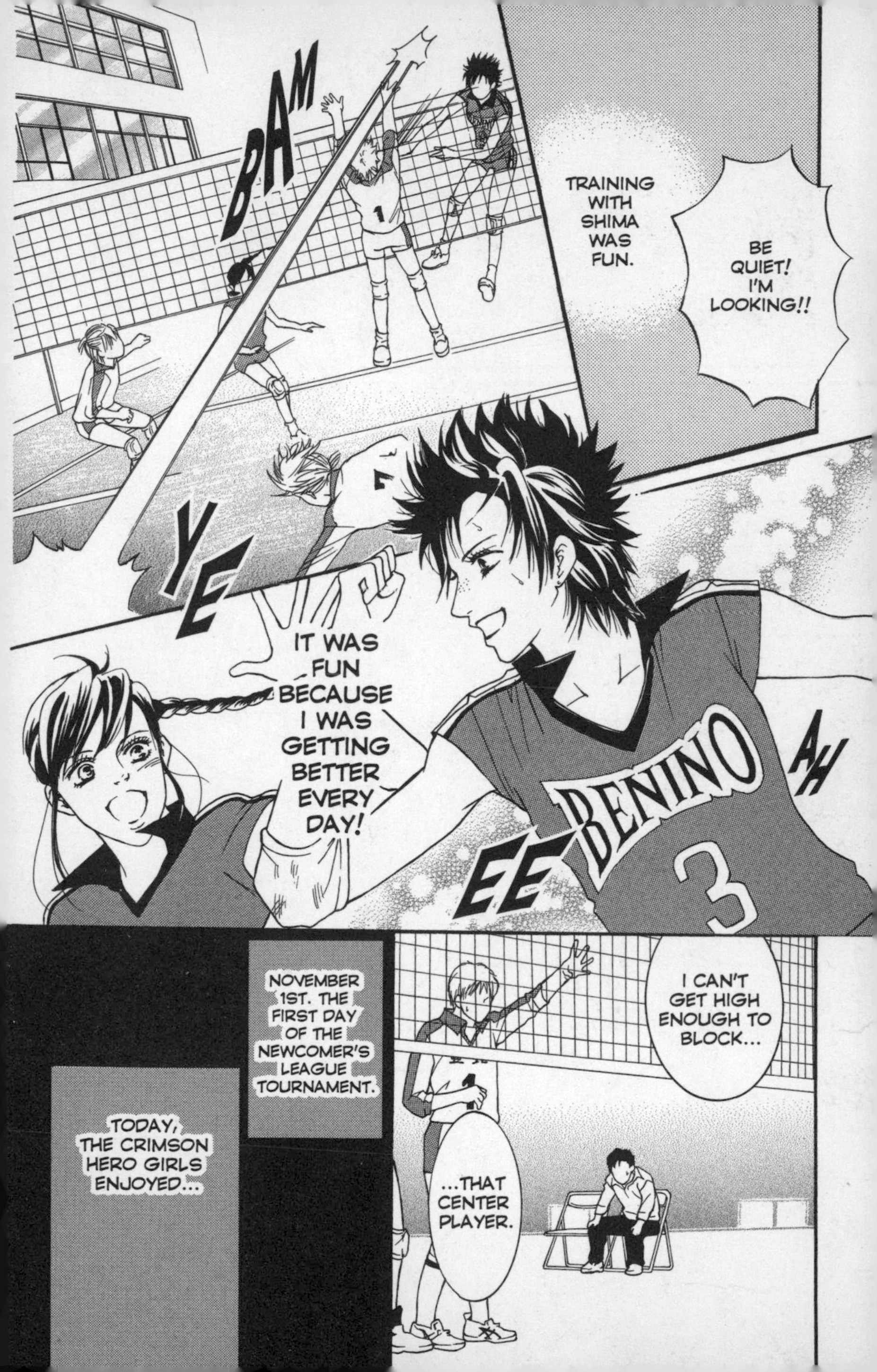
BE QUIET! I'M LOOKING!!
TRAINING WITH SHIMA WAS FUN.
BAM
YE
EE
AH
IT WAS FUN BECAUSE I WAS GETTING BETTER EVERY DAY!
BENINO 3
I CAN'T GET HIGH ENOUGH TO BLOCK...
...THAT CENTER PLAYER.
NOVEMBER 1ST. THE FIRST DAY OF THE NEWCOMER'S LEAGUE TOURNAMENT.
TODAY, THE CRIMSON HERO GIRLS ENJOYED...

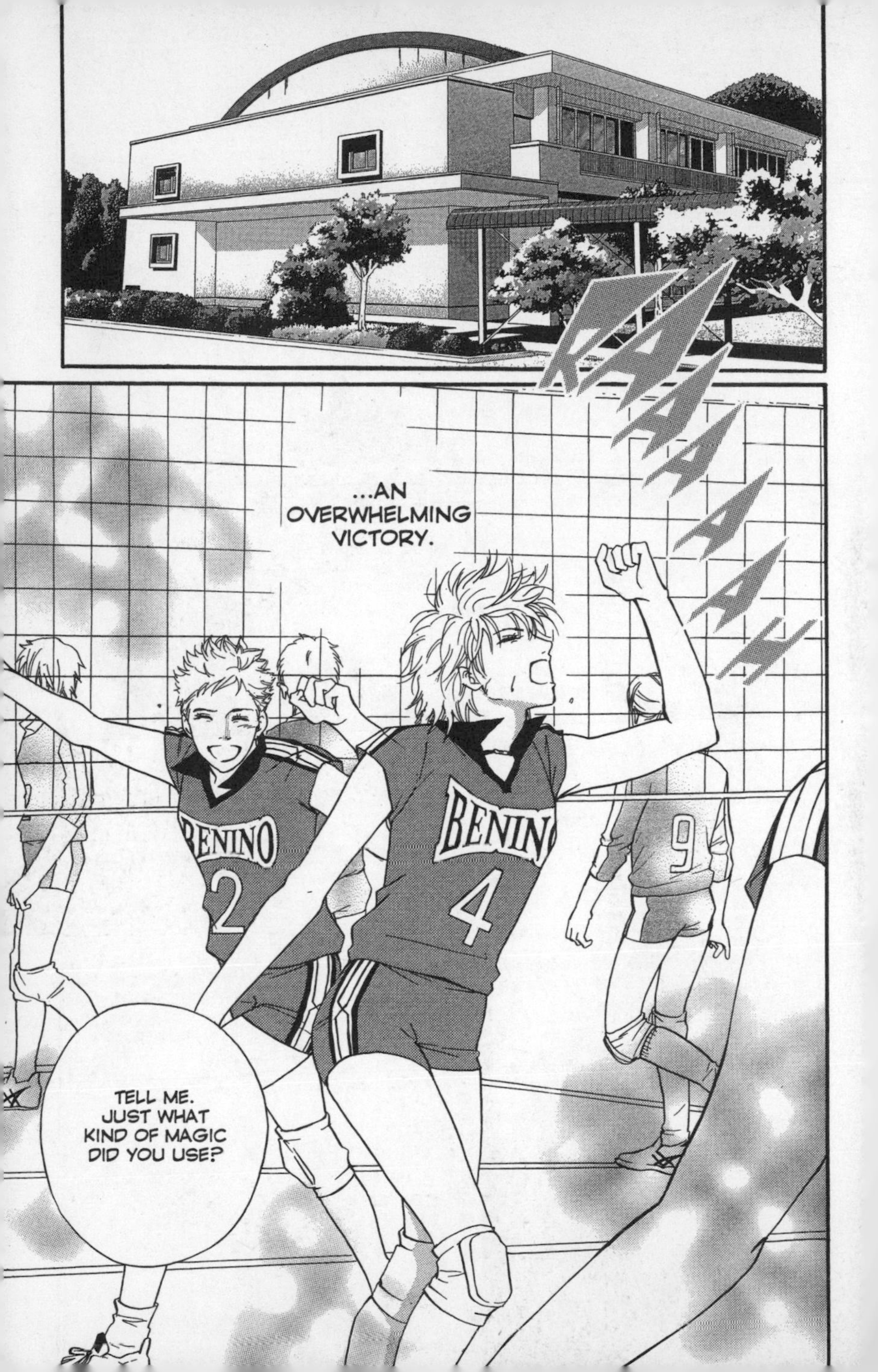
...AN OVERWHELMING VICTORY.
TELL ME. JUST WHAT KIND OF MAGIC DID YOU USE?

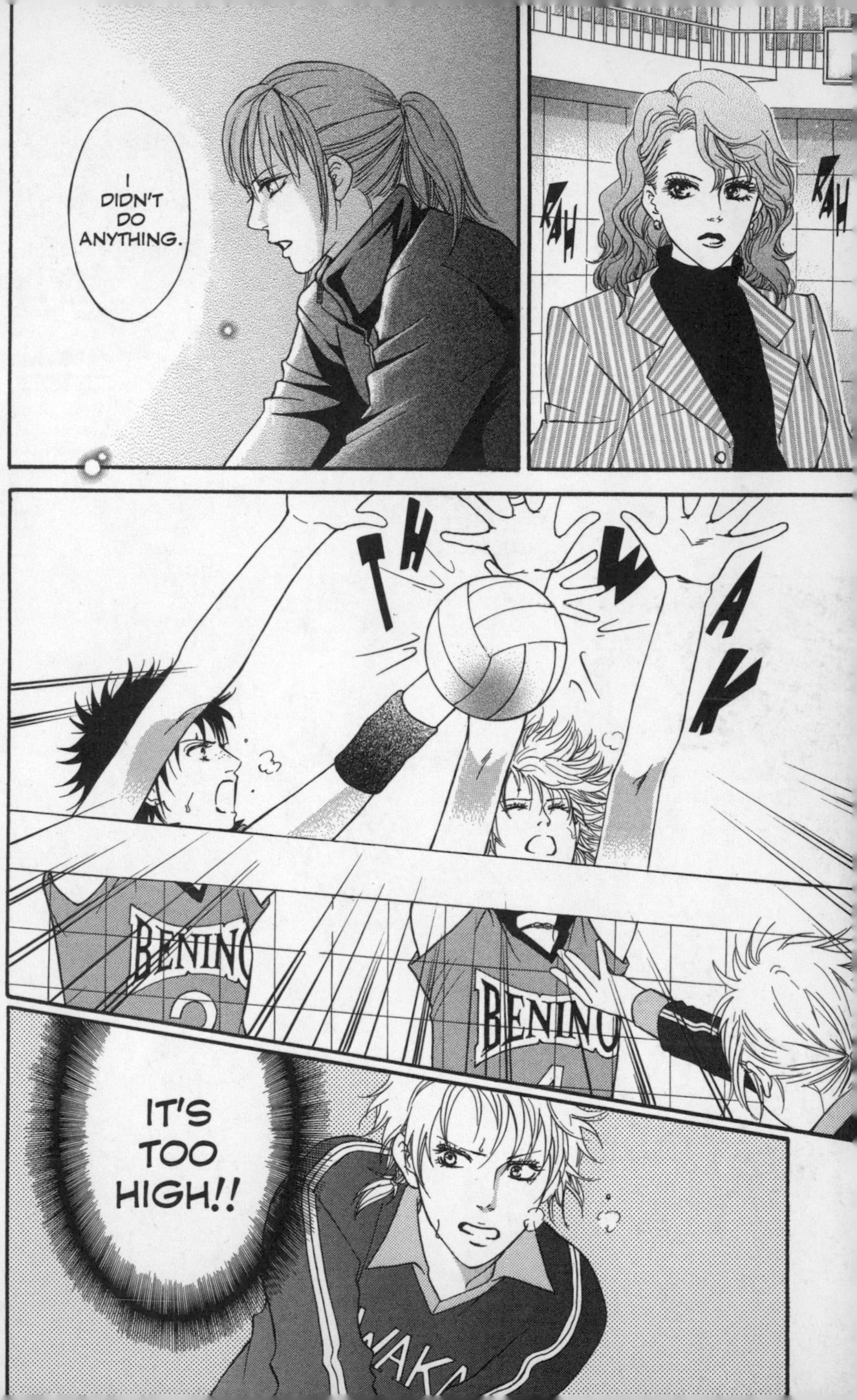
RAH
RAH
I DIDN'T DO ANYTHING.
THWAK
IT'S TOO HIGH!!

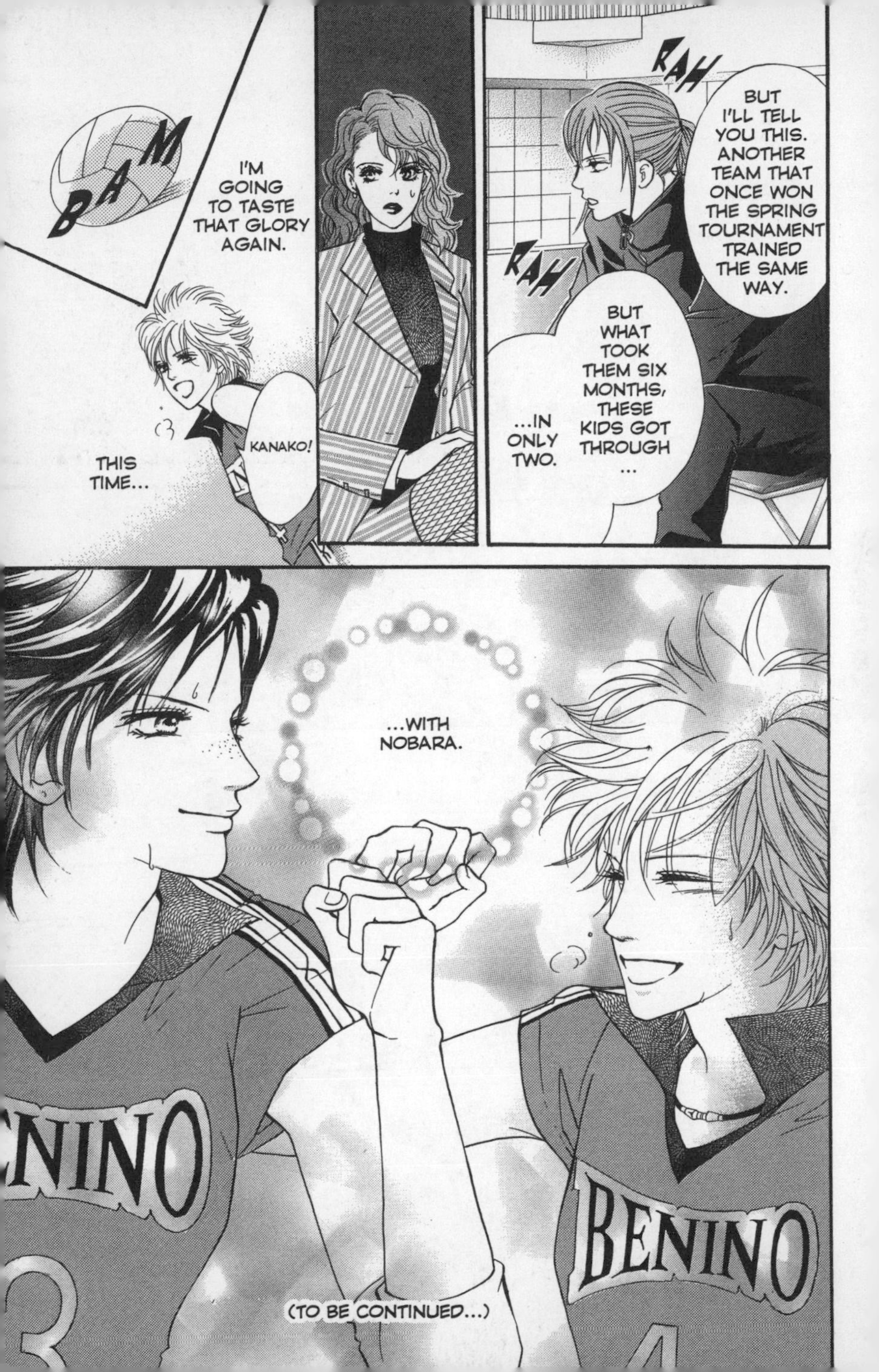
RAH
BUT I'LL TELL YOU THIS. ANOTHER TEAM THAT ONCE WON THE SPRING TOURNAMENT TRAINED THE SAME WAY.
RAH
BUT WHAT TOOK THEM SIX MONTHS, THESE KIDS GOT THROUGH ...
...IN ONLY TWO.
I'M GOING TO TASTE THAT GLORY AGAIN.
BAM
KANAKO!
THIS TIME...
...WITH NOBARA.
BENINO
BENINO
(TO BE CONTINUED...)

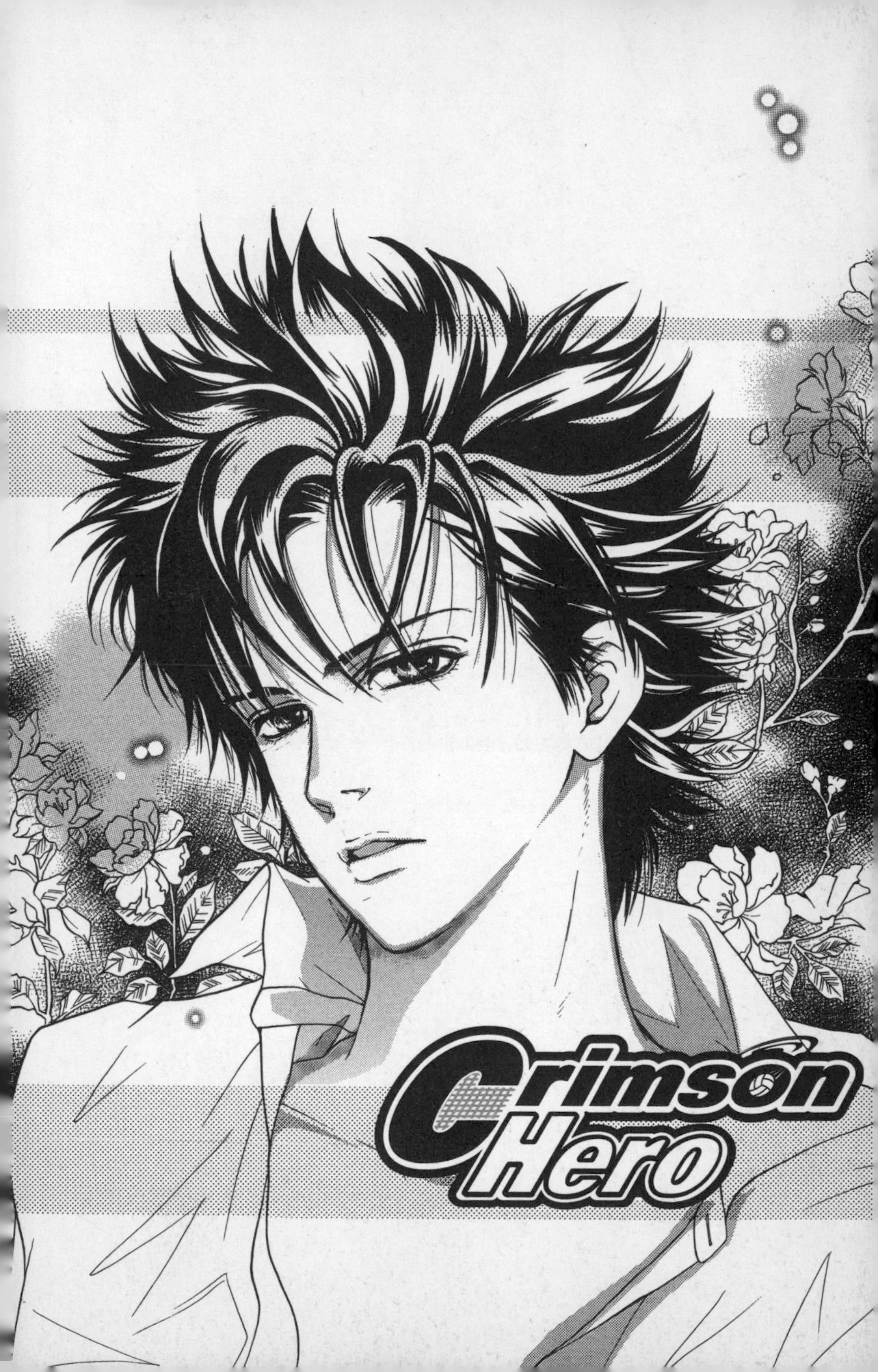
Crimson Hero

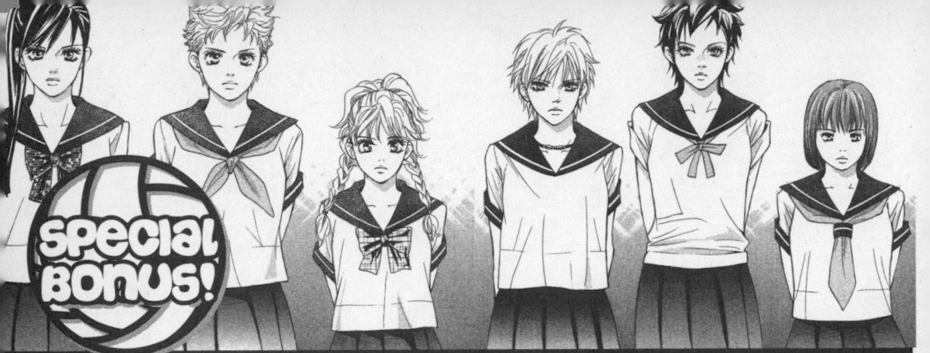
SPECIAL BONUS!

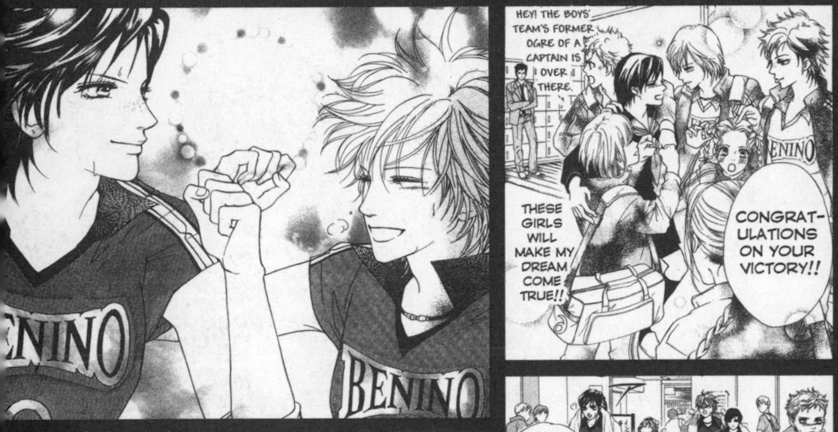
HEY! THE BOYS' TEAM'S FORMER OGRE OF A CAPTAIN IS OVER THERE.
CONGRATULATIONS ON YOUR VICTORY!!
THESE GIRLS WILL MAKE MY DREAM COME TRUE!!
WE'LL START HERE, WITH OUR DEFEAT.
I WANT TO PLAY VOLLEYBALL WITH YOU GUYS.

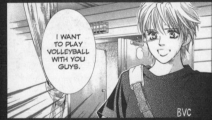

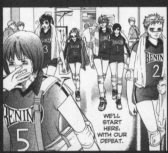

THE CRIMSON GIRLS: WHO'S WHO!

THE CRIMSON GIRLS STARTED AS A WEAK LITTLE TEAM, BUT THEY MANAGED TO IMPROVE ASTOUNDINGLY. HERE WE'LL INTRODUCE THE GIRLS AS THEY UNITE IN THEIR QUEST TO GET TO THE SPRING TOURNAMENT. THE SECRET BEHIND THEIR STRENGTH? TEAMWORK!

AMAZING ATHLETIC ABILILTY + PASSION FOR VOLLEYBALL=
AN ACE WITH BOUNDLESS POTENTIAL

NOBARA SUMIYOSHI

FIRST-YEAR

NOBARA

I WILL NEVER DO THIS AGAIN!

HER FAMILY RUNS A TRADITIONAL JAPANESE RESTAURANT AND OPPOSED HER PLAYING VOLLEYBALL, SO NOBARA RAN AWAY TO LIVE AND WORK IN CRIMSON DORM. HER ATHLETIC ABILITY IS TOP-NOTCH. HER WEAK POINT USED TO BE HER MENTAL STATE, BUT SHE OVERCAME THAT TO BECOME A TRUE ACE, READY TO LEAD HER TEAM TO VICTORY!

SHE BATTLED HERSELF AND EMERGED STRONGER!

NOBARA SHOWED AMAZING LATENT TALENTS IN MATCHES, BUT HER LACK OF CONFIDENCE KEPT HER FROM BEING ABLE TO REACH HER FULL POTENTIAL. AN INTENSIVE STINT OF TRAINING WITH THE EAGLES HELPED HER BREAK OUT OF HER SHELL, AND SHE GAINED A POWERFUL WEAPON: THE AIR FAKE!

HEIGHT: 5' 9   BLOOD TYPE: A
POSITION: LEFT   ACE ATTACKER

FUTURE MATRON OF THE TRADITIONAL RYOTEI, SEIRYU.
BROKE THE RECORD FOR THE HIGHEST JUMP.
LEFT THE ALL-JAPAN JUNIORS TRAINING CAMP PARTWAY THROUGH.

SHE'S FOUND A POWERFUL ALLY AS SHE AIMS FOR THE SPRING TOURNAMENT!

PLEASE TELL ME WHAT I NEED TO DO TO IMPROVE.

I'LL CHALLENGE YOU SIDEWAYS!!

PHILLIPS HEAD

NOBARA HAD LONG HARBORED UNREQUITED LOVE FOR HER FRIEND YUSHIN, BUT FINALLY THEY MANAGED TO SHARE THEIR FEELINGS FOR EACH OTHER. NOW THE TWO HAVE DOUBLE THE POWER. TOGETHER THEY'LL WORK HARD TO GET TO THE SPRING TOURNAMENT.

I...

I LOVE YOU TOO, YUSHIN.

THE GENIUS SETTER'S COMEBACK

TOMOYO OSAKA

SECOND-YEAR

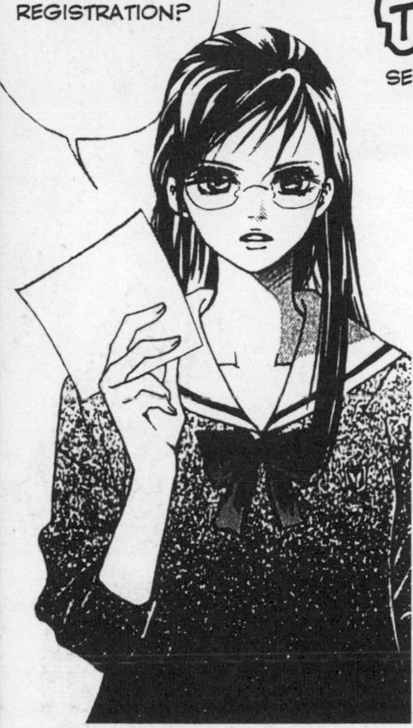
SO WHO'S IN CHARGE OF CLUB REGISTRATION?

TOMOYO

IN JUNIOR HIGH THEY CALLED HER A GENIUS SETTER, BUT SHE LEFT THE TEAM AFTER AN INJURY. WITH NO PLACE TO PLAY, SHE QUIT VOLLEYBALL. NOBARA'S PASSIONATE PLEAS MOVED HER TO TAKE UP VOLLEYBALL AGAIN. YOU'D NEVER GUESS SHE HAD A LONG BREAK FROM PLAYING. SHE IS THE TEAM'S COMMAND CENTRAL.

HEIGHT: 5' 7" BLOOD TYPE: O
POSITION: RIGHT CAPTAIN

CALLED THE GENIUS SETTER.
A FORMER MEMBER OF THE ALL-JAPAN JUNIORS.

SHE ONCE GAVE UP VOLLEYBALL.

EVERYONE CALLED HER A GENIUS UNTIL THE DAY SHE INJURED HERSELF. THEN NOBODY GAVE HER A SECOND LOOK. HER FEELINGS HURT AND HER SELF-CONFIDENCE GONE, SHE FELT TOO PARALYZED TO ACT.

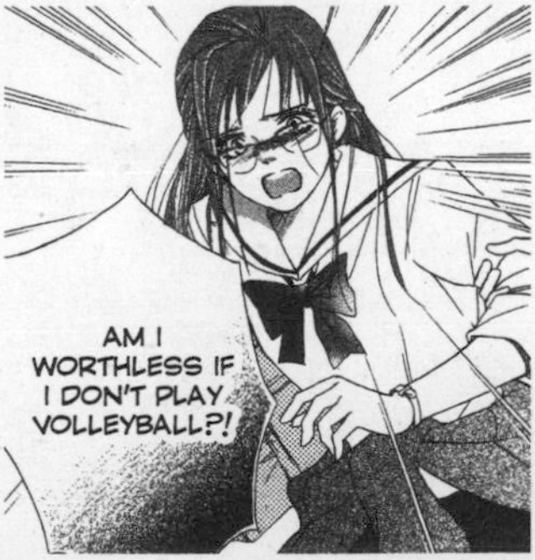
AM I WORTHLESS IF I DON'T PLAY VOLLEYBALL?!

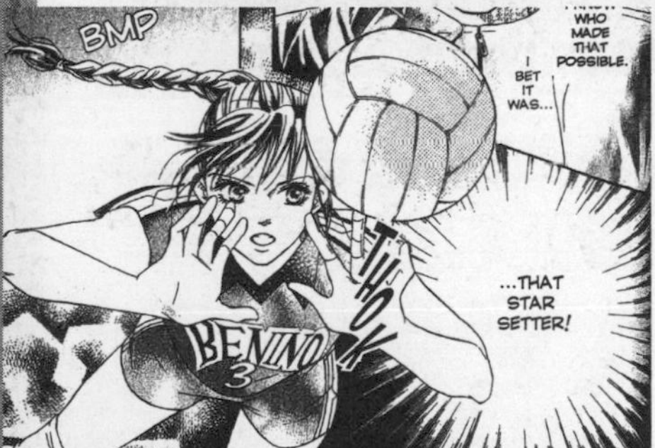
WHO MADE THAT POSSIBLE.
I BET IT WAS...
BMP
THWOK
...THAT STAR SETTER!
BENINO
3

SHE LEADS THE TEAM WITH HER KEEN INTUITION AND COOL HEAD!

THE ONCE-PATHETIC CRIMSON TEAM NOW DAZZLES WITH ITS ARRAY OF ATTACKS. IT'S THIS STAR SETTER'S BRILLIANT TOSSES THAT MAKE IT ALL POSSIBLE.

A RAPID RISE! CRIMSON'S NEW ACE! (SELF-PROCLAIMED)

KANAKO NODA

FIRST-YEAR

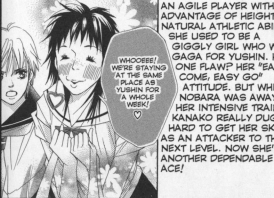

KANAKO

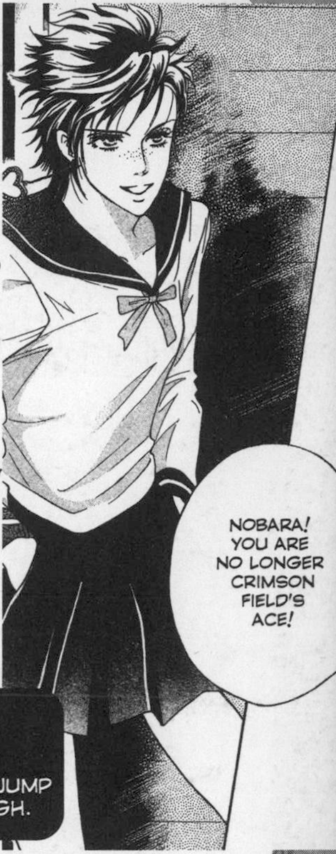
NOBARA! YOU ARE NO LONGER CRIMSON FIELD'S ACE!

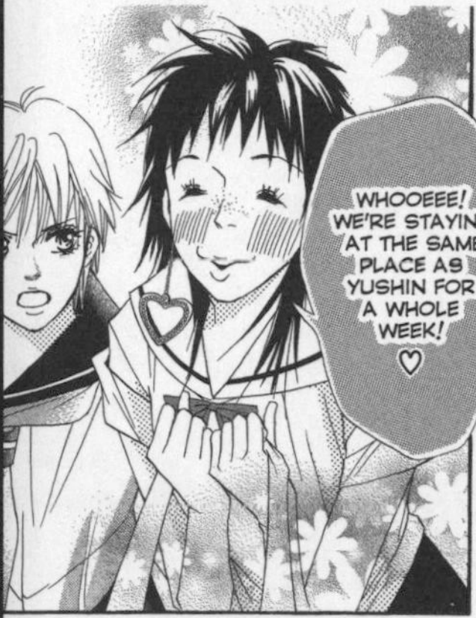
WHOOEEE! WE'RE STAYING AT THE SAME PLACE AS YUSHIN FOR A WHOLE WEEK! ♡

AN AGILE PLAYER WITH THE ADVANTAGE OF HEIGHT AND NATURAL ATHLETIC ABILITY. SHE USED TO BE A GIGGLY GIRL WHO WAS GAGA FOR YUSHIN. HER ONE FLAW? HER "EASY COME, EASY GO" ATTITUDE. BUT WHILE NOBARA WAS AWAY ON HER INTENSIVE TRAINING, KANAKO REALLY DUG IN HARD TO GET HER SKILLS AS AN ATTACKER TO THE NEXT LEVEL. NOW SHE'S ANOTHER DEPENDABLE ACE!

HEIGHT: 5' 8.7"
BLOOD TYPE: AB
POSITION: CENTER
HOLDER OF THE HIGH JUMP RECORD IN JUNIOR HIGH.

DETERMINED! SHE EVEN IMPROVED HER WEAK RECEPTION SKILLS!!

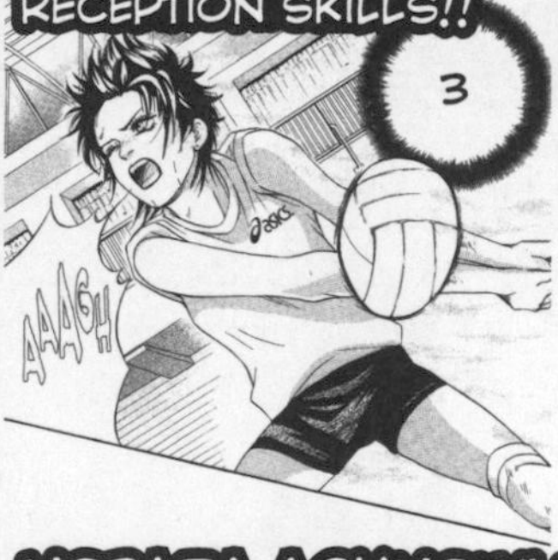
3
AAAGH

HER HEIGHT MADE RECEIVES HARD FOR HER. SHE SHOWED HER STUBBORN GRIT WHEN SHE HAD TO PULL OFF 50 SERVE RECEIVES!

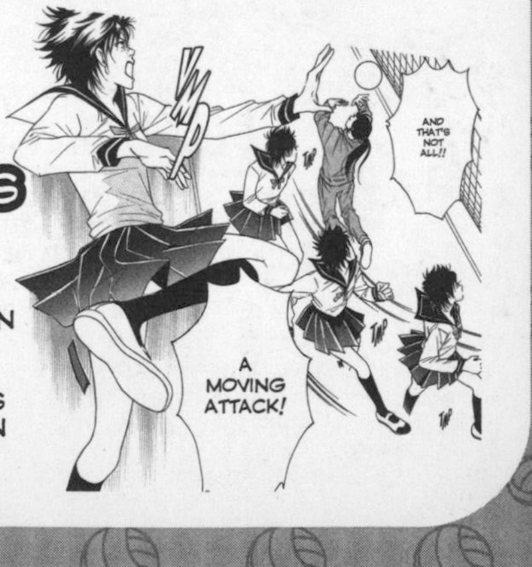
AND THAT'S NOT ALL!!
A MOVING ATTACK!

NOBARA ACKNOWLEDGES HER AS A RIVAL!

SHE SKIMPED ON SLEEP TO GET THREE NEW ATTACKS UNDER HER BELT, BUT THEN ALMOST THREW IT ALL AWAY BELIEVING SHE WAS NO MATCH FOR NOBARA. NOW THEY'VE ACKNOWLEDGED EACH OTHER AS HELPFUL RIVALS AND PROMISED TO TRAIN HARD TOGETHER.

THE POWERFUL ATTACKER WHO LOVES TO EAT.

AYAKO MOCHIDA

SECOND-YEAR

MOCHI

HEIGHT: 5' 7
BLOOD TYPE: B
POSITION: LEFT
VICE CAPTAIN

TOP POWER HITTER ON THE TEAM. ONCE PRONE TO GIVING UP WHEN THE GOING GOT ROUGH, A BITTER DEFEAT SPURRED AYAKO TO BELIEVE IN NOBARA AND JOIN HER IN GOING FOR THE TOP!

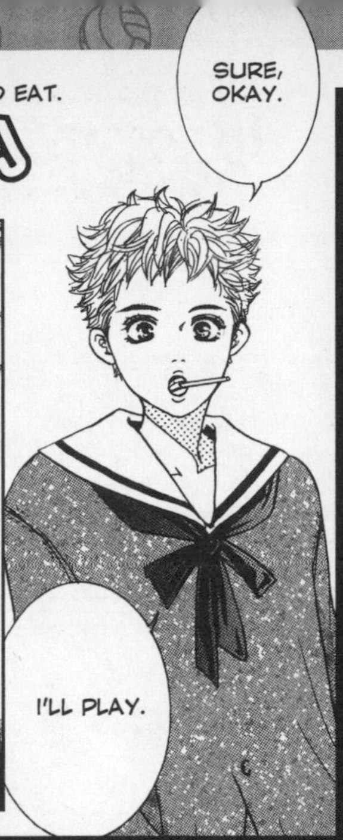
SURE, OKAY.
I'LL PLAY.

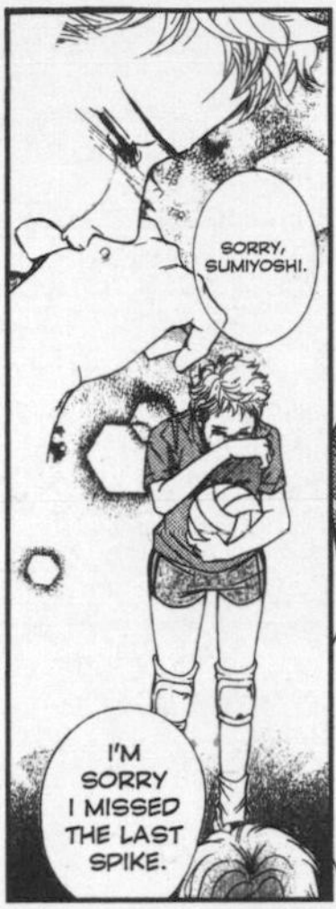
SORRY, SUMIYOSHI.
I'M SORRY I MISSED THE LAST SPIKE.

THE HARD-WORKING RECIEVER: BALANCING ATHLETICS AND ACADEMICS

KYOKA GOTO

FIRST-YEAR

GOCCHIN

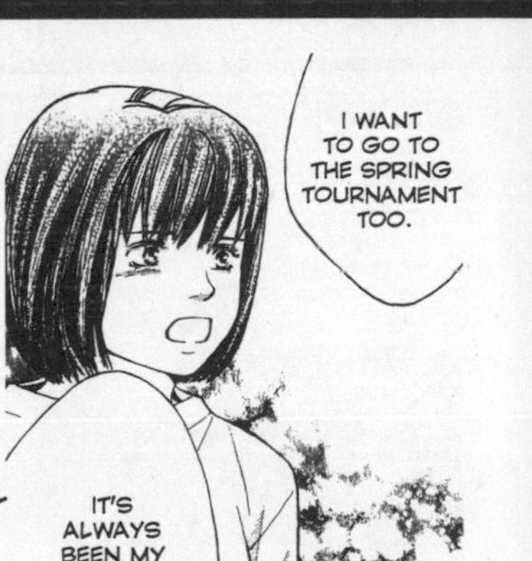
I WANT TO GO TO THE SPRING TOURNAMENT TOO.
IT'S ALWAYS BEEN MY DREAM!!

ALWAYS WALKING AROUND WITH FLASHCARDS, KYOKO STRUGGLED TO BALANCE VOLLEYBALL AND HER STUDIES. BUT SHE DECLARED HER INTENTION TO AIM FOR THE SPRING TOURNAMENT TO HER FATHER! WITH HER SERIOUS APPROACH TO PRACTICES, SHE'S THE TEAM'S SECRET POWERHOUSE.

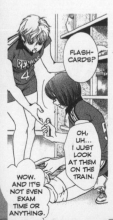

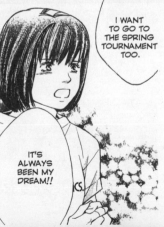

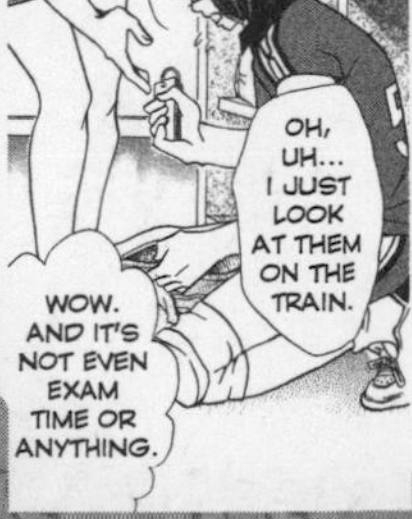
FLASH-CARDS?
OH, UH... I JUST LOOK AT THEM ON THE TRAIN.
WOW. AND IT'S NOT EVEN EXAM TIME OR ANYTHING.

HEIGHT: 5' 4" BLOOD TYPE: A
POSITION: RIGHT
BOTH PARENTS ARE EDUCATORS. HAS A SUCCESSFUL OLDER SISTER.

A FIGHTING SPIRIT WITHIN A SLENDER FRAME

RENA KOMIZO

FIRST-YEAR

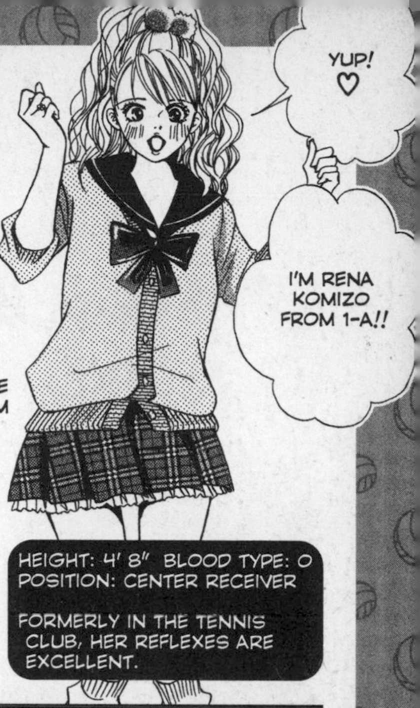
YUP! ♡
I'M RENA KOMIZO FROM 1-A!!

RENA

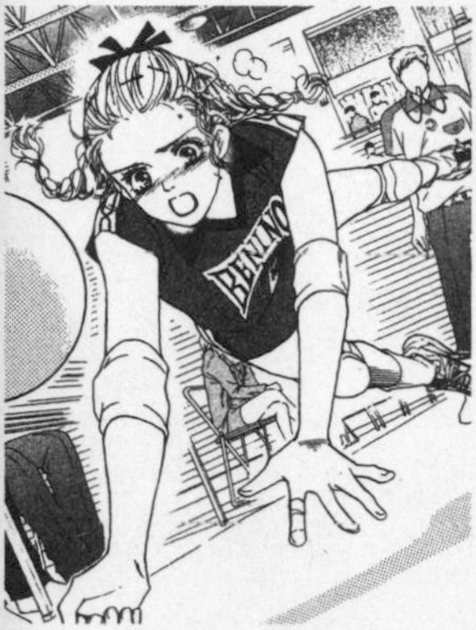

RENA JOINED AFTER BEING SMITTEN BY NOBARA'S PLUCKY SPIRIT. WITH HUGE DETERMINATION, SHE TRANSFORMED FROM A WEAK BEGINNER WHO DIDN'T EVEN KNOW THE RULES TO A DEPENDABLE PLAYER! SHE'S A GENTLE-HEARTED GIRL WHO HELPS KEEP THE PEACE.

HEIGHT: 4' 8" BLOOD TYPE: O
POSITION: CENTER RECEIVER

FORMERLY IN THE TENNIS CLUB, HER REFLEXES ARE EXCELLENT.

THE RELIABLE MANAGER WHO BUILT UP THE TEAM

YUI SUZUSHIRO

THIRD-YEAR

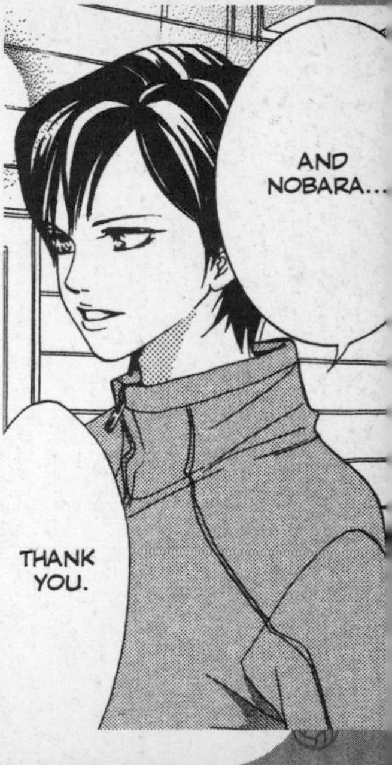
AND NOBARA...
THANK YOU.

YUI-SAN

FORMER CAPTAIN. SETTER. THE FORMER CAPTAIN OF THE BOYS' TEAM IS HER BOYFRIEND.

THE FORMER CAPTAIN. SHE WAS A PASSIONATE PLAYER FROM THE PRIOR GIRLS TEAM--THOUGH SOME OF THE BOYS CALLED THEM LOSERS. NOBARA GOT HER TO JOIN THE NEW GIRLS' TEAM, AND AFTER RETIRING, SHE BECAME THE MANAGER.

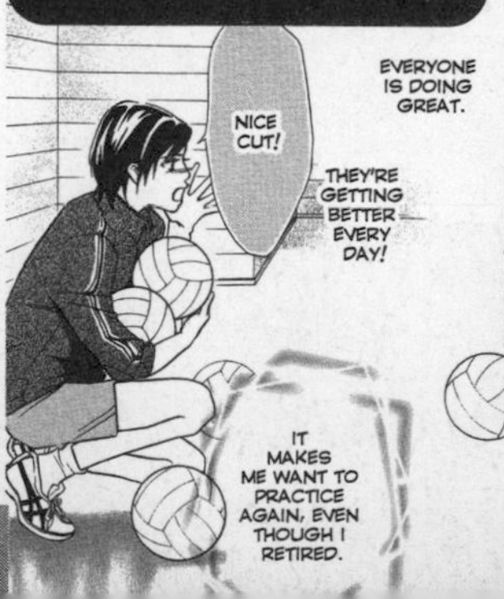
EVERYONE IS DOING GREAT.
NICE CUT!
THEY'RE GETTING BETTER EVERY DAY!
IT MAKES ME WANT TO PRACTICE AGAIN, EVEN THOUGH I RETIRED.

♥A mountain of reference photos… Somehow, they've taken over several shelves. Some I took myself. Others were shot by a professional. But of all these photos, few show the players on the court in their moment of joy. I've got to go take some like that. That's what I want to draw.

—Mitsuba Takanashi, 2006

At age 17, Mitsuba Takanashi debuted her first short story, *Mou Koi Nante Shinai* (Never Fall in Love Again), in 1992 in *Bessatsu Margaret* magazine and now has several major titles under her belt.

Born in the Shimane Prefecture of Japan, Takanashi now lives in Tokyo, where she enjoys taking walks, watching videos, shopping, and going to the hair salon. Takanashi has a soft spot for the Japanese pop acts Yellow Monkey and Hide, and is good at playing ping-pong.

CRIMSON HERO

VOL. 9
The Shojo Beat Manga Edition

This volume contains material that was originally published in English in
Shojo Beat magazine, April–August 2008 issues. Artwork in the magazine may have been
slightly altered from that presented here.

STORY AND ART BY
MITSUBA TAKANASHI

Translation & English Adaptation/Naoko Amemiya
Touch-up Art & Lettering/Mark Griffin
Graphics & Cover Design/Courtney Utt & Julie Behn
Editor/Nancy Thistlethwaite

Editor in Chief, Books/Alvin Lu
Editor in Chief, Magazines/Marc Weidenbaum
VP, Publishing Licensing/Rika Inouye
VP, Sales & Product Marketing/Gonzalo Ferreyra
VP, Creative/Linda Espinosa
Publisher/Hyoe Narita

Printed in Canada

Published by VIZ Media, LLC
P.O. Box 77010
San Francisco, CA 94107

Shojo Beat Manga Edition
10 9 8 7 6 5 4 3 2 1
First printing, October 2008

www.viz.com
store.viz.com

The gripping story — in **manga** format

Get the complete *Be With You* collection—
buy the manga and fiction today!

RATED
T
FOR
TEEN
ratings.viz.com

VIZ
MEDIA

www.viz.com

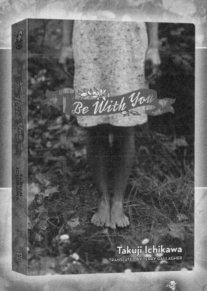

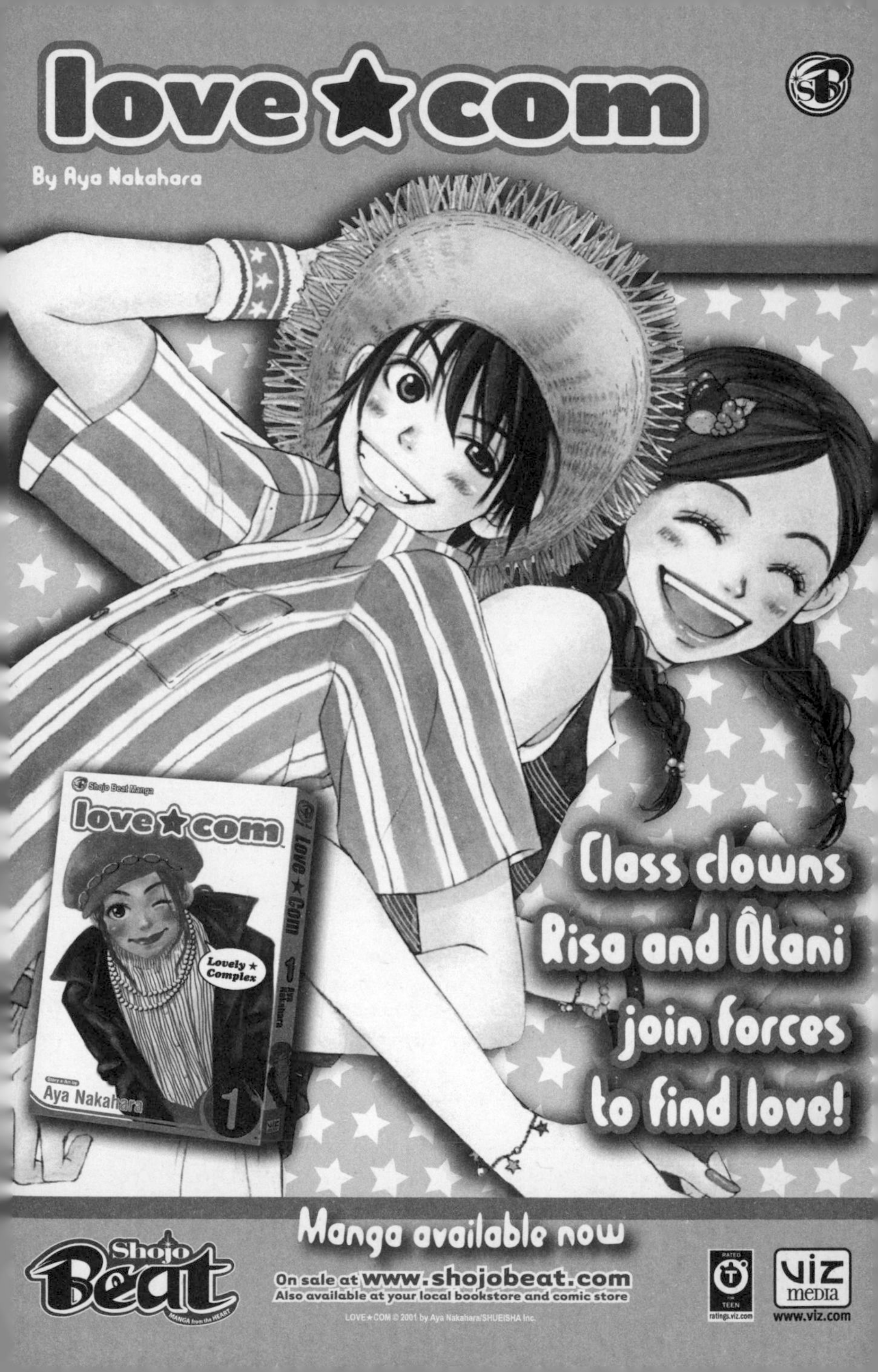
love★com
By Aya Nakahara
Shojo Beat Manga
love★com
Love★Com
Lovely★Complex
1
Aya Nakahara
Story & Art by
Aya Nakahara
1
Class clowns Risa and Ôtani join forces to find love!
Manga available now
Shojo Beat
MANGA from the HEART
On sale at www.shojobeat.com
Also available at your local bookstore and comic store
LOVE★COM © 2001 by Aya Nakahara/SHUEISHA Inc.
RATED T FOR TEEN
ratings.viz.com
VIZ media
www.viz.com

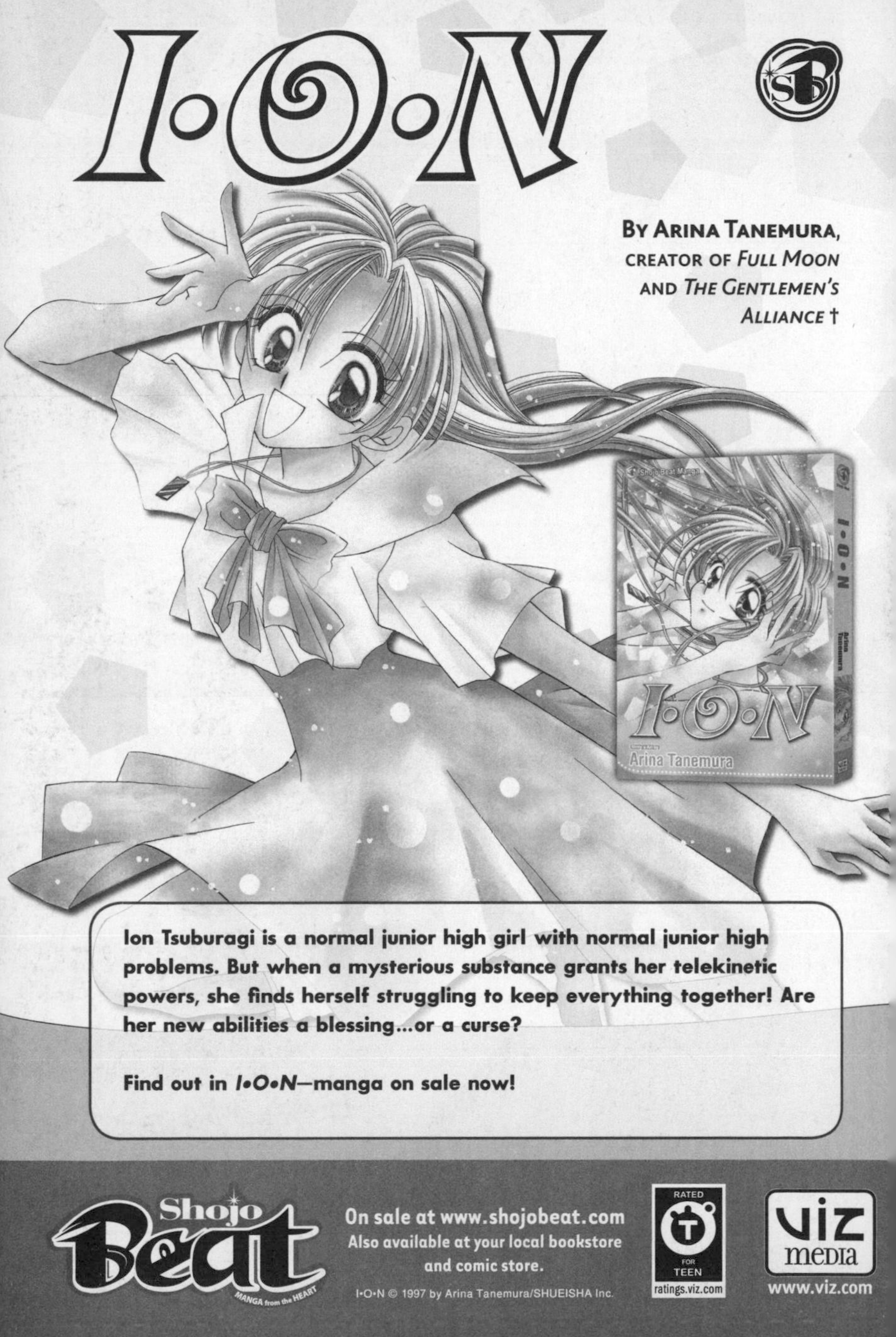
I•O•N
By Arina Tanemura,
creator of Full Moon
and The Gentlemen's
Alliance †
Shojo Beat Manga
I•O•N
Arina Tanemura
Ion Tsuburagi is a normal junior high girl with normal junior high problems. But when a mysterious substance grants her telekinetic powers, she finds herself struggling to keep everything together! Are her new abilities a blessing...or a curse?
Find out in I•O•N—manga on sale now!
Shojo Beat
MANGA from the HEART
On sale at www.shojobeat.com
Also available at your local bookstore and comic store.
I•O•N © 1997 by Arina Tanemura/SHUEISHA Inc.
RATED T FOR TEEN
ratings.viz.com
viz media
www.viz.com

Art book featuring
216 pages of beautiful
color images personally
selected by Tanemura

Read where Mitsuki's
pop dreams began
in the manga—all 7
volumes now available

Complete your
collection with the
anime, now on DVD

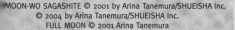

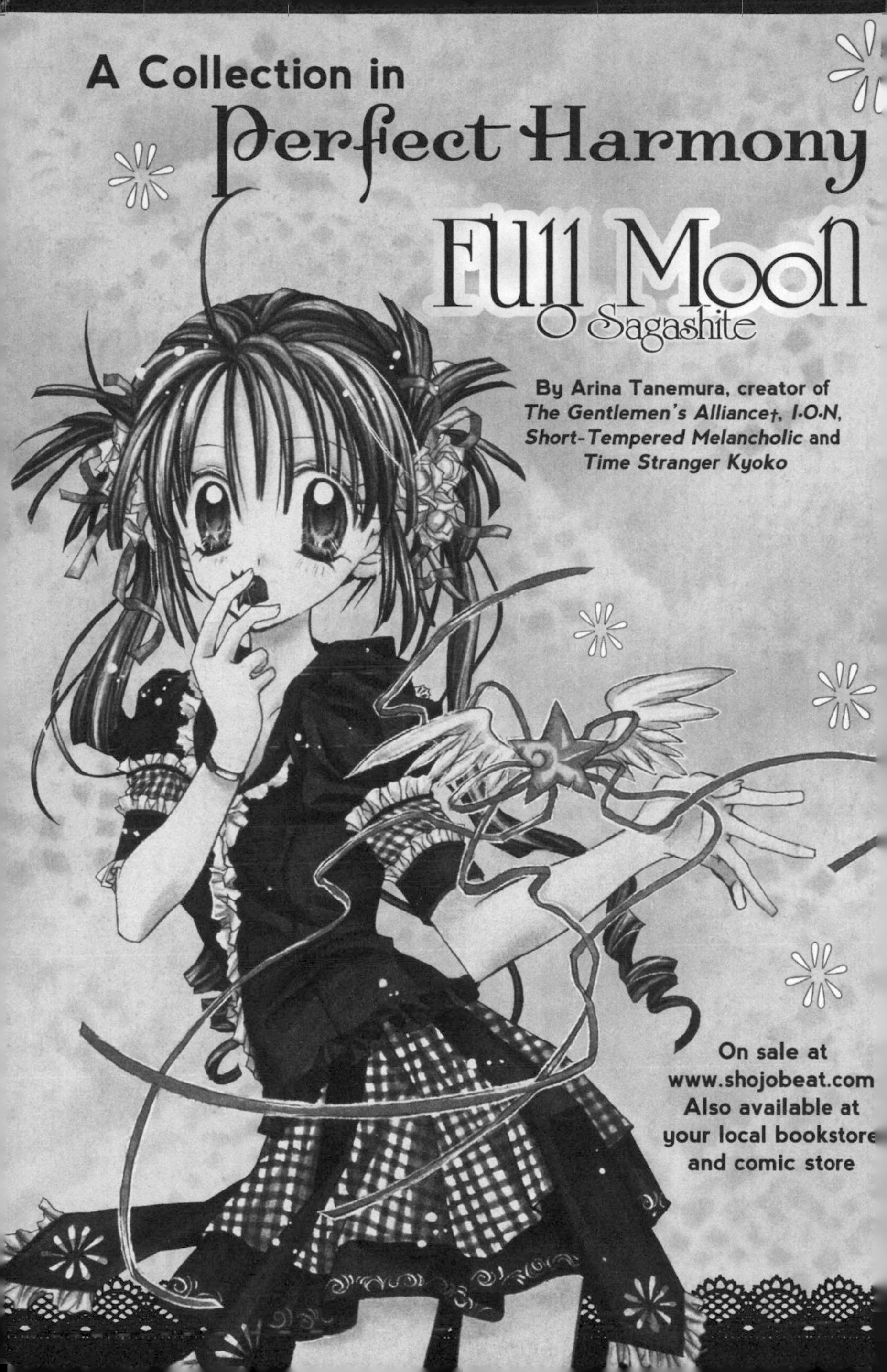
A Collection in
Perfect Harmony
Full Moon
O Sagashite
By Arina Tanemura, creator of
The Gentlemen's Alliance†, I·O·N,
Short-Tempered Melancholic and
Time Stranger Kyoko
On sale at
www.shojobeat.com
Also available at
your local bookstore
and comic store